The Psychology of Assessment Centers

The Psychology of Assessment Centers

Edited by
Duncan J. R. Jackson
The University of Seoul
Charles E. Lance
The University of Georgia
Brian J. Hoffman
The University of Georgia

NEW YORK AND LONDON

First published 2012
by Routledge
711 Third Avenue, New York, NY 10017

Simultaneously published in the UK
by Routledge
27 Church Road, Hove, East Sussex BN3 2FA

Routledge is an imprint of the Taylor & Francis Group, an informa business

Library of Congress Cataloging in Publication Data
The psychology of assessment centers / edited by Duncan J.R. Jackson, Charles E. Lance, Brian J. Hoffman.
p. cm.
1. Assessment centers (Personnel management procedure) 2. Psychology, Industrial.
I. Jackson, Duncan J. R. II. Lance, Charles E., 1954– III. Hoffman, Brian J.
HF5549.5.A78P77 2012
658.3'12—dc23
2012016033

ISBN: 978-0-415-87814-2 (hbk)

Typeset in Minion and Optima
by EvS Communication Networx, Inc.

To my family, friends, colleagues, and the occasional kind strangers who supported me both in New Zealand and during my move to South Korea. I've learned a great deal here and I couldn't have achieved that without you.

—Duncan Jackson

To my parents who supported my continued education.

—Chuck Lance

Thanks to my teachers and professors at Northeast Lauderdale Elementary, Brandon Middle School, Brandon High School, Hinds Community College, University of Southern Mississippi, and University of Tennessee for all that you taught me.

—Brian Hoffman

Contents

Foreword

Paul R. Sackett
University of Minnesota

Assessment centers have a long history of use in a wide variety of organizations worldwide for selection, promotion, and development purposes. Assessment centers prototypically involve multiple candidates whose performance is observed in multiple exercises (e.g., in-baskets, leaderless group discussions, one-on-one role plays) by multiple trained assessors who rate the candidates on multiple dimensions (e.g., oral communications, organizing and planning, decisiveness, leadership). Some assessment centers obtain dimension ratings at the conclusion of each exercise; these are commonly referred to as "post-exercise dimension ratings" (PEDRs). These PEDRs are subsequently combined, either mechanically or judgmentally, into overall dimension ratings. Other assessment centers do not use PEDRs, but rather postpone evaluation until all exercises are completed, at which time the assessors share dimension-relevant observations across exercises and judgmentally arrive at overall dimensions ratings. Thus both approaches produce overall dimension ratings. These overall dimension ratings may be further aggregated across dimensions to form overall assessment ratings.

The origins of this volume can be traced to an article that my colleague George Dreher and I published in 1982. Titled "Constructs and assessment center dimensions: Some troubling empirical findings," the article examined data from three assessment centers and found the same pattern in all three. In each center, a set of dimensions was rated at the conclusion of each exercise, and we found that within-exercise ratings of the various dimensions were more highly correlated than within-dimension ratings across exercises. Cast in multitrait-multimethod terms, with dimensions as traits and exercises as methods, hetrotrait-monomethods correlations were higher than monotrait-heteromethod correlations. Cast in factor-analytic terms, and using the exploratory factor analytic methods of the era, the factors emerging from these centers reflected exercises, rather than dimensions. While others had noticed this phenomenon, the Sackett and Dreher article gained attention due, I suspect, to its publication in a highly visible journal and to the replication across multiple assessment centers. The basic finding has now been widely replicated (Lance, Lambert, Gewin, Lieven, & Conway, 2004).

Dreher and I labeled these findings as "troubling," as they ran contrary to what we expected to find: as assessment centers were designed to evaluate candidate standing on dimensions, the factors underlying assessment center ratings would reflect dimensions. The article proved a touchstone, prompting a wide variety of differing reactions, and generating a large amount of research aimed at better understanding the constructs underlying assessment center ratings. It has been praised for prompting a more probing examination of assessment centers. It has been criticized for leading the field astray in search of a remedy for a non-existent problem. A few years ago, I saw reference to "the near-classic article by Sackett and Dreher." My first reaction was to puff up with pride at the term "classic," but that deflated quickly as I pondered the qualifier "near!"

Responses to the article can be grouped roughly into categories reflecting different ways of completing the following: "The finding that exercises dominate dimensions in accounting for variance in post-exercise dimension ratings…."

1. is a problem, and the solution is to change various aspects of the assessment center in pursuit of a center in which dimension variance dominates exercise variance;
2. is a problem, and the solution is to re-design assessment centers with an exercise focus, rather than a dimension focus;
3. is an artifact of data-analytic procedures used. The emergence and continuing refinement of confirmatory factor analysis procedures suggested more nuanced partitioning of variance, including both dimension and exercise factors;
4. is not a problem, as dimensions are simply convenient summary labels for categories of behavior. For a given dimension, the various exercises are not intended as parallel items; rather, each is intended to shed light on different behaviors relevant to the dimension. Thus high dimension correlations across exercises need not be expected.

Each of these perspectives is well-represented in the current volume. Jackson, Lance, and Hoffman have done a marvelous job of assembling a fine set of chapters clearly articulate each perspective. After an initial set of stage-setting chapters, we are presented with separate sections building the case for the traditional dimension-based design of assessment centers, for designing assessment centers with a focus on exercises, rather than dimensions, and for a dimension-exercise hybrid approach. Each section contains a useful blend of theory, research, and practice; I view this as an outstanding example of I/O psychology's scientist-practitioner model.

Before closing, I'd like to comment on the origins of the Sackett and Dreher article. It can be traced to a graduate school summer internship I held in the summer of 1977 at the company referred to as "Organization A" in the Sackett and Dreher article. One open-ended task assigned to me was to evaluate an ongoing assessment center. It occurred to me that post-exercise dimension ratings could be cast in multitrait-multimethod terms. I analyzed the data and, unexpectedly, found that exercises played a larger role than dimensions. The finding troubled me, and I suspected that this reflected an anomalous finding, suggesting a design flaw in this center. A fellow student had taken a job and was involved in running an assessment center in his organization. He provided data from that center, and I found exercise variance dominated dimension variance in that setting as well (Organization B in the article). So it wasn't specific to Organization A. A colleague connected me with the director of an ongoing center in Organization C; again, exercise variance dominated. I put this on the back burner as I conducted my dissertation research on another topic and headed off to my first job at the University of Kansas. There I met George Dreher, another new assistant professor. Conversations with George helped organize thinking about the assessment center findings, and we decided that the findings were worth trying to publish. I offer this back-story for two purposes. First, it illustrates a research model that I find occurring with some frequency, in which the phenomenon of interest emerges from being embedded in an organizational setting, rather a study being planned in advance. Second, that an influential finding emerged from an internship project may be of some encouragement to students: you never know when an interesting issue will present itself!

Finally, I note that my own thinking has evolved over time. In ongoing work with Nathan Kuncel, we argue that post-exercise dimension ratings are an intermediate step toward an overall dimension rating, and that it is the overall dimension rating that should be the focus of inquiry, as it is the basis for organizational action. Thus we shift focus from partitioning variance in post-exercise dimension ratings to partitioning variance in overall dimension ratings. Viewing overall dimension ratings as a composite of post-exercise ratings, we find that while exercise-specific variance dominates dimension variance in individual post-exercise ratings, dimension variance quickly overtakes exercise-specific variance as the dominant source of variance as ratings from multiple exercises are combined. Thus the perspectives reflected in this volume likely will not be the final word on this topic. They do, however, give us a clear picture of where we stand today.

Paul R. Sackett

References

Lance, C. E., Lambert, T. A., Gewin, A. G., Lievens, F., & Conway, J. M. (2004). Revised estimates of dimension and exercise variance components in assessment center post-exercise dimension ratings. *Journal of Applied Psychology, 89*, 377-385.

Sackett, P. R., & Dreher, G. F. (1982). Constructs and assessment center dimensions: Some troubling empirical findings. *Journal of Applied Psychology, 67*, 401-410.

About the Editors

Duncan J. R. Jackson is an Assistant Professor at the University of Seoul, South Korea, in the Human Resource Management Program. He is also Director of the Research Center for Personnel Selection and Promotion at Assesta Group. Duncan earned his Doctorate from Massey University in Auckland, New Zealand and served as a Senior Lecturer in New Zealand for six years prior to moving to Seoul. His primary research interest is in task-based assessment centers and on psychological and situational factors that affect work-related behavior. His work has been published in some of the top journals in industrial-organizational psychology including the *Journal of Occupational and Organizational Psychology*, *Human Performance*, and the *International Journal of Selection and Assessment*. Duncan has consulted to a broad range of large and small organizations in both the private and public sectors. He has developed assessment center programs for a range of organizations and has also served as an assessment center trainer and assessor.

Charles E. Lance is a Professor of I/O psychology at The University of Georgia. His work in the areas of performance measurement, assessment center validity, research methods, and structural equation modeling has appeared in such journals as *Psychological Methods, Organizational Research Methods (ORM), Journal of Applied Psychology, Organizational Behavior and Human Decision Processes, Journal of Management* and *Multivariate Behavioral Research*. Dr. Lance is also co-editor of *Performance Measurement: Current Perspectives and Future Challenges* (with Wink Bennett and Dave Woehr) and *Statistical and Methodological Myths and Urban Legends: Received Doctrine, Verity, and Fable in Organizational and Social Research* (with Bob Vandenberg) and *The Psychology of Assessment Centers* (with Duncan Jackson and Brian Hoffman). Dr. Lance is a Fellow of the Society for Industrial and Organizational Psychology (SIOP) and the American

Psychological Association and is a member of the Society for Organizational Behavior. He is currently Associate Editor of *ORM*, and on the editorial boards of *Personnel Psychology, Human Performance*, and *Group & Organization Management.*

Brian J. Hoffman is currently an Assistant Professor at the University of Georgia in the Industrial & Organizational Psychology Program. He earned his doctorate from the University of Tennessee. Brian's primary research interest is leadership assessment, with an emphasis on understanding the quality of information received from assessment centers and multisource performance ratings. His research has been published in top tier outlets, including *Personnel Psychology, Journal of Applied Psychology*, and *Academy of Management Journal.* He was the recipient of the 2011 Douglas W. Bray and Ann Howard Research Grant and serves on the planning committee of the International Congress for the Assessment Center Method. Over the past 10 years, Brian has served as an AC designer, administrator, and assessor/role player for a variety of large and small companies.

About the Contributors

Winfred Arthur, Jr. is a Full Professor of psychology and management at Texas A&M University. He is a Fellow of the Society for Industrial and Organizational Psychology, the Association of Psychological Science, and the American Psychological Association. His research interests are in human performance; training development, design, implementation, and evaluation; team selection and training; acquisition and retention of complex skills; testing, selection, and validation; models of job performance; personnel psychology; and meta-analysis. He received his Ph.D. in industrial/organizational psychology from the University of Akron in 1988.

Jurgen Bank is Director of Assessment, at BTS USA, Inc., Catalysts for Profitability & Growth. He previoulsy managed PDI Ninth House's Leadership Assessment service globally, providing consistent and marketable assessment solutions that impact individual and organizational effectiveness. He earned a terminal degree in Psychology, Diploma of Psychologist (Diplompsychologe), from Philipps University, Marburg, Germany in 1988. He has worked with ACs throughout his career. First, as management developer at Generali insurance, and later as external consultant with SHL and PDI Ninth House. Jurgen has led multi-national projects in North and South America, Europe, and Asia. He has designed and reviewed hundreds of assessment systems both for development as well as for selection and is a recognized expert for state-of the-art, innovative, and scalable leadership assessment solutions. Jurgen has published several articles and presented at industry conferences on practitioner issues in global assessment and use of technology for assessment.

Walter C. Borman received his Ph.D. in Industrial/Organizational Psychology from the University of California (Berkeley). He is currently Chief Scientist of Personnel Decisions Research Institutes and is Professor of Industrial-Organizational Psychology at the University of South Florida. He is a Fellow of the Society for Industrial and Organizational Psychology. Borman has written more than 350 books, book chapters, journal articles, and conference papers. He also has served on the editorial boards of several journals in the I/O field, including the *Journal of Applied Psychology, Personnel Psychology,* and the International Journal of Selection and Assessment. He is currently editor of *Human Performance.* Finally, he was the recipient of the Society for Industrial and Organizational Psychology's Distinguished Scientific Contributions Award for 2003, the M. Scott Myers Award for Applied Research in the Workplace for 2000, 2002, 2004 and 2010, and the American Psychological Foundation's Gold Medal Award for Life Achievement in the Application of Psychology in 2011.

Mark C. Bowler is currently an Assistant Professor in the Industrial/Organizational Psychology program at East Carolina University. He earned his doctorate in Industrial/Organizational Psychology from the University of Tennessee. His primary research interest is in the design and implementation of assessment centers with a focus on the statistical principles relating to the evaluation of their construct-related validity. His research in this area has been published in journals such as *Journal of Applied Psychology, Journal of Vocational Behavior,* and *Organizational Research Methods.*

Sarah Brock is the Offering Manager for PDI Ninth House's global development and succession assessment business. Sarah's focus is on developing and deploying offerings that help clients drive the highest impact and best development and succession decisions. Her primary research interest is in leadership assessment: exploring meaningful differences throughout the leadership pipeline, understanding drivers of readiness beyond skill, such as motivation, experience, derailers, and style, as well as examining the impact of development actions on performance and readiness. Sarah earned her doctorate from the University of Tulsa and has consulted internally with several organizations to develop assessment systems and global employee opinion surveys. She has spent the last 10 years with PDI NH designing, deploying, and delivering assessments with multinational corporations across the globe.

Neil Christiansen is a Professor of Psychology at Central Michigan University here he teaches courses in personnel psychology, personality psychology, and structural equation modeling. Neil's interests focus on the relationship between personality and work behavior, including the assessment of personality in the work place (e.g., the validity of personality tests, applicant faking of personality inventories, and alternative methods of assessing personality), the interaction of personality and work situations, and the accuracy of personality judgments. His research has been published in journals such as *Journal of Applied Psychology*, *Personnel Psychology*, *Journal of Organizational Behavior*, *Human Performance*, and the *International Journal of Selection and Assessment*.

Joy Hazucha leads PDI Ninth House's Research group supporting her firm's Thought Leadership about leaders and leadership development in the 21st century. This includes understanding how business and cultural context drive leadership requirements, investigating differences between different levels of leadership, assessing and developing performance, potential, readiness, and fit, and measuring outcomes. She earned her Ph.D. in I-O Psychology from the University of Minnesota. Her career at PDI has included consulting with clients across industries, leadership of our European offices, and assessment, especially at the C Suite level. Her publications include a chapter on Behavior Change in the *Handbook of Industrial and Organizational Psychology* (Dunnette & Hough, 1992), and one about the strategic management of global leadership talent in *Advances in Global Leadership*, Vol, 3 (2003).

Scott Highhouse is Professor and Ohio Eminent Scholar in the Department of Psychology, Bowling Green State University. He received his Ph.D. in 1992 from University of Missouri at St. Louis. Scott served as Associate Editor of *Organizational Behavior and Human Decision Processes* (OBHDP) from 2001-2007, and as Associate Editor of *Journal of Occupational and Organizational Psychology* from 2007-2009. Scott has been named a fellow of the American Psychological Association (APA), the Association for Psychological Science (APS), and the Society for Industrial Organizational Psychology (SIOP). He formerly worked in organizational development at Anheuser Busch Companies in St. Louis, Missouri. His primary areas of expertise are assessment/selection for employment, and human judgment/decision making, and his work has been featured in the *Washington Post*, *Wall Street Journal*, and *Chronicle for Higher Education*.

Paul G. W. Jansen is currently Professor of Industrial Psychology, Faculty of Economics and Business Administration, Vrije Universiteit Amsterdam, The Netherlands. Paul Jansen graduated, cum laude, in 1979, with specialization in Mathematical Psychology at the University of Nijmegen; Ph.D. in social sciences in 1983. Paul Jansen is one of the founders, and current board member of the *HRM Network NL*. Since 2006 he is chairman of the Amsterdam Center for Career Research (www.accr.nl). His research interests are in management development, careers, assessment (e.g., assessment centers, 360-graden feedback), and performance management. His work has been published in *Applied Psychology: An international Review*, *Applied Psychological Measurement*, *Career Development International*, *International Journal of Selection and Assessment*, *Journal of Applied Psychology*, *Journal of Organizational Behavior*, *Journal of Vocational Behavior*. *Psychometrika*, and *Small Business Economics*.

Martin Kleinmann has been a Professor at the Universität Zürich, located in Switzerland, and is currently the head of the Work and Organizational Psychology group. He has received several grants from the German Research Foundation and the Swiss National Science Foundation, has worked as a consultant for several years in the field of assessment centers and has been the president of the German Society of Industry and Organizational Psychology and the editor of the leading German journal of personnel psychology. His books about assessment centers are published in German and translated into Russian. His articles are published in the *Journal of Applied Psychology*, *Personnel Psychology*, and several other journals. His main research interests include construct-related validity of personnel selection, performance ratings in different contexts, impression management, and time management.

Filip Lievens is currently Professor at the Department of Personnel Management and Work and Organizational Psychology of Ghent University, Belgium. He is the author of over 100 articles in the areas of organizational attractiveness, high-stakes testing, and selection including assessment centers, situational judgment tests, and web-based assessment. He serves in the editorial board of both *Journal of Applied Psychology* and *Personnel Psychology* and was a past book review editor of the *International Journal of Selection and Assessment*. He was the first European winner of the Distinguished Early Career Award of the

Society for Industrial and Organizational Psychology (2006) and the first industrial and organizational psychologist to be laureate of the Royal Flemish Academy of Sciences and Arts (2008).

Klaus G. Melchers is an assistant professor for work and organizational psychology at Universität Zürich in Switzerland. He received his Ph.D. in experimental psychology from Philipps-Universität Marburg in Germany. His main research interests include personnel selection (with a focus on assessment centers and employment interviews), personality measurement in the work context, and rater training. His work has been published in *Personnel Psychology, Human Performance, Psychological Review*, and the *International Journal of Selection and Assessment*. In the past, he was also involved in various applied projects concerning the design, administration, and evaluation of assessment centers.

John P. Meriac is currently an Assistant Professor at the University of Missouri-St. Louis in the Industrial-Organizational Psychology Program. He earned his doctorate from the University of Tennessee. His primary areas of research are in the domains of personnel selection and performance management. In these areas, he has focused on the measurement of individual differences and job performance, particularly on the psychometric issues surrounding their measurement. He has published several journal articles and edited book chapters, and made numerous conference presentations. Over the past several years, John has also served various roles in both administrative and developmental assessment centers.

Kevin P. Nolan is currently finishing his Ph.D. in Industrial-Organizational Psychology at Bowling Green State University. His primary research interests are job choice and employee selection. Kevin's work has been published in several outlets including *Journal of Occupational and Organizational Psychology*. He was the recipient of the 2010 Bonnie A. Sandman Award for Outstanding I-O Psychology Student, and will join the faculty of Hofstra University as an Assistant Professor in the fall of 2011.

Nigel Povah, MSc, C.Psychol, AFBPsS (nigle.povah@adc.uk.com) is the CEO and founder of Assessment and Development Consultants Ltd (A&DC®), one of the UK's best known firms of Occupational Psychologists, and he is a leading expert in the Assessment Center field with over

30 years of experience. Nigel has written numerous books and articles on Assessment Centers, including: *Assessment & Development Centres,* co-authored with Iain Ballantyne (1995, 2004); *Succeeding at Assessment Centres for Dummies,* co-authored with his daughter, Lucy Povah (2009); and *Assessment Centres and Global Talent Management,* co-edited with George C. Thornton III (2011). He has presented numerous papers on Assessment Centers and helped to formulate the British Psychological Society's Best Practice Guidelines on the *Design, Implementation and Evaluation of Assessment and Development Centres,* (2003).

Lucy Povah, MSc, CPsychol is a Chartered Occupational Psychologist and a Senior Consultant for A&DC Ltd. While at A&DC, she has managed and delivered a range of UK, U.S., and international Talent Management projects. These projects include identification of future leaders and best practice end-to-end assessment and development processes, requiring the design and delivery of a considerable number of assessment centers. Lucy has written numerous articles and presented at a variety of conferences. Recent achievements include co-authoring, with her father Nigel Povah, the book *Succeeding at Assessment Centres for Dummies* (2009) and contributing to a related DVD for prospective candidates. Additionally, Lucy co-authored an article on context-centered Leadership for the *Human Resources People & Strategy Journal,* which won the Walker award for the best article in 2010. Her specific areas of interest include management/leadership talent identification and how to ensure that talent strategy is integrated with the wider business strategy.

Anuradha Ramesh is a research and assessment consultant with PDI Ninth House. She is responsible for conducting research to understand the value of assessments to organizations as well as research that informs the design and delivery of assessment and assessment centers. She has worked with numerous clients to develop assessment solutions including high potential identification and succession, to understand the impact of cultural differences on the assessment of individuals, and to evaluate the effectiveness of assessment solutions implemented by organizations. She also works directly with leaders by delivering in-depth assessment and feedback. Anu received her B.S. and M.S. in Applied Psychology from Delhi University and a Ph.D. in Industrial & Organizational Psychology from the University of Maryland. Her work has been published in the *Journal of Applied Psychology, International*

Journal of Testing, and *Perspectives on Science and Practice*. She has received multiple awards for her work.

Deborah E. Rupp is the William C. Byham Chair in Industrial/Organizational Psychology in the Department of Psychological Sciences, and an affiliated faculty member in the Krannert School of Managements at Purdue University. She received her PhD in Industrial/Organizational Psychology from Colorado State University, and was previously an Associate Professor of Psychology, Labor/Employment Relations, and Law at the University of Illinois at Urbana-Champaign Her assessment-related research focuses on validation, developmental assessment centers, and the use of technology to enhance assessment and development. She has co-authored the new edition of *Assessment Centers in Human Resource Management* with George Thornton and was the first recipient of the Douglas Bray/Ann Howard Award for research on leadership assessment and development. She also conducts research on organizational justice, corporate social responsibility, and emotions at work. She recently co-chaired the International Congress on Assessment Center Methods, and co-led the taskforce that prepared/published a revision to the *Guidelines and Ethical Considerations for Assessment Center Operations*. Her assessment center research was also cited in proceedings surrounding U.S. Supreme Court case *Ricci* v. *DeStefano et al.* Rupp is a Fellow within the Society for Industrial and Organizational Psychology and is currently serving as a SIOP representative to the United Nations. Her work has appeared in outlets such as *Journal of Applied Psychology, Academy of Management Review, Personnel Psychology*, and *Organizational Behavior and Human Decision Processes*. She is currently the Editor-in-Chief of *Journal of Management*.

Paul R. Sackett is the Beverly and Richard Fink Distinguished Professor of Psychology and Liberal Arts at the University of Minnesota. He received his Ph.D. in Industrial and Organizational Psychology at the Ohio State University in 1979. His research interests revolve around various aspects of testing and assessment in workplace, educational, and military settings. He has served as editor of two journals: *Industrial and Organizational Psychology: Perspectives on Science and Practice* and *Personnel Psychology*. He has served as president of the Society for Industrial and Organizational Psychology, as co-chair of the committee producing the Standards for Educational and Psychological Testing, as a member of the National Research Council's Board on Testing and

Assessment, as chair of APA's Committee on Psychological Tests and Assessments, and as chair of APA's Board of Scientific Affairs.

Carl J. Thoresen is Vice President of Cornerstone Management Resource Systems, a consulting firm located in Carnegie, Pennsylvania, which specializes in the development and implementation of task-based assessment centers (TBACs) and other leadership development initiatives for some of the world's leading organizations. Prior to joining Cornerstone, Carl was Assistant Professor of Industrial-Organizational Psychology at Tulane University in New Orleans, Louisiana. Carl's research has been published in numerous peer-reviewed journals, including *Psychological Bulletin, Journal of Applied Psychology, Personnel Psychology, Journal of Organizational Behavior, Journal of Personality and Social Psychology,* and *Human Performance.* Carl holds a B.A. in Philosophy from Northwestern University, an M.S. in Organizational Behavior from Cornell University, and a Ph.D. in Human Resource Management from the University of Iowa.

Joseph D. Thoresen, a licensed psychologist in the state of Pennsylvania for more than 30 years, is currently President and CEO of Cornerstone Management Resource Systems. He received his M.S. degree from the University of Tennessee and began his career as a practitioner in the corporate office of Rohm and Haas Company in Philadelphia. He left as Manager of Training and Organization Development to join Development Dimensions International, where he became one of the first full-time assessment center consultants. He founded Cornerstone Management Resource Systems in the mid-1980s. Throughout his career, he has worked to combine published research and his practical experience in many different organizations to improve the assessment center method. He developed and implemented his first task-based assessment center in 1999.

George C. Thornton III earned his Ph.D. in Industrial Psychology at Purdue University and is currently Professor Emeritus at Colorado State University. George's primary interests include the assessment center method and implications of employment discrimination litigation for personnel psychology practices. His recent publications include *Assessment Centers in Human Resource Management* with Deborah E. Rupp, and *Developing Organizational Simulations* with Rose Muller-Hanson. He is co-editor with Nigel Povah of *Assessment Centres: Strategies of*

Global Talent Management, which consists of chapters by more than 40 authors from 19 countries spanning 5 continents. He is the winner of the Distinguished Professional Contributions Award given by the Society of Industrial and Organizational Psychology. Over the past 40 years he has served as assessment center designer, administrator, assessor, and consultant. He has delivered presentations and workshops on assessment centers to diverse audiences in the United States, Canada, Germany, Switzerland, England, Israel, South Africa, Indonesia, Korea, Singapore, Brazil, Costa Rica, and China.

Andreja Wirz is a doctoral student at Universität Zürich in Switzerland. She is currently involved in a research project supported by a grant from the Swiss National Science Foundation that is concerned with the construct-related validity of assessment centers. Andreja is particularly interested in personnel selection and development and is currently working on her dissertation concerning the validity of assessment centers. Before, she has worked as a personnel consultant for the selection of IT professionals.

David J. Woehr is currently a professor in the Department of Management in the Belk College of Business at the University of North Carolina Charlotte. Dr. Woehr received the B.A. degree in Psychology from Trinity University and the M.S. and Ph.D. degrees in Industrial and Organizational Psychology from the Georgia Institute of Technology. Dr. Woehr's research interests are in the areas of performance measurement, managerial assessment, and applied psychometrics. His research has appeared in the *Journal of Applied Psychology, Personnel Psychology, Organizational Behavior and Human Decision Processes, Organizational Research Methods, Educational and Psychological Measurement, Journal of Vocational Behavior,* and others. He currently serves as the Associate Editor of *Human Performance* and is on the editorial board of *Organizational Research Methods and the European Journal of Work and Organizational Psychology.* Dr. Woehr is an elected fellow in the Society for Industrial and Organizational Psychology, the American Psychological Association, and the Association for Psychological Science.

Acknowledgments and Preface

Acknowledgments

An edited volume, by its very definition, is a shared task. As such, we would like to thank all of the contributors to this book who so very conscientiously and openly shared their invaluable insights and knowledge. We are also grateful to Ms. Anne Duffy and her staff at Routledge who offered guidance, encouragement, and support. Each of us would like to express thanks to our respective organizations; The University of Seoul and The University of Georgia, for providing support and advocacy from the beginning to the end of this project. Thanks especially to Dr. Stuart Carr for his original concept for this volume and his encouragement at its inception. We would also like to express our thanks to our ever-understanding families for providing us with the patience and support that we needed in order to complete this volume.

Duncan J. R. Jackson, Charles E. Lance, and Brian J. Hoffman

Preface

Research on the reliability and validity of assessment centers (ACs) has being ongoing for at least 50 years. One of the most heavily researched topics over the last 30 years has been the internal structure of AC ratings that assessors make on rating dimensions after the completion of each exercise (post-exercise dimension ratings or PEDRs). In a now classic article, Paul Sackett and George Dreher found in 1982 that factor analyses of PEDRs resulted in structures defined by exercises, not dimensions. Sackett and Dreher referred to these as "troubling" findings (p. 408) because, at least when viewed from a traditional multitrait-multimethod perspective, PEDRs seemed to reflect the influence of the method of eliciting the ratings (i.e., the exercises) and not the dimensions (traits) they were designed to assess. This pattern of findings, replicated often subsequently, led researchers to seek ways of making PEDRs more "construct valid," resulting in quite a large body of literature on AC construct validity. Not surprisingly, there grew in this literature several different perspectives on what the internal structure of ACs *should* look like and how ACs should be best engineered for the various goals of selection, assessment, promotion, and development. The editors of this volume were concerned that the journal literature was becoming unbalanced in terms of its acknowledgement of the different perspectives that were *really* being discussed in academic circles. Simply complaining about this lack of balance didn't seem like a fruitful approach. So, one of us sought advice.

The annual meeting of the Society for Industrial Organizational Psychology (SIOP) is an excellent venue to obtain advice. There are seasoned academics and practitioners from around the globe who attend the annual meeting and present and discuss their research with colleagues. Many of them are well known and well read authors of the textbooks and journal articles that are used in undergraduate and graduate I-O classes and who are sometimes sought out by current students who are eager to catch a glimpse of the real live human being behind the printed name in the publication that their professor set as compulsory reading. As such, SIOP, the great collective of I-O psychology knowledge from many corners of the planet, would provide a great opportunity for Duncan Jackson, a senior lecturer based at Massey University in New Zealand at the time, to scour the Earth's knowledge in a single concentrated forum.

It was 2010 and SIOP was being held in New Orleans. Jet lagged and fatigued from travelling across a large section of the globe, Duncan found himself sitting in a plane from Los Angeles to New Orleans with Dr. Stuart Carr, a professor from Massey University, New Zealand. The two hadn't spoken for a while. Duncan was based in Massey University's Business School and Stuart in Massey University's School of Psychology. They were worlds apart, separated by about a kilometer of cattle grazing fields. So, in a not-particularly-cost-effective-fashion, they met in mid-air somewhere above the United States. Duncan saw an opportunity and raised the issue of the AC debate. Stuart listened intently, considered for a while, and then announced:

"You need to bring all of the main authors in the AC literature together such that they might be better positioned to acknowledge the importance of the different perspectives on this issue."

"Okay, that sounds good. How about a dinner? Or a summer camp? A rock concert? How about an outing, like an assessment center picnic or something like that?" was Duncan's response.

"No, you need to edit a book."

"What?!?!?" Cold chills flashed through Duncan's body. He remembered his incapacity to file documents and the bedroom he rented that was so untidy it was barely recognizable as a room at all.

"I don't think I can do that. Really, I have trouble organizing my own breakfast."

Stuart offered encouragement. "You can do it and really it's the only way to facilitate progress on this important topic in our discipline. I think that you need to start this off."

"That sounds swell, Stuart." Contempt flashed across Duncan's face. Deep down, he was thinking that there was no way and no how. This just sounded like way too much effort and there didn't seem to be time to complete it anyway.

Stuart was undeterred. "A plane is no place to discuss this. We'll have to meet in a restaurant. We need to write things on paper napkins. That's how every big idea begins." Stuart was concocting a strategy on how this book might be structured.

It might have been Stuart's Scottish heritage that acted as the impetus for the resulting $2 meal that was supposed to constitute "dinner in a restaurant.". Picture here the dingiest, darkest, and strangest pizza joint in the whole of New Orleans and you have the setting for the scene that took place.

The conversation turned to the idea of the AC book. "Ah yes, the book. You need to get that off the ground. We'll need some paper to jot down ideas."

Resourceful as always, Stuart managed to secure some napkins and a pen. He began scribbling ideas on a napkin in black ink. Ball point pens do not function well on napkins. They're not designed for such terrain, and Duncan could hardly read a word that was written. But he listened carefully to what Stuart was saying and he liked what he heard.

"You need all of the big names in the field. If the big names are there, the book will get read. You need to start with a historical background and then lead into separate sections, one for each perspective. How many main perspectives are there?"

"Three."

"Okay, what are they called?"

"The dimension-based, task-based, and mixed-model perspectives."

"Good. So you'll have one section for each perspective and each section will present a separate chapter for theory, research, and practice. So that's three chapters per section."

Stuart was still scribbling while talking out loud and Duncan began to envision what this volume might look like and how it might assist the discipline to evolve and to become more open to alternative perspectives.

The next step was to think of big names. The idea occurred to Duncan that if he contacted one big name, then that might open doors to others. As it turned out, he didn't know any big names, but he knew Chuck Lance. Duncan must have thought that Chuck was a big name because at the previous SIOP he witnessed him being chased into an elevator by a young student who proclaimed: "Dr. Lance! I just read your article in the *Journal of Applied Psychology*. It was just wonderful. I really admire your work." Her eyes were beaming. She looked entranced.

"Thanks, I'm glad that you enjoyed it."

And it came to pass that Charles (Chuck) E. Lance was a good choice for Duncan in terms of garnering support from someone he knew and who had experience in organizing two previous edited volumes. The two had met in 2004 when they found that they both shared a similar task-based view on AC measurement. Duncan arranged to meet with Chuck after a meeting at SIOP.

"How about doing a book?" Duncan asked, half expecting rejection.

"Okay. What is it gonna be about?" This was an encouraging response and Chuck seemed to like the idea that Stuart had mapped out. "But we're going to need another editor, otherwise this is going to look unbalanced. You and I have very similar views. We need someone that thinks about these things a bit differently."

"I agree. Okay, who?"

"Well, how about Brian Hoffman?" Enter Brian Hoffman. Brian had extensive experience administering an AC while in graduate school at the University of Tennessee and was beginning to publish rather prolifically on ACs. Taking a mixed-model view of the AC phenomenon, Brian seemed to be just the person for the job. From this time, Duncan, Chuck, and Brian met regularly to plan who would contribute to the book and which chapters would be necessary to allow the story to unfold in the most meaningful and interesting ways possible. They assembled a crack team of expert contributors who delivered products of extremely high quality.

That, more or less, is how the editorial team was assembled for this volume. The structure of the book is much as it was mapped out in a dingy restaurant between Stuart Carr and Duncan Jackson in 2010, and so we thank Stuart for his insight and encouragement. After a general introduction and this introductory commentary, the book presents some general historical and methodological background to AC research as well as a general overview of modern AC research. Subsequently, there are nine chapters on the theory, research, and implementation each of dimension-based, task-based, and mixed model ACs. A final chapter provides an integrative overview of the books' preceding chapters. We do not purport to have ended the debates that are described in this volume, and readers will need to form their own opinions as to which approach yields the strongest arguments. We do, however, hope that this volume will facilitate a wider acceptance of different perspectives on assessment centers and on the study of human behavior in the workplace. Of course, we express our utmost gratitude to the chapter authors, the big names, the experts, the authorities whom we sought out and who agreed to participate in this effort. We couldn't have done it without you!

Duncan J. R. Jackson, Charels E. Lance, and Brian J. Hoffman

Part 1

A Context for Assessment Centers

1

What Are Assessment Centers and How Can They Enhance Organizations?

Nigel Povah and Lucy Povah

A&DC Ltd, UK

This chapter provides an introduction and overview of the "World of Assessment Centers (ACs)" by briefly describing the many facets of this well-established assessment methodology. We cover a range of topics: the basic principles, reasons for the popularity of ACs, benefits to individuals, organizational benefits and how they contribute to the achievement of the organization's corporate objectives, key challenges, legal implications, and recent variations in Assessment Center (AC) design principles.

What Defines an AC?

The AC has been around for well over half a century now, so what is it and what makes it so enduring in a world of fast-paced change? As almost every introduction to ACs says, it is not a place but a technique or process that is used to assess individual performance and potential. The Guidelines and Ethical Considerations for Assessment Center Operations (International Taskforce on Assessment Center Guidelines, 2009) cite the following definition:

> An AC consists of a standardized evaluation of behavior based on multiple inputs. Several trained observers and techniques are used. Judgments about behavior are made, in major part, from specifically developed assessment simulations. These judgments are pooled in a meeting among the assessors or by a statistical integration process. In an integration discussion, comprehensive accounts of behavior—and often ratings of it—are pooled. The discussion results in evaluations of the assessees' performance on the

> dimensions or other variables that the AC is designed to measure. Statistical combination methods should be validated in accordance with professionally accepted standards. (pp. 244–245)

The core elements of this definition are the focus on behavior, the use of multiple techniques (particularly job simulations), standardized evaluations from multiple observers (assessors) all of whom independently follow a consistent methodology, culminating in a structured integration session to determine individual performance against a set of discrete variables (dimensions/competencies).

Key Features and Components

Below we discuss the key features and components of an AC.

Focus on Job-Related Behavior. The aforementioned *Guidelines* (International Taskforce on Assessment Center Guidelines, 2009) state that it is essential to conduct job analyses in order to determine those dimensions or competencies which are important for success on-the-job. Indeed this is the starting point of any assessment process, as it is critical to know what it is that one is trying to assess and how the behavior of successful job incumbents differs from the less successful. These differentiating behaviors need to be observable, as they influence the AC design process and in particular the choice of appropriate tools and techniques (Thornton & Byham, 1982).

Use of Multiple Techniques. One of the strengths of the AC is that the conclusions reached about each participant are based on more than one assessment technique, which allows a picture of the individual to be built rather than relying on one data set only (Woodruffe, 2000). ACs can consist of psychometric tests, interviews, questionnaires, and most importantly, simulations. Simulations are the critical ingredient of an AC because they provide the participant with the opportunity to actually display behavior which is indicative of their capability. It is this feature that sets the AC apart from all other forms of assessment and it is incumbent upon the AC designer to establish the link between the desired behavior and both the dimensions and the simulations, as depicted in Figure 1.1.

Once the desired behaviors have been identified through job analysis, the designer can define the dimensions that are critical to

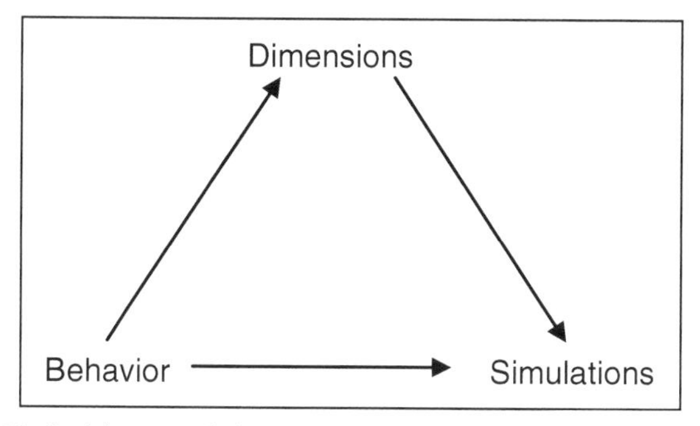

Figure 1.1 The link between behavior, dimensions and simulations.

successful job performance and at the same time, those situations in which these behaviors need to be displayed. The situations then form the basis of the simulations and the link to the relevant dimensions can be established.

There are of course many different working situations but it is helpful to recognize that they can be conveniently categorized under three headings:

1. Working in Groups
2. Working One-to-One
3. Working Alone

All working contexts fit under one of these three headings, and it is therefore self-evident that all simulations will also relate to one or more of these categories (Ballantyne & Povah, 1995, 2004). Typical simulations for the first category are group exercises and presentations; for the second category, we have interview simulations (role plays) and fact find exercises; and for the third category we have in-basket exercises, analysis exercises and scheduling exercises, amongst others.

According to the International Taskforce Guidelines (2009), in order for an assessment event to legitimately qualify as an AC it must contain at least one job-related simulation, although several would be ideal. One should include sufficient simulations to afford participants the opportunity to demonstrate behavior related to each dimension being assessed. One should also consider the different types of situations (or tasks) that are important to job success and look to include simulations that represent these. For example, if assessing leadership in a senior manager one might wish to observe how the individual inspires and motivates others in a presentation context, as well as how the individual provides direction and encouragement when tackling a performance problem with a direct report in a one-to-one interaction. These two different simulations (a presentation and a roleplay/interview simulation) would provide evidence of two different facets of the same dimension; in this case leadership. This example emphasizes the importance of ensuring that both the critical dimensions and job situations are represented in AC design. This important design principle introduces us to the existing debate of whether to approach AC design based on either dimensions or tasks (simulation exercises), or to employ a combination of the two. We will return to this debate below.

Multiple Observers. Another key feature of ACs is the use of multiple observers (assessors), mainly to avoid the risk of one individual's subjective bias adversely influencing the outcome. Having a number of observers independently assessing each participant ensures that the conclusions reached about each participant are based on a set of collective views (Connelly & Ones, 2008). This should enhance the objectivity of that conclusion, assuming the observers have been well trained and there is no evidence of collusion or undue influence from a domineering observer or chair person during data integration (Thornton & Rupp, 2006). When choosing observers a number of factors should be considered such as how many, who to choose, and what level of training is required. The number of observers will be influenced by a number of factors, such as: the nature and purpose of the AC, the availability of resources, the types of simulations to be used, and the skill levels of the observers. It is advisable to always train more observers than will be needed to account for illness, conflicting work demands and to allow for those individuals who do not seem willing or able to fulfill the observer role. When choosing observers, the need for a diverse group should be taken into account, especially if the participants themselves are a diverse group. The level of the observers within the organization is also important as observers need to understand what is required of the job role to make appropriate decisions. Observers should generally be one to two levels above the participants. For selection ACs with internal participants, it is best not to use participants' line managers as observers to help maximize objectivity (Ballantyne & Povah, 1995; 2004). There is however a strong case for using internal or external Psychologists on these occasions, as there is good evidence that their involvement enhances predictive validity (Gaugler, Rosenthal, Thornton, & Bentson,

1987; Lievens, 1998). However, the choice of internal or external observers is not a simple one, as it will often involve some trade-offs, with internal observers having greater familiarity with the organization and the target role, whereas external observers will usually be involved because of their greater level of experience and expertise as observers. One possible option here is to use a combination of both internal and external observers, in order to blend the advantages conferred by each group (Schlebusch & Roodt, 2008).

Data Integration. Data integration is an important and necessary part of an AC. It is important, because it is at this stage that the true value of an AC is achieved through determining meaningful conclusions about each participant which can then be used to make appropriate selection, promotion or development decisions, relating to that individual. It is necessary, because, up until this point, the data about each participant are spread amongst the different observers and the final aggregation of all of these data has yet to occur. The International Taskforce Guidelines (2009) clearly state that the integration of each individual's behaviors can be individual dimension scores aggregated across exercises, exercise specific scores, or potentially, depending on the purpose of the AC, across-exercise scores aggregated into an overall assessment rating. This highlights the fact that dimension-based and task-based ACs are both considered to be acceptable ways of interpreting the data. Whichever approach is favored, data need to be reviewed by pooling the observers' scores or through the use of a standard, professional, statistical process.

Multiple Participants. Given that the AC is sometimes referred to as "a multiple process" it is often thought that there must be multiple participants and this is generally the case, with centers frequently run for groups of 4, 6, or 8 participants and occasionally 10 or 12. However, it is perfectly legitimate to run a center for just one participant, so long as the other key features such as having multiple observers are still adhered to. The most common situations where there is only one participant are with senior roles, or with positions where there are few job applicants and there are problems in bringing them together at the same time. The only drawback with the single participant is the difficulty in conducting a group discussion exercise, unless volunteers from the organization or role-players are employed.

Impersonators

As the success and popularity of ACs has grown over the years, so too have the impersonators who lay claim to being ACs but fail to meet the minimum standards described in the International Taskforce Guidelines (2009), and summarized in this chapter. Lievens and Thornton (2005) cite some of the typical impersonators, which include:

1. Assessment events where there is no requirement for the participants to display overt behavioral responses and are therefore devoid of any true simulations.
2. Assessment events whose only simulations simply require the participant to provide multiple choice responses, such as with most electronic In-baskets.
3. Assessment events comprising solely of a battery of psychometrics and/or one or more interviews.
4. Assessment events which fail to adhere to the key features described previously and/or have one or more of the following characteristics: reliance on only one assessment technique, all assessments conducted by just one assessor, the absence of any integration of the data or preferring instead to treat each of the data sources about an individual independently.

Why do Organizations use Assessment Centers?

There isn't a single, simple answer to this question, as it will depend on what the organization is trying to achieve and how it perceives the associated benefits of using the AC approach. Many of the applications today can be linked to an organization's corporate strategy and more specifically its Talent Management objectives.

Different Uses of ACs

Since their conception in Europe in the 1940s the use of the AC approach has grown and during the 1990s businesses, predominantly in the US and UK, were using this approach on a regular basis. Today there are said to be over 50,000 operational ACs worldwide (Schlebusch & Roodt, 2008). Encouragingly, ACs are still said to be increasing in popularity.

Organizations use ACs for a range of purposes which fit into two broad categories: selection and development. Originally ACs were developed to assist organizations in making selection decisions and thus guiding decisions around which individual best fits a particular role. A couple of decades later, the AC methodology was adapted for use in a developmental context, often termed development centers (DCs) or developmental assessment centers (DACs).

ACs for selection could be used to recruit candidates for any level of role in any function, either from within and/or outside the organization. Additionally, this approach has been used to identify those individuals who will be let go during downsizing. ACs for development could be used to identify individual development needs for improved performance in a current role; to identify individuals with high-potential; to identify individuals for succession planning purposes; to audit the skills of a given group; or to provide individuals with appropriate Career Guidance.

In recent research on international AC practices (Assessment & Development Consultants, 2008), 437 respondents from 43 countries spanning five continents, were asked why their organization used AC methodology; the most frequently reported response was external recruitment for roles other than graduate level (57%), with diagnosing development needs (56%) coming a close second, and identifying high potential (50%) coming third. It was also evident that Europe, Australasia, and Asia mostly use ACs for recruitment (usually for graduates or other external applicants), whereas Africa and more recently the Americas, use them to evaluate the development needs of their employees (Assessment & Development Consultants, 2008; Krause & Thornton, 2008). In the case of the United States, this increasing trend of ACs being used more for development purposes may be due to selection activities placing greater emphasis on online assessment, except when ACs face technological challenges or for litigious reasons where some organizations revert to traditional interviews. In any event, research continues to support the notion that AC methodology is considered useful for meeting both selection and development objectives.

Contribution to the Talent Management Agenda

AC methodology entails observing an individual's behavior in order to determine their capability against a given benchmark. The principle of observing behavior to determine performance has a number of uses across the talent management or human resources management arena.

In the UK, organizations often develop a common behavioral language detailing the performance expected by people at certain job levels or in certain business functions, often termed a competency model or framework (Ballantyne & Povah, 2004). In the US, however, competency models often represent underlying psychological variables such as conscientiousness or openness (Hoffmann, 1999). Competency models help to provide a framework that can be used in ACs for making related talent management decisions; who to hire, promote, or let go. Additionally, DACs can be used to assist in an individual's career development, by identifying strengths and areas for improvement, which can help determine an appropriate career path. Another use for DACs is to aid an organization's succession planning process by identifying individuals with potential to take key roles in the organization in the future.

Benefits to the Organization

Numerous research papers (Harel, Arditi-Vogel, & Janz, 2003; Salgado, 1999; Schmidt & Hunter, 1998; Thornton & Rupp, 2006) have discussed the validity of the AC approach, with the predictive validity still reported as highly effective from 0.3–0.6, and the range generally being attributed to the variations in the design of the AC (Hermelin & Robertson, 2001). Alongside the validity argument there are numerous benefits to the organization of using such an approach.

As described above, the process requires the use of multiple assessors, meaning the process combines individual perspectives for a more objective view than a selection interview, which may have only one interviewer. Assessors have also often remarked about the useful skills they acquired when working on an AC. These skills include the ability to provide constructive behavioral feedback to colleagues and direct reports.

The AC process requires the collection and evaluation of behavioral evidence against a required standard and does not rely on self-reported evidence, like that collected in an interview or from a personality questionnaire. This results in a highly standardized process, as every candidate has the same opportunity to show their ability. The AC is therefore perceived to be a fair selection method by candidates and employers alike (Hausknecht, Day, & Thomas, 2004; Thornton & Rupp, 2006). Use of this approach has helped to project a positive, professional employer image to potential applicants (Thornton & Rupp, 2006), which is an important element of attracting and retaining key talent in a competitive marketplace.

Benefits to the Individual

It has also often been said that ACs help to create a 'two-way' selection process that allows both the candidate and employer to choose the best fit from their perspective (Hausknecht et al., 2004). We have already discussed the rich behavioral data collected, which allows an employer to make an informed decision, but what does the individual gain from this process?

ACs are comprised of job-related simulations that place the candidates in situations that require them to display similar behaviors to those expected from an effective performer in the actual role. This therefore, allows the candidate to obtain a realistic job preview of the role they are applying for. If they realize during the AC that they do not really enjoy the tasks they have been given, then they can consider whether this is the role for them, or conversely they may enjoy the tasks, confirming their choice of role. This preview is very difficult to obtain during any other type of selection approach, apart from work sampling, where an actual job extract is used.

As mentioned above, because of the realistic tasks set in ACs and the fact that candidates can show a range of abilities in the multiple exercises, they are perceived to be one of the fairest selection methods in use, providing employers with a rounded view of each individual and this is of course appreciated by the candidate.

Furthermore, candidates can learn a lot about themselves from the feedback provided after an event. While this obviously depends on the level of feedback given and the usefulness of the comments; if done well, individuals can gain useful insight into their strengths and development areas and their fit to different roles. This feedback should be based on behavioral evidence, not on their educational attainment or general intelligence, therefore presenting an opportunity for each individual to improve (Thornton & Mueller-Hanson, 2004).

It is widely recognized that AC popularity has grown, but it is difficult to attribute this to a particular reason (Briscoe, 1997; Lievens & Thornton, 2005). It could be a response to a fast-paced change with organizations requiring different skills that are best assessed behaviorally, or increased competition to get the best talent requiring a valid selection process or it could simply be down to the fact that this methodology is now better understood and appreciated. Whatever the rationale for the increase in popularity, ACs do not come without their challenges, which perhaps prevent their use from being even more widespread.

Key Challenges

Despite the effectiveness of ACs, they often need to overcome some key challenges before the commitment to proceed is secured. Such challenges can relate to a variety of matters, but are most commonly based on the parameters of cost, time and resources.

Cost

It is hard to deny that ACs are costly because of their duration, the number of resources involved and the sophistication of the process which demands careful preparation by skilled practitioners (be they internal or external). The key response to these costs is to provide a cost justification to illustrate the return on investment. Fortunately, the answer lies in a methodology called Utility Analysis which is well described by Cascio (1982) and Smith (1988). The method can be quite complicated and we cannot do justice to it in this chapter, but a good example to illustrate the calculation can be found in Ballantyne and Povah (2004). In simple terms, the method entails determining the degree to which a particular selection procedure in a specific context improves the quality of applicants chosen over random selection. Research into the utility of ACs by Hoffman and Thornton (1997) found that the results consistently demonstrated that ACs were superior to traditional selection techniques such as interviews and paper and pencil tests. They concluded that the benefits of ACs in selecting high-performing managers outweighed the design and administration costs, aided in part by them having significantly lower subgroup differences, thus enabling higher cut scores and providing greater utility. Indeed this observation highlights the fact that most utility analyses focus on the economic gains and far fewer refer to the non-economic factors that may influence the choice of an assessment technique, such as: acceptance of the process by candidates and managers, perceived fairness, or potential subgroup differences on statutory protected groups and legal defensibility (Cabrera & Raju, 2001). When the economic gains are calculated and these are combined with a consideration of these non-economic factors, a compelling case can be made for the use of ACs.

Time and Resources

Embarking on an AC is a serious commitment which cannot be undertaken lightly as it is undoubtedly a time-consuming and resource-hungry process. There are potentially five groups of people who are likely to be affected, namely the project or center manager, the center designers, the candidates or participants, the assessors, and in some cases the managers of participants. In the case of a traditional selection AC with external applicants, one is less concerned about the time impact on candidates so long as the center isn't so long as to discourage people from applying. Nor is there any impact on candidate line managers, so the major time investment principally affects the project or center manager, the center designers, and the assessors.

However, with DACs the impact is greater as both participants and their line managers are also affected by the need to invest time in the process. It is tempting to try to reduce the time commitment through the use of a number of different approaches, some of which are relatively safe with minimal detrimental impact and others which offer a false economy. These are listed in Table 1.1 along with an indication of the likely consequences of these actions.

With all of these attempts at saving time, it is important to evaluate the impact that these actions will have on the effectiveness of the center and its purpose; and most critical of all to ensure that such changes won't reduce the efficacy and legal defensibility of the process.

Implications for Legal Defensibility

It has long been recognized that any assessment process should be objective, free from bias and fair to all candidates, if only from a moral and ethical justification. This is perhaps further supported by the need for a diverse workforce, as organizations seek to emulate the diversity of their customer group (Cascio, Jacobs, & Silva, 2010).

Therefore, a constant concern when implementing an assessment process is that subgroup differences may occur (lower average scores for protected groups, resulting in lower selection rates). Such instances

TABLE 1.1 Consequences of Time-Saving Actions

Common time-saving actions	Consequences
Skimping on the Job Analysis.	Could end up measuring the wrong things and creating legal defensibility problems.
Reducing the number of simulations to shorten the Assessment Center (AC) duration.	Could result in inadequate coverage of the competencies, or measuring too many in each exercise and decreasing inter-rater reliability.
Using 'off-the-shelf', rather than customized simulation exercises.	Depends on the quality and fit of the simulations; safer with a Developmental Assessment Center (DAC).
Reducing exercise design time and failing to trial the exercises before going 'live'.	Exercises may contain errors or fail to provide adequate measurement of the designated competencies.
Reducing the time spent on Assessor Training.	Could lead to a decrease in inter-rater reliability and overall decline in validity.
Shortening the duration of the AC or DAC.	Feasible for an AC if the guiding principles are still followed. Could be detrimental to a DAC if participants don't feel it has a developmental feel/ purpose.
Using technology to ease the administrative burden eg compiling participant scores and feedback reports.	Fine if it works, although there needs to be a contingency plan in case of technological failure.

are rightly seen as discriminatory and need to be taken seriously. We will first position the issue of subgroup differences and then discuss how ACs fair against other assessment approaches in terms of legal defensibility.

The Key Legal Issues—Discrimination and Subgroup Differences

In any social context the issue of diversity is an important one that needs careful consideration and management. The term *diversity* covers physical characteristics, such as race or gender and non-physical characteristics such as sexual orientation or personality. To date, the legal system for workplace discrimination has mostly focused on physical diversity characteristics (Pyburn, Ployhart, & Kravitz, 2008).

Each country has its own laws and policies for managing diversity and protecting groups of individuals who might be subjected to discrimination. While there are some similarities between countries' laws, for example most countries have legislation relating to discrimination on the basis of race, gender, and disability; each country seeks to reflect its unique social context.

Additionally, there are bodies that produce codes of practice for organizations to follow, such as the Equal Opportunities Commission (in China), the Equality and Human Rights Commission (in the UK), and the Equal Employment Opportunity Commission (in the United States). Failure by an employer to adhere to all of these codes might not be unlawful but could result in a discrimination employment lawsuit.

The most common discrimination cases are related to selection decisions. Selecting the right quality of candidate while establishing diversity can be problematic; and this is often referred to as the diversity-validity dilemma (Cascio et al., 2010). This is because most selection methods are capable of disadvantaging groups of people. This does not automatically mean that the assessment method is intrinsically unfair, especially if the criterion score or pass rate is based on occupational requirement research (Ballantyne & Povah, 1995, 2004), but without this research, an employer could unfairly and disproportionately reject groups of applicants.

Comparing Assessment Centers with Other Selection Methods or Tools

When choosing selection tools it would make sense that employers should use the most relevant and valid tools yet, increasingly, employers are inclined to pick less valid tools in preference for those that are perceived to be legally fair to all potential applicants and therefore 'safe' from legal challenge.

By and large, the discussion of subgroup differences in relation to the AC method suggests that this approach shows smaller sub-group differences in comparison with written cognitive ability tests (Thornton & Rupp, 2006). Many cognitive ability tests can show Black-White differences of up to one standard deviation and yet, according to Dean, Roth, and Bobko's (2008) meta-analysis, Black-White differences were reduced to 0.52 standard deviation and Hispanic-White differences were reduced to 0.28 standard deviation, when using ACs.

Similarly, Bobko, Roth, and Buster (2005) compared racial differences for overall performance on work samples tests for two jobs, including the types of exercises used in ACs. They found Black-White mean differences of 0.70–0.73 standard deviations. Interestingly, the mean differnces varied when looking at scores per exercise type, ranging from near zero on a counseling exercise (for civil engineering managers) and a role play (for right-of-way specialists) to 0.80 for a managerial technical exercise and a specialist map reading exercise. The lack of Black-White differences for interpersonal exercises compared to technical exercises is salient, and suggests that the potential for subgroup differences could be higher in cognitively loaded exercises (Goldstein, Yusko, Braverman, Smith, & Chung, 1998).

Early studies looking at gender found no differences in AC ratings for men and women (Thornton & Byham, 1982; Thornton, 1992; Thornton & Rupp, 2006), however, Anderson, Lievens, Van Damm, and Born (2006) found that females scored higher in a leadership role assessment center. Melchers and Annen (in press) also found no differences in a military academy assessment center scores for candidates from German, French, or Italian-speaking regions of Switzerland.

The majority of subgroup difference research seems to support the notion that ACs offer a fair approach to assessment, producing lower sub-group differences than other approaches. However, as mentioned earlier, the perception of fairness of the assessment approach can be of equal importance in minimizing the risk of legal challenge.

In 1999, Terpstra, Mohamed, and Kethley reviewed the legal risks associated with nine different selection approaches (unstructured interviews, structured interviews, biographical information blanks (BIBs), cognitive ability tests, personality tests, honesty tests, physical ability tests, work sample/performance tests, and ACs) to determine where U.S. legal challenges against these selection methods had occurred and where these challenges had been successful (when the approach had been ruled discriminatory). Although this research was conducted over a decade ago and an up-to-date review is due, there were some useful findings to assist employers' decision making. They found that ACs were very infrequently challenged, especially compared to their usage. The techniques that were most frequently challenged were unstructured interviews, cognitive ability tests (e.g. specific ability/aptitude tests), and physical ability tests (e.g. fitness tests), all receiving numerous discriminatory rulings.

Once could therefore conclude that the numbers of complaints are higher when validity of approach is lower (as with unstructured interviews) and that applicants perceive some assessment approaches to be less fair (such as cognitive ability tests) and others to be more fair (such as work samples and ACs). Smither, Reilly, Millsap, Pearlman, and Stoffey (1993) also stated that those assessment approaches that are perceived as more fair, including ACs, faced fewer legal challenges.

Thornton, Wilson, Johnson, and Rogers (2009) conducted a recent review of 61 U.S. federal court cases involving ACs and found 53 rulings to be favorable to the AC method (in favor of the organization using the AC, approval of settlement agreements involving an AC, and the denial of injunctions against an AC) and 8 rulings to be unfavorable (failure to endorse an AC as an alternative promotional method and rulings against mismanaged ACs). This provides further evidence that well-managed ACs are viewed favorably by federal courts as a fair and robust assessment approach. In the case where rulings were unfavorable, the ACs were considered poorly designed and managed. Thornton et al. (2009) therefore concluded that it was the design and execution of these specific ACs that were at fault rather than the method itself.

Variations in AC Design

As the introduction to this volume explains, this book discusses the relative merits of three variations in AC design, namely the traditional dimension-based AC (DBAC), the task-based AC (TBAC) and the mixed-model AC (MMAC). Since the early days of AC practice the focus of all genuine ACs was on measuring the dimensions or competencies. However, the prolonged debate of the last three decades around the exercise effect has cast some doubt over the construct validity of ACs, which has given rise to the view amongst some, that we should focus more on the tasks being assessed, as reflected in the simulation content. This has led them to advocate the use of TBACs, while others have argued for more of a combined approach as depicted by MMACs, although the majority has remained loyal to the traditional DBAC. Indeed the legitimacy of these different approaches has recently gained some momentum thanks to their acknowledgement in the 2009 edition of the *International Taskforce Guidelines*, which states:

> *Behavioral classification*—Behaviors displayed by participants must be classified into meaningful and relevant categories such as behavioral

> dimensions, attributes, characteristics, aptitudes, qualities, skills, abilities, competencies or, knowledge. In these guidelines, the term 'dimension' is used as a general descriptor for each type of behavior category. Note that other classification schemes also may be used. For example, categories may reflect components of the target jobs or the assessment itself. (p. 245)

This suggests that it is acceptable to refer to how participants have performed on a job-related task, thus justifying that the behavioral data may be grouped in relation to performance within a simulation exercise such as an in-basket, interview simulation or group discussion.

However, it is worth noting that this stance isn't new, as many practitioners have long since recognized that both dimensions and exercises contribute valid data to the evaluation of each participant's performance (Ballantyne & Povah, 1995, 2004; Woodruffe, 1993, 2000). Indeed Joiner (2002) highlights the fact that there is more widespread support for the MMAC approach than might have been apparent when he points out that candidate scores will vary on a performance dimension such as *problem solving skills* depending on the types of exercises used to measure the dimension, because in effect the exercise further defines which aspect of the dimension is being measured.

In any event, Woodruffe (1993, 2000) makes the valid point that dispensing with dimensions in favor of exercises isn't really an option, as they are the basis of constructive, meaningful feedback about individual performance. No doubt the reader will form his or her own view on this interesting issue as they work through the contents of this book.

The Future for ACs

As mentioned earlier, AC use is growing and yet the future of ACs is not without its challenges. We see two significant factors which could have an increasing influence on how future ACs are designed and run.

The Impact of Technology

The ongoing rapid advance in the development of IT capability is continually presenting AC designers and practitioners with new ways of implementing their centers. For example, there are a number of software programs which can be used to design an AC and remove much of the difficulty in putting together an effective schedule that works for all interested parties. Although we have yet to encounter a program that does the whole task as well as an experienced human AC designer, there is no doubt that these programs can reduce some of the burden. There are also various tools, such as electronic inboxes, which can administer the AC to the participants through the medium of an email system, providing them with their personal schedule, any necessary briefing documentation and inviting them to attend various meetings. Also, with the use of a web-cam and access to the internet or a local area network (LAN), they can participate in a one-to-one role-play or be interviewed at their desk.

It is also possible to run a *virtual* AC at a designated test center where a candidate can be invigilated while undertaking a series of tasks, without ever meeting their interviewer or assessors in person and they can even be situated at different locations around the world! This of course saves on the time and expense of travel, as well as speeding up the whole process, which coincidentally simulates the contemporary virtual working world. With this increasingly electronic approach comes the risk that some behavioral cues might be missed due to not actually being in the same room. Also participants completing online application forms have described the experience as dehumanizing, with detrimental consequences, as they felt they weren't being treated as personal applicants, the process was perceived as unreal and they became carefree and tended to respond in a socially desirable way (Price & Patterson, 2003). Although this particular research relates to online application forms, it is quite possible that the same affect could apply with a virtual AC and this is undoubtedly an important area for further research.

Technology can also assist the assessors with the collation of data in the feedback report and there is scope for some automating of the scoring, such as selecting from a checklist those behavioral indicators which were displayed by the participant, but human intervention is still necessary to ensure that the final set of data is an accurate reflection of the participant's performance.

However, the biggest danger in all of this, apart from developing a reliance on technology (just as many drivers do with satellite navigation), is the risk of abandoning or diluting the adherence to the principles and high standards that have served ACs so well over the last 50 or so years. Nevertheless the boundaries of technology will keep rolling forward and it is futile to try to resist its impact on AC practice—we just need to ensure it is used well.

Global Influences

We live in a shrinking world and many organizations are giving greater consideration to how they will operate globally. This has significant implications for ACs as it means that many centers are being run to identify global talent, as organizations need people who can readily move from one country to another and quickly adapt to new cultures. As would be expected, this has implications for the content of an AC and the need to fully understand the demands that the successful candidates will face in working cross-culturally. This invariably means learning about new cultural norms and embracing the principles of diversity and this has implications for the team of assessors who need to be fully conversant with those cultures.

Organizations also face the challenge of trying to encourage a consistent approach in how the AC and associated processes are run. Most organizations favor a reasonable degree of consistency, so as to avoid variable standards. However, they also recognize that it can often be difficult to impose a totally uniform assessment approach across a wide range of countries, so some guidelines are usually provided as to which aspects of the methodology can be adapted and which aspects are "no go" or mandatory. For example, we have worked with a global multinational, who adopted a worldwide recruitment policy that required all recruitment activity included the use of a competency-based (behavioral event) interview and one other assessment tool with an established predictive validity of at least 0.25. This achieved the balance of imposing a standardized approach to interviewing, while allowing some freedom in the choice of a respectable, additional tool.

There is no doubt that AC researchers and practitioners will need to spend more and more time focusing on the numerous implications for ACs that will arise from increasing globalization and these two trends of IT and globalization will more than likely end up fueling one another.

Conclusion

The purpose of this chapter was to give the reader a brief introduction and overview of ACs. We have therefore provided an explanation of what an AC is and what it isn't, given the numerous occasions when it is, unfortunately, misrepresented. We expanded this explanation by describing the critical features which define an AC and we then reviewed why and how organizations use them; often with the aim of supporting their corporate strategies. Recently organizations have used ACs or DACs as integral selection or development activities within their broader talent management strategy.

We reviewed some of the key cost-benefit arguments that need to be considered when evaluating the viability of an AC, including issues around the legal defensibility of the AC method in comparison with other assessment tools.

We then touched on the topic of variations in AC design, with particular reference to the key theme running through this volume, of a comparison between the DBAC, TBAC, and mixed-model approaches to ACs. We highlighted the fact that, despite the longevity of the DBAC approach, there are many who would see the mixed-model approach as offering the 'best of both worlds', but readers will need to decide for themselves once they have reviewed the contents of the book.

We concluded our review of ACs by looking at two recent major developments, namely the impact of technology and the increasing demands for ACs to be run globally. Technology has already started to affect the way ACs are conducted, with computers being used to administer simulations, and in some cases remotely over the internet, creating a type of virtual AC. This particular feature also offers another option when it comes to the need to run ACs globally, as it is quite feasible to have the participants and assessors in different countries, all linked up via the internet. These two developments are still very much in their infancy in relation to established AC practice and there is little doubt that we will see more and more activity in these areas. Researchers will be evaluating their impact and implications and practitioners will be driven by their clients to test the boundaries of feasibility in order to contain costs and speed up the process. It will therefore be critical that the practitioners recognize the dangers of commercial pragmatism and they should ensure they heed the evidence coming from researchers who will be pointing out the inevitable risks associated with such practices. However, we are confident that while the AC may well need to continue on its evolutionary journey, it doesn't appear to be in any danger of extinction.

References

Anderson, N., Lievens, F., Van Dam, K., & Born, M. (2006). A construct investigation of gender differences in a leadership role assessment center. *Journal of Applied Psychology 91*, 555–566.

Assessment & Development Consultants. (2008). The global research report: An international survey of assessment center practices. Retrieved January 5, 2008, from http://www.adc.uk.com/page.aspx/26/interact (Go to Latest Research Findings)

Ballantyne, I., & Povah, N. (1995). *Assessment & Development Centres* (1st ed.). Hants, UK: Gower.

Ballantyne, I., & Povah, N. (2004). *Assessment & Development Centres* (2nd ed.). Hants, UK: Gower.

Bobko, P., Roth, P. L., & Buster, M. A. (2005). Work sample selection tests and expected reduction in adverse impact: A cautionary note. *International Journal of Selection and Assessment, 13,* 1–9.

Briscoe, D. R. (1997). Assessment centers: Cross-cultural and cross-national issues. *Journal of Social Behavior and Personality, 12,* 261–270.

Cabrera, E. F., & Raju, N. S. (2001). Utility analysis: Current trends and future directions. *International Journal of Selection and Assessment, 9,* 92–102.

Cascio, W. F. (1982). *Applied psychology in personnel management* (2nd ed.). Reston, VA: Reston Publications.

Cascio, W. F., Jacobs, R. & Silva, J. (2010). Validity, utility, and adverse impact: Practical applications from 30 years of data. In J. L. Outtz (Ed.), *Adverse impact: Implications for organizational staffing and high stakes selection* (pp. 271–288). New York, NY: Routledge, Taylor & Francis Group.

Connelly, B. S., & Ones, D. S. (2008, April). *Interrater unreliability in assessment center ratings: A meta-analysis.* Paper presented at the Annual Conference of the Society for Industrial and Organizational Psychology, San Francisco, CA.

Dean, M. A., Roth, P. L., & Bobko, P. (2008). Ethnic and gender subgroup differences in assessment center ratings: A meta-analysis. *Journal of Applied Psychology, 93,* 685–691.

Gaugler, B. B., Rosenthal, D. B., Thornton, G. C., III, & Bentson, C. (1987). Meta-analysis of assessment center validity. *Journal of Applied Psychology, 72,* 493–511.

Goldstein, H. W., Yusko, K. P., Braverman, E. P., Smith, D., & Chung, B. (1998). The role of cognitive ability in the subgroup differences and incremental validity of assessment center exercises. *Personnel Psychology, 51,* 357–374.

Harel, G. H., Arditi-Vogel, A., & Janz, T. (2003). Comparing the validity and utility of behavior description interview versus assessment center ratings. *Journal of Managerial Psychology, 18,* 94–104.

Hausknecht, J. P., Day, D. V., & Thomas, S. C. (2004). Applicant reactions to selection procedures: An updated model and meta-analysis. *Personnel Psychology, 57,* 639–683.

Hermelin, E., & Robertson, I., (2001). A critique and standardization of meta-analytic validity coefficients in personnel selection. *Journal of Occupational and Organizational Psychology, 74,* 253–277

Hoffman, C., & Thornton, G. C., III (1997). Examining selection utility where competing predictors differ in adverse impact. *Personnel Psychology, 50,* 455–470.

Hoffmann, T. (1999). The meanings of competency. *Journal of European Industrial Training, 23,* 275–285.

International Task Force on Assessment Center Guidelines (2009). Guidelines and ethical considerations for assessment center operations. *International Journal of Selection & Assessment, 17,* 243–253.

Joiner, D. (2002). Assessment centers: What's new? *Public Personnel Management, 31,* 179–185.

Krause, D. E., & Thornton, G. C., III (2008). International perspectives on adverse impact: Europe and beyond. In S. Schlebusch & G. Roodt (Eds.), *Assessment centres: Unlocking potential for growth* (pp. 349–374). Randburg, South Africa: Knowres Publishing.

Lievens, F. (1998). Factors which improve the construct validity of assessment centers: A review. *International Journal of Selection & Assessment, 6,* 141–152.

Livens, F. & Thornton, G. C. III (2005). Assessment centers: recent developments in practice and research. In A. Evers, O. Smit-Voskuijl, & N. Anderson (Eds.), *Handbook of Selection* (pp. 243–264). Oxford, UK: Blackwell.

Melchers, K. G. & Annen, H. (2010, April). *More than 2%! Incremental Validity of an AC beyond GMA.* Poster presented at the 25th Annual Conference of the Society for Industrial and Organizational Psychology, Atlanta, GA.

Price, R. & Patterson, F. (2003). On-line application forms: Psychological impact on applicants and implications for recruiters. *Selection and Development Review, 19,* April, 12–19.

Pyburn, K. M., Jr., Ployhart, R. E., & Kravitz, D. A. (2008). The diversity-validity dilemma: Overview and legal context. *Personnel Psychology, 61,* 143–151.

Salgado, J. F., (1999). Personnel selection methods. In C. L. Cooper & I. T . Robertson (Eds.), *International review of industrial and organizational psychology* (Vol. 16, pp. 39–53). New York, NY: Wiley.

Schlebusch, S., & Roodt, G. (2008). *Assessment centres: Unlocking potential for growth.* Randburg, South Africa: Knowres Publishing.

Schmidt, F. L., & Hunter, J. E. (1998). The validity and utility of selection methods in personnel psychology: Practical and theoretical implications of 85 Years of Research Findings. *Psychological Bulletin, 124,* 262–274.

Smith, M. (1988). Calculating the sterling value of selection. *Guidance and Assessment Review, 4*(1), February 6–8.

Smither, J. W., Reilly, R. R., Millsap, R. E., Pearlman, K., & Stoffey, R. W. (1993). Applicant reactions to selection procedures. *Personnel Psychology, 46,* 49–76.

Terpstra, D. E., Mohamed, A. A., & Kethley, R. B. (1999). An analysis of federal court cases involving nine selection devices. *International Journal of Selection and Assessment, 7,* 26–34.

Thornton, G. C., III. (1992). *Assessment centers in human resource management.* Reading, MA: Addison-Wesley.

Thornton, G. C., III, & Byham, W.C. (1982). *Assessment centers and managerial performance.* New York, NY: Academic Press.

Thornton G. C., III, & Mueller-Hanson, R. A. (2004). *Developing organisational simulations—A guide for practitioners and students.* Mahwah, NJ: Erlbaum.

Thornton, G. C., III, & Rupp, D. R. (2006). *Assessment centers in human resource management: Strategies for prediction, diagnosis, and development*. Mahwah, NJ: Erlbaum.

Thornton, G. C., III, Wilson, C. L., Johnson, R. M., & Rogers, D. A. (2009). Managing Assessment Center Practices in the Context of Employment Discrimination Litigation. *Psychologist-Manager Journal, 12*, 175–186.

Woodruffe, C. (1993). *Assessment Centres* (2nd ed.). London: Institute of Personnel Management.

Woodruffe, C. (2000). *Development and Assessment Centres* (3rd ed.). London: Chartered Institute of Personnel and Development.

2

One History of the Assessment Center

Scott Highhouse and Kevin P. Nolan
Bowling Green State University

Imagine that a WWII German officer candidate is required to pull on a metal spring with all of his might. As he pulls harder on the spring, it delivers an increasingly strong current of electricity throughout his body—all the while, a hidden camera is photographing his facial expressions. The military psychologists who administered this "character" test were not interested in how far the candidate could pull the metal spring or how long the candidate could endure the pain involved. Instead, the psychologists were interested in the degree of composure shown by the candidate as he completed the exercise. This curious procedure, and other similar ones employed by the German military, laid the initial foundation for what was to evolve into the modern-day assessment center for identifying and developing talent in organizations.

Character assessments like this one reflected a new school of thought referred to variously as organismic, gestalt, or holistic, which focused on the whole person and minimized the role of standardized tests of specific abilities or traits. The German psychologists believed that "intangible" aspects of character were more important than aptitudes or skill (Fitts, 1946, p. 153). This holistic concept of assessment, and the situational tests used to conduct it, inspired officer selection practices implemented by the Allies prior to the end of the war.[1] The British War Officer Selection Boards (a.k.a. WOSBs) borrowed the notion of multiple assessment procedures, but focused less on intrapsychic processes and more on the prediction of social skills. The Army psychiatrists pioneered the use of quasi-natural social situations to examine how people worked with others to solve problems encountered by actual soldiers in the field. In the United States, the Office of Secret Service (OSS) employed the services of Henry Murray, who was independently developing his own holistic view of personality assessment (see Ansbacher, 1941), to institute an elaborate method for selecting future spies and saboteurs. Murray and his colleagues borrowed many of the situational practices developed by the British and Germans, but also developed many of their own. Additionally, they inspired the use of pooled judgments made by multiple assessors (Taft, 1959). Many of these wartime practices found immediate application by industry in Australia, Britain, New Zealand, and in the United States (e.g., Brody & Powell, 1947; Fraser, 1947; Taft, 1948).

The most immediate forerunner to the modern-day assessment center was established by AT&T over a decade after the war ended.[2] Douglas Bray, inspired by the OSS report *Assessment of Men* (OSS, 1948), found an opportunity to apply the techniques in industry when he joined AT&T in 1956. Management at AT&T had the idea of conducting a longitudinal study of management careers, later known as the Management Progress Study (Bray, 1964), and approached Bray to lead the research project. It was for the purposes of this research that Bray conceived of the assessment center (Bray interviewed in Mayes, 1997). The first non-research assessment program in the United States was made operational at Michigan Bell Telephone Company in 1958 (Jaffee, 1965). This center modified the Management Progress center by eliminating the personality and projective tests, substituting the clinical interview for one that was based more on work experience and background, and emphasizing situational performance tasks (Bray, 1989).

Early assessment centers were implemented in Standard Oil of Ohio (SOHIO), Sears, General Electric, and IBM. Nevertheless, Byham (1977) reported that only 12 American corporations operated assessment centers by 1969. The procedure did not really take off on a large scale until after Byham published a *Harvard Business Review* article on the method in 1970. At about the same time, he founded with Bray an assessment center company to provide materials and know-how to organizations interested in developing in-house assessment centers (Bray, 1989). Standardized situational exercises first became available for purchase in 1973 from Development Dimensions, Inc. (DDI). By that time, hundreds of organizations were running assessment centers (Byham, 1977).

Organization of the Chapter

There are a number of ways to report the history of any selection technique. This is especially true of assessment centers, whose content tends to vary significantly from one application to another. One approach to reviewing the history of assessment centers has been to detail how the technique evolved from wartime to industrial applications (e.g., Thornton & Byham, 1982). Another approach has been to emphasize the origins of the holistic philosophy, and its influence on individual and group assessments for selection (Highhouse, 2002a). We believe it would be redundant at best (lazy at worst) to repeat these approaches. Consequently, we decided to approach the history of the assessment center method by studying the history of the exercises commonly used in them, and the evolution of the dimensions commonly assessed in them. This approach seems especially appropriate given the on-going controversies—documented in this book—concerning focus on dimensions, tasks, or both. First, we provide detailed historiographies of the most common families of assessment center exercises: *leaderless group discussions*, *role-play simulations*, and *in-baskets*. Following this, we examine the origin and evolution of the *dimensions* assessed. Our goal was to present a lively and relevant historical overview of the assessment center as we know it.

Exercises

A major distinguishing feature of assessment centers is the use of situational exercises. Finkle (1976) observed that the exercises had great appeal among managers in the United States. Post-war managers were highly skeptical of the value of ability and personality tests, and this attitude was encouraged by high profile indictments of employment testing in books published in the 1950s and early 1960s (i.e., *The Organization Man*, *Life in the Crystal Palace*, *The Brainwatchers*). Some exercises were used more commonly than others (e.g., the in-basket), but there was no universally-used situational exercise. As a matter of fact, by 1982, Tenopyr and Oeltjen lamented the fact that the label "assessment center" was indiscriminately applied to widely varying practices. In response to this confusion, Bray (1989) offered the following essential features of the assessment center (p. 18):

- Heavily based on individual and group behavioral exercises
- Behavior recorded and reported fully to all assessors
- All assessors consider all behavior
- Ratings of predetermined dimensions made in face-to-face meeting of assessors

Although assessment centers often employed standardized tests, and sometimes projective tests, Finkle (1976) noted that most assessment programs would "play down" the use of such tests (p. 864). In other words, the situational exercises were viewed as the defining feature of the assessment process.

Leaderless Group Discussions

The leaderless group discussion (LGD) is an inclusive label for a family of assessment center exercises in which a group of candidates is asked to discuss a topic of mutual interest. No one is appointed leader of the group, and assessors do not enter into the discussion once it begins. An early LGD used by AT&T, and described by Douglas Bray in a letter to Bernard Bass, involved assigning different colored vests to candidates. The candidates were instructed:

> From now on thru this problem you are Mr. Blue, Mr. Red, etc. You may take a seat at any one of the 6 chairs. We are interested in finding out how well you can present your point of view on some problem. Consequently, we are asking you to present a case for a man who is being considered for promotion within the company. (Bernard M. Bass Papers, May 7, 1964)

Candidates were each assigned a different imaginary person for whom they were to advocate for employment. Success on the task depended less on their ability to get their person promoted, but more on how they communicated their case. Assessors sat behind and at a distance from the candidates being assessed. They rated them on their overall approach, presentation, voice, vocabulary, forcefulness, stress tolerance, hand gestures, and eye contact.

The first LGD for selection purposes occurred in Germany around 1925 (Ansbacher, 1951). J. B. Rieffer, who directed German military psychology between 1920 and 1931, developed this "round-table" discussion technique to identify officer candidates for the Army after WWI. Although the Army seemed to lose interest in the practice when WWII began, the German Navy adopted it and assigned it considerable importance. Whereas the earlier versions of the LGD were put at the end of officer assessment and prompted candidates to freely discuss the testing process, the naval version prompted recruits to argue about the merits of things such as smoking cigarettes, and taking dance lessons. Ansbacher (1951) noted that the LGD found many civilian applications in Germany during and after the war.

Evidently inspired by the work of the German military, W. R. Bion instituted a number of leaderless group tests, including the LGD, in the assessment of officer candidates for the British Army (Bion, 1946). Bion was interested in an officer's capacity to engage in mature and independent social relationships (Sutherland & Fitzpatrick, 1945). He believed that leaderless situations created an internal conflict in the candidate—between the desire to achieve personal success and the desire to demonstrate the ability to work through others (Murray, 1990). The LGD used by the WOSB involved simply asking eight to ten candidates to select a subject for discussion and talk to each other about it (Garforth & De La, 1945). Other leaderless tests presented groups with physical problems (e.g., carrying equipment) and leaving the group to work out a solution. These problems together allowed the psychiatrists to observe tendencies that were considered group-cohesive and group-disruptive (Sutherland & Fitzpatrick, 1945). Similar procedures were adopted by the Australian military (Gibb, 1947).

In the United States, the OSS implemented an LGD in their main assessment center, "Station S." Candidates sat around a table while the assessors sat at the other end of the room. The candidates were instructed to answer the following question: "What are the major post-war problems facing the United States and (if you have time) along what lines do you think they should be solved?" (OSS, 1948, p. 129). Assessors were interested in each candidate's judgment and resourcefulness (referred to as "effective intelligence"), as well as his knowledge and understanding of current events. At the same time, candidates were rated on social skills and leadership in directing the discussion toward group goals. Finally, candidates were asked to vote on a secret ballot for the man or men they considered most effective.

On the domestic front, the LGD was gaining attention as an important selection technique in Britain. American psychologist Bernard Bass, who became known as a leading scholar on the LGD technique, explained how he came to know about it:

> What really got me started on my dissertation was a visit [to Ohio State University] by Richard Urbrock, a staff psychologist for Proctor and Gamble. He

> had just returned from England where he had observed the British Country House technique, the forerunner of assessment centers. A leaderless group discussion (LGD) was one of the techniques. (Bass interviewed in Hooijberg & Choi, 2000, p. 292)

The "Country House" technique that Bass referred to was developed by the National Institute of Industrial Psychology to select senior managers in coal distributing companies. The procedure, described by Fraser (1946, 1947), involved lodging candidates in a hotel where they were administered a battery of ability and personality tests. After dinner, the candidates were seated around a fireplace and asked to begin an informal discussion among themselves on any topic of common interest. Participants were asked to ignore the psychologist and two members of management who were seated in the rear of the room.

LGDs had been used in the United States prior to the early AT&T assessment center version described at the beginning of this section. The first tryouts occurred under the direction of Milton Mandell (1946) for possible use by the U.S. Civil Service Commission. The first operational LGD was implemented by the New York City Department of Health (Brody & Powell, 1947) as part of a battery of assessments for selecting health officers for training. Unlike the British counterparts, the American version involved discussion of topics directly relevant to the job in question. Five days prior to the actual LGD, candidates were assigned a medical problem involving public health (i.e., the control of rabies). Candidates were to prepare group recommendations and a short talk on one of eight topics relevant to the medical problem. At the actual LGD, the group was given little direction as how to proceed.

The early American versions generated limited enthusiasm (Gleason, 1957) and some critics (Douglas, 1950; Meyer, 1950). The prospects for the LGD as a replacement for interviewing and testing seemed slim. Bass noted that he discontinued his research program on LGDs because, "I did not think anyone was paying attention to it" (Bass interviewed in Hooijberg & Choi, 2000, p. 293). It seems that the technique might have remained a historical novelty if Bray (1964) had not implemented it into the AT&T assessment center.

Role-Play Simulations

Although the German and British armies experimented with tests that required officer candidates to give orders and direct assistants in accomplishing tasks (Fitts, 1946; Sutherland & Fitzpatrick, 1945), the intellectual father of the role play for use in assessment was J. L. Moreno. Moreno, who did not appear to suffer from humility (see Moreno, 1953), set out to introduce an entirely new science called Sociometry—the study of the individual in relation to the group. He is often credited with innovations such as psychodrama and group therapy. Although Moreno's work is rarely mentioned in the organizational psychology literature, he strongly influenced the post-war researchers of leadership and assessment. For instance, Bass (interviewed in Hooijberg & Choi, 2000) credits Moreno as one of the most significant contributors to leadership research in the 20th century.

The OSS researchers (OSS, 1948) acknowledged Moreno as the inspiration for their Station S improvisations, which represented the first formal use of the technique for selection. Prior to U.S. involvement in the war, Moreno had advocated the use of role play techniques for military selection and placement (Moreno, 1941). According to Moreno, through the use of improvisational, spontaneity tests, the artificial setting of (Binet) intelligence tests is "substituted for by the natural life-setting" (p. 385). In addition, Del Torto and Cornyetz (1944, p. 356) suggested that psychodrama could "release areas of information" that are not liberated by the interview and projective tests. The OSS procedure involved assigning candidates to role-play dyadic situations. The situations were personalized for each candidate, often to resolve doubts (e.g., suspected inability to take criticism or use tact) that the assessment staff still harbored about the candidate's fitness (MacKinnon, 1977). As an example, one candidate might be assigned the role of a small business owner who is interested in becoming a member of an exclusive club in town. The other candidate would be privately assigned the role of a club owner who had heard rumors of the person being "blackballed" by other clubs.

OSS assessors quickly dropped the use of rating forms for the role-plays, concluding that their intuitive impressions of that candidate's personality were more useful. Although the staff viewed the role play as an extremely valuable part of assessment, many industrial psychologists remained skeptical. Discussing various methods of personnel selection, Crissey (1949) noted:

> Other techniques, such as the various projective tests, role playing, sociometric techniques, observational methods, such as used in the O.S.S., may have possibilities, though so far the results have not been too promising. (p. 75)

Post-war applications of role play in industry tended to focus on supervisory training (Bradford & Lippitt, 1946). The ideas of spontaneity and experimenting with different personas were also fundamental contributors to the t-group movement in management development (Highhouse, 2002b).

Leadership scholars were also developing role-play simulations to study the effects of situations on leader effectiveness. J. K. Hemphill, who was an integral part of the Ohio State leadership studies of the 1940s, contributed the first simulation used in the AT&T assessment center (Mayes, 1997). This simulation, referred to as the "Manufacturing Problem," required each participant to play the role of a partner in a small manufacturing enterprise. The partners (i.e., assessees) had to coordinate activities to make as much money as possible for the group. Following this exercise, an example assessor report noted about a candidate:

> He was verbally active and kept up a steady flow of rather directive suggestions and orders which his peers came to follow. He was challenged for group leadership only once and succeeded in outtalking his opponent. Although he made most of the production decisions himself, he delegated most of the other jobs. (Bray, Campbell, & Grant, 1974, p. 22)

This business game simulation has fallen out of favor over the years, yet there are innumerable varieties of role-play simulations that continue to be used in assessment centers. One example is the simulated phone call, in which a candidate plays the role of a vendor who must convince a supplier (i.e., assessor) to purchase inventory. Another exercise requires the candidate to play the role of a customer service manager who must make a decision about whether to make exceptions to a return policy—the candidate is allowed to question an assessor to acquire relevant facts about the case. More generic leader role-plays include coaching a direct report or resolving an issue or problem with a peer (A. Howard, personal communication, May 4, 2010). The common thread in these exercises is that the candidate must assume another role, and must decide how to behave in that role.

In-Baskets

Sudden, unanticipated events that propel candidates into new and unfamiliar managerial roles have served as the context for the most popular of all assessment center exercises—the in-basket (Bender, 1973; Finkle, 1976). Consider the following scenario:

> Early this morning, your predecessor was killed in a car crash and you have been abruptly assigned to take his place. You have been given access to the contents of his in-basket (e.g., memos, letters, reports, etc.) and told that over the next few hours you will be evaluated with regards to how well you address the materials contained within. Good luck!

The in-basket is a "solitaire" management game that requires participants to behave in an imaginary environment as they would in real life, and commit themselves in writing to a specific course of action (Byham, 1977). The introductory device of killing off a hypothetical predecessor appears to be an artifact of its military origins; where it is not uncommon for officers to meet with a sudden catastrophe or be transferred unexpectedly (Lopez, 1966). It has been retained over the years to prevent the assessee from creating imaginary past relationships or conversations to bypass dealing with an item (A. Howard, personal communication, May 4, 2010). The imaginary situation usually takes place at night to necessitate the use of letters instead of phone calls, and time pressure is created by telling candidates that they have only two hours before they must catch a plane (Thornton & Byham, 1982).

In 1952, the Educational Testing Service (ETS) was contracted by the Air Force's Officer Education Research Laboratory to determine how well the Air Command and Staff School was achieving its training objectives. According to Frederiksen and his colleagues at ETS (Frederiksen, Saunders, & Wand, 1957), there was a clear need for an instrument that could measure:

- complex skills such as the ability to organize information
- ability to discover the problems implicit in a situation
- anticipation of events which may arise because of such problems
- arrival at decisions based on a large number of considerations

The first In-Basket Test was administered in 1953, and consisted of four two-hour sessions that required each cadet to assume four different director roles at a hypothetical military base. In developing the in-basket, Frederikson was influenced at least somewhat by the Melbourne Test 90, designed by Australian psychologist Paul Lafitte (1954). In Lafitte's test, university students assumed the role of "big business man" and solved two problems in writing for which they had been given assorted pieces of information. The first problem required them to determine where they would build their "super holiday camp."[3] The second problem required them to deal with a variety of things that had gone wrong in the first months of construction on the camp.

In order to create simulated problems for the Air Force officers to solve, Frederikson et al. (1957) studied a series of essays written by the students in the training center. According to authors, "Students were asked to describe some problem in the Air Force—how it arose the factors bearing on its solution, what had been done to solve it, and what remained to be done to complete its solution" (p. 6). These problems were translated into memos and reports that were presented to the in-basket participants. In reflecting on their participation in the in-basket exercise, many of the students responded positively. Others felt that they were provided insufficient background materials, and that the time constraints did not allow them to make considered judgments. The researchers concluded that the in-basket was a desirable criterion for evaluating the effectiveness of Air Force administrative officers, but they were hesitant to use the measure in its present form for assessment.

The first assessment center in-basket was developed by ETS, in conjunction with the AT&T staff. This in-basket, used in the Management Progress Study, provided three hours for the manager to address 25 distinct (but interrelated) items. Afterward, the assessee was interviewed to learn how he tackled the problems, what he learned from them, and the reasoning followed in the actions—or lack of actions—taken (Bray et al., 1974). Inaction seemed to weigh heavily on evaluations, as managers who relied excessively on "getting more information" were viewed as poor decision makers. The New York Port Authority was the first to use a fully quantitative scoring system for hiring police lieutenants (Lopez, 1966). Bentz (1967), in discussing the executive assessment program at Sears, commented on the difficulty of scoring an in-basket objectively:

> I'd like to mention that as one proceeds through scoring an In-Basket, a very strong subjective impression of the person's administrative style emerges. This is so strong that we believed these impressionistic data should be captured. Again, after considerable difficulty, we devised a means for converting this subjective impression into a kind of measurable index, and reports were written in an attempt to capture this subjective material. (p. 194)

In early assessment centers, no attempt was made to objectively score candidates' performance on the in-basket. The debriefing served as the basis for dimension ratings (Hinrichs, 1969).

Changes in the structure and responsibilities of managerial jobs have made some question the relevance of the technique for the modern workforce (Schneider, Huck, Seegers, & Ashworth, 1994). Over the years, several noteworthy attempts have been made to provide a facelift to the traditional in-basket format. Gibson (1961), for example, integrated in-basket materials with a motion picture devised to simulate the constant interruptions managers experience daily. In 1977, Lopez explored the use of auditory input by including telephone messages and allowing those taking the in-basket to make outgoing telephone calls to solicit information (Gill, 1979). The in-basket exercises of today have been meaningfully influenced by the proliferation of personal computers, where the inbox has replaced the in-basket.

Dimensions

As noted earlier in this chapter, the German assessment methods were based on a holistic view of personality. Little attention was given to individual traits. Max Simoneit, the father of German military psychology, did not believe that personality types had practical usefulness for prediction (Ansbacher, 1941). Instead, the focus of the German assessors was on the similarity of candidate's global character to that of past war heroes. The British, on the other hand, were opposed to traits because they did not want preconceived notions about attributes of successful officers to contaminate assessment of candidates. The WOSB assessors believed that the officer's job could be effectively carried out in various ways, and that competence was the main goal of assessment (Murray, 1990). Three primary demands of the officer's job were the focus of assessment: quality of social relations, stamina under stressful conditions, and competence in practical situations.

The OSS assessment staff recorded candidate performance ratings on a number of trait-like dimensions, including *Emotional Stability, Leadership,* and *Social Relations.* As Highhouse (2002a) noted, however, the psychologists were philosophically opposed to the idea of adding the ratings together into a composite score. They believed that only a trained psychologist could determine how the individual components made up a candidate's "whole personality" (OSS, 1948, p. 43). Table 2.1 presents the dimensions assessed by the OSS staff, along with the situational exercises designed to elicit behaviors reflective of these traits. The "X"s in the table show which exercises were used to elicit which traits. As the table shows, the interview—a lengthy comprehensive clinical interview—was the only "test" that is connected with every dimension. The psychodramas are not listed in the columns because they were

Table 2.1 Dimensions and Situations used by the OSS (1948) Assessment Staff

	Interview	LGD	Debate	Brook	Assigned Leader	Assigned Subordinate	Construction	Stress Interview	Post-Stress Interview	Obstacle Course
Energy & Initiative	X	X	X	X	X		X			X
Effective Intelligence	X	X	X	X	X	X				
Emotional Stability	X						X	X	X	
Social Relations	X	X	X	X	X		X			
Leadership	X	X	X	X	X		X			
Physical Ability	X			X						X
Security	X							X	X	
Propaganda Skills	X	X	X							

Note: *Observing and Reporting* was another dimension used by the OSS staff, but it was assessed with paper and pencil tests. Also, *Motivation for Assignment* began as a separate dimension, but was combined with Energy and Initiative.

not rated on the dimensions.[4] This reliance on the interview, and the importance placed on the role-plays for checking hunches about personality, shows the lack of regard the assessors had for standardized methods of assessment (see Eysenck, 1953).

The assessment center used in the original, 1956, Management Progress Study included 26 dimensions. Bray (1989) recalled that they had arrived at these dimensions by reviewing the management-selection literature and by interviewing behavioral scientists and top AT&T personnel executives. The Management Progress Study, directly inspired by the OSS center, was clinical in nature; including projective tests and in-depth interviews. These components were dropped when the assessment center was made operational for selection decisions at AT&T.[5] The transition from wartime selection boards to industrial assessment centers marked the movement away from global personality assessments, toward focus on specific dimensions of work-related behavior. Most subsequent assessment centers relied heavily on situational exercises to make ratings on behavioral dimensions (e.g., planning and organizing; sensitivity), and the number of dimensions assessed was commonly in the double digits (Thornton & Byham, 1982). This is despite the fact that Carter (1954) warned that assessors were only capable of rating three or, at most, four dimensions of behavior. Carter reviewed factor-analytic studies of assessor ratings of behavior in situational tests, and identified three observable dimensions: (a) *individual prominence and achievement*, (b) *aiding attainment by group*, and (c) *sociability*. Carter noted that situational exercises should not be used for jobs that did not require these behaviors as part of their performance criteria.

Dimension vs. Exercise Debate

The stability of dimension scores across situational exercises has been a concern throughout the history of the assessment center. Sakoda (1952) conducted a factor analysis of the ratings made by OSS assessors and concluded that dimension ratings were not meaningful unless they were considered in the context of situational types. For instance, a candidate could demonstrate effective intelligence in "active" situations (e.g., Brook, Assigned Leader), but not in "verbal" ones (e.g., Debate, LGD). According to Sakoda (1952, p. 851), "Instead of seeking 'primary' abilities, we can investigate the abilities required in a 'verbal' or 'active' situation." This work appeared to preface the debate that was to come, over whether assessors should focus on dimensions, exercises, or both.

The first application of the multitrait-multimethod matrix approach to assessment center ratings was done by Thomson (1970) as part of his doctoral dissertation at Case Western Reserve. Thomson used data from the SOHIO assessment center to examine whether final dimension ratings were correlated with supervisor ratings on the same dimension. Although Thomson found a severe lack of discriminant validity in the monomethod heterotrait comparisons, he emphasized the results in support of assessment center construct validity. The topic remained dormant for another 12 years, until two published studies (Sackett & Dreher, 1982; Turnage & Muchinsky, 1982) pushed the issue back into the forefront. These studies showed that the same dimensions rated across exercises were not correlated, and that different dimensions within exercises were highly correlated. This called into question the practice of making inferences about candidate abilities and traits based on their behavior in the exercises. The Sackett and Dreher (1982) article was especially lucid and forceful, and has subsequently been regarded as the seminal piece in the construct validity "crisis" that has lasted nearly three decades (see Lance, 2008).

Dimension Discussions

The team approach to assessment is one of the defining features of the assessment center method (Finkle, 1976). This approach had its origins in the OSS assessment program, of which Henry Murray was an integral part. Murray was originally a physician who often participated in "grand rounds," where the medical problems and treatment of a particular patient are presented to a team of doctors, residents, and medical students. In the 1930s, Murray applied this team approach to personality assessment at Harvard, using a team of psychologists, psychiatrists, and anthropologists. He brought a similar approach to the OSS for the assessment of future spies. Bray (1989) noted that he borrowed the approach for the assessment of AT&T managers in the Management Progress Study. He assembled his assessment team with psychologists from AT&T and university psychology departments. Assessments took place in the summers (between 1956 and 1958) so that the university-based psychologists would have adequate time in their schedules.

Because it would have been prohibitive to staff operational assessment centers with psychologists, the ones put into operation at most organizations including AT&T used managers (e.g., second-level supervisors) as assessors. Thornton and Byham (1982) described the typical process used in operational assessment centers: (a) assessors individually observe and rate exercises, (b) they derive consensus dimension ratings via group discussions, and (c) they integrate the dimension ratings to form a final overall assessment. In the typical group discussion, assessors are asked to report their preliminary dimension ratings. These are recorded on a flipchart for discussion to arrive at a consensus on the final dimension ratings. In the final stage, the team arrives at an overall assessment rating. The entire group discussion process can take several days to complete, and no mechanical or statistical formulas are used.

Considerable research in the area of personality assessment had already shown that assessor discussions were not an improvement over a simple mechanical combination of ratings (see Taft, 1959, for a review). Oldfield (1947) noted in regard to panel interviews: "Discussion of the merits of candidates merely amounts to a somewhat clumsy method of averaging the individual judgments of the members" (p. 129). The first to study this issue in the assessment center was Wollowick and McNamara (1969). The authors found that the subjectively-derived combination of tests, dimensions, and exercises (i.e., the Overall Assessment Rating) correlated .37 with the criterion, whereas a statistical combination of them provided a multiple correlation of .62. Subsequent research supported this finding (see Pynes, Bernardin, Benton, & McEvoy, 1988, for a review). Sackett and Wilson (1982) found that a simple average of dimension ratings predicted post-discussion ratings 93.5% of the time. Pynes et al. (1988) calculated that a police assessment center could save $6137.92 per year (in 1988 dollars) if it eliminated the team discussion meeting. Despite this, the consensus judgment process continues to be a staple of the assessment center. Perhaps Taft (1959, p. 345) was prescient when he suggested that "public relations considerations" would determine whether the clinical or mechanical procedures are used. Howard (1997) reported that "Many assessors report a potent sense of satisfaction from putting the evidence together and creating a holistic view of the assessee" (p. 36).

Conclusion

The assessment center of today is a descendent of procedures developed by maverick psychologists and psychiatrists who were dissatisfied with traditional psychometric methods of assessing abilities and traits. Like most selection procedures, many of the simulations used in assessment centers originated in the military. Their implementation in business reflected post-war efforts to predict leadership by examining the candidate "in action." Many of the early figures in the adaptation of these procedures to business, and ultimately to assessment center exercises (e.g., Bernard Bass, J. K. Hemphill, J. L. Moreno), were prominent figures in leadership theory and research. The connection between leadership theory and leader identification/selection is arguably weaker today (cf. Hogan & Kaiser, 2005).

The large number of dimensions used in the traditional assessment center was not aligned with the simultaneously emerging literature on personality assessment and cognition, showing that people could not handle rating more than a few broad dimensions. The quest for parsimony, which is characteristic of the psychometric tradition, was up against the holistic emphasis on the detailed, nuanced, ideographic evaluation of each person. Indeed, this tension between objective and subjective assessment is a current that runs throughout the history of the assessment center, and is reflected in debates that persist to this day.

Notes

1. Eysenck (1953) claimed that the Japanese followed many of the German procedures, but (similar to the Germans) provided little documentation of effectiveness. Hopkins (1944) suggested that similar procedures were conducted secretly by the Russians as well.
2. In an earlier article (Highhouse, 2002a), the first author mistakenly attributed the first use of the term "assessment center" to D. E. Super, who did not even use the term in the cited article. It appears that Murray and MacKinnon (1946; p. 80) made the first published use of the term in a selection context.
3. This first problem is more like a modern day "analysis problem" exercise, a very common type of assessment center exercise (A. Howard, personal communication, May 4, 2010).
4. Behavior after drinking hard liquor was also considered an important part of the evaluation of the role plays.
5. SOHIO continued to use projective tests and clinical interviews in their assessment centers (Finkle, 1976).

References

Ansbacher, H. L. (1941). Murray's and Simoneit's (German military) methods of personality study. *Journal of Abnormal Psychology, 36,* 589–592.

Ansbacher, H. L. (1951). The history of the leaderless group discussion technique. *Psychological Bulletin, 48,* 383–390.

Bass, Bernard M. Papers (1960–1967). Letter from Douglas Bray (M1242, folder #174). Archives of the History of American Psychology, University of Akron, Akron, Ohio.

Bender, J. M. (1973, July/August). What is typical of assessment centres. *Personnel,* 50–57.

Bentz, V. J. (1967). The Sears experience in the investigation description and prediction of executive behavior. In F .R. Wickert & D. E. McFarland (Eds.), *Measuring executive performance* (pp. 147–205). New York: Apppleton-Century-Crofts.

Bion, W. R. (1946). The leaderless group project. *Bulletin of the Menninger Clinic, 10,* 77–81.

Bradford, L. P., & Lippitt, R. (1946). Role-playing in supervisory training. *Personnel, 22,* 358–369.

Bray, D. W. (1964). The management progress study. *American Psychologist, 19,* 419–429.

Bray, D. W. (1989). History of the assessment center in the United States. In J. Wilson, G. Thomson, R. Millward, & T. Keenan (Eds.), *Assessment for Teacher Development* (pp. 15–24) Philadelphia: Falmer Press.

Bray, D. W., Campbell, R .J., & Grant, D. L. (1974). *Formative years in business: A long-term AT&T study of managerial lives.* New York: John Wiley & Sons.

Brody, W., & Powell, N. J. (1947). A new approach to oral testing. *Educational and Psychological Measurement, 7,* 289–298.

Byham, W. C. (1977). Application of the assessment center method. In J. L. Moses & W. C. Byham (Eds.), *Applying the assessment center method* (pp. 31–44). New York: Pergammon Press.

Carter, L. F. (1954). Evaluating the performance of individuals as members of small groups. *Personnel Psychology, 7,* 477–484.

Crissey, O .L. (1949). Personnel selection. In W. Dennis (Eds.), *Current trends in industrial psychology* (pp. 554-83). Pittsburgh, PA: University of Pittsburgh Press.

Del Torto, J., & Cornyetz, P. (1944). Psychodrama as expressive and projective technique. *Sociometry, 7,* 356–375.

Douglas, A. G. (1950). Shall civil service endorse science or novelty? *Public Administration Review, 10,* 78–86.

Eysenck, H J. (1953). *Uses and abuses of psychology.* Harmondsworth, Middlesex, UK: Penguin Books.

Finkle, R. B. (1976). Managerial assessment centers. In M. D. Dunnette (Ed.), *Handbook of industrial and organizational psychology* (pp. 861–888). Chicago: Rand McNally.

Fitts, P. M. (1946). German applied psychology during World War Two. *The American Psychologist, 1,* 151–161.

Fraser, J. M. (1946). An experiment with group methods in the selection of trainees for senior management positions. *Occupational Psychology, 20,* 63–67.

Fraser J. M. (1947). New-type selection boards in industry, *Occupational Psychology, 21,* 170–178.

Frederiksen, N., Saunders, D R., & Wand, B. (1957). The in-basket test. *Psychological Monographs, 71,* 1–28.

Garforth, G. I., & De La, P. (1945). War officer selection boards. *Occupational Psychology, 19,* 97–108.

Gibb, C. A. (1947). The principles and traits of leadership. *Journal of Abnormal and Social Psychology, 42,* 267–284.

Gibson, G. W. (1961). A new dimension for 'In-basket' training. *Personnel, 38,* 76–79.

Gill, R. W. (1979). The in-tray (in-basket) exercise as a measure of management potential. *Journal of Occupational Psychology, 52,* 185–197.

Gleason, W. J. (1957). Predicting army leadership ability by modified leaderless group discussion. *Journal of Applied Psychology, 41,* 231–235.

Highhouse, S. (2002a). Assessing the candidate as a whole: A historical and critical analysis of individual psychological assessment for personnel decision making. *Personnel Psychology, 55,* 363–396.

Highhouse, S. (2002b). A history of the t-group and its early applications in management development. *Group Dynamics: Theory, Research, and Practice, 6,* 277–290.

Hinrichs, J. R. (1969). Comparison of "real life" assessments of management potential with situational exercises, paper-and-pencil ability tests, and personality inventories. *Journal of Applied Psychology, 53,* 425–432.

Hogan, R., & Kaiser, R. B. (2005). What we know about leadership. *Review of General Psychology, 9,* 169–180.

Hooijberg, R., & Choi, J. (2000). From selling peanuts and beer in Yankee stadium to creating a theory of transformational leadership: An interview with Bernie Bass. *Leadership Quarterly, 11,* 291–306.

Howard, A. (1997). A reassessment of assessment centers: Challenges for the 21st century. *Journal of Social Behavior and Personality, 12,* 13–52.

Hopkins, P. (1944). Observations on army and air-force selection and classification procedures in Tokio, Budapest, and Berlin. *The Journal of Psychology, 17,* 31–37.

Jaffee, C. L. (1965). Assessment centers help find management potential. *Bell Telephone Magazine, 44*(3), 18–25.

Lafitte, P. (1954). Melbourne Test 90. *Australian Journal of Psychology,* Monograph Supplement 1, 1–107.

Lance, C. E. (2008). Why assessment centers do not work the way they are supposed to. *Industrial and Organizational Psychology, 1,* 98–104.

Lopez, F. (1966). *Evaluating executive decision making: The in-basket technique.* New York: American Management Association.

Mandell, M. M. (1946). The group oral performance test. *Public Personnel Review, 7,* 209–212.

Mayes, B. T. (1997). Insights into the history and future of assessment centers: An interview with Dr. Douglas W. Bray and Dr. William Byham. *Journal of Social Behavior and Personality, 12,* 3–12.

MacKinnon, D. W. (1977). From selecting spies to selecting managers—The OSS assessment program. In J. L. Moses & W. C. Byham (Eds.), *Applying the assessment center method* (pp. 13–30). New York: Pergammon Press.

Meyer, C. A. (1950). The group interview test: Its weakness. *Public Personnel Review, 11,* 147–154.

Moreno, J .L. (1941). The advantages of the sociometric approach to problems of national defense. *Sociometry, 4,* 384–391.

Moreno, J. L. (1953). How Kurt Lewin's "research center for group dynamics" started: A secession from the sociometric movement. *Sociometry, 16,* 101–104.

Murray, H. (1990). The transformation of selection procedures: The War Office Selection Boards. In E. Trist & H. Murray (Eds.), *The social engagement of social science: A Tavistock anthology* (pp. 45–67). Philadelphia: The University of Pennsylvania Press.

Murray, H. A., & MacKinnon, D. W. (1946). Assessment of OSS personnel. *Journal of Consulting Psychology, 10,* 76–80.

Office of Strategic Services (OSS) Assessment Staff. (1948). *Assessment of men: Selection of personnel for the Office of Strategic Services.* New York: Rinehart.

Oldfield, R. S. (1947). *The psychology of the interview.* London: Methuen.

Pynes, J., Bernardin, H. J., Benton, A. L., & McEvoy, G. M . (1988). Should assessment center dimension ratings be mechanically-derived? *Journal of Business and Psychology, 2,* 217–227.

Sackett, P. R., & Dreher, G. F. (1982). Constructs and assessment center dimensions: Some troubling empirical findings. *Journal of Applied Psychology, 67,* 401–410.

Sackett, P. R., & Wilson, M. A. (1982). Factors affecting the consensus judgment process in managerial assessment centers. *Journal of Applied Psychology, 67,* 10–17.

Sakoda, J. M. (1952). Factor analysis of OSS situational tests. *Journal of Abnormal and Social Psychology, 47,* 843–852.

Schneider, J. R., Huck, J. R., Seegers, J., & Ashworth, S. (1994, April). *The in-basket exercise in the face of changing managerial jobs: Has it outlived its relevance?* Paper presented at the 22nd International Congress on the Assessment Center Method.

Sutherland, J.D., Fitzpatrick, G.A. (1945). Some approaches to group problems in the British Army, *Sociometry, 8,* 205–217.

Taft, R. (1948). Use of the "Group Situation Observation" method in the selection of trainee executives, *Journal of Applied Psychology, 32,* 587–594.

Taft, R. (1959). Multiple methods of personality assessment. *Psychological Bulletin, 56,* 333–352.

Tenopyr, M., & Oeltjen, P. D. (1982). Personnel selection and classification, *Annual Review of Psychology, 33,* 581–618.

Thomson, H. A. (1970). Comparison of predictor and criterion judgments of managerial performance using the multitrait-multimethod approach. *Journal of Applied Psychology, 54,* 496–502.

Thornton, G. C., & Byham, W. C. (1982). *Assessment centers and managerial performance.* San Diego, CA: Academic Press.

Turnage, J. J., & Muchinsky, P. M. (1982). Transsitutaional variability in human performance within assessment centers. *Organizational Behavior and Human Decision Processes, 30,* 174–200.

Wollowick, H. B., & McNamara, W. J. (1969). Relationship of the components of an assessment center to management success. *Journal of Applied Psychology, 53,* 348–352.

3

Methods and Data Analysis for Assessment Centers

David J. Woehr
University of North Carolina Charlotte

John P. Meriac
University of Missouri, St. Louis

Mark C. Bowler
East Carolina University

What do assessment centers measure? How well do assessment center ratings predict job performance? How can the reliability and validity of assessment center ratings be optimized? These are the primary questions underlying the vast majority of the research literature on assessment centers. As established in the previous chapters, assessment centers (ACs) emerged and continue to be primarily used as an approach to the measurement of individual differences relevant to work performance. So like any measurement tool, a fundamental concern for ACs is establishing how well they measure the individual differences they purport to measure and the appropriateness of the inferences that are drawn from these measures. In essence, this defines the construct validation process (American Educational Research Association, American Psychological Association, & National Council on Measurement in Education, 1999; Society for Industrial and Organizational Psychology, 2003). Thus, a primary theme throughout the AC literature has been the accumulation of evidence pertaining to the interpretation of AC ratings. The primary goal of the present chapter is to present a general overview of the methods and analytic approaches that have been applied in this endeavor. Toward this end, we begin with a discussion of the scores that result from the use of the AC method, that is AC ratings. We then turn to the ways in which these ratings have been analyzed in order to address the underlying questions of interest.

Assessment Center Ratings

It is important to begin any discussion of AC ratings by acknowledging that while the AC method is recognized as a distinct and identifiable approach to the measurement of individual differences, there is tremendous variability in the design and implementation of specific ACs. Drawing on a relatively large body of research, Woehr and Arthur (2003) identify seven methodological factors and design characteristics on which there is considerable variability across operational ACs. These include: (a) the number of dimensions assessors are asked to observe and subsequently rate; (b) the number of exercises participants complete; (c) the ratio of participant to assessors; (d) the type of assessor, psychologists/HR professional vs. managers/supervisors; (e) occurrence and extent of assessor/rater training; (f) the AC purpose, selection/promotion vs. development; and (g) the point at which participants are evaluated by assessors, within vs. across exercises.

Of these seven, arguably the most important characteristics on which ACs may vary is the way in which participants are evaluated by assessors. Specifically, Sackett and Dreher (1982) identify two distinct evaluation processes commonly used in ACs. In the first, which Sackett and Dreher refer to as the "AT&T method" (aka across-exercise approach; Woehr & Arthur, 2003), assessors observe participant performance in each exercise, but no ratings are made until all exercises are completed. Following the completion of all exercises, assessors share their observations and then provide consensus ratings of participants on the set of dimensions. Such ratings have been referred to as final dimension ratings (Sackett & Dreher, 1982) or post consensus dimension ratings (PCDRs; Hoffman & Woehr, 2009). PCDRs may then be combined (either clinically or mechanically) to generate an overall assessment center rating (OAR). Sackett and Dreher identify the second approach as the 'within-exercise' rating method. In this approach, assessors observe participant performance and provide dimension ratings upon completion of each exercise. These preliminary ratings have been referred to as post-exercise dimension ratings (PEDRs; Lance, 2008). Following the completion of all exercises, PEDRs may be combined (either clinically or arithmetically) to generate final dimension ratings, which in turn may be combined (either clinically or arithmetically) to generate an OAR.

Similar to any measurement tool, evidence supporting the construct validity of AC ratings may be content-related, criterion-related, or construct-related. ACs have traditionally been viewed as an approach that lends itself to content-related validity evidence (Byham, 1980; Norton, 1977). For ACs, typical content-related evidence focuses the extent to which a job analysis is used to identify important dimensions of the targeted job as well as on the development of appropriate simulation exercises. Although the use of job analysis and the systematic development of exercises is an inherent component of most ACs, surprisingly little research has explicitly examined the adequacy of this process (cf. Norton, 1977). Thus, it is important to note that evidence pertaining to the validity of AC ratings has almost exclusively been of two types—criterion-related and construct-related. Moreover, these two types of evidence have tended to focus on different types of AC ratings. Specifically, criterion-related evidence has tended to look at the predictive validity of OARs and/or final dimension ratings with respect to various external, job-relevant criteria. Results of this research have generally been unequivocal in their support for the criterion-related validity of these ratings (see Arthur, Day, McNelly, & Edens, 2003; Gaugler, Rosenthal, Thornton, & Bentson, 1987; Meriac, Fischer, & Hoffman, 2010; and Meriac, Hoffman, Woehr, & Fleisher, 2008, for meta-analytic summaries of these findings). Moreover, because final dimension ratings as well as OARs are obtained in both the within- and across-exercise rating approaches, accumulated criterion-related validity evidence may be based on data from ACs using either approach. Construct-related evidence, however, has tended to emphasize the internal structure of AC ratings and thus almost exclusively utilizes PEDRs. That is, because only the within-exercise rating approach provides ratings on each dimension for each exercise, this approach has exclusively served as the basis for studies examining the underlying structure of AC ratings.

Although there is a substantial amount of literature with respect to both criterion- and construct-related validity, more evidence has been accumulated with respect to criterion-related validity. In an early meta-analysis focusing on OAR's, Gaugler et al. (1987) summarized 47 studies reporting 107 validity coefficients. More recently, Arthur et al. (2003) meta-analyzed the criterion-related validity of AC ratings at the dimension level and summarized 34 studies reporting 258 final dimension level validity coefficients Similarly, Meriac et al. (2008) examined the incremental validity of AC ratings, summarizing the findings of 48 studies. In contrast, recent meta-analytic reviews focusing on construct-related validity evidence (i.e., PEDRS) include substantially less data. For example, Bowler and Woehr (2006) summarize 24 studies reporting 35 independent sets of ratings and Lance, Lambert, Gewin, Lievens, and Conway (2004) summarize 26 studies reporting 39 sets of ratings.

The Multitrait-Multimethod (MTMM) Perspective

An important turning point for AC research stems from the work of Sackett and Dreher (1982). Discussing PEDRs stemming from ACs using a within-exercise approach, Sackett and Dreher stated: "The current article focuses on the preliminary judgments made by assessors upon completion of each exercise" (p. 402). More importantly, they were among the first to note that: "These ratings can be cast as a multitrait-multimethod matrix in which dimensions serve as traits and exercises as methods (Campbell & Fiske, 1959)" (p. 402). Thus, Sackett and Dreher (1982) were the first researchers to apply Campbell & Fiske's MTMM approach to construct-related validity evidence to AC ratings. With this approach, the pattern of correlations among PEDRs is examined for evidence of convergent and discriminant validity. Subsequently, empirical studies examining AC construct-related validity have almost exclusively focused on the internal structure of AC PEDRs. More importantly, unlike research examining the criterion-related validity of final dimension ratings and OARs, evidence with respect to the construct-related validity of PEDRs has been equivocal at best. That is, this research indicates that AC ratings generally do not reflect the dimensions they were intended to measure. This finding has been the focus of a great deal of recent attention and debate in the AC literature (e.g., see Lance, 2008, and corresponding commentaries). Given this focus, the remainder of the chapter focuses on the data analytic approaches used in examining the internal structure of AC ratings—factor analytic approaches (both exploratory and confirmatory) and ANOVA-based variance partitioning approach (both univariate and multivariate).

Factor Analysis and AC Ratings

The application of factor analysis to AC ratings goes back as far as the history of ACs in the United States. Early applications of factor analytic techniques to AC ratings focused on factoring matrices of final dimension ratings to identify factors underlying the relatively large number of dimensions used in many ACs. In the original Management Progress Studies, for example, Bray and Grant (1966) assessed a total of 25 dimensions across several simulation and paper-and-pencil exercises, as well as several cognitive and personality tests. In an attempt to determine "underlying constructs employed in making judgments" (p. 6), the authors conducted an exploratory factor analysis (EFA) on final dimension ratings. Specifically, the researchers expected that some broader set of constructs were operating despite ratings on more narrowly defined performance dimensions. They found that a core set of eight broad factors emerged, including, for example, "administrative skills," and "interpersonal skills" (p. 8). The authors speculated that these latent constructs may be what actually drives variation in the dimension ratings made by AC raters.

Similarly, Schmitt (1977) factor analyzed a set of 17 final dimension ratings. Results supported a three-factor solution as optimal for explaining variance in the dimension ratings. These three broad factors were labeled: (a) administrative skills, (b) interpersonal skills, and (c) activity/forcefulness. It should be noted that variations on a three-category taxonomy have emerged repeatedly in the AC literature (i.e., Gaugler & Thornton, 1989; Huck & Bray, 1976; Thornton & Byham, 1982). In addition, other models with fewer categories (e.g., Shore, Thornton, & Shore, 1990) or more categories (e.g., Arthur et al., 2003) have been postulated in the literature, and have only recently been examined using factor analysis (Meriac, Hoffman, & Woehr, 2009).

Here it is important to note that this line of research focuses on final dimension ratings (as opposed to PEDRs) and draws a distinction between the set of manifest dimensions assessed and the factors or constructs underlying these dimensions. Key to this distinction is the idea that the set of espoused dimensions purportedly being assessed may not be identical to the constructs actually underlying the ratings (Arthur, Day, & Woehr, 2008). Subsequent to Sackett and Dreher (1982), however, attention shifted to the modeling of PEDRs as a function of dimension and exercise factors. This shift was facilitated by the development and application of confirmatory factor analytic (CFA) approaches allowing for the testing of specific a priori models. A key difference between CFA and EFA applications, however, is that CFA models of AC ratings tend to equate espoused dimensions with the latent factors (i.e., dimensions factors) underlying the ratings. Moreover, this shift was so widely endorsed that nearly all studies examining the construct-related validity of AC ratings over the past 25 years have utilized applications of CFA to test MTMM-based models. Thus, we provide a more detailed consideration of these methods below.

Confirmatory Factor Analytic Models of AC Ratings

Typical applications of CFA to the analysis of AC PEDRs are based on the traditional MTMM conceptualization of Campbell and Fiske (1959). To illustrate, Figure 3.1 presents a illustrative hypothetical model in which a set of nine AC PEDRs are viewed as a function of a set of three latent dimension factors and a set of three latent exercise factors. Each observed AC PEDR is a function of one dimension factor and one exercise factor (as well as unique or residual variance which is not included in the figure). Furthermore, the relationship between PEDRs and dimension factors is defined by the loadings of the ratings on the dimension factors (represented by the *a* parameters in the figure). Similarly, the relationship between PEDRs and exercise factors is defined by the loadings of the ratings on the exercise latent variable (represented by the *b* parameters in the figure). Dimension factors are also assumed to be correlated (*c* parameters in the figure) as are the exercise factors (*d* parameters in the figure). Dimension and exercise factors are assumed to be uncorrelated.

Based on the model presented in Figure 3.1, equations for the correlations among the 9 observed PEDRs can be specified. These correlations form the typical MTMM matrix, which is comprised of three types of correlations:

(a) Correlations among PEDRs sharing a common dimension, but different exercises (i.e., monotrait-heteromethod [MTHM] correlations);
(b) Correlations among PEDRs sharing a common exercise, but different dimensions (i.e., heterotrait-monomethod [HTMM] correlations);
(c) Correlations among PEDRs that share neither dimensions nor exercises (i.e., heterotrait-heteromethod [HTHM] correlations).

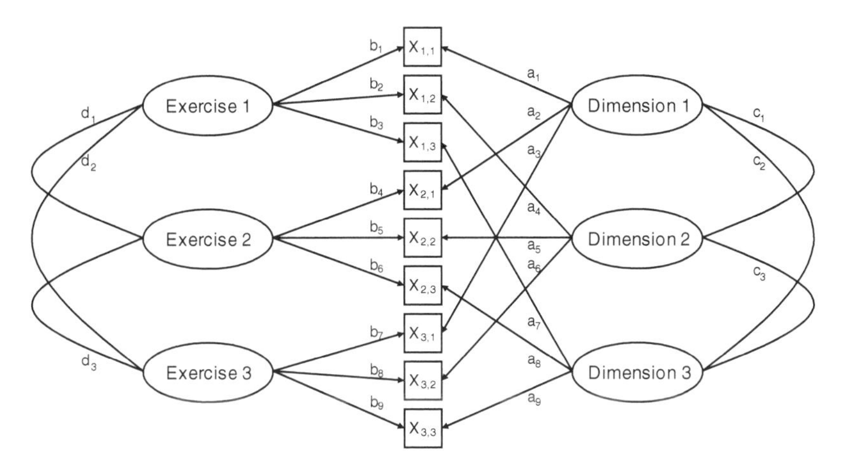

Figure 3.1 The traditional CFA model for evaluating assessment center PEDRs.

The equations for these correlations[1] based on the model are:

$$\text{MTHM } r = a^2 + b^2d \tag{3.1}$$

$$\text{HTMM } r = b^2 + a^2c \tag{3.2}$$

$$\text{HTHM } r = a^2c + b^2d \tag{3.3}$$

In addition, the variance in each rating attributable to dimensions and exercise factors (i.e., the observed variance minus the uniqueness or residual) is:

$$\sigma^2_{\text{observed}} - {}_{\text{residual}} = a^2 + b^2 \tag{3.4}$$

The primary goals of the CFA then are to assess the fit between the observed correlations among the PEDRs and a reproduced correlation matrix based on the model, and to provide estimates of the individual model parameters.

Alternative CFA Models

In addition to the more common MTMM model presented above, a number of alternative models have been consistently represented in the AC literature. These models are briefly described below.

Correlated Uniqueness Model. The correlated uniqueness (CU) model is an alternate approach at modeling exercise effects that relies on allowing uniqueness (i.e., error) variance estimates to correlate in common factor analysis. Specifically, with this approach dimension effects are explicitly modeled while exercise effects are not. This is undertaken in CFA approaches by allowing covariances among error terms to be freely estimated within exercise. Lievens and Conway (2001) employed this approach to model dimension and exercise effects, and in comparison with previous research at that time, concluded that exercise effects did not predominate. However, simulation research has demonstrated that this model tends to over-estimate dimension effects compared to alternate models (Lance, Woehr, & Meade, 2007). As a result, researchers (Lance et al., 2004; Lance et al., 2007) have recommended it not be used.

General Performance Model. Another alternative model that has been employed models a general performance factor (i.e., a person effect; Lance et al., 2007). Researchers that have used this model have speculated that this general factor might indicate overall performance, effort, or other systematic person effects that drive consistent performance within and across exercises. This approach involves modeling a general (g) factor in addition to exercise factors, dimension factors, or both dimension and exercise factors. Some researchers have postulated that assessees demonstrate overall effective performance across all dimensions or across all exercises. However, to the extent that external raters share common misperceptions of the ratee's performance, this could also be explained as a rater source effect.

Higher-Order Models. More recently, it has been suggested that second-order factor models may be appropriate for modeling MTMM data such as that represented in AC ratings (Eid, Lischetzke, Nussbeck, & Trierweiler, 2003; Lance et al., 2007). For example, one or more broad dimension factors may explain variance in lower-order dimension factors as one way of modeling dimension intercorrelations. These models may demonstrate that one or more general dimension factors may drive more narrowly focused dimension ratings. Although these have not been frequently employed in AC research, second-order factor models might explain covariance among dimensions.

Limitation of CFA Applications

Although the traditional MTMM factor analytic model largely serves as the 'default' model of AC ratings, a number of both conceptual and methodological concerns have been raised. Conceptually, Howard (2008) argues that ACs were never designed to conform to an MTMM model. Similar perspectives have been shared by other AC scholars (e.g., Thornton & Rupp, 2006), who argue that convergent and discriminant validity should be properly evaluated across methods, not within a single method (i.e., ACs with other non-AC methods). Specifically, the rationale of the AC design is that different exercises are more or less optimal for the evaluation of performance in different dimensions. Specifically, some forms of leadership and influence behavior may be more appropriately evaluated through interpersonal exercises, and some forms of analytical skills are more appropriately evaluated through paper-and-pencil exercises. A full treatment of such conceptual issues is beyond the scope of the present chapter.

More relevant are the set of analytic problems associated with the application of CFA to MTMM models. A recent study by Lance et al. (2007) helps to illustrate these concerns. Specifically, Lance et al. present a Monte Carlo study examining multiple "true" models postulated to underlie AC PEDRs. For each of three population models, Lance et al. generated 500 sample MTMM matrices. These 1,500 sample matrices were then separately analyzed via CFA with each sample matrix evaluated using parameterizations representing each of the three population models. Thus, Lance et al. were able to directly evaluate whether a CFA would produce convergent and admissible solutions when the correct model was applied to the respective sample matrix (i.e., does the right model fit the data?). Moreover, they were able to evaluate what happens when an incorrect model was applied to a sample matrix (i.e., does the wrong model actually fit the data?).

Results of the analyses presented by Lance et al. (2007) indicated that, regardless of whether the data underlying the AC ratings corresponded to the model specifications used, CFAs based on models with multiple dimension factors converged to an admissible solution for only 57% of the data matrices. Even more striking was that for all models that reached an admissible solution, regardless of whether the fitted model matched the population model on which the data was based, traditional model goodness of fit statistics (e.g., Root Mean Square Error of Approximation [RMSEA], Comparative Fit Index [CF I], Non-normed

Fit Index [NNFI], Expected Cross-validation Index [ECVI], etc.) indicated that the model provided a good fit to the data. Based on these results, Lance et al. concluded that a CFA of an MTMM matrix is a problematic analytical technique due to its propensity to produce results that conflict with the true nature of the data.

Here it is important to note that the analytic problems demonstrated by Lance et al. (2007), especially with respect to the high rate of improper solutions and failure to converge, are not unique to AC data and have been recognized in the more general MTMM CFA literature. That is, it is widely recognized that reliance on the traditional CFA model for the analysis of MTMM data often results in improper or unstable solutions particularly as the number of latent constructs increases (Kenny & Kashy, 1992; Marsh, 1989; Marsh & Bailey, 1991; Marsh & Grayson, 1995). This general issue, in combination with the specific results of the Lance et al. (2007) study, raises serious concerns for the continued exclusive reliance on the CFA-based approach for evaluating the internal construct validity of AC PEDRs, and calls for the use of alternative evaluation approaches. One such alternative is the use of random effects ANOVA models to assess the impact of multiple facets of measurement (e.g., dimensions and exercises). More detail on this alternative analytic approach is provided below.

In sum, factor analytic studies have been extensively utilized in examining the internal structure of ACs. Studies seeking broad categories (i.e., factors) that explain variance in dimensions have identified several theoretically sound models that may be useful for categorizing dimensions and making comparisons across studies (Meriac et al., 2009). However, recent research (i.e., Lance et al., 2007) suggests that due to several methodological limitations of CFA designs (i.e., the models used), caution should be taken in drawing inferences regarding the construct validity of ACs (or the lack thereof) based on internal structure.

Generalizability Theory and AC Ratings

Although the random-effects ANOVA model that provides the basis of Generalizability (G)-theory was once widely recognized as a potentially fruitful approach to the evaluation of MTMM data (e.g., King, Hunter, & Schmidt, 1980; Schmitt & Stults, 1986), over the past two decades, relatively few organizational research studies have utilized these approaches. In contrast, G-theory methods have remained popular in the analyses of MTMM data in educational measurement (e.g., Cronbach, Linn, Brennan, & Haertel, 1997; Shavelson, Baxter, & Gao, 1993; Webb, Schlackman, & Sugrue, 2000), in part because of such methods' ability to deal with complex measurement designs often confronted in educational research. The decline of ANOVA-based approaches for analyzing MTMM data in organizational research coincided with the rise of CFA-based strategies in the mid-1980s. As noted by authors at the time, CFA was viewed as a method that allowed researchers to relax some of the assumptions ANOVA-based approaches such as G-theory required, and generate parameter estimates for individual dimension-exercise units—something ANOVA-based approaches fail to provide (Schmitt & Stults, 1986). Unfortunately, as previously discussed, the added flexibility this approach provides researchers has come at a price (e.g., Lance et al., 2007), and as such it is important to reconsider the benefits of G-theory methods.

There are two variance partitioning approaches that are applicable to the evaluation of MTMM data: univariate and multivariate. The univariate model follows the more traditional understanding of the variance partitioning of AC PEDRs (cf. Arthur, Woehr, & Maldegen, 2000; Bowler & Woehr, 2009; D. J. R. Jackson, Stillman, & Atkins, 2005) and can be directly mapped onto the Campbell and Fiske (1959) conceptualizations of convergent and discriminant validity. The multivariate model steps beyond this understanding and provides additional information that is not available via the univariate model (e.g., dimension intercorrelations). One practical difficulty that may be preventing more widespread use of G-theory methods for analyzing MTMM data is the lack of a clear framework for implementing them with MTMM data, and linking them to concepts typically associated with MTMM data (e.g., MTMM correlations, construct validity, CFA). Thus, drawing on recent work by Woehr, Putka, and Bowler (2010), we next provide an overview of both univariate and multivariate applications of G-theory for the analysis of MTMM data in general and AC ratings in particular.

The Univariate G-theory Model and MTMM Data

Table 3.1 shows a simple, hypothetical MTMM correlation matrix illustrating typical data based on AC ratings. The model includes three dimensions (d1, d2, d3) each measured by three exercises (ex1, ex2, ex3). Researchers attempting to model these data via univariate

Table 3.1 Example MTMM Correlation Matrix

		Exercise 1			Exercise 2			Exercise 3		
		Dimension 1	Dimension 2	Dimension 3	Dimension 1	Dimension 2	Dimension 3	Dimension 1	Dimension 2	Dimension 3
Exercise 1	Dimension 1									
	Dimension 2	$r_{d2e1,d1e1}$								
	Dimension 3	$r_{d3e1,d1e1}$	$r_{d3e1,d2e1}$							
Exercise 2	Dimension 1	$\mathbf{r_{d1e2,d1e1}}$	$\mathrm{r_{d1e2,d2e1}}$	$\mathrm{r_{d1e2,d3e1}}$						
	Dimension 2	$\mathrm{r_{d2e2,d1e1}}$	$\mathbf{r_{d2e2,d2e1}}$	$\mathrm{r_{d2e2,d3e1}}$	$r_{d2e2,d1e2}$					
	Dimension 3	$\mathrm{r_{d3e2,d1e1}}$	$\mathrm{r_{d3e2,d2d1}}$	$\mathbf{r_{d3e2,d3e1}}$	$r_{d3e2,d1e2}$	$r_{d3e2,d2e2}$				
Exercise 3	Dimension 1	$\mathbf{r_{d1e3,d1e1}}$	$\mathrm{r_{d1e3,d2e1}}$	$\mathrm{r_{d1e3,d3e1}}$	$\mathbf{r_{d1e3,d1e2}}$	$\mathrm{r_{d1e3,d2e2}}$	$\mathrm{r_{d1e3,d3e2}}$			
	Dimension 2	$\mathrm{r_{d2e3,d1e1}}$	$\mathbf{r_{d2e3,d2e1}}$	$\mathrm{r_{d2e3,d3e1}}$	$\mathrm{r_{d2e3,d1e2}}$	$\mathbf{r_{d2e3,d2e2}}$	$\mathrm{r_{d2e3,d3e2}}$	$r_{d2e3,d1e3}$		
	Dimension 3	$\mathrm{r_{d3e3,d1e1}}$	$\mathrm{r_{d3e3,d2e1}}$	$\mathbf{r_{d3e3,d3e1}}$	$\mathrm{r_{d3e3,d1e2}}$	$\mathrm{r_{d3e3,d2e2}}$	$\mathbf{r_{d3e3,d3e2}}$	$r_{d3e3,d1e3}$	$r_{d3e3,d2e3}$	

Note. Cells with italicized text reflect heterotrait-monomethod (HT-HM) correlations. Cells with bold text reflect monotrait-heteromethod (MT-HM) correlations. Cells with no text formatting reflect heterotrait-heteromethod (HT-HM) correlations.

G-theory may conceive of the data collection design underlying these data as persons (*p*) crossed with dimensions (*d*) crossed with exercises (*e*), or in G-theory short-hand $p \times d \times ex$. That is, each person is rated on three dimensions, and each dimension is assessed via the same three exercises. The statistical model underlying univariate G-theory is a random-effects analysis of variance (ANOVA) model (Cronbach, Gleser, Nanda, & Rajaratnam, 1972; S. Jackson & Brashers, 1994). Based on this model, each person's observed score (X_{pde}) on a given dimension-exercise unit is modeled as a simple additive function (Brennan, 2001):

$$X_{pde} = \mu + \nu_p + \nu_d + \nu_e + \nu_{pd} + \nu_{pe} + \nu_{de} + \nu_{pde,r} \tag{3.5}$$

where μ is the grand mean score across all persons, dimensions, and exercises; ν_p is the person main effect and conceptually reflects the expected value of a person's score (expressed as a deviation from the grand mean) across the population of dimensions and exercises; ν_d is the dimension main effect and conceptually reflects the expected value of a dimension's effect (again, expressed as a deviation from the grand mean) across the population persons and exercises; ν_e is the exercise main effect and conceptually reflects the expected value of an exercise's effect (again, expressed as a deviation from the grand mean) across the population of persons and dimensions; ν_{pd} is the person $\times$ dimension interaction effect, and conceptually reflects differences in the ordering of persons' expected scores (averaged over exercises) across dimensions; ν_{pe} is the person $\times$ exercise interaction effect, and conceptually reflects differences in the ordering of persons' expected scores (averaged over dimensions) across exercises; ν_{de} is the dimension $\times$ exercise interaction effect, and conceptually reflects differences in the ordering of dimension's expected scores (averaged over persons) across exercises; and finally, $\nu_{pde,r}$ is the remaining residual after accounting for all other effects in the model.

The assumptions underlying this model reflect common random-effects ANOVA assumptions. Namely, all effects in the model are assumed to be independently and identically distributed with means of zero and variances of σ^2_p, σ^2_d, σ^2_{e}, σ^2_{pd}, σ^2_{pe}, σ^2_{de}, and $\sigma^2_{pde,r}$ respectively (S. Jackson & Brashers, 1994; Searle, Casella, & McCulloch, 1992). It is the latter *variance components* that are the focus of estimation efforts in G-theory. As noted here, each term in the model (i.e., each main effect term, each interaction term, and the residual term), has its own variance component. Given that each of the effects is assumed to be independent (and therefore uncorrelated with one another), the expected *total* variance in scores across all person × dimension × exercise combinations in the population (in the sample data, these reflect cells in the $p \times d \times e$ data matrix) may be expressed as a simple sum of these variance components:

$$\sigma^2_{\text{expected total}} = \sigma^2_p + \sigma^2_d + \sigma^2_e + \sigma^2_{pd} + \sigma^2_{pe} + \sigma^2_{de} + \sigma^2_{pde,r.} \quad (3.6)$$

Typically, in the context of modeling MTMM data, researchers are not interested in expected total variance, but rather expected *observed* variance in scores on dimension-exercise units *across* persons. The expected observed variance in scores *across* persons is the sum of only a subset of the variance components above, namely:

$$\sigma^2_{\text{expected observed}} = \sigma^2_p + \sigma^2_{pd} + \sigma^2_{pe} + \sigma^2_{pde,r.} \quad (3.7)$$

Note that dimension main effect variance (σ^2_d), exercise main effect variance (σ^2_e), and dimension × exercise interaction effect variance (σ^2_{de}) do not contribute to observed variance across persons because the aforementioned effects are constants *across* persons for any given dimension-exercise unit (i.e., these effects represent mean values and thus are constant across people). This is why it is essential when discussing variance component based decompositions of MTMM data researchers do not use the terms "dimension effects" and "exercise effects" loosely. In the case of the prototypical fully crossed MTMM design such as this, dimension *main* effects and exercise *main* effects have no impact on observed variance, but other effects involving dimensions and exercises (i.e., v_{pt} and v_{pm}) do. As we will note later, the "dimension effects" and "exercise effects" typically discussed in CFA-based decompositions of MTMM data manifest themselves as person × dimension and person × exercise interaction effects (respectively) in the context of univariate G-theory.

Linking Variance Components and Construct-related Validity. Recently, the link between the variance/covariance components that underlie G-theory and the traditional conceptualization of construct-related validity (i.e., Campbell & Fiske, 1959) has been clarified. As noted by Woehr et al. (2010), there are direct statistical associations between the observed variance produced via G-theory and the correlations found in a traditional MTMM matrix. Specifically:

$$\text{Average monotrait-heteromethod (MT-HM) } r = \sigma^2_p + \sigma^2_{pd,} \quad (3.8)$$

$$\text{Average heterotrait-monomethod (HT-MM) } r = \sigma^2_p + \sigma^2_{pe,} \quad (3.9)$$

$$\text{Average heterotrait-heteromethod (HT-HM) } r = \sigma^2_{p.} \quad (3.10)$$

These allow for clear links to be made between the variance components and convergent-discriminant validity. Regarding convergent validity, Campbell and Fiske recommend examining the MT-HM correlations and determining if they are significantly different from zero. The univariate G-theory analogue to this is examining the proportion of variance accounted for by the combination the person effect (σ^2_p) and the person by dimension interaction (σ^2_{pd}). Regarding discriminant validity, Campbell and Fiske recommend two strategies. First they suggest MT-HM correlations should be greater than the HT-HM corrections (i.e., Σ MT-HM r – HT-HM r). The G-theory analogue for this discriminant validity is simply the person by dimension interaction (σ^2_{pd}). Second, it is suggested the MT-HM correlations should be greater than the HT-MM correlations (i.e., Σ MT-HM r – HT-MM r). Subsequently, discriminant validity is also indexed by the difference between the person by dimension interaction (σ^2_{pd}) and the person by exercise interaction (σ^2_{pe}). Finally, Campbell and Fiske suggest that method variance is indicated by an examination of the differences between the HT-MM correlations and the HT-HM correlations (i.e., Σ HT-MM r – HT-HM r).

The Multivariate G-theory Model and MTMM Data

Given all of the constraints it imposes, as well as its general structure, one may argue that the univariate G-theory model only provides an overly simplified decomposition of the variance in each dimension-exercise unit. Arguably the univariate G-theory model, which is typically applied to assess the generalizability of scores from a measure of a single trait or construct, may be suboptimal in the case of AC ratings given that multiple dimensions are being assessed (e.g., D. J. R. Jackson, Ahmad, & Grace, 2010). For example, the univariate G-theory model (as applied here) implies that there will be no common variance between different dimensions (measured by different exercises) beyond that accounted for by a general person main effect.

Fortunately, the univariate G-theory model can easily be adjusted to not only systematically evaluate the constraints that the model imposes on the data (as described above), but to also evaluate whether a multivariate G-theory model may be more appropriate for one's data. Unlike traditional applications of both univariate and multivariate G-theory, one can frame the multivariate G-theory model within the context of

MTMM data in two different and very useful ways. Specifically, the multivariate G-theory model can be framed in ways that can help researchers and practitioners evaluate the relative appropriateness of *dimension-centric* and *exercise-centric* scoring of their MTMM data. This issue may be particularly salient in AC work, where one may often be faced with evaluating whether dimension-centric or exercise-centric scores (or some combination thereof) are most defensible; or in the case of multisource feedback, where one may be faced with evaluating whether rating dimension-centric or rating source-centric scores are most defensible. Though rarely discussed in the context of organizational research literature, one can view fitting a multivariate G-theory model to MTMM data as akin to fitting a univariate G-theory model for each dimension or exercise separately (depending on how one frames the model), while accounting for the fact that components of observed variance for each dimension-exercise unit will be correlated due to the fact the dimension share exercises in common and exercises share dimensions in common.

As was the case with univariate G-theory, there is an explicit link between the variance and covariance components that underlie multivariate G-theory and elements of a MTMM correlation matrix. More generally, Cronbach et al. (1972) noted relationships exist between variance and covariance components and the *average* variances and covariances among observed variables. In the case of MTMM data, these observed variables represent dimension-exercise units. Such relationships allow researchers to estimate the variance and covariance components underlying the multivariate G-theory model without the use of specific G-theory software (e.g., mGENOVA; Brennan, 2001) or SEM software.

Estimating Variance Components Underlying MTMM Data

As previously noted, the primary means of estimating variance components in the context of G-theory has historically been ANOVA-based procedures (e.g., Shavelson & Webb, 1991). These procedures required rather arduous manipulations of expected mean squares tables or highly specialized software that was idiosyncratic to G-theory (e.g., GENOVA, urGENOVA; Brennan, 2001). Fortunately, over the last four decades there have been several advances in variance component estimation that can greatly simplify the process (Searle et al., 1992). Procedures for the direct estimation of variance components are now widely available in common statistical packages, and clear examples of the ease with which variance components can be estimated using SAS and PASW (the software formerly known as SPSS) are provided by DeShon (2002) and Putka and McCloy (2008).

In addition to being easy to implement, modern methods of variance component estimation have another key advantage; they can readily deal with missing data and unbalanced designs (DeShon, 1995; Marcoulides, 1990; Putka, Le, McCloy, & Diaz, 2008). This is something that proves difficult for ANOVA-based estimators of variance components characteristic of the G-theory literature. Despite this benefit of modern methods, recent applications of G-theory to MTMM data by organizational researchers have unnecessarily discarded data to achieve a balanced design for purposes of estimating variance components (e.g., Arthur et al., 2000; Kraiger & Teachout, 1990; Lievens, 2001, 2002). Though modern methods of variance component estimation are clearly advantageous in several respects (see Searle et al., 1992, for a review), the most notable drawback of those methods—largely based on maximum likelihood—is that they can involve rather substantial memory requirements (Bell, 1985). This will make their use prohibitive for larger MTMM datasets. However, just as memory requirements for conducting SEM studies were a problem in the 1970s and 1980s, but are typically no longer a problem today, it is likely that the same will be true for G-theory applications in the future. Second, at least as implemented in SAS and PASW, the aforementioned variance component estimation methods don't readily allow researchers to test any of the assumptions underlying the G-theory model, nor evaluate its fit to a given MTMM dataset. In response to these concerns, Woehr et al. (2010) present an even simpler approach to estimating variance components that contribute to observed variance across persons. More specifically, they show an explicit the link between G-theory variance components and MTMM correlations, and demonstrate how both univariate and multivariate G-theory models can be expressed and estimated as structural models—which will allow researchers to assess model fit and the adequacy of G-theory model assumptions. They also demonstrate that these models are less susceptible to the estimation problems associated with traditional MTMM CFA models.

In sum, although ANOVA-based approaches (i.e., G-theory) continue to be widely used for the analysis of MTMM data in educational research, they have been applied infrequently and inconsistently in organizational research in general and in the analysis of AC ratings in particular. It is likely that the primary reason for this is the fact that these methods have been somewhat more difficult to implement and are somewhat more restrictive than more typical CFA based approaches. Nevertheless, recent developments in analytic approaches and software as well as with conceptual linkages to traditional notions of construct validity, especially with respect to MTMM data, moderate many of these limitations. Consequently, we believe that the more widespread use of these approaches, especially multivariate G-theory models, have the potential to positively contribute to the AC literature. Multivariate G-theory and recent advances in its SEM representation (Woehr et al., 2010) shows promise as an informative and reliable approach toward examining sources of variance in AC ratings.

Future Directions and General Conclusions

Over the past 50 years, ACs have emerged as a popular tool for evaluating individual differences related to managerial performance. Traditionally, ACs are more likely to be used for the selection or promotion of individuals into managerial jobs, but may also serve as the basis for training and development. As with any measurement method, a fundamental concern for ACs is establishing how well they measure the individual differences they purport to measure and the appropriateness of the inferences that are drawn from these measures. Thus, a primary theme throughout the AC literature has been the accumulation of evidence pertaining to the interpretation of AC ratings. The primary goal of the present chapter was to present a general overview of the methods and analytic approaches that have been applied in this endeavor.

Evidence pertaining to the validity of AC ratings has generally emerged from two approaches. Criterion-related evidence has generally focused on the relationship of OARS and final dimension ratings with various external, job-relevant criterion including ratings of job performance, ratings of potential, career advancement, salary increases, and training performance. Evidence supporting the criterion-related validity of AC ratings has been consistently documented (e.g., Arthur et al., 2003; Gaugler et al., 1987). Construct-related validity evidence has generally focused on the internal structure of AC PEDRs. This line of research has generated far more controversy and debate within the AC literature. Consequently, the bulk of this chapter focused on analytic approaches underlying this stream of research.

While some research has used exploratory factor analytic approaches to assess the dimensionality of final dimension ratings, the predominant approach to assessing the construct-related validity has been the use of confirmatory factor analysis (CFA) of a MTMM matrix based on AC PEDRs. More recently, alternative analytic approaches to the examination of the internal structure of AC ratings have been suggested. In particular, researchers have advocated the use of both univariate and multivariate variance partitioning approaches. To date, however, these approaches have been applied relatively infrequently and inconsistently. However, while these approaches show some promise, they are based on the same MTMM conceptual framework that underlies CFA approaches. Concern has been raised as to the appropriateness of this framework.

Finally, given the amount of empirical research examining the validity of AC ratings, both criterion-related and construct-related, the quantitative integration of these findings (i.e., meta-analysis) has also been evident in the AC literature. However, the application of meta-analytic techniques to AC ratings raises a number of concerns. Early meta-analyses (i.e., Gaugler et al., 1987) focused on the relationship of an OAR with external criterion. Across studies, however, OARs are based on widely different dimensions (both in terms of content and number). Specifically, Woehr and Arthur (2003) report that the number of dimensions rated across a set of 48 operational ACs ranged from 3 to 25 with a mean of 10.60. More importantly, they report a total of 129 different dimensions labels across studies (i.e., 129 different dimensions were rated across the 48 studies). Similarly, they report that the number of exercises used across studies ranged from 2 to 8 (mean = 4.78). The extent of the differences across ACs makes it extremely difficult to combine and integrate findings across studies, especially with respect to AC dimensions.

Several recent meta-analyses (i.e., Arthur et al., 2003; Bowler & Woehr, 2006; Meriac et al., 2008) have attempted to overcome this problem by collapsing the large number of dimensions found across studies into a smaller more manageable set of conceptually distinct dimensions. This research is consistent with findings of studies applying EFA to final dimension ratings which consistently indicate that the number of factors extracted does not correspond to the number of dimensions assessed. Moreover, this research has been generally supportive of the validity of AC dimensions (i.e., a reduced set), both construct-related as well as criterion-related, but is not without its critics (Lance, 2008).

Along these same lines, notably missing from the AC literature to date are attempts to bridge the gap between criterion-related validity studies (examining the relationship between final dimension ratings and external job-based criteria) and construct-related validity studies (examining the internal structure of PEDRs). Specifically, relatively few, if any, studies have examined relationships between final dimension ratings and measures of actual job performance. We believe that the literature would greatly benefit from more studies that examined both the underlying dimensionality of final dimension ratings as well as studies that examine the relationship between constructs assessed via ACs and non-AC methods.

Note

1. It is important to note that, for reasons of simplification, these formula assume that values of the parameters a, b, c, and d represent the parameter means across the model and thus formulae 1–3 represent mean correlations.

References

American Educational Research Association, American Psychological Association, & National Council on Measurement in Education (1999). *Standards for educational and psychological testing.* Washington, DC: American Educational Research Association.

Arthur, W., Jr., Day, E. A., McNelly, T. L., & Edens, P. S. (2003). A meta-analysis of the criterion-related validity of assessment center dimensions. *Personnel Psychology, 56,* 125–154.

Arthur, W. Jr., Day, E. A., & Woehr, D. J. (2008). Mend it, don't end it: An alternate view of assessment center construct-related validity evidence. *Industrial and Organizational Psychology: Perspectives on Science and Practice, 1,* 105–111.

Arthur, W., Woehr, D. J., & Maldegen, R. (2000). Convergent and discriminant validity of assessment center dimensions: A conceptual and empirical re-examination of the assessment center construct-related validity paradox. *Journal of Management, 26,* 813–835.

Bell, J. F. (1985). Generalizability theory: The software problem. *Journal of Educational Behavior and Statistics, 10,* 19–29.

Bowler, M. C., & Woehr, D. J. (2006). A meta-analytic evaluation of the impact of dimension and exercise factors on assessment center ratings. *Journal of Applied Psychology, 91,* 1114–1124.

Bowler, M. C., & Woehr, D. J. (2009). Assessment center construct-related validity: Stepping beyond the MTMM matrix. *Journal of Vocational Behavior, 75,* 173–182.

Bray, D. W., & Grant, D. L. (1966). The assessment center in the measurement of potential for business management. *Psychological Monographs: General and Applied, 80,* 1–27.

Brennan, R. L. (2001). *Generalizability theory.* New York: Springer-Verlag.

Byham, W. C. (1980). *Review of legal cases and opinion dealing with assessment centers and content validity.* Pittsburgh, PA: Development Dimensions International.

Campbell, J. P., & Fiske, E. (1959). Convergent and discriminant validation by the multitrait-multimethod matrix. *Psychological Bulletin, 56,* 81–105.

Cronbach, L. J., Gleser, G. C., Nanda, H., & Rajaratnam, N. (1972). *The dependability of behavioral measurements.* New York: Wiley.

Cronbach, L. J., Linn, R. L., Brennan, R. L., & Haertel, E. H. (1997). Generalizability analyses for performance assessments of student achievement or school effectiveness. *Educational and Psychological Measurement, 57,* 373–399.

DeShon, R. P. (1995, May). *Restricted maximum likelihood estimation of variance components in generalizability theory: Overcoming balanced design requirements.* Paper presented at the meeting of the Society of Industrial and Organizational Psychology, Orlando, FL.

DeShon, R. P. (2002). Generalizability theory. In F. Drasgow & N. Schmitt (Eds.), *Measuring and analyzing behavior in organizations* (pp. 189–220). San Francisco: Jossey-Bass.

Eid, M., Lischetzke, T., Nussbeck, F. W., & Trierweiler, L. I. (2003). Separating trait effects from trait-specific method effects in multitrait-multimethod models: A multiple-indicator CT-C (*M*-1) model. *Psychological Methods, 8,* 38–60.

Gaugler, B. B., Rosenthal, D. B., Thornton, G. C., III, & Bentson, C. (1987). Meta-analysis of assessment center validity. *Journal of Applied Psychology, 72,* 493–511.

Gaugler, B. B., & Thornton, G. C. III (1989). Number of assessment center dimensions as a determinant of assessor generalizability of the assessment center ratings. *Journal of Applied Psychology, 74,* 611–618.

Hoffman, B. J., & Woehr, D. J. (2009). Disentagling the meaning of multisource feedback source and dimension factors. *Personnel Psychology, 62,* 735–765.

Howard, A. (2008). Making assessment centers work they way they are supposed to. *Industrial and Organizational Psychology: Perspectives on Science and Practice, 1,* 98–104.

Huck, J. R., & Bray, D. W. (1976). Management assessment center evaluations and subsequent job performance of black and white females. *Personnel Psychology, 29,* 13–30.

Jackson, D. J. R., Ahmad, M. H., & Grace, G. M. (2010). *Are task-based assessments best represented by absolute situational-specificity?* Paper presented at the Society for Industrial Organizational Psychology, Atlanta, Georgia.

Jackson, S., & Brashers, D. E. (1994). *Random factors in ANOVA.* Thousand Oaks, CA: Sage.

Jackson, D. J. R., Stillman, J. A., & Atkins, S. G. (2005). Rating tasks versus dimensions in assessment centers: A psychometric comparison. *Human Performance, 19,* 213–241.

Kenny, D. A., & Kashy, D. A. (1992). Analysis of multitrait-multimethod matrix by confirmatory factor analysis. *Psychological Bulletin, 112*, 165–172.

King, L. M., Hunter, J. E., & Schmidt, F. L. (1980). Halo in a multidimensional forced-choice performance evaluation scale. *Journal of Applied Psychology, 65*, 507–516.

Kraiger, K., & Teachout, M. S. (1990). Generalizability theory as construct-related evidence of the validity of performance ratings. *Human Performance, 3*, 19–35.

Lance, C. E. (2008). Why assessment centers do not work the way they are supposed to. *Industrial and Organizational Psychology: Perspectives on Science and Practice, 1*, 84–97.

Lance, C. E., Lambert, T. A., Gewin, A. G., Lievens, F., & Conway, J. M. (2004). Revised estimates of dimension and exercise variance components in assessment center postexercise dimension ratings. *Journal of Applied Psychology, 89*, 377–385.

Lance, C. E., Woehr, D. J., & Meade, A. W. (2007). Case study: A monte carlo investigation of assessment center construct validity models. *Organizational Research Methods, 10*, 430–448.

Lievens, F. (2001). Assessors and use of assessment centre dimensions: A fresh look at a troubling issue. *Journal of Organizational Behavior, 22*, 203–221.

Lievens, F. (2002). Trying to understand the different pieces of the construct validity puzzle of assessment centers: An examination of assessor and assessee effects. *Journal of Applied Psychology, 87*, 675–686.

Lievens, F., & Conway, J. M. (2001). Dimension and exercise variance in assessment center scores: A large-scale evaluation of multitrait-multimethod studies. *Journal of Applied Psychology, 86*, 1202–1222.

Marcoulides, G. A. (1990). An alternative method for estimating variance components in generalizability theory. *Psychological Reports, 66*, 102–109.

Marsh, H. W. (1989). Confirmatory factor analysis of multitrait-multimethod data: Many problems and a few solutions. *Applied Psychological Measurement, 13*, 335–361.

Marsh, H. W., & Bailey, M. (1991). Confirmatory factor analyses of multitrait-multimethod data: A comparison of alternate models. *Applied Psychological Measurement, 15*, 47–70.

Marsh, H. W., & Grayson, D. (1995). Latent variable models of multitrait-multimethod data. In R. H. Hoyle (Ed), *Structural equation modeling: Concepts, issues, and applications* (pp. 177–198). Thousand Oaks, CA: Sage.

Meriac, J. P., Fischer, J., & Hoffman, B. J. (2010, April). *Assessment center validity: A meta-analysis of contextual and methodological moderators.* Paper presented at the meeting of the Society for Industrial-Organizational Psychology, Atlanta, Georgia.

Meriac, J. P., Hoffman, B. J., & Woehr, D. J. (2009, April). *A quantitative review and analysis of the constructs underlying assessment center ratings: What are we measuring?* Paper presented at the 24th annual conference of the Society for Industrial-Organizational Psychology, New Orleans, Louisiana.

Meriac, J. P., Hoffman, B. J., Woehr, D. J., & Fleisher, M. S. (2008). Further evidence for the validity of assessment center dimensions: A meta-analysis of the incremental criterion-related validity of dimension ratings. *Journal of Applied Psychology, 93,* 1042–1052.

Norton, S. D. (1977). The empirical and content validity of assessment centers vs. traditional methods for predicting managerial success. *Academy of Management Review, 2,* 442–453.

Putka, D. J., Le, H., McCloy, R. A., & Diaz, T. (2008). Ill-structured measurement designs in organizational research: Implications for estimating interrater reliability. *Journal of Applied Psychology, 93,* 959–981.

Putka, D. J., & McCloy, R. A. (2008, February). *Estimating variance components in SPSS and SAS: An annotated reference guide.* Alexandria, VA: Human Resources Research Organization. Retrieved from http://www.humrro.org/djp_archive/Estimating Variance Components in SPSS and SAS.pdf

Sackett, P. R., & Dreher, G. F. (1982). Constructs and assessment center dimensions: Some troubling empirical findings. *Journal of Applied Psychology, 67,* 401–410.

Searle, S. R., Casella, G., & McCulloch, C. E. (1992). *Variance components.* New York: Wiley.

Schmitt, N. (1977). Interrater agreement in dimensionality and combination of assessment center judgments. *Journal of Applied Psychology, 62,* 171–176.

Schmitt, N., & Stults, D. M. (1986). Methodological review: Analysis of multitrait-multimethod matrices. *Applied Psychological Measurement, 10,* 1–22.

Shavelson, R. J., Baxter, G. P., & Gao, X. (1993). Sampling variability of performance assessments. *Journal of Educational Measurement, 30,* 215–232.

Shavelson, R. J., & Webb, N. M. (1991). *Generalizability theory: A primer.* Newbury Park, CA: Sage.

Shore, T. H., Thornton, G. C., & Shore, L. M. (1990). Construct validity of two categories of assessment center dimension ratings. *Personnel Psychology, 43,* 101–116.

Society for Industrial and Organizational Psychology, Inc. (2003). *Principles for the validation and use of personnel selection procedures* (4th ed.). Bowling Green, OH: Author.

Thornton, G. C., III, & Byham, W. C. (1982). *Assessment centers and Managerial Performance.* San Diego, CA: Academic Press.

Thornton, G. C., III, & Rupp, D. R. (2006). *Assessment centers in human resource management: Strategies for prediction, diagnosis, and development.* Mahwah, NJ: Erlbaum.

Webb, N. M, Schlackman, J., & Sugrue, B. (2000). The dependability and interchangeability of assessment methods in science. *Applied Measurement in Education, 13,* 277–301.

Woehr, D. J., & Arthur, W. Jr. (2003). The construct-related validity of assessment center ratings: A review and meta-analysis of the role of methodological factors. *Journal of Management, 29*(2), 231–258.

Woehr, D. J., Putka, D., & Bowler, M. C. (2010). *An examination of G-theory methods for modeling multitrait-multimethod data: Clarifying links to construct validity and confirmatory factor analysis.* Unpublished manuscript.

4

Core Debates in Assessment Center Research

Dimensions Versus Exercises

Filip Lievens

Ghent University, Belgium

Neil Christiansen

Central Michigan University

In assessment center (AC) research, few issues have generated more discussion than the debate surrounding the use of dimensions and exercises when deriving scores and providing feedback to candidates. This chapter reviews the origins of this debate and the different research streams it has produced. Specifically, dimension-based, task-based, and mixed-model AC perspectives are covered to foster an understanding of how the different perspectives hold valuable insights into ACs and what they measure. In the final section, directions for future research are given. Accordingly, this chapter aims to provide a road map for the sections that follow in this book.

Origins of the Dimensions Versus Exercises Debate

What are the origins of the debate between dimensions and exercises? Although early references related to the debate can be found in Sakoda (1952), Neidig, Martin, and Yates (1979), and Archambeau (1979), the debate originated from the classic study of Sackett and Dreher (1982). They investigated AC ratings in three organizations and focused on one type of rating that until then had not been scrutinized, namely within-exercise dimension ratings (i.e., ratings that assessors make on dimensions in each exercise). Sackett and Dreher reasoned that ratings of candidates on a dimension such as communication should at least show some consistency across the exercises. Conversely, they also expected that different dimensions measured in the same exercise should be rated relatively distinctly from each other. The within-exercise dimension ratings were placed in a multitrait-multimethod (MTMM) matrix and exploratory factor analysis (EFA) was applied to discover the underlying patterns.

In each of the three organizations, Sackett and Dreher (1982) discovered the same pattern in the correlations. They found low correlations among ratings of a single dimension across exercises (i.e., weak convergent validity) and high correlations among ratings of various dimensions within one exercise (i.e., weak discriminant validity). Furthermore, exploratory factor analyses indicated more evidence for exercise factors than for dimension factors. Or to put it differently, much more variance in AC ratings could be attributed to exercises than to dimensions. However, it should also be noted that the predominance of exercise variance did not preclude finding some evidence supporting the notions of consistency and discrimination in the dimension ratings. Specifically, although the correlations were lower than might be expected, the dimension ratings did converge across exercises and the relatively high correlations of dimension ratings within exercises did not approach unity.

Sackett and Dreher (1982) drew the following conclusion "The findings suggest severe problems for assessment centers: In all three centers, method variance predominates" (p. 406). Although these findings were regarded as troublesome, Sackett and Dreher underlined that they did not imply that ACs lack construct-related validity. Almost 20 years later, Sackett and Tuzinski (2001) again cautioned for this misinterpretation of the basic findings, noting: "Assessment centers do not lack "construct validity," but rather lack clear consensus as to the constructs they assess" (pp. 117–118).

Importance of the Dimensions Versus Exercises Debate

As of February 2010, inspection of the Web of Science database showed that the Sackett and Dreher article had been cited 135 times. This is remarkable as ACs are typically regarded as "alternative" selection procedures and continue to be less widely used as cognitive ability tests or personality inventories. It is also extraordinary in that the Sackett and Dreher article presented only internal validity evidence based on relationships within ACs, rather than criterion-related validity evidence which was seen as the gold standard at that time. How can the impact of this article on AC research in particular and on the area of personnel selection in general be explained?

First, the impact of the Sackett and Dreher (1982) article can be understood by the fact that many regarded it as providing a key test of the theory underlying ACs. That is, it was generally believed that the theory underlying ACs emphasizes the dimensions (as opposed to exercises) as the cornerstones of the approach to assessment. As such, dimensions were seen as stable individual-difference attributes, whereas exercises were merely alternative platforms for the dimensions to be measured. Although this is a simplification of AC theory (see Gibbons & Rupp, 2009; Howard, 2008), it does represent the way AC theory has at times been vulgarized. In this light, it is understandable that any study showing that the dimensions as hallmarks of ACs did not function as purported would receive considerable research attention in the years to come.

Second, the impact of the Sackett and Dreher (1982) article can be framed in the context of the growing impact that constructs have begun to play in personnel selection research. Although personnel selection was long regarded as an applied area with a heavy emphasis on predictive efficiency, the construct-driven approach has gained in importance following key publications by Binning and Barrett (1989), Klimoski (1993), as well as Schmitt and Chan (1998). A tenet of the construct-driven approach is that high predictive validity of selection practices is certainly desirable, but that it is also crucial to understand why selection devices work and what constructs are being measured. As noted above, the Sackett and Dreher study showed that evidence for dimensions as constructs (i.e., as psychological bundles of behavior across situations) was lacking. On a more general level, this result challenges the construct-oriented approach, explaining why future research has scrutinized it more closely.

Third, the internal validation of within-exercise dimension ratings has received substantial research attention through the years because evidence for the consistency of dimension ratings across exercises is deemed to be necessary for aggregating these ratings (either via consensus discussion or mathematically) into final dimension ratings. For example, recent meta-analyses on both the criterion-related validity (Arthur, Day, McNelly, &, Edens 2003) and incremental validity (Meriac, Hoffman, Woehr, & Fleisher, 2008) of ACs used final dimension ratings as the main units of analysis. For these results to be meaningful, it is generally regarded as important that there is evidence that these ratings assess the dimensions consistently across the various exercises. The same argument applies when final dimension ratings are placed in a nomological network with other predictors such as cognitive ability tests or personality inventories.

Fourth, there are practical reasons as to why the debate between dimensions and exercises has received continued journal coverage. Many scholars have argued that it is important to ascertain that dimensions are measured in ACs because the developmental feedback given to candidates is typically formulated around dimensions. The reasoning is that feedback and subsequent action plans might actually have detrimental effects if the dimensions are not valid indicators of managerial abilities. Apart from the type of feedback provided, similar arguments of the outcomes of the dimension-exercise debate can be made for other components of ACs (e.g., a dimension-based vs. task-based job analysis approach, a dimension-based vs. exercise-based rating approach).

It should be noted that many of the implications of the Sackett and Dreher (1982) findings are really "potential" implications. For instance, no study has tested whether dimension-based feedback is indeed detrimental (see fourth implication). Similarly, no research has investigated whether assessors indeed have trouble clinically aggregating dimension ratings across exercises into a final dimension rating (see third implication).

Revisiting the Dimensions Versus Exercises Debate

Many studies have focused on replicating and/or remedying the original Sackett and Dreher (1982) findings of dimensions being less important components than exercises. The results described have proven to be robust as they were found in both selection and developmental ACs. In addition, they have been found in ACs conducted all over the world. Apart from the United States (Bycio, Alvares, & Hahn, 1987; Harris, Becker, & Smith, 1993; Joyce, Thayer, & Pond, 1994; Kudisch, Ladd, & Dobbins, 1997; Reilly, Henry, & Smither, 1990; Sackett & Dreher, 1982; Schneider & Schmitt, 1992; Silverman, Dalessio, Woods, & Johnson, 1986), these results have been established in the United Kingdom (Anderson, Lievens, van Dam, & Born, 2006; Crawley, Pinder, & Herriot, 1990; Robertson, Gratton, & Sharpley, 1987), Germany (Kleinmann &

Koller, 1997; Kleinmann, Kuptsch, & Koller, 1996), Belgium (Lievens & Van Keer, 2001), France (Borteyrou, 2005; Rolland, 1999), Australia (Atkins & Wood, 2002), New Zealand (Jackson, Stillman, & Atkins, 2005), China (Wu & Zhang, 2001), and Singapore (Chan, 1996). Finally, similar results have been reported regardless of the statistical technique applied (MTMM correlations, EFA, CFA, analysis of variance, variance component analysis, etc.).

Given the vast amount of studies that aimed to replicate the construct-related validity findings, it comes to no surprise that researchers have also aimed to quantitatively summarize the research base. So far, three quantitative studies have been conducted. First, Lievens and Conway (2001) reanalyzed 34 MTMM matrices of AC ratings. Their main conclusion was that a model consisting of exercises and dimensions represented the best fit to the data. In this model, exercises and dimensions explained the same amount of variance (34%). A second quantitative review (Lance, Foster, Gentry, & Thoresen, 2004) came to different conclusions as a model with exercises and one general dimension prevailed, with exercise variance (52%) being more important than dimension variance (14%). Third, Bowler and Woehr (2006) used meta-analytical methods to combine 35 MTMM matrices into one single matrix. The best fit was obtained for a model with dimensions and exercises. Exercises explained most of the variance (33%), although dimensions also explained a substantial amount of variance (22%). Some dimensions (i.e., communication, influencing others, organizing and planning, and problem solving) explained significantly more variance than others (i.e., consideration of others, drive). Note that dimensions were found to correlate highly (.79).

In light of these relatively robust findings, different research perspectives have emerged over the years. Prior to discussing these various perspectives, however, the next section puts the dimensions versus exercises debate in a broader historical context.

Putting the Dimensions Versus Exercises Debate in Context

Analogous to the disappointment that AC researchers experienced when confronted with the correlations between dimension ratings computed across exercises, personality psychologists were rocked by the claims of Walter Mischel in his 1968 book *Personality and Assessment.* Mischel argued that the cross-situational consistency in behavior that is required for supporting trait constructs was lacking or perhaps even nonexistent. Although one can quibble with the merits of the interpretations, Mischel's characterization of the magnitude of cross-situational consistency effects has proven to be relatively accurate: on average the correlation between behavioral observations in one situation and another is probably around .19 or .20 (e.g., Richard, Bond, & Stokes-Zoota, 2003). However, the amount of cross-situational consistency has been shown to vary considerably with the characteristics of the situations involved and the behavioral observations being considered.

Perhaps the most important determinant of cross-situational consistency is the similarity of the situations involved (Bem & Funder, 1978). For example, Mischel (1985) reported behavioral consistency correlations of approximately .50 for aggressiveness when situations were highly similar. As such, Mischel's position is not that consistency does not exist, but that it will only be observed when we take careful account of situational factors. However, such situational effects can be subtle, with even the presence or absence of a single salient person in the room reducing such estimates to a size consistent with the average estimate (e.g., .22 in Mischel & Peake, 1982). Similarity effects in the AC literature can be seen in the work of Highhouse and Harris (1993) as well as applications of Trait Activation Theory (see below, Haaland & Christiansen, 2002; Lievens, Chasteen, Day, & Christiansen, 2006).

Before AC researchers and practitioners are tempted to design their exercises to be as similar as possible, there are some reasons for caution. When one designs or identifies situations that are highly similar in terms of the psychological features, the behavioral ratings will demonstrate much better cross-situational consistency (Bem & Funder, 1978; Mischel & Peake, 1982). However, because the ratings are "context-dependent," they will tend to predict behavior well only in other highly similar situations. If one is interested in behavior in a very different setting, or across a range of disparate situations, prediction will suffer (Wood, 2007).

Consistent with this, research has shown that composites of the behavioral ratings that displayed the best cross-situational consistency may not be those that best predict relevant external criteria (Funder & Colvin, 1991). In ACs, this may be problematic in that the actual work situations faced by managers every day are quite varied (e.g., dealing with subordinates, completing reports under deadline, meeting with key stakeholders from other units). In order to predict success across these seemingly different situations, behavioral ratings would need to be based on observations across a range of situations.

This caution can be extended to efforts to reconcile traits and situations such as may be found in the notion of conditional dispositions described by Wright and Mischel (1987). In this approach, more specific traits are defined as a function of both the trait and situation. For example, from the approach of conditional dispositions it may be that ratings of Stress Tolerance as elicited by Time Pressure in one situation, and ratings of Stress Tolerance as activated by Evaluative Pressure in another, represent distinct constructs and should not be construed as the same if cross-situational consistency is to be expected. From this perspective, convergence across exercises could only really be achieved if exercises were so similar as to seem redundant. However, designing ACs that take this into account by including highly similar exercises in the service of creating cross-situational consistency may not be desirable as there is no guarantee that the two more narrow constructs would predict managerial effectiveness any better than a single broader construct assessed across disparate situations.

Thus, from the perspective of research on behavioral consistency in personality psychology, the puzzle of AC validity frequently debated in the I-O literature has a different perspective. High cross-situational consistency in and of itself may not be desirable if prediction across different situations is the goal. Furthermore, it is the very different exercise demands necessary to provide the observations that will predict across situations that are likely to create strong exercise effects. Taken together, the typically low monotrait-heteromethod correlations that are surpassed by heterotrait-monomethod correlations may be less disconcerting than they have been to some AC researchers. Given the large amount of exercise variance generated by the design of ACs, a more telling comparison may be for monotrait-heteromethod correlations to be higher than heterotrait-heteromethod correlations. This expectation of construct validity of ACs has tended to be supported (Bowler & Woehr, 2006).

Another important aspect of the cross-situational consistency of behavioral ratings involves the level of specificity in the behaviors and is directly related to the bandwidth and fidelity issues we drew attention to earlier. Research has convincingly shown that ratings that represent broader domains of behavior demonstrate more cross-situational consistency than those that reflect more precise and narrow domains (Funder & Colvin, 1991; Jackson & Paunonen, 1985). This extends beyond just having more broad categories, but also allowing ratings that have more psychological depth (e.g., allowing raters to differentiate interrupting someone out of rudeness versus due to impulsivity).

However, even at the very broad level of the dimensions of the Five-Factor Model (FFM), expectations that monotrait-heteromethod validity coefficients will exceed the heterotrait-monomethod correlations may be difficult to support. For example, Biesanz and West (2004) found that the average correlation between FFM dimensions rated by peers and parents were .38 and .33, respectively. In contrast, the cross-method validity coefficients averaged only .28. Although the finding in personality assessment that method effects are stronger than trait effects (including self-report) is not uncommon, personality assessments have been validated successfully against a remarkable array of outcomes besides job performance, including physical health symptoms (e.g., coronary artery disease; Bogg & Roberts, 2004; Caspi, Roberts, & Shiner, 2005; Hampson, Andrews, Barckley, Lichtenstein, & Lee, 2000), psychological health (e.g., Quirk, Christiansen, Wagner, & McNulty, 2003), and interpersonal relationships (e.g., conflict, abuse, dissolution; Karney & Bradbury, 1995). Given the wide array of predictive relationships, it may not be surprising that no one in the personality literature has suggested abandoning trait dimensions based on the method effects surpassing the trait effects.

Although the use of very broad dimensions may seem antithetic to the AC method, a reasonable compromise might be to report results at both narrow and broad levels. The more narrow dimensions would provide the feedback useful for developmental purposes, whereas broader dimensions might display better cross-situational consistency and be more predictive across a range of external outcomes. At the extreme, some personality researchers have suggested that even the FFM can be organized into two very broad dimensions loosely called *alpha* and *beta* (Digman, 1997), with the former including Emotional Stability, Agreeableness, and Conscientiousness and the latter Extraversion and Openness to Experience. Although we can anticipate considerable resistance to the suggestion, in ACs the dimensions could be organized into Motivation (involving dimensions related to drive, organizing and planning, and consideration of others) and Social Problem Solving (involving dimensions associated with communication, influencing others, and problem solving). Such an organization of narrow dimensions underneath more broad constructs might allow different uses to leverage the advantages of each.

Apart from framing the dimension-exercise debate in personality and social psychology, it should be noted that findings of situation-specific variance being larger than construct variance are not unique to ACs. Similar results have also been obtained for other method-driven predictors such as structured interviews (Conway & Peneno, 1999; van Iddekinge, Raymark, Eidson, & Attenweiler, 2004) and situational judgment tests (Trippe & Foti, 2003). For example, in the interview field, convergence between the same construct measured by different types of structured interviews (behavior description and situational interviews) has been lower than mean correlations across constructs within the same interview (Huffcutt, Weekley, Wiesner, Degroot, & Jones, 2001). Even when the *same* type of interview is used the results can be disappointing when the benchmarks of MTMM analysis are applied. For example, van Iddekinge and his colleagues evaluated customer service candidates on two behavior description interviews measuring the same dimensions. Variance explained by traits (9%) was overshadowed by which interview form (29%) and interviewer (19%) were used. However, this does not suggest that dimensions in the interview cannot correlate higher with the intended dimensions measured by other assessments (see van Iddekinge, Raymark, & Roth, 2005).

Moreover, the findings seem to extend to all fields wherein different constructs are measured in multiple performance-based exercises. For example, predominance of situation-specific variance over construct variance has been found in studies about patient-management problems for physicians (e. g., Julian & Schumacher, 1988), military examinations (e.g., Shavelson, Mayberry, Li, & Webb, 1990), hands-on science tasks (e.g., Baxter, Shavelson, Goldman, & Pine, 1992), bar examinations (e.g., Klein, 1992), and direct writing assessments (e.g., Dunbar, Koretz, & Hoover, 1991).

In conclusion, problems with the expectation that correlations between behavioral observations assessed across very different situations (or methods) will be high are commonplace in the psychological literature (Funder, 2009; Meyer et al., 2001). Although situations can be designed to be highly similar in order to observe stronger cross-situational consistency, this may not have intended effect of improving the usefulness of AC ratings for predicting external outcomes. Such considerations should temper expectations about trait and situational sources of variance and shift focus to whether validity coefficients exceed heterotrait-heteromethod correlations. Finally, organizing AC dimensions into more broad constructs may improve both cross-situational consistency and prediction of external criteria, leaving the narrow dimensions intact for developmental purposes.

Current Research Perspectives

As a response to the typical AC construct-related findings, three research perspectives can be broadly distinguished, as reflected in the structure of this book. Some scholars posit that we should keep working with dimensions and focus on AC design to improve the measurement of the dimensions (the dimension-based AC approach). Others argue that dimensions do not work in ACs and that we should abandon using them and focus solely on exercises (the task-based AC approach). A third group uses a hybrid approach which focuses on the AC behavior itself, which is then a result of the interaction between both exercises and dimensions (the mixed-model AC approach). Next, we review the rationales and research evidence of each of these different paradigms.

Focusing on Improved Dimension Measurement in ACs

A first stream of studies has assumed that the construct-related validity findings result from poor AC design. For example, poorly designed ACs (e.g., inadequate training of assessors, asking assessors to rate a large number of dimensions) might result in assessors being prone to halo bias when rating the candidates, which in turn might lead to strong exercise factors. Woehr and Arthur (2003) provide an excellent summary of this perspective by noting that "assessment centers as measurement tools are probably only as good as their development, design, and implementation." (p. 251).

A logical consequence of this perspective is that potential flaws in AC design should be identified and fixed. Basically, research adhering to this perspective has taken up the longstanding call of Klimoski and Brickner (1987) "to establish if, or under what conditions, ACs can be made to produce valid measures of constructs" (p. 255). Examples of factors that have been manipulated in past studies include using behavioral checklists, reducing the assessor-assessee ratio, making dimensions transparent, using psychologists as assessors, providing longer training to assessors, using frame-of-reference training, using task-based dimensions, and providing within-exercise dimension ratings only when assessees have completed all exercises.

This line of research has been the dominant research paradigm in the AC field for quite some time. Both quantitative (Lievens & Conway, 2001; Woehr & Arthur, 2003) and qualitative review studies (Lievens,

1998; Sackett & Tuzinski, 2001) have been conducted to summarize the effects of AC design changes on construct-related validity results. Two common threads run through the conclusions of these reviews. On the one hand, it seems fruitful to reduce assessors' limited information processing capacity. This is evidenced by interventions to support assessors in their observation and evaluation activities. Examples are limiting the number of dimensions or using behavioral checklists to ease the observation process. On the other hand, it appears beneficial to tackle assessors' schemas for categorizing the information observed. Examples are using psychologist as assessors and frame-of-reference training which aims to provide them with common standards as a reference for evaluating assessee performance. The success of the improved design/dimension measurement approach is best exemplified by the study of Arthur, Woehr, & Maldegen (2000). After implementing many of the above design recommendations (most notably asking assessors to provide within-exercise dimension ratings only when assessees had completed all exercises), they found clear evidence of dimension factors in an operational AC.

Although this perspective has generated a large strand of studies and various recommendations for improving dimension measurement, it is not without problems. First, even well-designed ACs have exhibited weak evidence of construct-related validity. For example, the analyses of Schneider and Schmitt (1992) revealed that most of the variance in AC ratings was explained by exercises instead of dimensions, even though they carefully implemented various recommendations for improving construct-related validity (e.g., limiting the number of dimensions, using behavioral checklist, and providing thorough assessor training). Similarly, Chan's (1996) rigorous AC design did not improve construct-related validity. These results can be explained by the fact that many of these design considerations have only small effects (but see Arthur et al., 2000, for an exception). That is, they do not change the basic pattern that discriminant validity coefficients are higher than convergent validity coefficients.

Second, one might question whether all of these design interventions have beneficial effects on the criterion-related validity. In fact, most of these design interventions have been tried out in ACs conducted in laboratory settings where candidates are typically rated on the basis of a limited number of exercises and dimensions. Yet, limiting the number of dimensions might detract from the criterion-related validity of actual ACs in the field. More generally, it has been argued that implementing these narrow design considerations might lead to ACs that are not found in practice.

Removing Dimensions and Focusing on Tasks: The Task-Based Approach

A second stream of research has taken a more radical decision as a response to the typical construct-related AC results. Instead of fixing and tweaking AC design, proponents of task-based ACs posit to simply remove the dimensions from the AC framework and focus solely on the exercises. Goodge (1987, 1988) and Lowry (1997) were among the first to argue in favor of such task-based ACs. Task-based ACs are composed of several work simulations in which general exercise performances rather than dimensions are assessed. It is argued that dimension ratings never had a place in situational work exercises (e.g., work samples). So, why should they play a role in an AC?

Thus, proponents of the task-based AC approach argue in favor of removing dimensions in ACs for at least three reasons. First, this decision is based on the robust exercise effects found across a myriad of studies and many ACs over the last decades. Indeed, as noted above, a vast amount of studies showed that exercise models (exercises-only models or exercises model with one general performance factor) typically provide a better fit to AC ratings than pure dimension-based models. Lance (2008) cogently summarized this body of research by stating that dimension do not work in ACs and will probably never do so. Contrary to the large amount of studies that tried to fit exercises versus dimensions model to AC ratings, few studies have directly compared task-based ACs to their dimension-based counterparts. As an exception, Jackson et al. (2005) made a direct comparison of the psychometric characteristics of task-based ACs with those of dimension-based ACs. Both models yielded similar psychometric qualities, although only the task-based model provided an acceptable theoretical fit for the data, suggesting that this model offers a better conceptualization of ACs.

Second, the task-based approach is defended on the basis of research showing that exercise variance does not constitute unwanted method bias in ACs. In three studies, Lance and colleagues (Lance et al., 2000; Lance et al., 2004; Lance, Foster, Nemeth, Gentry, & Drollinger, 2007) correlated exercise factors with external variables such as job performance, personality, and cognitive ability. Exercise factors exhibited positive relations with such external performance criteria, indicating that they do not reflect unwanted method bias. Recently, Lievens, Dilchert, and Ones (2009) further showed that exercises contributed not only more variance than dimensions in AC ratings but were also more valid in predicting a key criterion such as salary. Thus, these results confirm that exercise factors do not represent unwanted method bias. Instead, they seem to reflect valid true performance differences.

As a third reason for no longer investing in improved dimension measurement, proponents of the task-based AC approach posit that research endeavors to enhance dimension measurement (see first perspective) are misguided because assessors are not to blame. That is, it is argued that the construct-related validity findings do not primarily result from flawed AC design and biased assessors. Research by Lievens (2002) that examined both the effects of type of assessee performances and type of assessor speaks to this issue. In that study, large differences were found in evidence for convergent and discriminant validity across assessee performances. In fact, convergent validity was established only for consistent performances across exercises, whereas discriminant validity was established only for differentiated performances across dimensions. Evidence for convergent and discriminant validity also varied across type of assessor (psychologists, managers, and students) but these differences were much smaller. If one views the construct-related validity findings in this perspective, “there may be nothing wrong with assessment center’s construct validity after all” (Lance, Foster et al., 2004, p. 23).

Although task-based AC approaches have emerged as a viable alternative to dimension-based ACs, there are still a lot of things that we do not know about exercise-based assessment (Lievens, 2008). One key issue is that little is known about the main component of task-based ACs, namely the AC exercise. Specifically, research has only started examining the personal and situational factors that impact on exercise performance (Jackson, Stillman, & Englert, 2010; Schneider & Schmitt, 1992).

In addition, it is still unclear whether the task-based approach uses exactly the same exercises (albeit labeled as “tasks”) as in traditional ACs. Although the task-based approach considers an AC to be nothing more than a collection of work samples, the crux of this issue is that traditional AC exercises are at a more middling level of fidelity, whereas work samples are purported to be high in fidelity. Although we agree that dimensions have never had a place in narrow work samples, it remains to be seen whether dimensions may be required to make sense of observations across more generic AC exercises.

Focusing on AC Behavior: The Mixed Model Approach

A third stream of research has focused on candidate behavior and its determinants. In particular, the mixed-model AC approach aims to examine conditions wherein candidates might perform consistently across exercises. To shed light on these issues, mixed-model researchers have relied on interactionist theories that posit that behavior is a function of both the interaction between the person and the situation.

In personality and social psychology, the Cognitive-Affective Personality System (CAPS) theory (Mischel & Shoda, 1995, 1998) has emerged as one of the most comprehensive interactionist theories. The CAPS theory takes people's cross-situationally inconsistent behavior as a point of departure, namely the notion that "the data over the course of a century, however, made it increasingly evident that the individual's behavior varies considerably across different types of situations" (Mischel, Shoda, & Mendoza-Denton, 2002, p. 50). Next, the CAPS theory posits that nominal features of situations activate a series of mental representations (both cognitive and affective). On the basis of the particular interconnected and interacting CAPS units being activated (e.g., encodings), behavioral scripts are triggered (so-called If … then patterns). The key implication of CAPS theory is that situations are differently perceived by individuals, resulting in variability in their subsequent behaviors and performance. Jansen, Lievens, and Kleinmann (2009) applied the CAPS theory to the AC domain. They discovered that relevant traits were triggered only when candidates perceived the situation demands correctly. In particular, Jansen et al. showed that agreeableness (as measured by a personality inventory) was related to ratings on cooperation in AC exercises only among people who perceived that the situation demanded agreeable behavior. Similar results were obtained for the relationship between participants' standing on conscientiousness and their AC rating on planning and organizing. Future research should further explore how people's perceptions of the situation and the CAPS units they activate relate to candidate behavior and assessor ratings.

On the other hand, Trait Activation Theory (TAT; Tett & Burnett, 2003; Tett & Guterman, 2000) is an interactionist approach that has already made stronger inroads in ACs (Lievens, Tett, & Schleicher, 2009). TAT shows many parallels to the CAPS theory. TAT explains behavior based on responses to trait-relevant cues found in situations. A key characteristic of trait activation theory is that situational similarity is described in a trait-like manner, namely through the notion of *trait activation potential* (i.e., the capacity to observe differences in trait-relevant behavior within a given situation, Tett & Guterman, 2000). The trait activation potential of a given situation is primarily determined by the *relevance* and *strength* of that situation. A situation is considered relevant to a trait if it provides cues for the expression of trait-relevant behavior. Apart from situation relevance, situational strength also impacts on the variability and consistency of behavior (Mischel, 1973, 1977). In particular, strong situations involve unambiguous behavioral demands, resulting in few differences in reactions to the situation, whereas weak situations are characterized by more ambiguous expectations, enabling more variability in behavioral responses.

In TAT terms, dimensions measured in ACs are no longer seen as stable traits. Instead, they are conceptualized as conditional dispositions (Mischel & Shoda, 1995). This means that stable candidate performances on dimensions can be expected only when the exercises elicit similar trait-relevant situational cues. Exercises are no longer viewed as parallel measures but as triggers of trait-relevant behavior. In addition, TAT provides a theoretical explanation for the variability in candidate performances across different AC exercises. It posits that we should expect only strong convergence among dimension ratings between exercises when the exercises elicit similar trait-relevant situational cues (i.e., are high in trait activation potential for that trait).

Is there evidence in ACs for the propositions behind trait activation theory? Haaland and Christiansen (2002) were the first to examine the convergent validity of AC ratings in light of trait activation theory. They conducted a small-scale investigation of a promotional AC ($N = 79$). Their findings pointed out that convergence between dimension ratings in exercises that were judged to be high in trait activation potential was stronger than convergence between dimension ratings in exercises low in trait activation. These results provided support for the relevance of trait activation theory for understanding ACs. A reanalysis of 30 existing AC studies also confirmed the propositions of trait activation theory (Lievens et al., 2006). That is, convergence was stronger between exercises that both provided opportunity to observe behavior related to the same trait. Findings further showed that trait activation worked best for dimensions which were related to extraversion and conscientiousness.

A key drawback of these two prior studies is that they evaluated AC exercises in existing operational ACs; that is, without manipulation of trait activation potential in different exercises. Thus, so far, there have been no tests of the actual implementation of trait activation theory in AC exercise design. This post hoc use of trait activation theory might also explain the relatively small effects found in these two prior studies.

Directions for Future Research

The previous sections illustrate that three research perspectives have emerged as a result of the debate between dimensions and exercises in ACs. Clearly, the main question is *not* which perspective is best. The question is: How might these different perspectives make a good assessment tool even better? Indeed, it is our conviction that all of these three diverging perspectives shed light on different components of the AC framework. At the same time, these perspectives prompt intriguing directions for future research.

The *dimension-based AC approach* is useful because it places high quality AC design on top of the agenda. Everyone who was ever involved in an AC will acknowledge that "good" AC design is necessary and that continued efforts are warranted to further improve and fine-tune AC technology. Thanks to this perspective, various design recommendations have emerged. Where should the dimension-based approach go from here? Inspection of the design factors manipulated in ACs over the years reveals one important hiatus. Specifically, the dimensions themselves have received almost no attention (see Joyce et al., 1994, for an exception). As argued by Arthur, Day, and Woehr (2008) almost any dimension is promoted and espoused to a psychological "construct" status in ACs. Clearly, it deserves attention in future research to examine the effects of using more established constructs. Along these lines, the taxonomy of Arthur et al. (2003) and his theory of AC dimensions in this book are very useful leads. On a broader level, such research might also frame the AC dimension space in established taxonomies of the job performance domain.

The *task-based AC approach* has demonstrated that good AC design is only one—albeit important—part of the construct-related validity puzzle. Moreover, the task-based AC approach is valuable because it emphasizes AC exercises. So far, exercises are under-researched components of ACs. Indeed, as compared to our knowledge about assessors and AC rating aids we do not know a lot about exercises. Therefore, we urge task-based AC research to scrutinize the "tasks" and/or exercises given to assessees. To this end, future research might benefit from integrating the task-based approach into the extant work sample literature (Callinan & Robertson, 2000). Another key research need in the task-based AC literature consists of examining the effects of providing participants with task-based feedback on feedback acceptance and performance improvement and transfer across jobs. More broadly, we believe that the task-based AC approach should not only be compared to the traditional dimension-based AC approach but should follow an independent research path.

Similar to the dimension-based and task-based AC approaches, we believe that the *mixed-model AC approach* also shows huge promise for ACs. One reason is that it might shed insight onto the reasons as to why assessees do not perform consistently across exercises. Another reason is that the application of modern interactionist theories such as the CAPS and TAT provides a window of opportunities for AC research and practice. The critique that ACs are a-theoretical is long overdue. Therefore, we need to take this chance of providing ACs with a stronger theoretical background. Future research might use these interactionist theories in a proactive and prescriptive way (i.e., to change AC practices). Along these lines, Lievens et al. (2009) delineated how TAT might be used in key AC decisions such as selection of dimensions, design of exercises, observation/rating process, assessor selection, assessor training, and development of feedback reports.

Conclusion

At a deeper level, we believe that the three AC perspectives that have emerged from the longstanding debate between dimensions and exercises have more in common than their respective proponents often assert. All three AC perspectives acknowledge the key underlying idea that candidate behavior in ACs results from an interaction between person variables and situational variables, a notion that is central to the mixed-model AC approach. There therefore appears to be agreement with respect to the underlying determinants of candidate behavior to be observed (regardless whether the behavior is afterwards captured in an exercise-rating or dimension-rating approach).

The perspectives do differ in their emphasis placed on modeling these person and situational variables in AC practices. In the dimension-based AC approach, the person variables are explicitly measured as AC dimensions, whereas the situational variables (AC exercises) are seen as an alternate way of measuring these dimensions. Conversely, in the task-based approach, only the situational variables (AC exercises) are formally modeled, whereas the person variables (AC dimensions) are not formally measured. Finally, in the mixed-model AC approach, both dimensions and exercises are formally modeled. However, their interpretation substantially differs from that one in the dimension-based approach. In the mixed-model paradigm, the dimensions are regarded as conditional dispositions and the exercises as behavior-triggering situational cues.

These differences notwithstanding, this chapter shows that all three perspectives can substantially advance AC research and practice. Continued research on all three perspectives to ensure that ACs remain valuable as selection, promotion, development, and training tools in human resource management. In the long run, in order to better evaluate the merits of each perspective, focus needs also to shift to predicting behavior and outcomes outside of the AC and on direct comparisons of ratings derived from dimension, task, and hybrid approaches.

References

Anderson, N., Lievens, F., van Dam, K., & Born, M. (2006). A construct-driven investigation of gender differences in a leadership-role assessment center. *Journal of Applied Psychology, 91*, 555–566.

Archambeau, D. J. (1979). Relationships among skill ratings assigned in an assessment center. *Journal of Assessment Center Technology, 2*, 7–20.

Arthur, W. Jr., Day, E. A., & Woehr, D. J. (2008). Mend it, don't end it: An alternate view of assessment center construct-related validity evidence. *Industrial and Organizational Psychology: Perspectives on Science and Practice, 1*, 105–111.

Arthur, W., Day, E. A., McNelly, T L., & Edens, P. S. (2003). A meta-analysis of the criterion-related validity of assessment center dimensions. *Personnel Psychology, 56*, 125–154.

Arthur, W., Jr., Woehr, D. J., & Maldegen, R. (2000). Convergent and discriminant validity of assessment center dimensions: An empirical re-examination of the assessment center construct-related validity paradox. *Journal of Management, 26*, 813-835.

Atkins, P. W. B., & Wood, R. E. (2002). Self- versus others' ratings as predictors of assessment center ratings: Validation evidence for 360-degree feedback programs. *Personnel Psychology, 55*, 871–904.

Baxter, G. P., Shavelson, R. J., Goldman, S. R., & Pine, J. (1992). Evaluation of procedure-based scoring for hands-on science assessment. *Journal of Educational Measurement, 29*, 1–17.

Bem, D. J., & Funder, D. C. (1978). Predicting more of the people more of the time: Assessing the personality of situations. *Psychological Review, 85*, 485–501.

Biesanz, J. C., & West, S. G. (2004). Towards understanding assessments of the big five: Multitrait-multimethod analyses of convergent and discriminant validity across measurement occasion and type of observer. *Journal of Personality, 72*, 845–876.

Binning, J. F., & Barrett, G. V. (1989). Validity of personnel decisions: A conceptual analysis of the inferential and evidential bases. *Journal of Applied Psychology, 74*, 478–494.

Bogg, T., & Roberts, B. W. (2004). Conscientiousness and health-related behaviors: A meta-analysis of the leading behavioral contributors to mortality. *Psychological Bulletin, 130*, 887–919.

Borteyrou, X. (2005). *Intelligence, personnalité, mises en situation et prédiction de la réussite professionnelle: La construction d'un centre d'évaluation pour des officiers de marine.* Unpublished doctoral dissertation, Université Victor Segalen Bordeaux, Bordeaux.

Bowler, M. C., & Woehr, D. J. (2006). A meta-analytic evaluation of the impact of dimension and exercise factors on assessment center ratings. *Journal of Applied Psychology, 91*, 1114–1124.

Bycio, P., Alvares, K. M., & Hahn, J. (1987). Situational specificity in assessment center ratings: A confirmatory factor analysis. *Journal of Applied Psychology, 72*, 463–474.

Callinan, M., & Robertson, I. T. (2000). Work sample testing. *International Journal of Selection and Assessment, 8*, 248–260.

Caspi, A., Roberts, B. W., & Shiner, R. L. (2005). Personality development: Stability and change. *Annual Review of Psychology, 56*, 453–484.

Chan, D. (1996). Criterion and construct validation of an assessment centre. *Journal of Occupational and Organizational Psychology, 69*, 167–181.

Conway, J. M., & Peneno, G. M. (1999). Comparing structured interview question types: Construct validity and applicant reactions. *Journal of Business and Psychology, 13*, 485–506.

Crawley, B., Pinder, R., & Herriot, P. (1990). Assessment center dimensions, personality and aptitudes. *Journal of Occupational Psychology, 63*, 211–216.

Digman, J. M. (1997). Higher-order factors of the big five. *Journal of Personality and Social Psychology, 73*, 1246–1256.

Dunbar, S. B., Koretz, D. M., & Hoover, H. D. (1991). Quality control in the development and use of performance assessments. *Applied Measurement in Education, 4*, 289–303.

Funder, D. C. (2009). Persons, behaviors and situations: An agenda for personality psychology in the postwar era. *Journal of Research in Personality, 43*, 120–126.

Funder, D. C., & Colvin, C. R. (1991). Explorations in behavioral consistency: Properties of persons, situations, and behaviors. *Journal of Personality and Social Psychology, 60*, 773–794.

Gibbons, A. M., & Rupp, D. E. (2009). Dimension consistency: A new (old) perspective on the assessment center construct validity debate. *Journal of Management, 35*, 1154–1180.

Goodge, P. (1987). Assessment centres: Time for deregulation. *Management Education and Development, 18*, 89–94.

Goodge, P. (1988). Task based assessment. *Journal of European Industrial Training, 12*, 22–27.

Haaland, S., & Christiansen, N. D. (2002). Implications of trait-activation theory for evaluating the construct validity of assessment center ratings. *Personnel Psychology, 55*, 137–163.

Hampson, S. E., Andrews, J. A., Barckley, M., Lichtenstein, E., & Lee, M. E. (2000). Conscientiousness, perceived risk, and risk-reduction behaviors: A preliminary study. *Health Psychology, 19*, 496–500.

Harris, M. M., Becker, A. S., & Smith, D. E. (1993). Does the assessment center scoring method affect the cross-situational consistency of ratings. *Journal of Applied Psychology, 78*, 675–678.

Highhouse, S., & Harris, M. M. (1993). The measurement of assessment center situations: Bem's template matching technique for examining exercise similarity. *Journal of Applied Social Psychology, 23*, 140–155.

Howard, A. (2008). Making assessment centers work the way they're supposed to. *Industrial and Organizational Psychology: Perspectives on Science and Practice, 1*, 98–104.

Huffcutt, A. I., Weekley, J. A., Wiesner, W. H., Degroot, T. G., & Jones, C. (2001). Comparison of situational and behavior description interview questions for higher-level positions. *Personnel Psychology, 54*, 619–644.

Jackson, D. J. R., Stillman, J. A., & Atkins, S. G. (2005). Rating tasks versus dimensions in assessment centers: A psychometric comparison. *Human Performance, 18*, 213–241.

Jackson, D. J. R., Stillman, J. A., & Englert, P. (2010). Task-based assessment centers: Empirical support for a systems model. *International Journal of Selection and Assessment, 18*, 141–154.

Jackson, D. N., & Paunonen, S. V. (1985). Construct validity and the predictability of behavior. *Journal of Personality and Social Psychology, 49*, 554–570.

Jansen, A., Lievens, F., & Kleinmann, M. (2009, June). *The importance of situation perception in the personality - performance relationship.* Paper presented at the annual conference of the Society for Industrial and Organizational Psychology, New Orleans, LA.

Joyce, L. W., Thayer, P. W., & Pond, S. B. (1994). Managerial functions: An alternative to traditional assessment center dimensions. *Personnel Psychology, 47*, 109–121.

Julian, E. R., & Schumacher, C. F. (1988, March*). CBT pilot examination: Results and characteristics of CBX*. Paper presented at the conference of the National Board of Medical Examiners on Computer-based Testing in Medical Education and Evaluation, Philadelphia.

Karney, B. R., & Bradbury, T. N. (1995). The longitudinal course of marital quality and stability: A review of theory, methods, and research. *Psychological Bulletin, 118*, 3–34.

Klein, S. P. (1992, April). *The effect of content area and test type on bar exam scores.* Paper presented at the National Conference of Bar examiners, Chicago.

Kleinmann, M., & Koller, O. (1997). Construct validity of assessment centers: Appropriate use of confirmatory factor analysis and suitable construction principles. Journal *of Social Behavior and Personality, 12,* 65–84.

Kleinmann, M., Kuptsch, C., & Koller, O. (1996). Transparency: A necessary requirement for the construct validity of assessment centres. *Applied Psychology: An International Review, 45,* 67–84.

Klimoski, R. J. (1993). Predictor constructs and their measurement. In N. Schmitt & W. C. Borman (Eds.), *Personnel selection in organizations* (pp. 99–135). San Francisco: Jossey-Bass.

Klimoski, R. J., & Brickner, M. (1987). Why do assessment centers work? The puzzle of assessment center validity. *Personnel Psychology, 40,* 243–260.

Kudisch, J. D., Ladd, R. T., & Dobbins, G. H. (1997). New evidence on the construct validity of diagnostic assessment centers: The findings may not be so troubling after all. *Journal of Social Behavior and Personality, 12,* 129–144.

Lance, C. E. (2008). Why assessment centers (ACs) don't work the way they're supposed to. *Industrial and Organizational Psychology: Perspectives on Science and Practice, 1,* 84–97.

Lance, C. E., Foster, M. R., Gentry, W. A., & Thoresen, J. D. (2004). Assessor cognitive processes in an operational assessment center. *Journal of Applied Psychology, 89,* 22–35.

Lance, C. E., Foster, M. R., Nemeth, Y. M, Gentry, W. A., Drollinger, A. (2007). Extending the nomological network of assessment center construct validity: Prediction of cross-situationally consistent and specific aspects of assessment center performance. *Human Performance, 20,* 345–362.

Lance, C. E., Lambert, T. A., Gewin, A. G., Lievens, F., & Conway, J. M. (2004). Revised estimates of dimension and exercise variance components in assessment center postexercise dimension ratings. *Journal of Applied Psychology, 89,* 377–385.

Lance, C. E., Newbolt, W. H., Gatewood, R. D., Foster, M. R., French, N. R., & Smith, D. E. (2000). Assessment center exercise factors represent crosssituational specificity, not method bias. *Human Performance, 13,* 323–353.

Lievens, F. (1998). Factors which improve the construct validity of assessment centers: A review. *International Journal of Selection and Assessment, 6,* 141–152.

Lievens, F. (2002). Trying to understand the different pieces of the construct validity puzzle of assessment centers: An examination of assessor and assessee effects. *Journal of Applied Psychology, 87,* 675–686.

Lievens, F. (2008). What does exercise-based assessment really mean? *Industrial and Organizational Psychology: Perspectives on Science and Practice, 1,* 117–120.

Lievens, F., & Conway, J. M. (2001). Dimension and exercise variance in assessment center scores: A large-scale evaluation of multitrait-multimethod studies. *Journal of Applied Psychology, 86,* 1202–1222.

Lievens, F., & Van Keer, E. (2001). The construct validity of a Belgian assessment centre: A comparison of different models. *Journal of Occupational and Organizational Psychology, 74,* 373–378.

Lievens, F., Chasteen, C. S., Day, E. A., & Christiansen, N. D. (2006). Large-scale investigation of the role of trait activation theory for understanding assessment center convergent and discriminant validity. *Journal of Applied Psychology, 91,* 247–258.

Lievens, F., Dilchert, S., & Ones, D. S. (2009). The importance of exercise and dimension factors in assessment centers: Simultaneous examinations of construct-related and criterion-related validity. *Human Performance, 22,* 375–390.

Lievens, F., Tett, R. P., & Schleicher, D. J. (2009). Assessment centers at the crossroads: Toward a reconceptualization of assessment center exercises. In J. J. Martocchio & H. Liao (Eds.), *Research in personnel and human resources management* (pp. 99–152). Bingley: JAI Press.

Lowry, P. E. (1997). The assessment center process: New directions. *Journal of Social Behavior and Personality, 12,* 53–62.

Meriac, J. P., Hoffman, B. H., Woehr, D. J., & Fleisher, M. S. (2008). Further evidence for the validity of assessment center dimensions: A meta-analysis of the incremental criterion-related validity of dimension ratings. *Journal of Applied Psychology, 93,* 1042–1052.

Meyer, G. J., Finn, S. E., Eyde, L. D., Kay, G. G., Moreland, K. L., Dies, R. R., … Reed, G. M. (2001). Psychological testing and psychological assessment: A review of evidence and issues. *American Psychologist, 56,* 128–165.

Mischel, W. (1968). *Personality and assessment.* Hoboken, NJ: Wiley.

Mischel, W. (1973). Toward a cognitive social learning reconceptualization of personality. *Psychological Review, 80,* 252–283.

Mischel, W. (1977). The interaction of person and situation. In D. Magnussen & N. Endler (Eds.), *Personality at the crossroads: Current issues in interactional psychology* (pp. 333-352). Mahwah, NJ: Erlbaum.

Mischel, W. (1985, October). *Diagnosticity of situations.* Paper presented at the meeting of the Society for Experimental Social Psychology, Eston, IL.

Mischel, W., & Peake, P. K. (1982). Beyond déjà vu in the search for cross-situational consistency. *Psychological Review, 89,* 730–755.

Mischel, W., & Shoda, Y. (1995). A cognitive-affective system theory of personality: Reconceptualizing situations, dispositions, dynamics, and invariance in personality structure. *Psychological Review, 102,* 246–268.

Mischel, W., & Shoda, Y. (1998). Reconciling processing dynamics and personality dispositions. *Annual Review of Psychology, 49,* 229–258.

Mischel, W., Shoda, Y., & Mendoza-Denton, R. (2002). Situation-behavior profiles as a locus of consistency in personality. *Current Directions in Psychological Science, 11,* 50–54.

Neidig, R. D., Martin, J. C., & Yates, R. E. (1979). The contribution of exercise skill rating to final assessment center evaluations. *Journal of Assessment Center Technology, 2,* 21–23.

Quirk, S. W., Christiansen, N. D., Wagner, S. H., & McNulty, J. L. (2003). On the usefulness of measures of normal personality for clinical assessment: Evidence of the incremental validity of the revised NEO personality inventory. *Psychological Assessment, 15,* 311–325.

Reilly, R. R., Henry, S., & Smither, J. W. (1990). An examination of the effects of using behavior checklists on the construct validity of assessment center dimensions. *Personnel Psychology, 43,* 71–84.

Richard, F. D., Bond, C. F., Jr., & Stokes-Zoota, J. J. (2003). One hundred years of social psychology quantitatively described. *Review of General Psychology, 7,* 331–363.

Robertson, I., Gratton, L., & Sharpley, D. (1987). The psychometric properties and design of managerial assessment centers: Dimensions into exercises won't go. *Journal of Occupational Psychology, 60,* 187–195.

Rolland, J. P. (1999). Construct validity of in-basket dimensions. *European Review of Applied Psychology, 49,* 251–259.

Sackett, P. R., & Dreher, G. F. (1982). Constructs and assessment center dimensions: Some troubling empirical findings. *Journal of Applied Psychology, 67,* 401–410.

Sackett, P. R., & Tuzinski, K. (2001). The role of dimensions and exercises in assessment center judgments. In M. London (Ed.), *How people evaluate others in organizations* (pp. 111–129). Mahwah, NJ: Erlbaum.

Sakoda, J. M. (1952). Factor analysis of OSS situational tests. *Journal of Abnormal and Social Psychology, 47,* 843–852.

Schmitt, N., & Chan, D. (1998). *Personnel Selection: A theoretical approach.* Thousand Oaks, CA: Sage.

Schneider, J. R., & Schmitt, N. (1992). An exercise design approach to understanding assessment center dimension and exercise constructs. *Journal of Applied Psychology, 77,* 32–41.

Shavelson, R. J., Mayberry, P., Li, W., & Webb, N. (1990). Generalizability of job performance measurements: Marine Corps rifleman. *Military Psychology, 2,* 129–144.

Silverman, W. H., Dalessio, A., Woods, S. B., & Johnson, R. L. (1986). Influence of assessment center methods on assessors' ratings. *Personnel Psychology, 39,* 565–578.

Tett, R. P., & Burnett, D. D. (2003). A personality trait-based interactionist model of job performance. *Journal of Applied Psychology, 88,* 500–517.

Tett, R. P., & Guterman, H. A. (2000). Situation trait relevance, trait expression, and cross-situational consistency: Testing a principle of trait activation. *Journal of Research in Personality, 34,* 397–423.

Trippe, D. M., & Foti, R. J. (2003, April). *An evaluation of the construct validity of situational judgment tests.* Paper presented at the conference of the Society for Industrial and Organizational Psychology, Orlando, Florida.

Van Iddekinge, C. H., Raymark, P. H., & Roth, P. L. (2005). Assessing personality with a structured employment interview: Construct-related validity and susceptibility to response inflation. *Journal of Applied Psychology, 90,* 536–552.

Van Iddekinge, C. H., Raymark, P. H., Eidson, C. E., & Attenweiler, W. J. (2004). What do structured selection interviews really measure? The construct validity of behavior description interviews. *Human Performance, 17,* 71–93.

Woehr, D. J., & Arthur, W. (2003). The construct-related validity of assessment center ratings: A review and meta-analysis of the role of methodological factors. *Journal of Management, 29,* 231–258.

Wood, D. (2007). Using the PRISM to compare the explanatory value of general and role-contextualized trait ratings. *Journal of Personality, 75,* 1103–1126.

Wright, J. C., & Mischel, W. (1987). A conditional approach to dispositional constructs: The local predictability of social behavior. *Journal of Personality and Social Psychology. Special Issue: Integrating Personality and Social Psychology, 53,* 1159–1177.

Wu, Z. M., & Zhang, H. C. (2001). The construct validity and structure modeling of assessment center. *Acta Psychologica Sinica, 33,* 372–378.

Part 2

Dimension-Based Assessment Centers

5

Dimension-Based Assessment Centers

Theoretical Perspectives

Winfred Arthur, Jr.
Texas A&M University

The objective of this chapter is to provide the reader with a brief discussion of the theoretical and conceptual basis for assessment center dimensions. The orientation of this chapter is embedded within the perspective that dimensions have historically served as the foundational basis of assessment centers. This is in sharp contrast to a task-based perspective that calls for a "redesign of assessment centers toward task- or role-based assessment centers and away from traditional dimension-based assessment centers" (Lance, 2008a, p. 84). The issue of task-based assessment centers is discussed elsewhere in this volume (e.g., see Chapters 9, 10, and 11, this volume).

The historical nature and preeminence of dimension-based assessment centers is reflected in the International Task Force on Assessment Center Guidelines' (2009) definition of assessment centers as "a process employing multiple techniques and multiple assessors to produce judgments regarding the extent to which a participant displays selected behavioral dimensions" (p. 253). A noteworthy distinguishing feature embedded in this definition is the use of multiple exercises (i.e., methods/techniques) to obtain multiple dimension scores. Hence, the standard design and use of assessment centers is to cross dimensions and exercises, often partially, and then collapse performance across exercises to obtain dimension scores from a "single" method as illustrated in Figure 5.1. Consequently, the triangulation of dimensions through the use of multiple methods and multiple assessors is, in fact, the major defining characteristic of assessment centers. These dimension scores have then subsequently served as the focus for the various uses of assessment centers in human resource management including recruitment, selection, performance appraisal, training and development, and human resource planning, layoffs, and organizational development (e.g., see Eurich, Krause, Cigularov, & Thornton, 2009; Joiner, 2002; Spychalski, Quinones, Gaugler, & Pohley, 1997; Thornton & Rupp, 2006).

A Theory of Assessment Center Dimensions?

Surprisingly, in spite of the historical eminence of dimension-based assessment centers, a literature search undertaken to identify empirical and conceptual writing in the extant literature on the theory of assessment center dimensions highlighted the paucity and scarcity of any such works. Specifically, an electronic search of PsycINFO using the keywords *assessment center, dimension, and theory, theoretical, or foundation* resulted in the identification of three published articles and three dissertations. However, a detailed review of these works indicated that none of them spoke directly of a theory of assessment center dimensions. So, this then begs the question: How come and why are assessment centers historically and traditionally based on dimensions?

The historical background of assessment centers is embedded within the military *psychology* efforts on the part of Germany's, and then the British War Office Selection Boards, and the United States Office of Strategic Services (OSS; Thornton & Byham, 1982) in the selection of military personnel and intelligence agents. The OSS endeavor in turn was the key source of inspiration for the assessment center methodology used in the American Telephone and Telegraph's (AT&T) Management Progress Study. The Management Progress Study, which began in 1956, moved the assessment center methodology from a war setting and the selection of military personnel and intelligence agents to a civilian organizational setting and the selection and promotion of managers (Howard & Bray, 1988). Consequently, the traditional use of assessment centers in civilian settings has been in *managerial* contexts for administrative purposes, although its flexibility has led to its use in a wide variety of other settings and purposes.

The managerial origins of assessment centers is suggestive of the fact that the broader managerial performance literature informs the reasons why assessment centers are based on dimensions and indeed, even the type of dimensions that are assessed. However, in spite of these origins, it would seem that contemporary assessment center researchers have failed to acknowledge, integrate, and possibly gain insights from the broader research, theories, and models of managerial performance. This is alluded to by Arthur, Day, and Woehr (2008) when they state that "it is astonishing that despite the robust literatures and scientific disciplines devoted to areas like judgment and decision making, communication, and leadership, we have not seen the developers of assessment centers consulting these literatures when defining their similarly labeled dimensions" (p. 107). Nevertheless, the focus of assessment centers on behavioral dimensions is consonant with the taxonomic and behavioral approaches of the time. Indeed, the resulting behavioral dimensions in assessment centers (e.g., Thornton & Byham's, 1982, list of "33 commonly used dimensions"; see Table 5.1) bear a strong resemblance to their counterparts in the leader behavior literature (cf. initiating structure and consideration) and taxonomic efforts to describe managerial performance (Borman & Brush, 1993; see also Campbell, 1990).

For instance, based on previous conceptualizations in the leadership literature, Mumford, Campion, and Morgeson (2007) proposed a model of leadership skill requirements that consisted of cognitive skills, interpersonal skills, business skills, and strategic skills. They also tested for and obtained support for a "strataplex" by demonstrating that different categories of leadership skill requirements emerge at different organizational levels, and that jobs at higher levels of the organization require higher levels of all leadership skills. This latter framing is quite similar to that presented by the U.S. Office of Personnel Management (OPM) in terms of the leadership competencies required for managerial positions in the U.S. federal government (see Table 5.2).

Relatedly, early behavioral theories of leadership—the Ohio State and Michigan Leadership studies—seem to have converged on two-dimension theories of leadership with one dimension representing behaviors that relate to other individuals and relationships, and the other dimension representing behaviors that relate to task performance. Specifically, the two leadership dimensions posited by the Ohio State Leadership studies were initiating structure and consideration (Kerr, Schreisheim, Murphy, & Stogdill, 1974; Stogdill, 1950; also see Judge, Piccolo, & Illies, 2004). Consideration is the extent to which leaders express concern, respect, appreciation, and support to their followers whereas initiating structure is the extent to which leaders clearly communicate role expectations (Fleishman, Harris, & Burtt, 1955). On the other hand, the Michigan Studies focused on person- versus

Table 5.1 Primary Study Dimension Labels Sorted Into the Specified Dimension Categories

Level 1 Dimensions	Level 2 Dimensions (Thornton and Byham's, 1982, list of commonly used dimensions)	Level 3 Dimensions (Original primary study dimension labels)
Communication The extent to which an individual conveys oral and written information and responds to questions and challenges	Oral communication Oral presentation Written communication	Communication Oral communication Oral defense Oral presentation Presentation skills Written communication
Consideration/ Awareness of others The extent to which an individual's actions reflect a consideration for the feelings and needs of others as well as an awareness of the impact and implications of decisions relevant to other components both inside and outside the organization	Extra-organizational awareness Extra-organizational sensitivity Organizational awareness Organizational sensitivity Recognition of employee safety needs Sensitivity	Awareness of social environment Bell value system orientation Building relationships Company orientation Confrontation Empowerment Fostering open communication Interpersonal communication skills Interpersonal contact Interpersonal skills Interpersonal sensitivity Organizational orientation Participative leadership Participative management Perception of social cues Sensitivity Sensitivity to diversity Social objectivity Social sensitivity Team building Team orientation Team work Understanding people Willingness to communicate with group Working with others
Drive The extent to which an individual originates and maintains a high	Career Ambition Energy Initiative Job Motivation	Aggressiveness Amount of participation Career commitment Career motivation Career orientation

Level 1 Dimensions	Level 2 Dimensions (Thornton and Byham's, 1982, list of commonly used dimensions)	Level 3 Dimensions (Original primary study dimension labels)
activity level, sets high performance standards and persists in their achievement, and expresses the desire to advance to higher job levels	Tenacity Work standards	Drive Driving for continuous improvement Driving for results Energy Energy level Forcefulness Initiative Inner work standards Need for advancement Perseverance and initiative Persistence Personal motivation Potential Primacy of work Results management Results orientation Self-direction Work drive Work quality Work standards
Influencing others The extent to which an individual persuades others to do something or adopt a point of view in order to produce desired results and takes action in which the dominant influence is one's own convictions rather than the influence of others' opinions	Independence Integrity Leadership	Autonomy Change oriented leadership Character/personality Gaining team commitment Goal oriented communication Group leadership Impact Independence/dependence Influencing others Inspiring trust Integrity Leadership Leading courageously Negotiation Personal impact Persuasion and negotiation skills Persuasiveness Self confidence Transactional leadership Transformational leadership

(continued)

Table 5.1 Continued

Level 1 Dimensions	Level 2 Dimensions (Thornton and Byham's, 1982, list of commonly used dimensions)	Level 3 Dimensions (Original primary study dimension labels)
Organizing and planning The extent to which an individual systematically arranges his/her own work and resources as well as that of others for efficient task accomplishment; and the extent to which an individual anticipates and prepares for the future	Control Delegation Development of subordinates Planning and organization	Administrative ability Attracting and developing talent Coaching Conscientiousness Controlling Delegation Managing execution Organizing Organizing and planning Organization Organizational ability Planning Planning and organization Planning and organizing Planning and scheduling Recognizing priorities Shaping tactical plans Strategic focus Strategic planning Strategic thinking Supervising others and people management Tactical planning Thoroughness Thoroughness of performance Time sensitivity
Problem solving The extent to which an individual gathers information; understands relevant technical and professional information; effectively analyzes data and information; generates viable options, ideas, and solutions; selects supportable courses of action for problems and situations; uses available resources in new ways; and generates and recognizes imaginative solutions	Analysis Creativity Decisiveness Judgment Practical learning Range of interests Technical and professional knowledge	Analysis Analytical ability Breadth of interests Business savvy Business sense Cognitive analytical skills Creativity Decision making Decisive Decisiveness Fact finding Functional General mental ability Innovative thinking Intelligent systematic approach Interpreting information Judgment Openness Orientation to detail Originality Perception

Level 1 Dimensions	Level 2 Dimensions (Thornton and Byham's, 1982, list of commonly used dimensions)	Level 3 Dimensions (Original primary study dimension labels)
		Personal breadth Problem analysis Problem detection Problem solving Problem solving and decision making Range of interests Seasoned judgment Technical and functional skills Willingness to learn
Tolerance for stress/ Uncertainty The extent to which an individual maintains effectiveness in diverse situations under varying degrees of pressure, opposition, and disappointment	Adaptability Resilience Risk taking Tolerance for stress	Adaptability Behavior flexibility Change oriented Coping with stress Flexibility Flexibility and adaptability Good actions in a crisis Need for structure Resilience Resistance to stress Risk taking Social flexibility Stress management Stress tolerance Stress tolerance in conflict situations Tolerance for uncertainty
Unable to classify 42 (15)		Ability to delay gratification Coaching and team building Communication and impact Cultural political skills Development orientation Educational values Financial orientation Goal flexibility Generalist International know-how Need for peer approval Need for security Need for superior approval Open commercial attitude Personal acceptability Quality of participation Realism of expectations Relationship with authority Scholastic aptitude Self objectivity Stability

Table 5.2 U.S. Office of Personnel Management Leadership Competencies.

Leadership Level and Required Competencies			
Basic Competencies	Supervisory Competencies (First-Level)	Managerial Competencies (Mid-Level)	Executive Competencies (Senior-Level)
Flexibility	Human Resources Management	Creativity/Innovation	Vision
Resilience	Cultural Awareness	Financial Management	External Awareness
Service Motivation	Conflict Management	Technology Management	Strategic Thinking
Continual Learning	Team Building	Partnering	Entrepreneurship
Integrity/Honesty	Customer Service		Political Savvy
Decisiveness	Technical Credibility		
Oral Communication	Problem Solving		
Written Communication	Accountability		
Interpersonal Skills	Influencing/Negotiating		

task-oriented behaviors. Task-oriented behaviors emphasize performance, and include behaviors such as establishing objectives, structuring tasks, and evaluating outcomes. Relationship-oriented behaviors on the other hand emphasize personal relationships (Bowers & Seashore, 1966). Task- and relationship-orientation were initially conceptualized as opposite poles of a single dimension, but were later reconceptualized as two independent dimensions. In summary, these two streams of research are quite similar in their recognition of a focus on relationships and task performance for effective leadership. Interestingly, variations of these two leadership dimensions or foci, at lower levels of specificity, are present in most models and assessments of leadership and managerial performance including assessment centers.

Concerning managerial performance, Borman and Brush (1993) present an inductively derived taxonomy of performance requirements that was based on empirical studies conducted on different managerial jobs in several different organizations. Specifically, 187 managerial performance dimensions were extracted from a number of empirical studies. Twenty-five industrial/organizational (I/O) psychologists then sorted them into categories on the basis of their content similarity and a factor analysis of the correlation matrix resulted in an 18-factor solution which Borman and Brush described as mega-dimensions (see Table 5.3).

The brief review of exemplar works from the leadership (Mumford et al., 2007) and managerial performance (Borman & Brush, 1993) literatures and a perusal of the resultant dimensions leads one to conclude that although I was unable to locate or find any writing on the theory of assessment dimensions that directly linked the two, one could reasonably posit that given their historical origins in AT&T's Management Progress Study, assessment centers were designed to measure dimensions common to and important for success in the general managerial performance domain. This is highlighted by the similarity and overlap in construct labels represented in Thornton and Byham's (1982) list of 33 commonly used assessment center dimensions presented in Table 5.1, Mumford et al.'s (2007) list of 5 leadership skills, and Borman and Brush's (1993) taxonomy of 18 managerial performance requirements (see Table 5.3). Thus, whether the clustering of behaviors that represent the performance domain into manageable meaningful components (constructs or dimensions) is done theoretically (e.g., Borman & Brush, 1993; or Campbell, 1990), using behavioral observation as in the Ohio State and Michigan Leadership studies (Kerr et al., 1974; Stogdill, 1950), or via factor analysis (McCauley, Lombardo, & Usher, 1989), the results

Table 5.3 Borman and Brush's (1993) Taxonomy of Managerial Performance Requirements

18-Factor Mega-Dimension Solution
Planning and organizing
Guiding, directing, and motivating subordinates and providing feedback
Training, coaching, and developing subordinates
Communicating effectively and keeping others informed
Representing the organization to customers and the public
Technical proficiency
Administration and paperwork
Maintaining good working relationships
Coordinating subordinates and others resources to get the job done
Decision making/problem solving
Staffing
Persisting to reach goals
Handling crises and stress
Organizational commitment
Monitoring and controlling resources
Delegating
Selling/influencing
Collecting and interpreting data

of this clustering reveal dimensions that are quite similar to those routinely used in assessment centers.

In summary, given that assessment centers are intended to be simulations of the management/leadership domain, an overlap with the broader managerial performance domain should be expected, and is arguably, quite desirable. In essence, although, amongst others, assessment centers are predicated on a content-related validity approach because the exercises and activities model those for managers' jobs, the associated high levels of psychological fidelity results in a content representation that reflects the behavioral dimensions (or constructs) that are important to success in managerial and leadership roles. Thus, the match between the constructs measured in assessment centers and that required for success in the focal criterion domain is important. So again, why are assessment centers historically and traditionally based on dimensions? Although there may not be explicit theories of assessment center dimensions, it can reasonably be concluded that the historical origins and focus on the selection and promotion of managers served as the logical impetus for a focus on dimensions that were deemed to be important to success as a manager or leader.

The Role of Dimensions in Assessment Centers and the Construct/Method Distinction

A discussion of the role of dimensions in assessment centers or the "theory" of assessment centers requires a discussion of the distinction between predictor constructs and predictor methods (Arthur & Villado, 2008). Generally speaking, a predictor is a specific behavioral domain, information about which is sampled via a specific method. Thus, depending on one's focus, predictors can be represented in terms of *what* they measure, and *how* they measure what they are designed to measure. Specifically, any given predictor can be conceptualized as either a construct or a method. Consequently, the term "predictor construct" (or "construct") refers to the behavioral domain being sampled, and "predictor method" (or "method") refers to the specific process or techniques by which domain-relevant behavioral information is elicited and collected (Arthur, Day, McNelly, & Edens, 2003; Arthur & Doverspike, 2005; Arthur, Edwards, & Barrett, 2002; Campbell, 1990).

In the present chapter, the terms "dimension" and "construct" are used somewhat interchangeably primarily because although "construct" is generally used to refer to that which tests and measures measure, in the assessment center literature, the term "dimension" more so than "construct," is the label used to describe what assessment centers measure. Consequently, within the predictor construct/predictor method framework, an assessment center is best conceptualized as a method that is used to obtain information on multiple dimensions—in spite of the fact that by design, it consists of multiple exercises (methods). This is because as illustrated in Figure 5.1, performance is collapsed across exercises to obtain dimension scores from a "single" method. That being said, as previously noted, traditional assessment center theory and practice specifies the behavioral domain or content of assessment centers (i.e., what they measure) in terms of behavioral dimensions (although some of the recent practitioner literature also uses the term "competencies"; e.g., see International Task Force on Assessment Center Guidelines, 2009). Hence, the dimension-based perspective of assessment centers is based on an interpretation of dimensions as the conceptual basis of behaviors that are presumed to underlie job performance and other criteria of interest.

The preceding can again be contrasted with the espoused task-based perspective of assessment centers which by implication would conceptualize assessment centers "as a series of exercises designed to assess effectiveness in a variety of important managerial roles such as negotiator, counselor, fact-finder, and persuader, among others" so that "rather than ending up with a series of global dimension ratings, the product is

	EXERCISES				ASSESSOR RATINGS	
DIMENSIONS	A	B	C	D	Initial Rating	Final Rating
1						
2						
3	———	———	———	———	———	→
4						
5						
6						
OVERALL RATING/SCORE						

Figure 5.1 Dimension H exercise matrix that serves as the defining characteristic of assessment centers. It should be noted that not all dimensions may be observable in all exercises.

a series of assessments of effectiveness in exercises or role simulations" (Sackett & Dreher, 1984, p. 189). Hence, human resource and other organizationally-based decisions, including developmental feedback, would be made in terms of one's performance on exercises and not one's standing on specified dimensions.

From one perspective, a task-based perspective in assessment centers is not particularly new or that recent. For instance, as noted by Arthur et al. (2003), the criterion-related validities of assessment centers have typically been in the form of the correlation between the overall assessment rating (OAR) and the criterion (e.g., Aamodt, 2004; Gaugler, Rosenthal, Thornton, & Bentson, 1987; Hardison & Sackett, 2007; Hermelin, Lievens, & Robertson, 2007; Hunter & Hunter, 1984; Schmitt, Gooding, Noe, & Kirsch, 1984); and the OAR basically represents method-level information (albeit collapsed across exercises and dimensions). The focus on the OAR is quite different from the approach taken by those studies that have retained information at the dimension level and reported the criterion-related validities accordingly (e.g., Arthur et al., 2003; Meriac, Hoffman, Woehr, & Fleisher, 2008). These differences in approaches more likely than not contribute to the wide range in effect sizes obtained from meta-analyses of ostensibly the same predictor (Arthur & Day, 2011).

Dimensions and the Centrality of Constructs to Psychology as a Science, and Industrial/Organizational Psychology as an Applied Science

The centrality of constructs as a subject of study in the field of psychology is very well established (Anastasi & Urbina, 1997; Murphy & Davidshofer, 2001; Nunnally & Bernstein, 1994). Subsequently, as a subspecialty of psychology, identifying the human requirements (i.e., constructs/dimensions) that underlie effective task and role performance is and should be fundamental to the field of I/O psychology as well (Arthur et al., 2008; Howard, 1997). So, what is a dimension? Like a construct (Cronbach & Meehl, 1955), a dimension can be conceptualized as an explanatory variable that cannot be directly observed. It also does not have a single observable referent, but instead, consists of a covarying cluster of observable behaviors that are considered to be indicators or markers of the dimension in question. For instance, Thornton and Byham (1982) define dimensions as "cluster[s] of behaviors that are specific, observable, and verifiable, and that can be reliably and logically classified together"

(p. 117). And so whereas we cannot directly observe "problem solving" as an assessment center dimension, we can identify and observe the clusters of specific behaviors or activities (see Table 5.4 for an illustrative list) that together are considered to represent this dimension. Consequently, an important feature of assessment centers is a focus on *observable* behaviors and the linkages to the dimensions of interest.

Furthermore, in terms of its relationships to tasks, dimensions represent the cluster of specific behaviors that a person performs (i.e., "samples" as per Wernimont and Campbell, 1968) in the accomplishment of a task. As a result of this, in practice, assessors observe and

Table 5.4 Problem Solving Definition and Examples of Behavioral Indicators

PROBLEM SOLVING
The extent to which an individual gathers information; understands relevant technical and professional information; effectively analyzes and uses data and information; generates viable options, ideas, and solutions; selects supportable courses of action for problems and situations; uses available resources in new ways; and generates and recognizes imaginative solutions.
Identifies underlying as well as surface problems
Gathers available data
Sifts relevant data from irrelevant data
Pays close attention to significant details
Considers data gaps
Weights conflicting needs
Brings associated information to bear on problem
Explores problem: source roles, courses, impact
Supports assumptions with logic
Deals with constraints
Develops alternatives
Addresses short and long term impact of alternatives
Uses sound criteria to select or reject alternatives
Makes clear identification of trade-offs
Establishes clear and logical relationship between the decision and the analysis behind it
Uses creative parallels
Generates breakthrough solutions
Puts familiar things together in unfamiliar ways
Moves past imposed constraints (instructions, procedures, policies)
Makes unconventional or novel proposals or suggestions
Is the first to suggest ideas in the group
Proposes whole new approaches (beyond boundaries of current practices)
Uses creative argumentation
Derives new thoughts from others' ideas
Redefines a problem so that new solutions/options can be considered
Proposes non-incremental problem solving
Finds ways to do more with less
Stimulates innovative thinking in others
Sees and supports innovative thinking in others

record assessee behaviors during the assessment center exercises and subsequently, upon completion of the exercises, categorize the recorded behaviors into dimensions. This process may be facilitated by the use of behavioral checklists (e.g., Donahue, Truxillo, Cornwell, & Gerrity, 1997; Lievens & Conway, 2001; Reilly, Henry, & Smither, 1990). Indeed, this strong emphasis on observable behaviors is reflected in the widespread use of the term "behavioral dimensions" in the extant literature (e.g., see Thornton & Byham, 1982). Thus, assessment center dimensions are behavioral-, not trait-based; phrased another way, they can be described as focusing on samples of behavior instead of signs (Wernimont & Campbell, 1968).

The emphasis on behaviors in assessment centers can be contrasted with trait theory because whereas they share some similarities, they obviously have some profound differences as well. First, like traits, dimensions are posited to be constructs on which individuals differ (e.g., some people are better at solving problems than others). Second, although they are posited to manifest some level of consistency within the individual, dimensions are not posited to have the stable long-term enduring characteristic that is represented in the relatively long term stability of traits. Indeed, the behavioral foci of dimensions serves as the basis for the intervention-based focus of developmental assessment centers which are, by design, intended to assist and guide individuals to modify or change their dimension-related behaviors and thus, their standing on the specified dimensions. Third, traits have historically been associated with an individual's personality although they can and have been broadened to encompass ability-based traits (such as intelligence) as well. Dimensions on the other hand, are again specified in terms of direct observable behaviors and as a result, encompass a wider constellation of proficiencies, competencies, and skills (International Task Force on Assessment Center Guidelines, 2009; Thornton & Rupp, 2006), as commonly represented in I/O psychology science and practice.

Thornton and Byham (1982) summarize the distinction between traits and dimensions by noting that "[u]sually traits are thought to be *underlying personality constructs* that determine behavioral consistency across situations. They are assumed to be 'causal' variables that define a person's stable and enduring nature at work, at home, or during leisure time. Although some dimension labels look like traits, they are behaviorally defined and observed and do not require judgments about underlying personality constructs." (p. 118). The last sentence of the preceding quote is noteworthy because contrary to it, a close examination of dimensions, as used in practice, leaves one with the impression that many of them appear more to be trait-based dimensions (e.g., sensitivity, integrity, need for advancement, openness, conscientiousness) and less so behaviorally-based. This is illustrated in Arthur et al.'s (2003) list of assessment center dimension labels from their meta-analysis. Specifically, they identified a set of 168 dimensions from 34 primary studies that reported dimension-level criterion-related validities. These dimensions, along with the various levels of specificity into which they were categorized are presented in Table 5.1. A close review of the Level 3 dimension labels, which are the primary study dimension labels, indicates that several of these are quite trait-like. This not withstanding, at least in theory, dimensions are supposed to be behaviorally-based. That is, in assessing participants on a dimension such as "problem solving" as an example, assessors look for (observe), record, and rate direct *behavioral* indicators of this dimension (e.g., see Table 5.4). Thus, a dimension-based assessment center that adheres to the tenets of sound science and practice in assessment center design and development should focus on behaviors. One does not administer a test or measure (i.e., "sign") of problem solving to operationalize this dimension in an assessment center. Instead, one uses a performance-based exercise or activity that produces samples of observable behaviors that are indicators of problem solving or lack thereof.

The Assessment Center Construct-Related Validity Issue

A discussion of dimension-based assessment centers de facto also requires a discussion of the construct-related validity of assessment center ratings. In this chapter, we draw a distinction between *validity* or *construct validity* as the umbrella term, and *construct-related validity* as a specific validation procedure. Thus, validity or construct validity in its broadest form speaks to the appropriateness of inferences that are drawn from the test scores (American Educational Research Association, American Psychological Association, and National Council on Measurement in Education, 1999; Messick, 1989) which is in turn, inherently tired to the theoretical understanding of what a test purports to measure (Borsboom, Mellenbergh, & van Heerden, 2004). In contrast, *construct-related validity* is more narrowly construed and is just one of several *specific evidential approaches* or inferential strategies that can be used to contribute to our understanding of the construct validity of a test (Society for Industrial and Organizational Psychology, 2003). Hence, construct-related validity is a specific validation strategy or approach that focuses on specific measure-construct links, most commonly evidenced in the form of convergent and discriminant validity evidence.

A discussion of the construct-related validity of assessment center ratings is pivotal to dimension-based assessment centers because it fundamentally speaks to the core of the viability of a dimension-based perspective. Construct-related validity in this context pertains to the extent to which assessment centers are actually measuring that which they are designed to measure and the resultant appropriateness of the inferences that are drawn from said scores, such as providing dimension-based developmental feedback. Interestingly, unlike the consensus on the adequacy of the evidence supporting content-related and criterion-related validity of assessment centers, a recurring and persistent controversial issue, which has been actively and strongly debated, is the lack of construct-related validity evidence—that is, the extent to which assessment centers measure the dimensions they are purported to measure (e.g., see Lance, 2008a, 2008b; and Arthur et al., 2008; Brannick, 2008; Connelly, Ones, Ramesh, & Goff, 2008; Howard, 2008; Jones & Klimoski, 2008; Lievens, 2008; Melchers & König, 2008; Moses, 2008; Rupp, Thornton, & Gibbons, 2008; Schuler, 2008; and also Lievens, 2009).

In its simplest form, the apparent lack of construct-related validity is reflected in the observation that although assessment centers are designed to assess individuals on specific dimensions across multiple exercises, the robust finding in the extant literature is that correlations among ostensibly different dimensions within exercises are typically larger than correlations among the same dimensions across exercises. Thus, contrary to the tenets of the dimension-based approach, which posits that assessment center participants' behaviors should be cross-situationally consistent (e.g., see Figure 5.1), these results suggest that participants' behaviors are instead cross-situationally specific. The potential lack of construct-related validity evidence has several important implications but from a theoretical perspective, it is certainly essential to know whether assessment center ratings should be conceptualized as representing dimensions or exercises.

Several explanations have been provided for the weak construct-related validity evidence observed for assessment center ratings (e.g., see Arthur & Day, 2011; Arthur et al., 2008; Lievens, 2009; Woehr & Arthur, 2003, for reviews). These explanations have typically been either methodological or design-related, or conceptual and substantive in nature. The methodological and design-related factors that have been advanced include (a) the number of dimensions assessors are asked to observe, record, and subsequently rate; (b) the conceptual distinctiveness of dimensions; (c) the transparency of dimensions; (d) the choice and design of exercises, and the type and number of exercises; (e) the participant-to-assessor ratio; (f) the scoring and rating approach; (g) the type of assessor used; and (h) assessor training.

Likewise, conceptual and substantive explanations have included (a) the use of espoused versus actual constructs (Arthur et al., 2008); (b) the misspecification of the target constructs; (c) issues with analytical approaches specifically, the use of post-exercise dimension ratings to represent assessment center scores, and the misapplication of the multitrait-multimethod design (Arthur et al., 2008; Bowler & Woehr, 2006; Howard, 2008; Lance, Woehr, & Meade, 2007); and (d) differential activation of traits depending on the demands of a particular exercise (Lievens, 2009; Lievens, Chasteen, Day, & Christiansen, 2006).

There are obviously contrarian opinions about the adequacy of the above explanations for the weak construct-related validity evidence observed for assessment center ratings (e.g., Lance, 2008a, 2008b) and detailed treatment of these issues can be found in Chapter 5 and Chapter 7 of this volume. Nevertheless, I will conclude this section by noting that because of its theoretical and applied implications, the importance of the resolution of the present construct-related validity issue cannot be overstated. For instance, it is fair to note that certainly in terms of the volume of studies, in most cases, dimensions do not correlate across exercises with the result conclusion that exercises appear to explain more information than dimensions. For a host of reasons, some of which were articulated in Arthur et al. (2008), it is our position that the issue is not one of a failure of dimension-based assessment center theory, but instead a failure to engage in appropriate tests of said theory. And from another perspective, if one accepts the premise that assessment centers are methods, then they must be measuring some content, which in scientific terms are "constructs". Thus, again "we find it particularly ascientific to resign ourselves to a position that (to paraphrase) states that 'assessment centers measure something, we just do not know what it is' or that the scores represent exercises when exercises are not constructs" "a situation that is analogous to stating that scores on some paper-and-pencil tests represent performance in paper-and-pencil situations" (Arthur et al., 2008, p. 109). We certainly cannot be much of a scientific discipline if we are willing to accept a situation where the content of such an important measurement tool is unknown.

Where Do Dimensions Used in a Given or Specific Assessment Center Come From?

The choice of assessment center dimensions, like the content of other assessment tools in personnel psychology and human resource management, is typically arrived at inductively primarily by means of a job analysis (Doverspike & Arthur, in press). So, in the development of an assessment center, information obtained via a job analysis serves as the basis for dimension identification and the subsequent selection of exercises to measure said dimensions. And acknowledging that there is no such thing as *the* assessment center or *a single* assessment center, Figure 5.2 illustrates a typical sequence of steps that one would follow in arriving at the specified assessment center dimensions.

Job analysis is recognized as the first critical step in any personnel-related test development and validation effort because it allows for an identification and examination of the characteristics that make an optimal person-job match possible (Binning & Barrett, 1989). So, the scientific basis for basing dimension selection on a job analysis is that it ensures a conceptual linkage between the dimensions and the focal job or position in question (Doverspike & Arthur, in press). Sound professional practice and legal guidelines also recommend the use of a thorough and up-to-date job analysis. According to Section 14A of the *Uniform Guidelines* (Equal Employment Opportunity Commission, 1978), "Any validity study should be based upon a review of information about the job for which the selection procedure is to be used. The review should include a job analysis …" (p. 38300). The International Task Force on Assessment Center Guidelines (2009) also stipulate the collection of appropriate job analysis information to determine the assessment center dimensions. The central role of job analysis in the choice of dimensions in reflected in the results of Eurich et al. (2009) and Spychalski et al. (1997) which indicated that 90% and 93%, respectively, of the organizations they surveyed reported conducting a job analysis as part of their assessment center design and development.

The third step in Figure 5.2 indicates the identification of the critical knowledge, skills, abilities, and other characteristics (KSAOs) necessary for successful job performance. The next step then calls for the identification of the behavioral dimensions related to the identified KSAOs. In this context, KSAOs can be conceptualized as being at a lower level of specificity compared to dimensions (or competencies, which may in turn be conceptualized as being at a higher level of specificity than dimensions). The generation of KSAO lists and linkages to

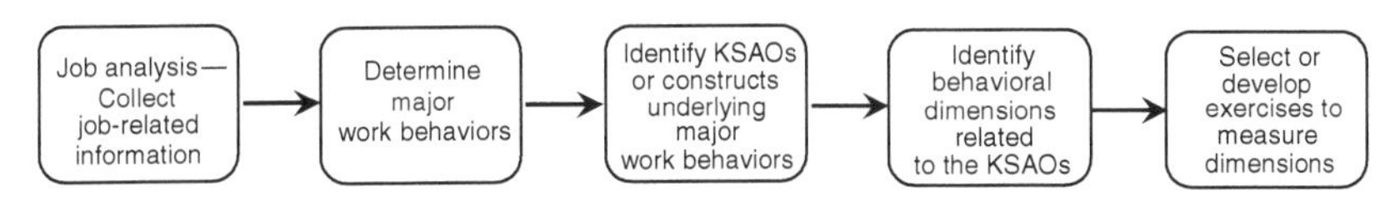

Figure 5.2 Dimension and exercise development/identification sequence.

specified dimensions is a rational and judgmental process that relies on the expertise of the assessment center developer as an individual with specialized knowledge in the study of human behavior. However, this process is also typically supplemented with task-KSAO, and KSAO-dimension linkage questionnaires that are completed by specified subject matter experts (SMEs) who provide the requisite job analysis ratings (Doverspike & Arthur, in press). The results from the subsequent analyses of these data then provide guidance on the choice and selection of the final set of dimensions or competencies. For purposes of selection and promotion, the dimensions should reflect abilities that underlie potential, whereas knowledge- and skill-based dimensions are more applicable for training and development purposes.

The implementation of the identification, labeling, and definition of dimensions step is a particularly critical one in the development of the assessment centers since it has been identified as a weak link in the assessment center design and development process because of the proclivity to rely on espoused dimensions (constructs; Arthur et al., 2008). Specifically, the assessment center literature appears to be a domain in which assertions about the dimensions being measured are rarely, if ever subjected to the psychometric standards that characterize test development in other domains (Arthur et al., 2008; Brannick, 2008). Thus, merely labeling data as reflecting a particular dimension does not mean that **is** the dimension being assessed. As noted by Arthur et al. (2008), the formulation and explication of dimension definitions should not be approached casually, and support for the construct representation of the assessment center's content should be demonstrated using multi-stage data collection and refinement efforts before the assessment center is put into operational or research use. Thus, it should be noted that contrary to common practice, efforts to establish the construct-related validity of the assessment center dimension ratings should be undertaken *before* the assessment center is put into operational or research use.

The final step in Figure 5.2 entails the selection or development of exercises to measure the behavioral dimensions that were identified. It is worth noting that whereas the assessment center developer may have limited control in terms of what the final dimensions may be—they are determined, after all, by the results of the job analysis—she/he has a lot more leeway in determining the exercises to be used. Consequently, in deciding on the exercises, the developer should take into account their trait activation potential (Lievens, 2009), face validity, reliability, fidelity, usability, cost, and practicality.

Although the preceding highlights the importance of job analysis in the choice and selection of assessment center dimensions, one can envisage situations in which the choice of dimensions is driven primarily by organizational desires and policy. So, for instance, in the case of a developmental assessment center, an organization may be motivated by the wish to inculcate and develop specified skills and competencies in its employees as per the examples represented by some of the dimensions presented in Table 5.2 and Table 5.3. Whereas there may be some debate as to exactly what they are and what they are not, competency models can be described as a form of job analysis that is focused at a much higher level of specificity. Thus, competency models attempt to identify variables related to overall organizational fit and subsequently, identify individual characteristics consistent with the organization's vision (Cascio & Aquinis, 2011; Schippmann et al., 2000). Thus, unlike the preceding job analysis-based sequence of steps, competency modeling is a top-down deductive approach that starts with focus on what the organization needs to be effective and competitive. Consequently, these skills and competencies are then the initial building blocks that guide the development or selection of the specified dimensions. However, even in this instance, one would suggest that some form of a job analysis should be undertaken to confirm the relevance and job-relatedness of the dimensions to the organization's goals and objectives.

Conclusions and Future Directions

A dimension-based focus has historically and traditionally been the dominant perspective in assessment center research and practice. Thus, it was quite surprising that an extensive electronic search of the extant literature failed to identify any works that spoke directly of a theory of assessment center dimensions. However, given origination of civilian assessment centers in AT&T's Management Progress Study with its focus on managerial performance, it is not surprising, and is indeed to be expected that the dimensions or at least the dimension labels commonly used in assessment center research and practice closely parallel those that are deemed to be important for effectiveness as a leader or manager. That notwithstanding, it could be argued that a furthering of a dimension-based perspective would benefit from a taxonomy or classification scheme of assessment dimensions. However, the assessment center literature has been characterized by an enormous proliferation of espoused dimension labels with no clear underlying structure or framework. So, for instance, Arthur et al. (2003) extracted 168 dimension labels from 34 assessment centers, and Woehr and Arthur (2003) 129 from 48 assessment centers. Although human behavior is certainly complex, it seems unlikely that 129 to 168 different dimensions are required to explain managerial performance. On a more favorable note, it would seem researchers have responded to Arthur et al.'s call to use and where warranted, refine and add to their assessment center dimension classification scheme (see Table 5.2). For instance, an electronic search of PsycINFO and Web of Science identified three meta-analyses (i.e., Bowler and Woehr, 2006; Lievens et al., 2006; Meriac et al., 2008), two primary studies (i.e., Hagan, Konopaske, Bernardin, & Tyler, 2006; Lievens, Dilchert, & Ones, 2009) and one study that used both primary and meta-analytic data (i.e., Dilchert & Ones, 2009), that have used Arthur et al.'s framework for organizing assessment dimensions.

Additional relevant and promising taxonomies can be found in the works of Borman and Brush (1993), Hoeft and Schuler (2001), Kolk, Born, and van der Flier (2004), and Mumford et al (2007) amongst others. For instance, a perusal of the dimension labels presented in Tables 5.1, 5.2, and 5.3, along with Kolk et al.'s (2004) triadic feeling, thinking, and power taxonomy, indicates a fairly high degree of overlap in these labels and descriptors. Hence, attempts to integrate and use these organizing frameworks are further encouraged.

Finally, from a dimension-based perspective, consonant with the centrality of constructs in the study and understanding of behavior, we echo Arthur and Day's (2011) call for a stronger focus and emphasis on dimension-level data and results in assessment center research and practice. Thus, we concur with their recommendation that overall assessment center rating (OAR)-*only* research should be discouraged and instead, whenever OAR results and data are reported, dimension-level data and results should be reported as well. This call is motivated by the fact that the use of OARs (a) results in a loss of dimension (construct)-level information, (b) means that one in effect has a method-level score, and (c) obscures the fact that some dimensions may be more predictive of performance than others (Arthur et al., 2003). It is acknowledged that for selection and other administrative purposes, a composite score is required to aid in decision making. However, because assessment center dimensions represent different constructs, the procedures used to generate composite scores can be the same as those typically used to combine scores from multi-predictor batteries such as the use of multiple regression or other means of assigning weights to different dimensions (e.g., see Arthur et al., 2003; Arthur, Doverspike, & Barrett, 1996; Bobko, Roth, & Buster, 2007; and Meriac et al., 2008).

References

Aamodt, M. G. (2004). *Research in law enforcement selection.* Boca Raton, FL: Brown Walker.

American Educational Research Association, American Psychological Association, and National Council on Measurement in Education. (1999). *Standards for educational and psychological testing.* Washington, DC: American Educational Research Association.

Anastasi, A., & Urbina, S. (1997). *Psychological testing* (7th ed.). Upper Saddle River, NJ: Prentice-Hall.

Arthur, W., Jr., & Day, E. A. (2011). Assessment centers. In S. Zedeck (Ed.), *APA Handbook of industrial and organizational psychology: Volume 2, Selecting and developing members for the organization* (pp. 205–235). Washington, DC: APA.

Arthur, W., Jr., Day, E. A., McNelly, T. L., & Edens, P. S. (2003). Meta-analysis of the criterion-related validity of assessment center dimensions. *Personnel Psychology, 56,* 125–154.

Arthur, W., Jr., Day, E. A., & Woehr, D. J. (2008). Mend it, don't end it: An alternate view of assessment center construct-related validity evidence. *Industrial and Organizational Psychology: Perspectives on Science and Practice, 1,* 105–111.

Arthur, W., Jr., & Doverspike, D. (2005). Achieving diversity and reducing discrimination in the workplace through human resource management practices: Implications of research and theory for staffing, training, and rewarding performance. In R. L. Dipboye & A. Colella (Eds.), *Discrimination at work: The Psychological and organizational bases* (pp. 305–327). San Francisco: Jossey-Bass.

Arthur, W., Jr., Doverspike, D., & Barrett, G. V. (1996). Development of a job analysis-based procedure for weighting and combining content-related tests into a single test battery score. *Personnel Psychology, 49,* 971–985.

Arthur, W., Jr., Edwards, B. D., & Barrett, G. V. (2002). Multiple-choice and constructed response tests of ability: Race-based subgroup performance differences on alternative paper-and-pencil test formats. *Personnel Psychology, 55,* 985–1008.

Arthur, W., Jr., & Villado, A. J. (2008). The importance of distinguishing between constructs and methods when comparing predictors in personnel selection research and practice. *Journal of Applied Psychology, 93,* 435–442.

Binning, J. F., & Barrett, G. V. (1989). Validity of personnel decisions: A conceptual analysis of the inferential and evidential bases. *Journal of Applied Psychology, 74,* 478–494.

Bobko, P., Roth, P. L., & Buster, M. A. (2007). The usefulness of unit weights in creating composite scores: A literature review, application of content validity, and meta-analysis. *Organizational Research Methods, 10,* 689–709.

Borman, W. C., & Brush, D. H. (1993). More progress toward a taxonomy of managerial performance requirements. *Human Performance, 6,* 1–21.

Borsboom, D., Mellenbergh, G. J., & van Heerden, J. (2004). The concept of validity. *Psychological Review, 111,* 1061–1071.

Bowers, D. G., & Seashore, S. E. (1966). Predicting organizational effectiveness with a four-factor theory of leadership. *Administrative Science Quarterly, 11,* 238–263.

Bowler, M. C., & Woehr, D. J. (2006). A meta-analytic evaluation of the impact of dimension and exercise factors on assessment center ratings. *Journal of Applied Psychology, 91,* 1114–1124.

Brannick, M. T. (2008). Basic to basics of test construction and scoring. *Industrial and Organizational Psychology: Perspectives on Science and Practice, 1,* 131–133.

Campbell, J. P. (1990). Modeling the performance prediction problem in industrial and organizational psychology. In M. D. Dunnette & L. M. Hough (Eds.), *Handbook of industrial and organizational psychology* (2nd ed., Vol. 1, pp. 687–732). Palo Alto, CA: Consulting Psychologists Press.

Cascio, W. F., & Aguinis, H. (2011). *Applied psychology in human resource management* (7th ed.). Upper Saddle River, NJ: Prentice Hall.

Connelly, B. S., Ones, D. S., Ramesh, A., & Goff, M. (2008). A pragmatic view of assessment center exercises and dimensions. *Industrial and Organizational Psychology: Perspectives on Science and Practice, 1,* 121–124.

Cronbach, L. J., & Meehl, P. E. (1955). Construct validity in psychological tests. *Psychological Bulletin, 52,* 281–302.

Dilchert, S., & Ones, D. S. (2009). Assessment center dimensions: Individual differences correlates and meta-analytic incremental validity. *International Journal of Selection and Assessment, 17,* 254–270.

Donahue, L. M., Truxillo, D. M., Cornwell, J. M., & Gerrity, M. J. (1997). Assessment center construct validity and behavioral checklists: Some additional findings. *Journal of Social Behavior and Personality, 12,* 85–108.

Doverspike, D., & Arthur, W. Jr. (in press). The role of job analysis in test selection and development. In M. A. Wilson, R. J. Harvey, G. M. Alliger, & W. Bennett, Jr. (Eds.), *The handbook of work analysis in organizations: The methods, systems, applications, and science of work measurement in organizations.* New York: Routledge Academic.

Equal Employment Opportunity Commission, Civil Service Commission, Department of Labor, and Department of Justice. (1978). Uniform guidelines on employee selection procedures. *Federal Register, 43,* 38290–38309.

Eurich, T. L., Krause, D. E., Cigularov, K., & Thornton, G. C., III. (2009). Assessment centers: Current practices in the United States. *Journal of Business and Psychology, 24,* 387–407.

Fleishman, E. A., Harris, E. F., & Burtt, H. E. (1955). Leadership and supervision in industry; an evaluation of a supervisory training program. *Ohio State University, Bureau of Educational Research Monograph, 33,* 1–110.

Gaugler, B. B., Rosenthal, D. B., Thornton, G. C., III, & Bentson, B. (1987). Meta-analysis of assessment center validity. *Journal of Applied Psychology, 72,* 493–511.

Hagan, C. M., Konopaske, R., Bernardin, H. J., & Tyler, C. L. (2006). Predicting assessment center performance with 360-degree, top-down, and customer-based competency assessments. *Human Resource Management, 45,* 357–390.

Hardison, C. M., & Sackett, P. R. (2007). Kriterienbezogene Validität des Assessment Centers: Lebendig und wohlauf? [Assessment center criterion-related validity: Alive and well?]. In H. Schuler (Ed.), *Assessment Center zur Potenzialanalyse* [Assessment center for the analysis of potential] (pp. 192–202). Göttingen, Germany: Hogrefe.

Hermelin, E., Lievens, F., & Robertson, I. T. (2007). The validity of assessment centres for the prediction of supervisory performance ratings: A meta-analysis. *International Journal of Selection and Assessment, 15,* 405–411.

Hoeft, S., & Schuler, H. (2001). The conceptual basis of assessment centre ratings. *International Journal of Selection and Assessment, 9,* 114–123.

Howard, A. (1997). A reassessment of assessment centers: Challenges for the 21st century. *Journal of Social Behavior and Personality, 12,* 13–52.

Howard, A. (2008). Making assessment centers work the way they are supposed to. *Industrial and Organizational Psychology: Perspectives on Science and Practice, 1,* 98–104.

Howard, A., & Bray, D. W. (1988). *Managerial lives in transition: Advancing age and changing times.* New York: Guilford Press.

Hunter, J. E., & Hunter, R. F. (1984). Validity and utility of alternative predictors of job performance. *Psychological Bulletin, 96,* 72–98.

International Task Force on Assessment Center Guidelines. (2009). Guidelines and ethical considerations for assessment center operations. *International Journal of Selection and Assessment, 17,* 243–253.

Joiner, D. A. (2002). Assessment centers: What's new? *Public Personnel Management, 31,* 179–185.

Jones, R. G., & Klimoski, R. J. (2008). Narrow standards for efficiency and the research playground: Why either-or conclusions do not help. *Industrial and Organizational Psychology: Perspectives on Science and Practice, 1,* 137–139.

Judge, T. A., Piccolo, R. F., & Illies, R. (2004). The forgotten ones? The validity of consideration and initiating structure in leadership research. *Journal of Applied Psychology, 89,* 36–51.

Kerr, S., Schreisheim, C. A., Murphy, C. J., & Stogdill, R. M. (1974). Toward a contingency theory of leadership based upon the consideration and initiating structure literature. *Organizational Behavior & Human Performance, 12,* 62–82.

Kolk, N. J., Born, M. P., & van der Flier, H. (2004). A triadic approach to the construct validity of the assessment center: The effect of categorizing dimensions into a feeling, thinking, and power taxonomy. *European Journal of Psychological Assessment, 20,* 149–156.

Lance, C. E. (2008a). Why assessment centers do not work the way they are supposed to. *Industrial and Organizational Psychology: Perspectives on Science and Practice, 1,* 84–97.

Lance, C. E. (2008b). Where have we been, how did we get there, and where shall we go? *Industrial and Organizational Psychology: Perspectives on Science and Practice, 1,* 140–146.

Lance, C. E., Woehr, D. J., & Meade, A. W. (2007). Case study: A Monte Carlo investigation of assessment center construct validity models. *Organizational Research Methods, 10,* 430–448.

Lievens, F. (2008). What does exercise-based assessment really mean? *Industrial and Organizational Psychology: Perspectives on Science and Practice, 1,* 112–115.

Lievens, F. (2009). Assessment centres: A tale about dimensions, exercises, and dancing bears. *European Journal of Work and Organizational Psychology, 18,* 102–121.

Lievens, F., Chasteen, C. S., Day, E. A., & Christiansen, N. D. (2006). Large-scale investigation of the role of trait activation theory for understanding assessment center convergent and discriminant validity. *Journal of Applied Psychology, 91,* 247–258.

Lievens, F., & Conway, J. M. (2001). Dimension and exercise variance in assessment center scores: A large-scale evaluation of multitrait-multimethod studies. *Journal of Applied Psychology, 86,* 1202–1222.

Lievens, F., Dilchert, S., & Ones, D. S. (2009). The importance of exercise and dimension factors in assessment centers: Simultaneous examinations of construct-related and criterion-related validity. *Human Performance, 22,* 375–390.

McCauley, C. D., Lombardo, M. M., & Usher, C. J. (1989). Diagnosing management development needs: An instrument based on how managers develop. *Journal of Management, 15,* 389–403.

Melchers, K. G., & König, C. J. (2008). It is not yet time to dismiss dimensions in assessment centers. *Industrial and Organizational Psychology: Perspectives on Science and Practice, 1,* 125–127.

Meriac, J. P., Hoffman, B. J., Woehr, D. J., & Fleisher, M. S. (2008). Further evidence for the validity of assessment center dimensions: A meta-analysis of the incremental criterion-related validity of dimension ratings. *Journal of Applied Psychology, 93,* 1042–1052.

Messick, S. J. (1989). Validity. In Linn. R. L. (Ed.), *Educational Measurement,* (pp. 13–103). New York: Macmillian.

Moses, J. (2008). Assessment centers work, but for different reasons. *Industrial and Organizational Psychology: Perspectives on Science and Practice, 1,* 134–136.

Mumford, T. V., Campion, M. A., & Morgeson, F. P. (2007). The leadership skills strataplex: Leadership skill requirements across organizational levels. *Leadership Quarterly, 18,* 154–166.

Murphy, K. R., & Davidshofer, C. O. (2001). *Psychological testing: Principles and applications* (5th ed.). Upper Saddle River, NJ: Prentice-Hall.

Nunnally, J. C., & Bernstein, I. H. (1994). *Psychometric theory* (3rd ed.). New York: McGraw-Hill.

Reilly, R. R., Henry, S., & Smither, J. W. (1990). An examination of the effects of using behavior checklists on the construct validity of assessment center dimensions. *Personnel Psychology, 43,* 71–84.

Rupp, D. E., Thornton, G. C., III., & Gibbons, A. M. (2008). The construct validity of the assessment center method and usefulness of dimensions as focal constructs. *Industrial and Organizational Psychology: Perspectives on Science and Practice, 1,* 116–120.

Sackett, P. R., & Dreher, G. F. (1984). Situation specificity of behavior and assessment center validation strategies: A rejoinder to Neidig and Neidig. *Journal of Applied Psychology, 69,* 187–190.

Schippmann, J. S., Ash, R. A., Battista, M., Carr, L., Eyde, L. D., Hesketh, B., et al. (2000). The practice of competency modeling. *Personnel Psychology, 53,* 703–740.

Schmitt, N., Gooding, R. Z., Noe, R. A., & Kirsch, M. (1984). Meta-analysis of validity studies published between 1964 and 1982 and the investigation of study characteristics. *Personnel Psychology, 37,* 407–421.

Schuler, H. (2008). Improving assessment centers by the trimodal concept of personnel assessment. *Industrial and Organizational Psychology: Perspectives on Science and Practice, 1,* 128–130.

Society for Industrial and Organizational Psychology, Inc. (2003). *Principles for the validation and use of personnel selection procedures* (4th ed.). Bowling Green, OH: SIOP.

Spychalski, A. C., Quinones, M. A., Gaugler, B. B., & Pohley, K. (1997). A survey of assessment center practices in organizations in the United States. *Personnel Psychology, 50,* 71–90.

Stogdill, R. M. (1950). Leadership, membership and organization. *Psychological Bulletin, 47,* 1–14.

Thornton, G. C., III, & Byham, W. C. (1982). *Assessment centers and managerial performance.* San Diego, CA: Academic Press.

Thornton, G. C., III, & Rupp, D. E. (2006). *Assessment centers in human resource management: Strategies for prediction, diagnosis, and development.* Mahwah, NJ: Erlbaum.

U.S. Office of Personnel Management Leadership Competencies. (n.d.). http://www.dtc.dla.mil/wfd/ldrshpdv/2.htm

Wernimont, P. F., & Campbell, J. P. (1968). Signs, samples, and criteria. *Journal of Applied Psychology, 52,* 231–258.

Woehr, D. J., & Arthur, W., Jr. (2003). The construct-related validity of assessment center ratings: A review and meta-analysis of the role of methodological factors. *Journal of Management, 29,* 231–258.

6

How to Apply a Dimension-Based Assessment Center

Paul G. W. Jansen
Vrije Universiteit Amsterdam

An assessment center (AC) has been defined as:

> A standardized evaluation of behavior based on multiple inputs. Several trained observers and techniques are used. Judgments about behavior are made, in major part, from specifically developed assessment simulations. These judgments are pooled in a meeting among the assessors or by a statistical integration process. In an integration discussion, comprehensive accounts of behavior—and often ratings of it—are pooled. The discussion results in evaluations of the assessees' performance on the dimensions or other variables that the assessment center is designed to measure. Statistical combination methods should be validated in accordance with professionally accepted standards. (International Task Force on Assessment Center Guidelines, 2009, pp. 244–245)

In practice the label "AC" is mostly used to denote the simulations that comprise part of a more elaborate procedure in which interviews and psychological tests are also often incorporated.

By combining several situational exercises, the AC has a high predictive validity for promotion, career potential, or job performance appraisal by a senior manager (Arthur, Day, McNelly, & Edens, 2003; Gaugler, Rosenthal, Thornton, & Bentson, 1987; Meriac, Hoffman, Woehr, & Fleisher, 2008), even when the promotion criterion is measured after very long time gaps (Hinrichs, 1978; McEvoy & Beatty, 1989; Mitchel, 1975; Jansen & Stoop, 2001; Jansen & Vinkenburg, 2006).

In this chapter, I first describe the AC as a grid of personal dimensions that are reflected in situational exercises. This conceptualization allows us to introduce a number of basic concepts, in particular the concepts of a dimension and of a dimension-based AC (DBAC). In the section on research findings, I list a number of troubling research findings, for instance the generally low cross-exercise consistency of AC dimensions and, for each finding, present a number of appropriate actions to deal with it. For instance, how should the limited consistency of dimensional ratings across AC exercises be dealt with in a DBAC? Since a DBAC almost invariably contains a consensus meeting of assessors, I deal with the question of how to structure, in practice, the evaluation processes in a DBAC by reviewing results from research. The chapter ends with a brief summary of the most important practical lessons learned.

Personal Dimensions and Situational Exercises

The AC Matrix

Work may be conceived as consisting of a limited number of critical work situations/tasks that have to be dealt with effectively. The situations are critical since (a) they have a decisive impact on effective job functioning, and thereby on criteria of organizational success, and (b) employee behavior varies in such situations. The latter implies that it is possible to provide examples of effective and ineffective behaviors. For instance, it is critical for job success as a sales manager that one is able to handle work situations such as making a presentation, conducting a sales interview, and writing a new business plan. It has been argued that every job consists of about ten such critical situations, tasks, or roles (Jansen & de Jongh, 1997).

Work situations, such as making a presentation or conducting a sales interview, in some way call on various qualities such as a worker's interpersonal sensitivity. However, effective mastery of the first-mentioned situation requires more: the presentation has to be prepared, and the speech has to be organized in such a way that, in a few minutes, the message is clearly conveyed. These requirements call on additional personal attributes, or dimensions, such as problem solving and judgment (all the example dimensions in this chapter are taken from the taxonomy presented by Arthur et al., 2003). Such dimensions are even more required when writing a new business plan, whereas this does not require any interpersonal sensitivity.

It is possible to cross the three personal dimensions of interpersonal sensitivity, problem solving, and judgment, with the three job situations of making a presentation, conducting a sales interview, and writing a new business plan (see Table 6.1). In the cells one finds the observed

Table 6.1 Work Behavior as a Grid of Personal Dimensions by Situational Tasks

		Situation (job task)		
		Making a presentation	Conducting a sales interview	Writing a business plan
Dimension (personal attribute)	interpersonal sensitivity	+	++	0
	problem solving	0	+	+
	judgment	+	0	++

Note. ++ = very much required, + = required, 0 = useful to have

basic behavior of a person, and this cannot be subdivided further given the present set of dimensions and tasks.

Every AC can be represented as such a grid constituted by crossing personal dimensions with situational exercises; with job tasks replaced by AC exercises. During the final evaluation phase of the AC, all observations in the matrix have to be combined to obtain a final evaluation of the candidate's behavior. The procedure to summarize the center can either work horizontally across exercises to yield a *dimensional profile* of the candidate, or vertically across dimensions to produce a *situational profile*. To determine the *overall assessment rating* (OAR), whichever of the dimensional and situational profiles was created is weighted according to a pre-established criterion, for instance being able to manage in the field of commerce at the level of a senior department supervisor. The OAR, and corresponding dimensional or situational profiles, are reported back to the candidate and/or the AC principal, who can use the AC results in personnel decisions such as recruitment, rejection, training, or transfer. In a DBAC, only dimensional profiles are used.

To summarize, I distinguish with respect to the measurement criteria associated with ACs.

1. *Dimensional criteria*: Dimensions such as interpersonal sensitivity, persistence, and leadership. These are more or less stable characteristics of a person that repeat across different work situations. Dimensions can be viewed as *personal inputs* to the job.
2. *Situational criteria*: Abilities related to the actual *work situation* that can be described by verbs such as planning, negotiating, or controlling. Abilities are situation-specific, and are limited in space and time. For instance, negotiating is not something someone does all day, but is a very specific activity that may be done within, for instance, one hour. Situational criteria refer to how the job task is actually done, that is how an assigned task is transformed to output by means of personal inputs.

3. *Output criteria*: Results such as turnover, market share, and number of complaints. These outputs are connected to the function and measure the *effectiveness* of a person in their work.

Personnel Assessment using Dimensional Criteria

From the matrix in Table 6.1, a dimension can be defined as a specific meaningful aggregate of candidate behaviors across AC exercises; the specificity is determined by the dimension being considered, for instance taking initiatives or acting decisively. As such, a dimension rating in a DBAC represents the general tendency of the candidate to act in a specific way (e.g., to be interpersonally sensitive) across a set of AC created situations. A DBAC produces personnel assessments in the sense of "*Across situations such as …, (s)he generally acts in a …* (personal adjective) *way. Therefore (s)he may be denoted as being …* (personal adjective)." Note that these assessments are based on concrete behaviors in distinct AC situations. Overall, the outcome of a DBAC is a set of dimension ratings obtained across the exercises. These are then used to decide on, for instance, promotion into a management position. Dimensional assessment using a DBAC is mandatory when the aim is to make general statements about a person that are valid across several job situations.

The construction of a DBAC starts by drawing up a set of critical job dimensions, for instance by a thorough job analysis. Subsequently, situational exercises are acquired or constructed in such a way that these measure the desired dimensions. If this is achieved, the DBAC is said to have construct validity. In this approach, situational exercises need not to have that much in common with the function at hand. What counts is the degree to which the desired dimensions are probed by the simulated situations. The gap between the dimensions and the actual job is bridged through anchoring the relationship in psychological theories of personality, attitudes, and motivation. So the reasoning is: *Exercises X and Y produce a valid measure of dimension A. Dimension A is critical for proficiency in management. Therefore, an assessment of dimension A based on a DBAC with exercises X and Y will yield a valid prediction of management success.*

An important advantage of using dimension-based ACs is that psychological theories are almost invariably phrased in terms of personal constructs such as openness to experience, or growth-need strength, or proactivity, which are equivalent to AC dimensions in the sense that they describe how a person tends to act across a number of situations. Psychological constructs are generally measured using questionnaires consisting of a number of items in which the construct is operationalized in a concrete situation. For instance, in case of proactivity: "*I am constantly on the lookout for new ways to improve my life*," or "*Wherever I have been, I have been a powerful force for constructive change.*" Respondents are asked to indicate the degree to which the description applies to them. A measure of the construct is obtained by averaging item scores, which is equivalent to measuring an AC dimension by averaging dimension scores across exercises.

DBAC and Construct Validity

The foregoing argument requires AC dimensions to have construct validity. However, studies have repeatedly found that the correlation between different dimensions in one assessment situation is larger than the correlation between results for one dimension assessed over different situations. As such, the construct validity of the AC is low (e.g., Fletcher & Dulewicz, 1984; Klimoski & Brickner, 1987; Neidig & Neidig, 1984; Robertson, Gratton, & Sharpley, 1987; Sackett & Harris, 1988). This limited construct validity of AC dimensions is troublesome for DBACs in which dimensional ratings are intended to serve as a basis for providing participants with developmental feedback. The crux is that this feedback, and any resulting action plans, might be flawed if the ACs do not provide a consistent and distinct measurement of the dimensions (Lievens, Chasteen, Day, & Christiansen, 2006).

There is, however, a large variation; there are ACs with a somewhat better construct validity (Lievens & Conway, 2001). These tend to have fewer dimensions and involve more experienced assessors. In their meta-analysis, Bowler and Woehr (2006) estimated that dimensions generally account for 22% of the rating variance, and exercises generally account for 34%, implying that AC construct validity is not that bad.

Limited construct validity is not the only troublesome finding in terms of DBACs. In the section on research findings, I present an overview of previous findings associated with dimensions. Note, however, that the focus of that section is not on providing an overview of AC research but, rather, on how to apply a DBAC and deal with the research outcomes. For instance, how should the limited consistency of dimensional ratings across AC exercises be dealt with in a DBAC?

Research Findings on Dimension-Based Assessment Centers and Appropriate Actions

Based on a number of recent studies (Bowler & Woehr, 2006; Haaland & Christiansen, 2002; Lance, Lambert, Gewin, Lievens, & Conway, 2004; Lievens, 2002; Lievens et al., 2006; Lievens & Conway, 2001), the following causes of, and corresponding remedies (actions) for, the lack of AC construct validity are distinguished.

Limited Cognitive Capacity of Assessors

During an ongoing situational exercise, such as a group discussion, an assessor may have to observe, for about an hour, six candidates who are involved in a complicated social process. The assessor has to note relevant behavioral observations, and then regroup these while weighting them according to perhaps five to seven dimensions. Even for experienced assessors this is a very challenging task. Nevertheless, research suggests that candidates do vary their behaviors between AC exercises rather than between assessors (Lance et al., 2004). Candidate behavior is typically cross-situationally specific. This suggests that assessors' judgments tend to be veridical.

Action 1. Limit the number of dimensions to no more than five meta-dimensions. Several studies have shown that between two and four factors typically underlie an assessor's ratings (see e.g. Thornton & Byham, 1982; Shore, Thornton, & McFarlane Shore, 1990). Based on their investigation, Shore et al. (1990, p. 111) are in favor of "*grouping assessment dimensions into broad interpersonal- and performance-style categories*." These "*meta-dimensions*" embrace:

1. intelligence, thinking (with several interpretations: analytical, creative, social, problem solving, intellectual);
2. social orientation (interpersonal sensitivity, consideration, and awareness of others), and social capability (interpersonal effectiveness, interpersonal skills, influencing others, communication);
3. independence and strength (decisive, firm, resistant, leadership, adaptability, and resilience);
4. ambition (motivated, involved, drive, committed);
5. operational competence (productive, effective, systematic, planning and organizing, results orientation).

These general categories should be formulated in a language that fits the company's management style. In AC applications, the meta-dimensions are not represented by some sort of short label but, rather, by corresponding examples of concrete behaviors in the context of the situational exercise. The same "supra-competencies" are also reported by Arthur et al. (2003). An additional advantage of using meta-dimensions is that manager assessors, who generally have expertise in the jobs, need less time to understand the dimensions.

Action 2. In order to have dimensions that are conceptually distinct and sufficiently specific to be the most relevant for the target job, provide assessors with behavioral checklists, that is translations of the dimensions into concrete situational exercise behaviors.

Action 3. Provide sufficient assessor training, use assessors for whom appraising people is part of their daily job (e.g., psychologists). Take care that assessors are familiar with the exercise, preferably choose people who have sufficient working experience in the simulated job situation (such as managers). Lievens and Conway (2001) found that the variance among the dimensions was larger with psychologists than with managers as assessors, indicating that psychologists are better at discriminating among the dimensions. Since this contributes to the discriminant validity of the dimension ratings, it is a good idea to have a psychologist in the team of assessors, for instance as the chair of the assessor consensus meeting.

Feedback Specificity

Feedback should be timely, specific, and constructive (e.g., Kinicki, Prussia, Wu, & McKee-Ryan, 2004). Feedback specificity refers to the level of information present in the appraisal statement. Since a DBAC produces personnel assessments in the sense of "*In situations such as ..., (s)he generally acts in a ... way,*" feedback in a DBAC will be less specific than feedback in an exercise-based AC. Goodman, Wood, and Hendrickx (2004) compared the effect of specific, situational feedback to the effect of more general dimensional feedback, that is less specific because it is generalized across several tasks or situations (DBAC), on both immediate performance improvements and long-term learning and generalization to other tasks. They found essentially that specific feedback is good for immediate performance but bad for long-term learning, whereas less-specific feedback is bad for immediate performance and good for long-term learning and generalization to other similar tasks. Specific feedback induces a *performance orientation* (Dweck & Legget, 1988), and this is detrimental to learning. In line with operant conditioning theory, specific positive feedback increases the *replication* of behaviors. Thus, increasing feedback specificity (exercise-based AC) may contribute to initial performance but discourage exploration and learning in the longer term. An advantage of less-specific feedback (DBAC) is that performers, since they will more often experience errors, will be stimulated to search for alternative actions in order to find the correct reaction and in that way develop strategies for avoiding future errors (Goodman & Wood, 2004). As such, less-specific feedback stimulates a *learning or mastery orientation.* Specific feedback stimulates practicing the same task; less-specific feedback stimulates modifying the task.

Action 1. Choose a specific type of AC that reflects the type of learning required, and adapt the specificity of feedback to the type of AC. Essentially, the reasoning is:

1. Mastery orientation: long-term learning required → less specific (dimensional) feedback → DBAC.
2. Performance orientation: increase/improve immediate performance → specific (situational) feedback → excise-based AC.

As a consequence, one should not be afraid to give less-specific feedback in a DBAC, that is, feedback that is poor in situational referents: "*In general, you tend to ... (description of dimension).*" Naturally, it should always remain an option to explain this general dimension assessment in terms of concrete, exercise-related behaviors: "*In a situation that emphasizes interpersonal sensitivity in the sense of understanding another person on account of written materials (e.g., in-basket) you did ..., but in a situation that emphasizes interpersonal sensitivity in the sense of active listening (e.g., simulated employee interview with a role player) you did ... Taken together, this implies with respect to the dimension of interpersonal sensitivity that you in general tend to....*"

Strong Correlations between Different Dimensions within the Same Exercise.

Discrimination among ratings within exercises is generally better when the dimensions are not expressing the same underlying traits. There will, for instance, be more overlap between the dimensions of persuasiveness and personal impact, since both relate to "influencing others," than between persuasiveness and "innovative thinking" dimensions since the first refers to "influencing others" and the second to "problem solving" (Arthur et al., 2003).

Action 1. Reduce content overlap between dimensions by using fewer dimensions (see above) and by using dimensions that are quite different. This implies using a few (e.g., no more than five) abstract, high-level dimensions.

Dissimilar Exercises

The measurement model within a dimension-based AC assumes that the same dimensions underlie behaviors in different exercises. Since a dimension is supposed to be tapped by several exercises, exercises should have dimensional overlap. However, in general, assessment center exercises such as In-Basket, Group Discussion, or Analysis/Presentation, represent quite dissimilar situations that place different psychological demands on participants. This dissimilarity arises because of the demand that exercises should simulate various critical job tasks. As a consequence, an assessee may be assessed as quite interpersonally sensitive in a small-group situation such as the Analysis/Presentation exercise, but as less interpersonally sensitive in a large group situation such as the Leaderless Group Discussion where many cognitive and interpersonal inputs have to be processed. Nevertheless, if person A is, *in general,* more interpersonally sensitive than person B, the rank-order on interpersonal sensitivity, A > B, should be seen both in exercises that very much tap this dimension (such as Group Discussions) and exercises that to a lower degree appeal to this dimension (such as In-Baskets), although in the latter case the rank-order will be much less reliably measured. The more dissimilar exercises are, the harder it becomes to measure a dimension consistently across them.

Action 1. Take care that exercises have an overlap in underlying traits, rather than in behaviors. According to trait-activation theory (Tett & Guterman, 2000), situations provide cues for the expression of trait-relevant behavior, and dissimilar situations differ in such trait relevance. A good convergence among assessment center ratings is most likely between high trait activating exercises that provide opportunities to observe behavior related to the same trait (Haaland & Christiansen, 2002). Therefore, exercises should be designed such that a non-trivial degree of trait *overlap* is guaranteed. Note that this does not imply that exercises should invoke the same behaviors, but rather that exercises should elicit adequate *trait-related behaviors*. For instance, the In-Basket test might be accompanied by an interview in which the assessee is asked to explain his or her actions and deliberations. In this way, it would be possible to measure interpersonal sensitivity. Alternatively, the In-Basket example might contain a few items in which the assessee has to demonstrate sensitive interpersonal behavior, for instance by having to write a letter to a complaining customer. Note that, in this approach, dimensions are assumed to indicate traits.

Exercise Design

Action 1. Design exercises to reflect situations that invoke or activate AC dimensions. Exercises should be designed not so much as good accurate examples of critical work behaviors, but as situations that invoke or activate relevant AC dimensions. More specifically, this implies designing exercises that involve challenging interactions with others (i.e., Analysis/Presentation Exercises, Leader Group Discussions) and that elicit a wide range of behaviors (Lievens et al., 2006). Such exercises generally tend to elicit two broad Big Five traits, namely Extraversion (communication, influencing others) and Conscientiousness (organizing and planning), that are found to be more easily observable and consequently offer greater construct validity than Openness to Experience, Emotional Stability (drive), or Agreeableness (consideration, awareness of others; Bowler and Woehr, 2006; Lievens et al., 2006).

Action 2. Use exercises that provide valid measures of the core dimensions. In a dimension-based AC, one could even work with a standard set of exercises as long as these provide valid measures of the core dimensions. Note that this would lead to one of the AC guidelines not being complied with: namely, that AC exercises should be *specially developed* assessment simulations. This is, however, not a problem since a dimension-based AC does not require exercise content validity, but, rather, dimension construct validity. Still, both for legal reasons (sample validity will much easier to uphold in court than construct validity) and for reasons of face validity (acceptability of AC exercises to candidates), DBACs tend to be based on exercises that, although not specific to the organization, are nevertheless specific to key elements of the job type at hand. Based on a large number of studies, Bartram (2005) proposed the Great Eight competencies as a general framework for situational performance criteria or job criteria (Table 6.2). These can also be viewed as eight general but critical job situations: leading tasks, interacting tasks, enterprising tasks etc. As such, Table 6.2 can be considered as a candidate list of all possible exercises in a dimension-based AC.

Table 6.2 Great Eight Competencies

1 Leading and Deciding
Takes control and exercises leadership. Initiates action, gives direction, and takes responsibility.

2 Supporting and Cooperating
Supports others and shows respect and positive regard for them in social situations. Puts people first, working effectively with individuals and teams, clients, and staff. Behaves consistently with clear personal values that complement those of the organization.

3 Interacting and Presenting
Communicates and networks effectively. Successfully persuades and influences others. Relates to others in a confident, relaxed manner.

4 Analyzing and Interpreting
Shows evidence of clear analytical thinking. Gets to the heart of complex problems and issues. Applies own expertise effectively. Quickly takes on new technology. Communicates well in writing

5 Creating and Conceptualizing
Works well in situations requiring openness to new ideas and experiences. Seeks out learning opportunities. Handles situations and problems with innovation and creativity. Thinks broadly and strategically. Supports and drives organizational change.

6 Organizing and Executing
Plans ahead and works in a systematic and organized way. Follows directions and procedures. Focuses on customer satisfaction and delivers a quality service or product to the agreed standards.

7 Adapting and Coping
Adapts and responds well to change. Manages pressure effectively and copes well with setbacks.

8 Enterprising and Performing
Focuses on results and achieving personal work objectives. Works best when work is related closely to results and the impact of personal efforts is obvious. Shows an understanding of business, commerce, and finance. Seeks opportunities for self-development and career advancement.

Note. From Bartram (2005).

Action 3. When designing a dimension-based AC, the measurement of a limited set of dimensions should be the criterion in selecting situational exercises, and not the complete coverage of critical job situations. The suggested procedure is:

1. Determine which dimensions are going to be assessed. This can be based on dimensions that are essential if one is to be effective in present or future critical job situations (selective AC), or on dimensions that are only weakly developed in a person (developmental AC).
2. Determine which set of exercises will best measure the selected dimensions: which combination of exercises will yield dimension ratings with high construct validity?
3. Select exercises in such a way that every dimension will be measured through at least two exercises.

Since, in practice, a DBAC almost always contains an assessor consensus meeting in which dimension ratings from each exercise have to be integrated into an overall dimensional profile of the candidate across all AC exercises, I deal, in the following section, with the question of how best to organize the final evaluation process in a DBAC.

Process during the AC Consensus Meeting in a Dimension-Based AC

The AC Consensus Meeting

The typical application of a dimension-based AC requires assessors to assess dimensions per exercise, and then formulate a general assessment of each dimension by generalizing across exercises. This is normally done during a consensus meeting. During such an AC consensus meeting, assessors have to deal with questions such as:

1. How should the various dimensional ratings per exercise (the cells in Table 6.1) be combined to form, on the one hand, one end rating per exercise (bottom row in Table 6.1) and, on the other, one end rating per dimension (right-hand column in Table 6.1)?
2. How should these exercise and dimension ratings subsequently be combined to produce a single OAR (bottom right-hand cell in Table 6.1)?
3. How should conflicting assessments of the same dimension from different situations be resolved? Which situational exercise should be dominant in the decision process?

4. Which dimensions should be decisive?
5. What to do in the event of differences of opinion between assessors of a candidate's performance, even when they have observed this candidate in the same simulated management situation?

Assessor training should essentially focus on the distinction between observing behavior and evaluating behavior. In achieving this, an assessor learns to use the grid shown in Table 6.1 to observe and register the candidate's primary behavior. It can then serve as a support for the registration, assessment, and reporting of observed behavior. Also, assessor training helps prepare assessors for the consensus meeting.

Only in a few of the numerous studies on ACs have the decision-making processes that take place during the assessors' consensus meeting been investigated. Mechanistic or formal procedures for combining AC assessments to a single OAR, such as averaging assessor ratings, are seen as superior to clinical or informal methods with respect to predictive validity (Ganzach, Kluger, & Clayman, 2000; Feltham, 1988; McEvoy, Beatty, & Bernardin, 1987; Pynes, Bernardin, Benton, & McEvoy, 1988; Russell, 1985). This superiority of statistical over clinical prediction has been recognized since Meehl (1955). Other studies have found that comparisons of assessors' ratings prior to and after the consensus meeting indicate that either managers have almost no mutual influence or that changes in the ratings have no impact whatsoever on the predictive validity of the AC (Wingrove, Jones, & Herriot, 1985). Thus, it would appear that a consensus meeting contributes little to increasing the predictive power of the AC over determining the OAR by a simple computation that averages across assessors. Further, Jones, Herriot, Long, and Drakeley (1991) found that procedural changes in the AC decision-making process did not affect the predictive validity of the OAR (for training criteria). They concluded that the OAR is valid because it summarizes a very large set of behavioral evidence (i.e., the cells in Table 6.1).

A Procedure for the Assessment Consensus Meeting

Although having an end discussion is debatable in terms of prediction objectives, validity (or efficiency) is not the only criterion for evaluating the contribution of a DBAC to the organization. Maybe for that reason, in practice, most DBACs continue to 'stubbornly' (Highhouse, 2008) rely on assessment center end discussions to reach dimension ratings and an OAR. Boxall and Purcell (2003) presented the following useful classification of norms for evaluating HRM interventions:

1. productivity (costs, efficiency, effectiveness),
2. flexibility (learning, change capacity), and
3. legitimacy (with relevant stakeholders).

While assessment center evaluation meetings may be hard to defend on productivity (validity) grounds, they are defendable on legitimacy or acceptability grounds. They can ensure that assessors feel committed to the DBAC outcomes, and also provide rational defense in the event of some candidates making legal challenges. Another positive side-effect of the consensus meeting is that it provides an opportunity to hear other managers talk about which types of behavior are, and for what reasons, effective in their organization, and which are ineffective or simply not necessary (cf. Table 6.3). Having such discussions may contribute to the criterion of learning and change since the assessors/managers may themselves gain in terms of personal effectiveness by being confronted with alternative actions in critical business situations, and being challenged about their own actions.

The following step-by-step procedure could help ensure that a DBAC consensus meeting is efficient and productive (in that it will produce valid end ratings), and also that it will contribute to acceptability and legitimacy of the DBAC results with users. It was applied in the ACs that were reported in longitudinal validity studies by Jansen and Stoop (2001) and by Jansen and Vinkenburg (2006).

Step 1. For every exercise, assessors will provide quantitative ratings of assessee behavior using a limited (maximum 5) number of

Table 6.3 Types of Discussions during AC Consensus Meetings

Input	Problem	Solution	Criterion
observation	different observations	add or remove	assessor observation report
categorization	different classifications	reclassify	dimension definition
evaluation	different evaluations	revaluate	what works in this situation
organizational effectiveness	different visions on what 'works' in the organization	norming discussion	what works in this organization (how do we do things here: culture)

non-overlapping and general dimensions. For instance, a candidate's behavior in a group discussion could be rated for its degree of 'interpersonal sensitivity' on a 5-point scale ranging from 1 (not at all present/observed) to 5 (very much present/observed). The ratings would be supported by a report on behavioral observations.

Step 2. Start with the first exercise, for instance a group discussion. Dimension ratings for a candidate on that exercise are compared and clarified using the behavioral observations. In the event that ratings differ significantly, for instance by more than 1 point on a 5-point scale, the discussion moves to compare observations for that dimension. Reasons for different assessors having different observations for a dimension can be (see also, Table 6.3):

1. Assessors have *different observations* of the same candidate. In this case, assessors have to check and clarify their observation reports, add missing observations to their personal list of observation notes, or remove observations when they were wrongly noted, for instance when the assessor erred as to the candidate for whom the observation was made. This can occur with a group discussion where several managers are observing several candidates;
2. Although assessors have the *same observations* for the same candidate (e.g., "*He frequently interrupted in the group discussion*") these pieces of behavior are classified in different dimensions. For instance, some assessors judge interrupting behavior to be an indicator of low *interpersonal sensitivity* while others see it as an indicator of a strong focus on *impact*. In this case, assessors have to discuss the basis for classification, that is, the definitions of the dimensions, and re-categorize wrongly categorized observations using the agreed definition of the dimensions. Frequently, the director of the consensus meeting will be able to refer the assessors to the agreed definitions of the dimensions as practiced during the assessors' training;
3. Assessors make the same observations (e.g., "*He frequently interrupted in the group discussion*") and place these in the same dimension (e.g., *impact*', but they *evaluate* the behavior differently. That is, although assessors agree that the candidate interrupted a lot, they disagree about what this says about the candidate's level of impact. For some assessors, interrupting is an indicator of a low focus on impact because the candidate is easily distracted from his main point but, for others, the same behavior indicates a strong focus on impact because the candidate has the courage to interrupt in a lengthy discussion which threatens to digress. Essentially, this discussion is about the local, that is, with respect to a particular AC situation, effectiveness of a candidate's behavior. The

action in this case is to get agreement among the assessors about, in this instance, whether frequent interrupting really has an impact in the particular job situation, and revaluate the dimension accordingly;

4. Finally, it is possible that assessors agree on their observations, their evaluations, and also on the fact that certain behaviors are effective in the exercise situation, but *disagree on the effectiveness* of a specific behavior in a specific *organizational context*. In this type of discussion, assessors mostly argue with their own organization as an implicit or explicit background: "*Although in general it can be very effective to interrupt in a lengthy (group) discussion, in our type of organization interrupting is simply not done!*" Note that, here, it is not effectiveness that works, but appropriateness, that is, what is done or not done, that counts. In this situation, the consensus meeting will require a discussion about cultural norms for effective management in the organization at hand. Note also that assessors will have to specify which type of behavior is both effective (works) and accepted (done) in that particular situation. For instance, in a lengthy discussion it may be better not to bluntly interrupt but to wait your turn and then change the subject by asking a colleague to follow-up a line of argument that they proposed earlier but that got lost in the ensuing discussion.

In an efficient consensus meeting, the majority of the discussion should be on the latter two aspects of disagreement. Assessors should talk about their observations and evaluations, both within the framework of the AC at hand and with respect to the context of their own organization, rather than about the classification of behavioral observations or about the meaning of dimensional denotations. The outcome of the four actions above should consist of an agreed-upon set of dimension observations, evaluations, and quantitative ratings for that exercise.

Step 3. Move on to the second, and then the third etc., exercise and repeat the procedure described in Step 2.

Step 4. Compare the outcomes of discussions on the within-exercise dimension ratings across different exercises in order to conclude how an assessee behaves *in general* with respect to that dimension. This amounts to assessing how (s)he *typically* behaves with respect to a given dimension across a set of critical job situations (i.e., those constituting the core of a managerial job). For instance, (s)he tends to act sensitively in the interpersonal aspects of managerial jobs. Here two approaches may be taken, including (a) the mechanical approach where final general dimension ratings are computed as the non-weighted average of corresponding within-exercise dimension ratings, and (b) the clinical approach, where the procedure described in Step 2 is repeated to obtain an agreed-upon common-rating and corresponding evaluation based on all within-exercise dimension ratings and evaluations. A complication here is that not all assessors will have been present during all the exercises. In some cases, some assessors will have to rely on the observational reports of others.

Although, as discussed earlier, research has shown that the mechanical approach is generally as good as or even better than the clinical approach, clinical procedures may still be adopted to ensure the commitment of the assessors to the OAR. A compromise could be that the outcome of the mechanical approach serves as an input to the clinical approach.

Conclusion

The foregoing research-based discussion on how to apply a DBAC can be summarized by the following take-home advice.

1. Limit the number of dimensions to no more than five, and avoid excessive content overlap between the dimensions. If this is difficult, or if you cannot avoid the same dimension being measured in several exercises, take care that the overlap in the exercises is in the underlying dimensions, and not in overt, concrete behaviors.
2. Give clear definitions of the dimensions (many can be found in the applied literature on assessment centers, e.g., Jansen & de Jongh, 1997) and also supply behavioral examples in terms of concrete exercise behavior.
3. Exercises should not be designed as faithful examples of critical work behaviors but, rather, as situations that invoke or activate relevant AC dimensions. Only use exercises that contain key elements of the job type at hand for legal reasons or to make the AC exercises acceptable to candidates and managers/assessors.
4. Use assessors who are familiar with personnel appraisal processes and with the exercises, and provide adequate assessor training.
5. Be clear about the type of feedback that will be given. It should be based on the goals to which the AC is expected to contribute, for instance improving immediate performance or long-term learning.
6. Organize an assessment center consensus meeting; not so much for reasons of productivity (validity) but more in order to increase legitimacy and acceptability of AC outcomes.

7. Start the AC consensus meeting by presenting computed (weighted) average dimension ratings across assessors that can then serve as an input for the discussion that may well modify these ratings.

To conclude, DBACs fit in a person-centered approach to assessment and have clear links to notions drawn from developmental psychology and elsewhere. As such, DBACs are closely connected to development center-based applications of ACs. However, since a DBAC is primarily a center for person *assessment*, one should remain alert to the measurement issues discussed in the present chapter.

References

Arthur, W., Jr, Day, E. A., McNelly, T. L., & Edens, P. S. (2003). A meta-analysis of the criterion-related validity of assessment center dimensions. *Personnel Psychology, 56*, 125–154.

Bartram, D. (2005). The great eight competencies: A criterion-centric approach to validation. *Journal of Applied Psychology, 90*, 1185–1203.

Boxall, P., & Purcell, J. (2003). *Strategy and human resource management*. New York: Palgrave MacMillan.

Bowler, M. C., & Woehr, D. J. (2006). A meta-analytic evaluation of the impact of dimension and exercise factors on assessment center ratings. *Journal of Applied Psychology, 91*, 1114–1124.

Dweck, C. S., & Legget, E. L. (1988). A social-cognitive approach to motivation and personality. *Psychological Review, 95*, 256–273.

Feltham, R. (1988). Assessment centre decision making: Judgmental vs. mechanical. *Journal of Occupational Psychology, 61*, 237–241.

Fletcher, C .A., & Dulewicz, V. (1984). An empirical study of a UK based assessment centre. *Journal of Management Studies, 21*, 83–97.

Ganzach, Y., Kluger, A. N., & Clayman, N. (2000). Making decisions from an interview: expert measurement and mechanical combination. *Personnel Psychology, 53*, 1–20.

Gaugler, B. B., Rosenthal, D. B., Thornton, G. C., III, & Bentson, C. (1987). Meta-analysis of assessment centre validity. *Journal of Applied Psychology, 72*, 493–511.

Goodman, J. S., & Wood, R. E. (2004). Feedback specificity, learning opportunities, and learning. *Journal of Applied Psychology, 89*, 809–821.

Goodman, J. S., Wood, R. E., & Hendrickx, M. (2004). Feedback specificity, exploration, and learning. *Journal of Applied Psychology, 89*, 248–262.

Haaland, S., & Christiansen, N. D. (2002). Implications of trait-activation theory for evaluating the construct validity of assessment center ratings. *Personnel Psychology, 55*, 137–163.

Highhouse, S. (2008). Stubborn reliance on intuition and subjectivity in employee selection. *Industrial and Organizational Psychology: Perspectives on Science and Practice*, 1, 333–342.

Hinrichs, J. R. (1978). An eight-year follow-up of a management assessment center. *Journal of Applied Psychology*, *63*, 596–601.

International Task Force on Assessment Center Guidelines. (2009). Guidelines and Ethical Considerations for Assessment Center Operations. *International Journal of Selection and Assessment*, *17*, 243–253.

Jansen, P. G. W., & de Jongh, F. (1997). *Assessment centres: A practical handbook*. Chichester, West Sussex, UK: Wiley.

Jansen, P. G. W., & Stoop, B. A. M. (2001). The dynamics of AC validity: Results of a 7-year study. *Journal of Applied Psychology*, *86*, 741–753.

Jansen, P. G. W., & Vinkenburg, C. J. (2006). Predicting management career success from AC data: a longitudinal study. *Journal of Vocational Behavior*, *68*, 253–266.

Jones, A., Herriot, P., Long, B., & Drakeley, R. (1991). Attempting to improve the validity of a well-established assessment centre. *Journal of Occupational Psychology*, *64*, 1–21.

Kinicki, A. J., Prussia, G. E., Wu, B., & McKee-Ryan, F. M. (2004). A covariance structure analysis of employees' response to performance feedback. *Journal of Applied Psychology*, *89*, 1057–1069.

Klimoski, R., & Brickner, M. (1987). Why do assessment centres work? The puzzle of assessment centre validity. *Personnel Psychology*, *40*, 243–260.

Lance, C. E., Lambert, T. A., Gewin, A. G., Lievens, F., Conway, J. M. (2004). Revised estimates of dimension and exercise variance components in assessment center postexercise dimension ratings. *Journal of Applied Psychology*, *89*, 377–385.

Lievens, F. (2002). Trying to understand the different pieces of the construct validity puzzle of assessment centers: An examination of assessor and assessee effects. *Journal of Applied Psychology*, *87*(4), 675–686.

Lievens, F., Chasteen, C. S., Day, E. A., & Christiansen, N. D. (2006). Large-scale investigation of the role of trait activation theory for understanding assessment center convergent and discriminant validity. *Journal of Applied Psychology*, *91*, 247–258.

Lievens, F., & Conway, J. M. (2001). Dimension and exercise variance in assessment center scores: A large-scale evaluation of multitrait-multimethod studies. *Journal of Applied Psychology*, *86*, 1202–1222.

Meehl, P. E. (1955). *Clinical vs. statistical prediction*. Minneapolis: University of Minnesota Press.

Meriac, J. P., Hoffman, B. J., Woehr, D. J., & Fleisher, M. S. (2008). Further evidence for the validity of assessment center dimensions: A meta-analysis of the incremental criterion-related validity of dimension ratings. *Journal of Applied Psychology, 2008*, *93*, 1042–1052.

McEvoy, G. M., Beatty, R. W., & Bernardin, H. J. (1987). Unanswered questions in assessment center research. *Journal of Business and Psychology*, *2*, 97–111.

McEvoy, G. M., & Beatty, R .W. (1989). Assessment centres and subordinate appraisal of managers: A seven year examination of predictive validity. *Personnel Psychology, 42*, 37–52.

Mitchel, J. O. (1975). Assessment center validity: A longitudinal study. *Journal of Applied Psychology, 60*, 573–579.

Neidig, R. D., & Neidig, P. J. (1984). Multiple assessment center exercises and job relatedness. *Journal of Applied Psychology, 69*, 182–186.

Pynes, J., Bernardin, H. J., Benton, A. L., & McEvoy, G. M. (1988). Should assessment center dimension ratings be mechanically-derived? *Journal of Business and Psychology, 2*, 217–227.

Robertson, I., Gratton, L., & Sharpley, D. (1987). The psychometric properties and design of managerial assessment centres: Dimensions into exercises won't go. *Journal of Applied Psychology, 60*, 187–195.

Russell, C. J. (1985). Individual decision processes in an assessment center. *Journal of Applied Psychology, 70*, 737–746.

Sackett, P. R., & Harris, M. M. (1988). A further examination of the constructs underlying assessment center ratings. *Journal of Business and Psychology, 3*, 214–229.

Shore, T. H., Thornton, G. C., III, & McFarlane Shore, L. (1990). Construct validity of two categories of assessment center dimension ratings. *Personnel Psychology, 43*, 101–116.

Tett, R. P., & Guterman, H. A. (2000). Situation trait relevance, trait expression, and cross-situational consistency: Testing a principle of trait activation. *Journal of Research in Personality, 34*, 397–423.

Thornton, G. C., III, & Byham, W. C. (1982). *Assessment centers and managerial performance*. New York: Academic Press.

Wingrove, J., Jones, A., & Herriot, P. (1985). The predictive validity of pre- and post-discussion assessment centre ratings. *Journal of Occupational Psychology, 58*, 189–192.

7

Research into Dimension-Based Assessment Centers

George C. Thornton III

Colorado State University

Deborah E. Rupp

Purdue University

The research literature on dimension-based assessment centers (ACs) is voluminous: at least 10 books, scores of book chapters, hundreds of published articles, countless doctoral dissertations and masters' theses, regular presentations at conferences and workshops around the world, and untold numbers of technical and unpublished reports. PsycINFO currently lists 522 works with assessment centers in the title, and surely many other publications deal with the method. More recent publications have emerged which we will weave into this review. To do justice to this huge body of research, we have chosen to focus our coverage on evidence of the validity of dimension-based ACs for three main purposes.

We begin with a description of how ACs have been used for prediction, diagnosis, and development. Then we clarify what we mean by evidence of validity. This sets up the next three sections where we review evidence supporting inferences that dimension-based ACs have validity for different purposes, along with suggestions for further research. We conclude with a discussion of the advantages of using dimensions as the currency of ACs consistent with the theme of this book. Throughout the chapter we discuss a number of theories, concepts, and frameworks in order to highlight the complex psychological processes embedded in dimension-based ACs. Additional details about theoretical perspectives on (Arthur, Chapter 5, this volume) and applications of (Jansen,

Chapter 6, this volume) dimension-based ACs are presented in companion chapters in this book.

Primary Uses of Dimension-Based Assessment Centers

For at least 55 years, dimension-based assessment centers have been and continue to be used worldwide, in both the public and private sectors (Delmestri & Walgenbach, 2009; Eurich, Krause, Cigularov, & Thornton, 2009; Lievens & Thornton, 2005). The dimension-based AC method encompasses a versatile set of techniques involving multiple trained assessors who observe and evaluate the overt behavior of individuals in multiple situational exercises with moderate to high psychological fidelity. Judgments about behavior are aggregated in one of several ways to provide assessments on dimensions determined to be important to jobs of interest. Sometimes, an overall assessment rating (OAR) representing a summary evaluation of dimension scores is obtained.

Some History

For over 50 years, dimension-based ACs have been used for a variety of purposes (Thornton & Rupp, 2006). Initially, the AC method was used by AT&T to study adult development, and then, after decades of longitudinal research with samples of men and women, practical applications of the AC method emerged (Bray, Campbell, & Grant, 1974; Howard & Bray, 1988). The method was used to identify individuals who had long-range potential to move into middle-management positions and then to aid in making promotions into first-level supervision and executive positions. Along the way, organizations realized that the rich assessment information collected in assessment centers provides potential insights into the strengths and developmental needs of individuals. This diagnostic information then began to be used to lay out development plans for individuals' subsequent training on and off the job. It also became apparent that participants sometimes were incidentally learning from the AC experience, gaining self-insight about the dimensions and improving their performance on them. Subsequently, the next generation of AC applications employed systematic procedures to maximize learning. These ACs have been labeled *developmental assessment centers* (DACs; International Task Force, 2009).

Aside from these applications focusing on the assessment and development of individuals, organizations have also used the dimension-based AC method to foster organizational outcomes. The process of developing an AC forces an organization to clarify the knowledge, skills, and abilities it is seeking in target-level positions and, consequently, to identify the human attributes that are embedded in organizational competency models. In addition, training middle- and higher level managers to be assessors led to development of their skills at behavioral observation, evaluation, and coaching. When managers from different parts of the organization work together on assessor teams, they gain cross-functional insights, and the movement of key staff members across units is facilitated. In short, development and implementation of an AC may also serve as an organizational development intervention. Rupp (2005) discusses how the dimension-based AC framework can be used as a structure for creating fully integrated HR systems, with the job-relevant competencies or dimensions informing selection, training, performance appraisal, and succession planning practices.

Prediction for Selection and Promotion Decisions

When ACs are used to aid in prediction during personnel selection and promotion, the main outcome of interest is the overall assessment rating (OAR). Continuing research is showing that the way in which the OAR is derived must be considered in order to understand its validity (Thornton & Rupp, 2006). In some ACs, assessors follow the behavior-reporting method, wherein they report observations made in various exercises and then come to consensus on overall dimension ratings and the final OAR. This was the method used in the original assessment programs of the Office of Strategic Services to select field agents in World War II (Fiske, Hanfmann, MacKinnon, Miller, & Murray, 1948), as well as in the AT&T managerial ACs that followed. In other programs, assessors follow the within-exercise method, wherein one or more assessors make ratings of dimensions after each exercise and those post-exercise dimension ratings (PEDRs) are combined statistically, first across exercises and then across dimensions to yield the OAR. Other integration processes involve both statistical combination and consensus discussion. For each of these approaches, dimensions provide the foundation for observing, integrating, and evaluating behavior. That is, dimension-relevant behaviors are noted by assessors as they observe assessees in exercises, these behavioral observations are categorized according to dimensions, and then these sets of dimension-relevant behaviors are used as evidence for making dimension ratings (within or across exercises).

Diagnosis of Dimension Proficiency

When dimension-based assessment centers are used to diagnose strengths and weaknesses and to lay out plans for development, the outcomes of interest are follow-up actions. While questions have raged about whether ACs have validity to measure specified performance dimensions, research continues to emerge that assessor ratings are measuring what they are intended to measure—namely dimensions such as "problem-solving," "organizing and planning," "drive," and "communication." These diagnostic programs have been referred to as *development centers* in the past. However, because development per se may be only an incidental result of this type of program, we prefer to restrict the term *developmental assessment center* to programs systematically designed to foster learning and development, as described next.

Development of Dimension Proficiency

Developmental assessment centers (DAC) have the express purpose of fostering learning both within and after the program. The structure of DACs is quite different from traditional ACs designed for prediction or diagnosis. Typically, participants go through a series of exercises, receive immediate feedback on behaviors relevant to dimensions, participate in a second set of parallel exercises, and receive further feedback. The outcomes of interest are change in participants' behavior, understanding, and attitudes.

Definition of Validity and Validation

Despite decades of discussion about validity and validation processes, as well as the publication of numerous authoritative documents on the topic, considerable variation exists in the use of these terms. Thus, we set forth our definitions, which match currently accepted authoritative documents which emphasize evidence related to the inferences made from test scores. (For recent statements about alternative definitions of validity, which emphasize the property of tests rather than test score interpretation, see Borsboom, Mellengergh, & van Heerden, 2004.)

We subscribe to the holistic and unified view of validity codified in the most widely accepted authority in testing, namely the *Standards for Educational and Psychological Testing* (AERA, APA, ACME, 1999). The *Standards* defines validity as the accumulated evidence about whether a measurement technique supports the inferences one wishes to draw from the results. Thus, validity is not an inherent property of the assessment method but rather a conclusion that is made in light of the various forms of evidence supporting the various inferences that are made based on the resultant scores. Thus we present several different bodies of research evidence to support alternative inferences from ratings from dimension-based ACs.

Traits Versus Methods

In order to interpret the evidence supporting the inference made from dimension-based AC ratings, it is important to make the distinction between *traits* and *methods* (Arthur & Villado, 2008). In the same way that a paper and pencil test with multiple-choice questions is a method that can be designed to measure different abilities, a self-report questionnaire with Likert-type response options for descriptive terms is a method that can measure different personality characteristics, and a situational judgment test is a method that can assess different behavioral intentions, the AC is a method that can measure different attributes. When an AC is used to make predictions about future job performance, the OAR is a measure of general ability in that domain. The analogy of a general mental ability test is apt here (Thornton & Gibbons, 2009). Intelligence tests provide an overall score, sometimes called *IQ* or *g*. Such tests measure a composite of several facets of intellectual ability such as verbal and quantitative reasoning, spatial visualization, perceptual speed, and knowledge of words. In like manner, the OAR from a dimension-based managerial AC may be thought of as a measure of g_{mgmt}—a general managerial ability. To make this overall assessment, observation of a wide variety of behavior in exercises is adequate. To extrapolate, g_{mgmt} from an AC with two assessors observing 10 behaviors relevant to five dimensions in four exercises is actually a 400-item test ($2 \times 10 \times 5 \times 4 = 400$). The omnibus content taps several classes of behaviors relevant to managerial effectiveness.

Because many selection and promotion ACs were set up to make these types of overall assessments, there was no expectation that the assessment would provide differential diagnosis of separate dimensions. Thus, the findings that we review later, showing a lack of clear convergent and discriminant validity in internal analyses of post-exercise dimension ratings, should not be surprising. ACs designed for this purpose never intended the assessors' judgments to meet that narrow standard of what others have called construct validity.

When the AC method is used for diagnosis or development, the unit of interest is the final across-exercise rating on each dimension. These dimension ratings are derived from observations of behavior in several exercises by multiple assessors. If two assessors observe 10 behaviors relevant to a dimension in four exercises, we have an 80-item measure. Reliability and content coverage are attained by taping dimension-relevant behavior in several situations. Thus, we must consider not only the relevance of the dimensions chosen for the target job but also the ability of the exercises to elicit dimension-relevant behaviors. Given the unique distinction between methods and traits in AC contexts, we move to a discussion of the evidence that the AC method measures these different units of analysis, namely OARs and final dimension ratings.

Validity for Selection: Evidence Related to the Overall Assessment Rating (OAR)

Assessment centers have been used extensively to help make employment decisions such as initial selection, promotion, certification, reductions in force, and job restructuring. The basic inference in such applications is that the overall assessment rating (OAR) is predictive of some future indicator of performance, such as training success, job performance, promotion in rank, salary, attendance, and retention/turnover. The OAR is conceived to be a measure of general ability to perform effectively in one or more possibly unknown and often ill-defined future assignments.

Representative Content

Considerable evidence exists that the content of dimension-based ACs is representative of the domain of jobs for which they are applied. The content, along with the level of difficulty and context, is selected to elicit behavior relevant to performance dimensions in a variety of simulations including individual and group exercises (Thornton & Mueller-Hanson, 2004). Job analysis and competency modeling are routinely used to identify the dimensions to be assessed, the type of exercises to use, and the content of problems built into the AC (Krause & Thornton, 2009; Thornton & Krause, 2009). Typically, the exercises are simulations of aspects of target jobs, but they are not exact replicas of any one position and not actual work samples. Thus, they possess relatively high psychological fidelity. Instructions, role-player prompts, and follow-up questions by assessors are designed to elicit behavior relevant to dimensions. The simulations evoke assessee behaviors that provide assessors the opportunity to observe, classify, and evaluate dimension-related behavior.

Correlation of the OAR with Other Methods

A meta-analysis by Collins et al. (2003) showed that the OAR was correlated with a complex variety of other measures known to be related to managerial and leadership effectiveness. Uncorrected and corrected correlations of the OAR with five variables were reported: cognitive ability (.43/.67), extraversion (.36/.50), emotional stability (.26/.35), openness (.18/.25), and agreeableness (.12/.17). Melchers and Annen (2010) did not detect a relationship between the OAR and general mental ability, but the OAR contributed uniquely to predictions of job performance.

Criterion-Related Validity Evidence

The clearest set of evidence to support dimension-based ACs used for prediction comes from scores of studies showing the correlation of OARs with a variety of subsequent criteria, including success in training, job performance, career progression, salary, and so forth (Thornton

& Rupp, 2006). Studies have been carried out with numerous jobs (e.g., factory workers, supervisors, managers, sales staff), and meta-analytical validity estimates at the construct level range from .27 to .64 (Thornton & Gibbons, 2009). Similarly, in a recent study Melchers and Annen (2010) found the OAR correlated with performance in a military officer training academy (.40) and later military performance (.28).

Incremental Prediction Over Other Methods

The OARs from dimension-based ACs have shown incremental validity over supervisory ratings (Chan, 1996), personality tests (Goffin, Rothstein, & Johnston, 1996; Hardison, 2005), biodata (O'Connell, Hattrup, Doverspike, & Cober, 2002), the behavioral description interview (Lievens, Harris, Van Keer, & Bisqueret, 2003), and cognitive ability tests (Dayan, Kasten, & Fox, 2002; Krause, Kersting, Heggestad, & Thornton, 2006; Melchers & Annen, 2010). Whereas some have claimed that the incremental validity of ACs over general ability tests is negligible (e.g., 2% or less; Hardison, 2005; Schmidt & Hunter, 1998), Melchers and Annen (2010) reported larger estimates (i.e., 7–15%). These authors also found that the OAR predicted training and military performance better than ratings on any of the individual six exercises. These sorts of findings provide criterion-related validity evidence of the dimension-based ACs as a method, over and above other methods measuring general and specific abilities and personality traits.

Avoiding Unintended Negative Consequences

One of the potential unintended negative consequences of personnel selection techniques is the occurrence of adverse impact—that is, lower average scores for legally protected groups, which may result in inordinately lower selection rates. Until recently, the widely expressed consensus among researchers was that the AC method yielded much lower subgroup differences in comparison with written cognitive ability tests (Thornton & Rupp, 2006). Whereas Blacks tend to score approximately one standard deviation below Whites on many cognitive ability tests, the differences have been found to be much smaller for AC ratings. In a meta-analysis of 27 AC studies, Dean, Roth, and Bobko (2008) found a .52 standard deviation difference between Whites and Blacks and a .28

standard deviation difference between Whites and Hispanics on OARs (see also Povah and Povah, Chapter 1, this volume).

Looking beyond race, early studies focused on gender showed no differences in AC ratings for men and women (Thornton, 1992; Thornton & Byham, 1982; Thornton & Rupp, 2006). By contrast, Anderson, Lievens, van Dam, and Born (2006) found that females scored higher in a leadership role assessment center. Melchers and Annen (2010) found no differences in assessment center scores for candidates from German-, French-, and Italian-speaking regions of Switzerland contending for the military academy. Furthermore, there was no differential validity in prediction of training performance or later military performance.

Research demonstrating fairness of OARs is one important bit of evidence in the validity argument. This is especially true when ACs are used for high-stakes decisions.

Research Needs: Controversies and Emergent Questions

Research is needed to address controversial areas that have shown mixed findings in past research on dimension-based ACs and topics that have not been empirically examined (Thornton & Gibbons, 2009). One of the biggest needs comprised the theme of this book: to compare the relative advantages and disadvantages of dimensions and exercises as the basic structure for deriving OARs in ACs. By carefully articulating the issues inherent to this comparison, we are certain that a number of new important research questions will emerge.

Other research questions include: Is transparency an asset or a liability in selection? To what extent are ACs measures of maximal and/or typical performance? What are the advantages and disadvantages of the integration method used? What are the effects of coaching assessees to improve performance, and on what dimensions or exercises does coaching have the most effect? What are the dangers of reusing various types of exercises (Rupp & Searle, 2011), and how can we build parallel exercises (Brummel, Rupp, & Spain, 2009)? How important is standardization of administration of each type of AC? To what extent are AC dimensions and exercises subject to impression management and faking? What are the effects of retesting (Rupp & Searle, 2011)?

Despite the need for more research, over 50 years of accumulated evidence have shown that OARs derived from dimension-based ACs predict a variety of job-related performance criteria. These longitudinal studies have been conducted in private and public organizations in several countries. There is substantial evidence that, for the purposes of selection and promotion, dimension-based ACs are working the way they are supposed to work.

Validity for Diagnosis: Evidence Regarding Across-Exercise Ratings of Dimensions

Because the purpose, design, and nature of assessment centers used for selection, diagnosis, and development are quite different, the nature of validity evidence needed to demonstrate their effectiveness differs. Diagnostic and developmental assessment centers both use dimension scores (as opposed to the OAR) as the unit of analysis. For a diagnostic AC, the criterion of interest is accuracy in dimension ratings. For a developmental AC, both accuracy of dimension ratings and the ability of the program to impact learning and improvement must be considered. In the sections that follow, we will discuss both of these types of validity evidence.

Relationship Between Across-Exercise Dimension Ratings and Other Methods

Research on dimension-based ACs has compared across-exercise dimension scores obtained via the AC method with measures of similar and dissimilar constructs measured via alternative methods. One of the first studies of this kind was conducted by Shore, Thornton, and Shore (1990), who explored the external convergent and discriminant validity of final AC dimension scores via data from 500 petroleum company employees who participated in an AC and completed a battery of cognitive ability and personality assessments. These researchers categorized dimensions as either "interpersonal style" (e.g., personal acceptability, understanding of people) or "performance style" (e.g., recognizing priorities, originality) and predicted that interpersonal dimensions would have relatively stronger relationships with personality facets yet relatively weaker relationships with cognitive ability, whereas performance dimensions would have relatively stronger relationships with cognitive ability yet relatively weaker relationships with personality facets. The data supported this a priori nomological network.

The evidence from Shore et al. (1990) is buttressed by two recent meta-analyses (Dilchert & Ones, 2009; Meriac, Hoffman, Woehr, & Fleisher, 2008). Using a set of six core dimensions derived by Arthur, Day, McNelly, and Edens (2003), these studies reported operational and corrected meta-analytic correlations among dimensions, cognitive ability, and Big Five personality traits. At the construct level, these results show that the dimensions are moderately correlated with either cognitive ability or personality, which is to be expected given the nature of dimensions (see Jones & Born, 2008). For dimensions that were more like cognitive ability, correlations with cognitive ability were shown to be larger than correlations with personality. For dimensions that were more like personality, correlations with personality were shown to be larger than correlations with cognitive ability. For example, Dilchert and Ones (2009) found the dimension "problem solving" to relate to cognitive ability ($r = .32$), but minimally with Big Five personality traits. The opposite trend was observed for dimensions such as "drive," "influencing others," and "consideration of others," which were unrelated to cognitive ability but more strongly related to the personality traits.

Relationships With Job Performance Criteria

Recent analyses, summarized in Table 7.1, provide evidence of the relationship between across-exercise dimension ratings and job-related

Table 7.1 Criterion-Related Validity of AC Dimensions

	Arthur et al, 2003 Meta-analysis[a]	Meriac et al, 2008 Meta-analysis[a]	Connelly et al, 2008 N = 3100	Lievens et al., 2009
Communication	.26/.33	.25/.27	.10	X
Consideration/ Awareness of Others	.20/25	.22/.24	.16	.21
Drive	.24/.31	.15/.16	.22	X
Influencing Others	.30/.38	.29/.31	.24	.08
Planning and Organizing	.29/.37	.33/.35	X	.15
Problem Solving	.30/.39	.31/.32	.25	.18
Stress Tolerance	X	.16/.18	X	X

[a]Sample-weighted correlation/Corrected value
X = not assessed in this study

criterion measures such as supervisory ratings of job performance, promotion, and salary. Arthur, Day, et al. (2003) used meta-analysis to collapse the AC dimension labels from 34 articles into six categories. Meriac et al. (2008) employed this dimension framework to meta-analyze data from 48 samples. As shown in Table 7.1, corrected and uncorrected sample-weighted average correlations were similar in nature, and the results of these two studies appear to be consistent. Each of the dimensions (with the exception of "stress tolerance") shows at least a moderately high correlation with job performance and explain variance beyond each other. In two studies, variance in predicting salary due to dimensions remained after accounting for variance due to exercises. Connelly, Ones, Ramesh, and Goff (2008) derived criterion-related validity estimates from 3,100 managers. The correlations for "drive," "influencing others," and "problem solving" are comparable to the meta-analyses. Lievens, Dilchert, and Ones (2009) made similar estimates from a sample of 520 employees. The correlations were significant, but some were lower than those in the other studies cited here.

Incremental Prediction Over Other Methods

Three analyses show evidence of the incremental predictive validity of across-exercise dimension ratings. Dilchert and Ones (2009) found that six AC dimensions added incremental validity over measures of cognitive ability and personality. The "problem solving" and "communication" dimensions added the highest incremental value over personality, whereas "influencing others" added the highest value over cognitive ability. Meriac et al. (2008) regressed job performance onto seven AC dimensions after entering general mental ability and personality measures. Doing so increased the percent of variance accounted for in-job performance from 20% to 30% ($\Delta R^2 = .10$). Forward selection of the individual dimensions into the regression equation showed that the following ordered six dimensions added significant accuracy: "organizing and planning," "problem solving," "drive," "influencing others," "consideration," and "stress tolerance." Lievens, Tett, and Schleicher (2009) found that four exercise factors explained more variance in the criterion (R = .49) than four dimension factors (R = .22) but that the dimension factors added unique explanatory power.

Summary

In short, evidence from dimension-based ACs supports both the inferences commonly made with across-exercise dimension ratings and the conclusion that ACs are working the way they are intended. As noted by Meriac et al. (2008), the available evidence suggests that AC dimensions are moderately correlated with, albeit quite distinct from, cognitive ability and personality, and they account for a significant proportion of the variance in job performance, over and above cognitive ability and personality.

Evidence of the Relationships Among Post-Exercise Dimension Ratings

In many (but not all) ACs, assessors make ratings of dimensions after observing behavior in each exercise. One or more assessors may make these *post-exercise dimension ratings* (PEDRs). In this section we trace the decades-long history of internal analyses of ratings within an AC. We will summarize results of some of these internal analyses which show that PEDRs measure the intended constructs (i.e., behavioral dimensions). We will also point out why many of the analyses of PEDRs do not reflect the theory and rationale of the AC method.

Post-Exercise Dimension Ratings

As the collection of PEDRs became popularized, it became possible for psychometricians to analyze the resulting matrix of exercise-by-dimension ratings according to Campbell and Fiske's (1959) *multi-trait-multi-method* (MTMM) model of construct validity. This provided a convenient way to consider the intercorrelations of dimensions within exercises (considered by some researchers to provide information regarding discriminant validity), as well as the correlations of single dimensions across exercises (considered by some researchers to provide information regarding convergent validity).

By treating dimensions as traits and exercises as methods, researchers were able to apply MTMM matrix techniques to study assessment center data in a way not possible for most other forms of assessment (Jones & Born, 2008). This led to a large number of correlational, factor-analytic, and meta-analytic studies, which all seemed to provide evidence that the original intention of assessment centers—to assess dimensions—may not have been realized (see Lance, 2008a). This research revealed that, when considering PEDRs as the unit of analysis, dimensions rated within an exercise were highly correlated (evidence against discriminant validity), and the correlation of a single dimension across exercises, although moderate, was not as strongly related as would be expected (evidence against convergent validity). Such findings have been confirmed meta-analytically, and subsequent factor-analytic studies have shown that modeling exercise factors fit MTMM matrix data better than does modeling dimensions.

These conclusions led a number of researchers to seriously question what dimension-based ACs were actually measuring and even to go as far as to call for a re-engineering of the method. Although these findings gave AC researchers much to debate over the decades, a number of counter-arguments have emerged from this dialogue (see Volume 1, Issue 1 of *Industrial and Organizational Psychology: Perspective in Science and Practice*). One such argument is that PEDRs should never have been and should never be the unit of analysis used to draw inferences about the accuracy of dimension assessments (Jones & Born, 2008; Rupp, Thornton, & Gibbons, 2008). Although there may be intuitive appeal in treating post-exercise dimension ratings as "traits" and AC exercises as "methods" in an MTMM framework, it is important to point out that, in most actual dimension-based AC contexts, a post-exercise dimension rating by one assessor after one exercise is not used as a "score" for prediction, diagnosis, or developmental purposes.

A PEDR by one assessor after one exercise would not be expected to be reliable. Such a rating defies the spirit of the assessment center method as a rigorous behavioral assessment technique that aggregates information across assessors and situations. Putting weight on such PEDRs is akin to putting weight on a single-item measure; we would never expect such a metric to completely represent the content domain of interest. For this reason, Thornton and Rupp (2006) argue that construct-validity evidence for dimensions is more appropriately deduced from analyses of across-exercise (final) dimension ratings. MTMM approaches may be appropriate, but only if the assessment center is considered the "method" in comparison with other methods, and final across-exercise dimension scores are considered the "traits" (such as the research reviewed in the previous section). Other debates about construct validity of dimension-based ACs require more consideration of the complexities of the AC context, which we address next.

Partitioning Multiple Sources of Variance

Bowler and Woehr (2009) argued that factor analyzing PEDRs considers only the variance associated with dimensions and exercises. As a result, variance attributable to additional sources, such as assessees, assessors, and the interactions between all of these sources, is ignored. For example, an assessee by dimension interaction would indicate the extent to which individuals show different patterns of proficiency across dimensions, whereas a dimension by exercises interaction would indicate the extent to which some dimensions are better assessed in some exercises than others. To examine their point, these authors analyzed post-exercise dimension ratings of three assessment center programs and compared results from analyses using the traditional CFA-based approach to a generalizability theory-based variance-partitioning approach where the additional sources of variance and interaction effects mentioned above could be estimated. As expected, the CFA-based analyses replicated past findings. That is, results showed evidence for exercise effects, with dimension factors playing only a minor role. However, with the variance partitioning approach, both dimensions and exercises contributed substantially to the variance in post-exercise dimension ratings. These results showed meaningful portions of variance due to persons, dimensions, the person-by-dimension interaction, and the dimension-by-exercise interaction. This means that assessees can be reliably differentiated with respect to their overall performance, their performance on specific dimensions, and specific profiles of dimension performance. It also means that dimension performance varies by exercises. Combined, these effects accounted for more variance in ratings than the variance accounted for by exercises and assessors combined, showing more evidence for the convergent and discriminant validity of post-exercise dimension ratings than concluded by researchers using CFA approaches.

More importantly, Kuncel and Sackett (in press) found that when post-exercise dimension ratings are aggregated across exercises to form an overall dimension rating, following the typical practice, dimension variance typically dominates over exercise variance. They conclude that the alleged problem of construct validity of assessment centers (based on studies of PEDRs) never existed.

Dimensions Are Not Completely Trait-Like and Are Non-Independent

Correlations of PEDRs may not be large or consistent because dimensions are not all completely trait-like and are not independent. Jones and Born (2008) point out that Campbell and Fiske (1959) spoke to the importance of establishing an a priori theory of how the traits in the matrix should and should not be related to one another. AC dimensions may include elements of knowledge/skills as well as abilities, may vary in the extent to which they are permanent or transitory, may be broad or narrow, and may be highly related to one another or highly unrelated. Social psychologists might refer to dimensions as "fuzzy sets" of categories of behavior (Brown, 1986). This speaks to the true complexity of both dimensions and the AC method and illustrates the limited value of seemingly simplistic MTMM approaches. Lance (2008b), in his response to the commentaries on his focal article (2008a), stated, "the alleged construct validity problem is not a problem with the way ACs work but with the MTMM urban legend's association of dimensions with traits and exercises with methods in an MTMM framework" (p. 141).

Across Exercises Dimension Inconsistency May Reflect Stable Individual Differences

Given many of the issues reviewed above, recent research has also recommended that we reconsider sources of variance that had been in the past considered "error" in AC validity studies. Two particular sources of variance include dimension inconsistency and dimension differentiation (Gibbons, 2008; Gibbons & Rupp, 2009). The former refers to inconsistency in observed proficiency on a dimension across exercises, and the latter refers to the extent to which individuals show differentiated proficiency across dimensions. Similar to arguments made in the personality literature (Bem & Allen, 1974; Fleeson, 2001), inconsistency and differentiation may actually represent stable individual differences, and the extent to which individuals display consistency and differentiation may be predictive of important work behaviors above and beyond their mean level of proficiency on the dimensions.

Gibbons, Rupp, and Schleicher (2006) conducted four studies to explore this issue. Their first study used NCAA basketball statistics to provide evidence for within-person stability in performance consistency. They found that basketball players reliably differed in the consistency of their performance on a number of criteria across games and that this consistency predicted variance in both individual and team performance over and above their mean performance on these criteria. Study 2 developed an index of consistency and differentiation for the purpose of analyzing assessment center data and tested it using Monte Carlo-like data simulation methods. In a third study, these indices were computed using data from two operational assessment centers. Results showed that assessees reliably differed in consistency and, to a lesser extent, differentiation across dimensions. In a final study, the data reported in Schleicher, Day, Mayes, and Riggio (2002) were reanalyzed in order to compute individual differences in consistency and differentiation, as well as their impact on performance. Results indicated that individual consistency incrementally predicted supervisor ratings of job performance, over and above an individual's mean-level dimension performance. Analyses of MTMM matrices made up of PEDRs do not account for these important aspects of behavior across exercises.

The Purpose of the AC Program May Also Be Relevant

Relatively little research has been conducted to evaluate the effect of the purpose of the AC on relationships among PEDRs. We would expect that diagnostic and developmental ACs would yield better evidence of convergent and discriminant relationships among PEDRs than selection and promotional ACs, where emphasis is on the final overall assessment rating (OAR). Mixed support for this expected pattern exists. In a meta-analysis, Woehr and Arthur (2003) found no difference in the level of convergent validity between the ACs for these different purposes, but, contrary to expectations, selection/promotion programs showed better discriminant validity than training/development programs.

Guenole and colleagues (Guenole, Chernyshenko, Stark, & Cockerill, 2004; Guenole, Chernyshenko, Stark, Cockerill, & Drasgow 2011) noted that the majority of early MTMM matrix studies questioning construct validity were conducted before 1998 using data from selection/promotion centers which were designed to produce an OAR, not diagnostic dimension scores. By contrast, their data on 1,205 executives in an AC designed specifically for diagnostic purposes and involving certified assessors with extensive assessor training showed substantially stronger dimension factors as opposed to exercise factors. The results of these studies suggest that further research is needed to examine the purpose of the AC as an explanatory variable in affecting the relationships among PEDRs.

Summary and Future Research: The Accuracy and Relevance of Dimension Ratings

The evidence reviewed in this section shows that dimensions are highly variable classes of competencies. Although they are job-related and behaviorally defined, any set of dimensions used by a particular AC program may contain some dimensions that are more trait-like, as well as some that are closer to abilities and hence more cognitively loaded. They also may differ in breadth, with some dimensions potentially representing sub-components of other dimensions. Further, research has shown that we can expect both within- and between-person variance on dimension proficiencies, and different types of exercises—as well as different exercise stimuli—may facilitate or hinder the manifestation of various dimensions.

Individuals, dimensions, and exercises interact in complex ways. Despite these complexities, evidence continues to amass that assessors' ratings of dimensions are measuring important constructs (i.e., they predict performance and show incremental validity over cognitive ability and personality) and that the pattern of relationships between dimensions—and between dimensions and other, external constructs—supports that AC developers are successfully measuring what they have set out to measure.

Although this research shows continued promise for dimension-based assessment centers, more research is certainly needed. Theories should set forth the *nature* of dimensions (e.g., knowledge/skill vs. ability), how they are expected to relate to one another, and the extent to which each should be expected to be more or less permanent or transitory. Predictions could be made regarding the expected within-person consistency of each dimension and whether each would be more or less appropriate for a prediction, diagnostic, or developmental context. Finally, each dimension could be discussed in terms of its potential for trait activation, and each exercise must be scrutinized to determine whether it provides stimuli to activate the trait (Lievens et al., 2009).

Evidence Supporting Inferences Made Using Dimension-Based DACS

Developmental assessment centers (DACs) are focused not only on obtaining an accurate assessment of job-relevant behavioral dimensions but also on providing experiential learning opportunities coupled with intermittent feedback, with the goal of increasing proficiency on the dimensions. These additional goals lead to a number of additional considerations that must be made when developing and validating DACs.

Choosing the Appropriate Dimensions

First, the dimensions chosen for DAC programs must be appropriate. Rupp, Snyder, Gibbons, and Thornton (2006) point to three criteria for DAC dimensions. First, they should represent performance dimensions that are relevant for the job, jobs, or organizational context. Second, because DACs are geared toward *improvement* on dimension proficiency, it is also necessary that the dimensions are those on which change would be expected. Thus DACs are more apt to be successful if the dimensions represent knowledge and skills rather than crystallized traits or abilities that would not be expected to change over the course of a DAC program. Third, the dimensions should be those for which DACs provide a viable training method. If there are other training formats better suited to develop knowledge and skill for some dimensions, then these formats should be used instead (see Arthur, Bennett, Edens, & Bell, 2003). Finally, to truly maximize the chances that individuals will learn and improve on the dimensions over the course of the DAC program, it is also necessary that the candidates are able to develop self-efficacy for improving themselves on each dimension.

Fostering Improvement in Proficiency in Dimensions

Evidence supports the effectiveness of DAC programs to foster learning and improvement on dimension proficiency, with differential change rates for different dimensions. For example, Engelbrecht and Fischer (1995) compared supervisor performance ratings of two groups of managers—one group who had participated in a DAC and an equivalent group who had not. Three months following the DAC program, they detected improvement in the dimensions "action orientation," "probing," and “development.” Further, the improvement detected was significantly greater than it was for the control group. They did not detect improvement for the dimensions “synthesis” or “judgment,” which they described as more cognitive in nature and therefore more resistant to change.

Rupp et al. (2006) reported results from an operational DAC where feedback was given halfway through the program and assessees participated in a second round of exercises with the goal of improving their performance on the dimensions. The program was embedded within a broader multisource feedback program, allowing for multisource ratings to be collected before and after DAC participation. The program also contained a second, parallel DAC, which participants went through 1 year following their first experience. This allowed for the detection of dimension proficiency improvement (a) across the span of a DAC (e.g., from morning to afternoon), (b) between the two DACs spaced 1 year apart, and (c) throughout the year by comparing multisource ratings collected on participants who did and did not participate in the program.

Analyses of these data showed improvement on all the dimensions: “information seeking,” “planning and organizing,” “problem solving,” “oral communication,” “leadership,” “conflict management,” and “cultural adaptability.” Different patterns of results were shown for different dimensions. Depending on the dimension, different sources (e.g., self, assessor, supervisor) were more or less able to detect improvement, and dimensions differed in terms of the time needed for improvement to be detected (e.g., one day, a few months, a year).

Jones and Whitmore (1995a,b) used career advancement as a criterion to assess the validity of a DAC program. Their initial results showed no difference in career advancement for groups that did and did not participate in the DAC. However, the number of dimension-based developmental recommendations made after the DAC that were actually followed by participants predicted career advancement. Further, recommendations that were followed regarding “career motivation” and “working with others” showed significant career impact. This shows not only the differential impact DACs have on the proficiency improvement on various dimensions but also the need to consider participant motivation along with DACs’ potential training effectiveness.

Effects on Motivation, Engagement, and Self-Other Agreement

Participants’ motivation for improving on various dimensions is an extremely important factor to consider when developing and validating

DACs. Although it would be the hope of DAC administrators that participants would spend maximal effort following feedback and improving themselves on those dimensions on which they were found to be the weakest, research has detected that negative feedback can be especially de-motivating in assessment center contexts (e.g., see Abraham, Morrison, & Burnett, 2006; van Emmerik, Bakker, & Euwema, 2008). In addition, the extent to which participants agree with assessor ratings also impacts their responsiveness to feedback and engagement in subsequent development. For example, Woo, Sims, Rupp, and Gibbons (2008) tracked middle managers following a DAC program. Consistent with the studies cited above, they found that behavioral engagement was higher for those who received more favorable feedback. In addition they found less subsequent engagement for over-raters (those who rated themselves higher on dimensions than did the assessors). Fletcher (2011) summarizes a number of studies exploring the impact of DACs on various indicators of candidate motivation, well-being, and self-awareness.

Alpha, Beta, and Gamma Change on Dimensions

Dimension-based DACs have been shown to induce in candidates a more complete understanding of the dimensions important for effective performance. Change in understanding of performance constructs may be an integral step in developing a skill and thus is an important training outcome. Brodersen and Thornton (2011) studied alpha, beta, and gamma change (Golembiewski, Billingsley, & Yeager, 1976) in middle managers' understanding of managerial competencies as a result of being assessed on and receiving feedback about their performance on dimensions in a DAC. Participants showed differential amounts of change on all six dimensions comprising the DAC. More than half of the managers showed some form of change. Gamma change (i.e., re-conceptualization of the dimension, showing a fundamental change in the meaning of the dimension) was experienced most frequently by the managers: for example, 33% on "information seeking," 31% on "problem solving," and 25% on "planning and organizing." Beta change (i.e., understanding the possible range of dimension performance such that what the person initially saw as average may later be seen as quite mediocre) was experienced by 43% on "leadership." This study suggests that a dimension-based AC provides assessors and participants alike a meaningful structure to characterize performance and that the AC itself can lead to a deeper understanding of dimensions as performance constructs.

Integrating DAC Validation and Training Evaluation

Other ways in which DACs have been evaluated are according to the training evaluation criteria specified in the training and development literature (e.g., Kirkpatrick, 1998; Kraiger, Ford, & Salas, 1993). For example, Rupp et al. (2006) applied Kirkpatrick's four levels of effectiveness criteria (reaction criteria, learning criteria, behavioral criteria, and results criteria) to present validity evidence of an operational DAC program. They showed that (a) participant reactions to the DAC program were positive, (b) participants showed evidence of learning on some dimensions within the time frame of the DAC, and (c) participants showed behavioral change on the dimensions over time as evidenced by multisource ratings following the DAC. Although the study design precluded the collection of results criteria, Rupp et al. discuss how future programs might develop innovative ways to collect clean measures of unit-level performance with which to assess the broader impact of DAC programs on organizational-level outcomes. Other concepts of training effectiveness (see Kraiger et al., 1993; Ford, Kraiger, & Merritt, 2010) point to additional criterion measures that could be used to evaluate/validate DAC programs. In sum, this research articulates the value of assessing not only behavioral outcomes but also cognitive, skill, and affective outcomes.

A final area where DACs and the training literature have intersected involves third-generation instruction. As explained by Kraiger (2008), third-generation instruction puts greater emphasis on the learner. The idea is for training experiences to be highly experiential and involve a process of social negotiation that is often initiated by the learner. DACs are well suited to this model in that, when used purely for development, DACs can be structured so that the participants are responsible for extracting the dimensions from the challenges they are presented in the exercises, thus facilitating the social construction of knowledge. We see evidence for this from the gamma change research summarized above (Brodersen & Thornton, 2011). Further, DACs allow for a great deal of self-assessment on the dimensions, and feedback sessions are very interactive. These sorts of third-generation instructional opportunities can be further enabled in DAC programs through the use of technology—allowing participants to observe themselves via video-recorded exercises in order to develop a deeper understanding of the dimensions and to receive a richer learning experience for both gaining self-awareness and improving themselves on the dimensions (Reynolds & Rupp, 2010; Rupp, Gibbons, & Snyder, 2008).

Summary and Future Research

Indeed, considering dimensions within a DAC context presents a brave new world within which to study a variety of psychological phenomena. The current body of research is limited in size and scope, and thus research is needed that systematically evaluates the most appropriate dimensions for DAC contexts. We have reason to believe, for example, that not all six core dimensions identified by Arthur, Bennett, et al. (2003) would be appropriate for a DAC. All dimensions have not been methodically tested to determine the extent to which they are developable, nor assessed in terms of which are best assessed/developed in DACs as opposed to alternative training contexts. Rich research evidence supporting DACs as a tool for developing proficiency on dimensions will require longitudinal data and studies that incorporate a wide range of effectiveness criteria (acceptance, attitudes, learning, behavior, results) at varying points in time and at varying levels of analysis. The use of technology to facilitate learning on DAC dimensions should also be systematically studied, including the comparison of the effectiveness of high- versus low-tech formats.

Dimensions as the Currency of ACs

The vast majority of ACs for which we have empirical research have been built with dimensions as the intended basic structure. Thus, any conclusions about the usefulness and utility of ACs rest on the foundation of research on dimension-based ACs. Research that has been undertaken on assessors' ratings, even research that has questioned the "construct validity" of assessors' ratings, has always used data gathered from dimension-based ACs. Until recently, no research has been based on ACs developed with any other structure. This is not to say that ACs built upon the foundation of any variables other than dimensions, such as tasks, roles, exercises, and so forth, would not have validity or usefulness. But that foundation is only now being built. Furthermore, to our knowledge, no comparative studies have examined the relative advantages of an AC built from scratch using dimensions against an AC built from scratch using some other structure.

Advantages of Dimensions as the Structure of ACs

There are a number of advantages to using dimensions to structure ACs. Dimensions appear to be an integral part of the natural language of discourse about performance effectiveness in work organizations. Dimensions are used in the typical language of managers, human-resource specialists, psychologists, and even people in general when describing effective performance in a variety of tasks, jobs, organizations, settings, and cultures. A natural language is the everyday language used in spoken and written communication by groups of people with common experiences and interests (Clarke, 2003; ter Muerlen, 2001). An example of the universality of dimensions in a variety of natural languages in several countries comes from the groundbreaking studies of McCrae and Costa (1997) in their derivation of the Big Five personality traits. Social psychologists who study natural categories in language tell us these categories are not mutually exclusive but rather are ill-defined "fuzzy sets" (Brown, 1986). This may explain the correlations among ratings of different AC dimensions. Dimensions also provide a parsimonious set of variables for organizing the observation of behavior in performance-based assessments, as compared to task lists. The longest lists of dimensions, numbering about 12 to 15, appear in the earliest ACs (see Thornton & Byham, 1982). Very soon thereafter, most ACs assessed no more than 8 to 10 dimensions. Recent research suggests that these can be encapsulated even further into four to five clusters of similar dimensions. By contrast, lists of tasks that might be assessed in alternatively structured ACs appear to be quite extensive. Task-based job analysis methods typically involve scores or even hundreds of tasks for any one job, and the lists of tasks vary from one job to another. Thus, it would appear to be a challenge to identify a relatively small number of tasks applicable to several jobs.

Dimension-based ACs provide a framework for assessing the potential of candidates to fill one of a number of similar positions in the future (e.g., middle management or leadership in an organization). Any one position may involve myriad tasks, and it would appear to be extremely complex to design ACs to assess behavior relative to the tasks in a variety of unknown, potential future positions.

Furthermore, in light of the ever-changing nature of work, especially in the global context, the tasks that managers may be asked to handle in the future are often unknown or only vaguely understood. When identifying individuals with long-range potential for advancement into upper management and executive positions, decision makers often do not know the exact challenges in the future state of the organization. Thus, dimensions that cut across tasks and functional areas provide a valuable level of generality.

Dimensions also provide a common frame of reference for numerous human-resource management functions. We have already shown how the assessments from dimension-based ACs provide diagnostic information that forms the basis for launching training activities. Likewise, behavioral observations organized by dimensions provide rich feedback to participants in developmental ACs. That feedback can then be generalized to performance in a wide variety of job activities, not tied to any specific tasks depicted in specific exercises.

Overall Summary and Conclusions

Three considerable and separate bodies of evidence support the validity of dimension-based assessment centers. Inferences from the scores in dimension-based assessment centers about prediction, assessment of dimensions, and impact on development appear justified on the basis of multiple strands of evidence for each of the three main purposes of ACs. Post-exercise dimension ratings show construct validity. Overall assessment ratings predict long-range job-related criteria and add predictive accuracy over other methods. Across-exercise ("final") dimension ratings (a) are related to similar constructs measured by other methods, (b) predict job-related criteria, and (c) add incremental explanatory power over other methods measuring related constructs. Assessment centers designed to develop dimensions (DACs) promote changes in behavior, attitudes, motivation, and job performance. Dimension-based assessment centers are working the way they are intended to work.

References

Abraham, J. D., Morrison, J. D., Jr., & Burnett, D. D. (2006). Feedback seeking among developmental assessment center participants. *Journal of Business and Psychology, 20*, 383–394.

American Educational Research Association, American Psychological Association, & American Council on Measurement in Education. (1999). *Standards for educational and psychological tests.* Washington, DC: American Psychological Association.

Anderson, N., Lievens, F., van Dam, K., & Born, M. (2006). A construct investigation of gender differences in a leadership role assessment center. *Journal of Applied Psychology, 91*, 555–566.

Arthur, W., Jr., Bennett, W., Jr., Edens, P. S., & Bell, S. T. (2003). Effectiveness of training in organizations: A meta-analysis of design and evaluation features. *Journal of Applied Psychology, 88*, 234–245.

Arthur, W., Jr., Day, E. A., McNelly, T. L., & Edens, P. S. (2003). A meta-analysis of the criterion-related validity of assessment center dimensions. *Personnel Psychology, 56*, 125–154.

Arthur, W., Jr., & Villado, A. J. (2008). The importance of distinguishing between constructs and methods when comparing predictors in personnel selection research and practice. *Journal of Applied Psychology, 93*, 435–442.

Bem, D. J., & Allen, A. (1974). On predicting some of the people some of the time: The search for cross-situational consistencies in behavior. *Psychological Review, 81*, 506–520.

Borsboom, D., Mellenbergh, G. J., & van Heerden, J. (2004). The concept of validity. *Psychological Review, 111*, 1061–1071.

Bowler, M. C., & Woehr, D. J. (2009). Assessment center construct-related validity: Stepping beyond the MTMM matrix. *Journal of Vocational Behavior, 75*, 173–182.

Bray, D. W., Campbell, R. J., & Grant, D. L. (1974). *Formative years in business: A long-term AT&T study of managerial lives.* New York: Wiley.

Brodersen, D. A., & Thornton, G. C. III. (2011). An investigation of alpha, beta, and gamma change in developmental assessment center participants. *Performance Improvement Quarterly, 25*(2), 25–48, .

Brown, R. (1986). *Social psychology* (2nd ed.). New York: The Free Press.

Brummel, B., Rupp, D. E., & Spain, S. (2009). Constructing parallel simulation exercises for assessment centers and other forms of behavioral assessment. *Personnel Psychology, 62*, 135–170.

Campbell, D. T., & Fiske, D. W. (1959). Convergent and discriminant validation by the multitrait-multimethod matrix. *Psychological Bulletin, 56*, 81–105.

Chan, D. (1996). Criterion and construct validation of an assessment centre. *Journal of Occupational and Organizational Psychology, 69*, 167–181.

Clarke, D. S. (2003). *Sign levels: Language and its evolutionary antecedents.* Boston, MA: Kluwer.

Collins, J. M., Schmidt, F. L., Sanchez-Ku, M., Thomas, L., McDaniel, M. A., & Lee, H. (2003). Can basic individual differences shed light on the construct meaning of assessment center evaluations? *International Journal of Selection and Assessment, 11*, 17–29.

Connelly, B. S., Ones, D. S., Ramesh, J., & Goff, M. (2008). A pragmatic view of assessment center exercises and dimensions. *Industrial and Organizational Psychology, 1*, 121–124.

Dayan, K., Kasten, R., & Fox, S. (2002). Entry-level police candidate assessment center: Efficient tool or a hammer to kill a fly? *Personnel Psychology, 55*, 827–849.

Dean, M. A., Roth, P. L., & Bobko, P. (2008). Ethnic and gender subgroup differences in assessment center ratings: A meta-analysis. *Journal of Applied Psychology, 93*, 685–691.

Delmestri, G., & Walgenbach, P. (2009). Interference among conflicting institutions and technical-economic conditions: The adopting of the assessment center in French, German, Italian, UK, and US multinational firms. *The International Journal of Human Resource Management, 20*, 885–911.

Dilchert, S., & Ones, D. S. (2009). Assessment center dimensions: Individual differences correlates and meta-analytical incremental validity. *International Journal of Selection and Assessment, 17*, 254–270.

Engelbrecht, A. S., & Fisher, A. H. (1995). The managerial performance implications of a developmental assessment center process. *Human Relations, 48*, 387-404.

Eurich, T. L., Krause, D. E., Cigularov, K., & Thornton, G. C. III. (2009). Assessment centers: Current practices in the United States. *Journal of Business and Psychology, 24*, 387–407.

Fiske, D. W., Hanfmann, E., MacKinnon, D. W., Miller, J. G., & Murray, H. A. (1948). *Selection of personnel for clandestine operations: Assessment of men.* Walnut Creek, CA: Aegean Park Press (Reprinted).

Fleeson, W. (2001). Toward a structure- and process-integrated view of personality: Traits as density distributions of states. *Journal of Personality and Social Psychology, 80*, 1011–1027.

Fletcher, C. (2011). The impact of ACs and DCs on candidates. In N. Povah & G. C. Thornton III (Eds.), *Assessment centres and global talent management* (pp. 115–129). Farnham, UK: Gower.

Ford, J. K., Kraiger, K., & Merritt, S. M. (2010). An updated review of the multi-dimensionality of training outcomes: New Directions for training evaluation research. In S. W. J. Koslowski & E. Salas (Eds.), *Learning, training, and development in organizations* (pp. 135–201). New York: Routledge.

Gibbons, A. M. (2008). Inconsistency in assessment center performance: Measurement error or something more? ProQuest Information & Learning. *Dissertation Abstracts International: Section B: The Sciences and Engineering, 68*(7-B), 4874–4874.

Gibbons, A. M., & Rupp, D. E. (2009). Dimension consistency as an individual difference: A new (old) perspective on the assessment center construct validity debate. *Journal of Management, 35*, 1154–1180.

Gibbons, A. M., Rupp, D. E., & Schleicher, D. J. (2006, September). *Inconsistency in assessment center performance: Measurement error or something more*? Paper presented at the 2006 International Congress on the Assessment Center Method, London.

Goffin, R. D., Rothstein, M. G., & Johnston, N. G. (1996). Personality testing and the assessment center: Incremental validity for managerial selection. *Journal of Applied Psychology, 81*, 746–756.

Golembiewski, R. T., Billingsley, K., & Yeager, S. (1976). Measuring change and persistence in human affairs: Types of change generated by OD designs. *Journal of Applied Behavioral Science, 12*, 133–157.

Guenole, N., Chernyshenko, O., Stark, S., & Cockerill, T. (2004). *Assessment centers can measure dimensions: MTMM CFA evidence from the leadership domain*. Unpublished paper, Department of Psychology, Goldsmiths University of London.

Guenole, N., Chernyshenko, O., Stark, S., Cockerill, J., & Drasgow, F. (2011). We're doing better than you might think: A large scale demonstration of assessment centre convergent and discriminant validity. In N. Povah & G. C. Thornton III (Eds.), *Assessment centres and global talent management* (pp. 15–46). Farnham, UK: Gower.

Hardison, C. M. (2005). *Construct validity of assessment center overall ratings: An investigation of relationships with and incremental criterion related validity over Big 5 personality traits and cognitive ability*. Unpublished doctoral dissertation, University of Minnesota, Minneapolis.

Howard, A., & Bray, D. W. (1988). *Managerial lives in transition: Advancing age and changing times*. New York: Guilford Press.

International Task Force on Assessment Center Guidelines. (2009). Guidelines and ethical considerations for assessment center operations. *International Journal of Selection and Assessment, 17*, 243–254.

Jones, R. G., & Born, M. P. (2008). Assessor constructs in use as the missing component in validation of assessment center dimensions: A critique and directions for research. *International Journal of Selection and Assessment, 16*, 229–238.

Jones, R. G., & Whitmore, M. D. (1995a). Evaluating developmental assessment centers as interventions. *Personnel Psychology, 48*, 377–388.

Jones, R. G., & Whitmore, M. D. (1995b). "Evaluating developmental assessment centers as interventions": Errata. *Personnel Psychology, 48*, 562–562.

Kirkpatrick, D. (1998). *Evaluating training programs: The four levels* (2nd ed.). San Francisco: Berrett-Koehler.

Kraiger, K. (2008). Transforming our models of learning development: Web-based instruction as enabler of third-generation instruction. *Industrial and Organizational Psychology: Perspectives on Science and Practice, 1*, 454–467.

Kraiger, K., Ford, J. K., & Salas, E. D. (1993). Application of cognitive, skill-based, and affective theories of learning outcomes to new methods of training evaluation. *Journal of Applied Psychology, 78*, 311–328.

Krause, D. E., Kersting, M., Heggestad, E. D., & Thornton, G. C., III. (2006). Incremental validity of assessment center ratings over cognitive ability tests: A study at the executive management level. *International Journal of Selection and Assessment, 14*, 360–371.

Krause, D. E., & Thornton, G. C., III. (2009). A cross-cultural look at assessment center practices: A survey in Western Europe and North America. *Applied Psychology: An International Review*, 58, 557–585.

Kuncel, N. R., & Sackett, P. R. (in press). Resolving the assessment center construct validity problem. *Journal of Applied Psychology*.

Lance, C. E. (2008a). Why assessment centers do not work the way they are supposed to. *Industrial and Organizational Psychology: Perspectives on Science and Practice, 1,* 84–97.

Lance, C. E. (2008b). Where have we been, how did we get there, and where shall we go? *Industrial and Organizational Psychology: Perspectives on Science and Practice, 1,* 140–146.

Lievens, F., Dilchert, S. & Ones, D. S. (2009). The importance of exercise and dimension factors in assessment centers: Simultaneous examination of construct-related and criterion-related validity. *Human Performance, 22,* 375–390.

Lievens, F., Harris, M. M., Van Keer, E., & Bisqueret, C. (2003). Predicting cross-cultural training performance: The validity of personality, cognitive ability, and dimensions measured by an assessment center and a behavior description interview. *Journal of Applied Psychology, 88,* 476–489.

Lievens, F., Tett, R. P., & Schleicher, D. J. (2009). Assessment centers at the crossroads: Toward a reconceptualization of assessment center exercises. *Research in Personnel and Human Resources Management, 28,* 99–152.

Lievens, F., & Thornton, G. C., III. (2005). Assessment centers: Recent developments in practice and research. In A. Evers, N. Anderson, & O. Voskuijl (Eds.), *Handbook of personnel selection* (pp. 243–264). Malden, MA: Blackwell.

McCrae, R. R., & Costa, P. T., Jr. (1997). Personality trait structure as a human universal. *American Psychologist, 52,* 509–516.

Melchers, K. G., & Annen, H. (2010). Officer selection for the Swiss army: An evaluation of validity and fairness issues. *Swiss Journal of Psychology, 69,* 105–115.

Meriac, J. P., Hoffman, B. J., Woehr, D. J., & Fleisher, M. S. (2008). Further evidence for the validity of assessment center dimensions: A meta-analysis of the incremental criterion-related validity of dimension ratings. *Journal of Applied Psychology, 93,* 1042–1052.

O'Connell, M. S., Hattrup, K., Doverspike, D., & Cober, A. (2002). The validity of "mini" simulations for Mexican retail salespeople. *Journal of Business and Psychology, 16,* 593–599.

Reynolds, D. H. & Rupp, D. E. (2010). Advances in technology-facilitated assessment. In J. C. Scott & D. H. Reynolds (Eds.), *Handbook of workplace assessment: Evidence-based practices for selecting and developing organizational talent* (pp. 609–641). San Fransisco: Jossey-Bass.

Rupp, D. E. (2005). Assessment centers, competencies, and integrated HR systems. *Human Capital Management* (Korean), *24,* 16–17.

Rupp, D. E., Gibbons, A. G., & Snyder, L. A. (2008). The role of technology in enabling third-generation training and development. *Industrial-Organizational Psychology, 1,* 495–499.

Rupp, D. E., & Searle, R. H. (2011). Using assessment centres to facilitate collaborative, quasi-standardized, industry-wide selection: lessons learned from medical specialty placement in the UK. In N. Povah & G. C. Thornton (Eds.), *Assessment centres and global talent management* (pp. 209–223). Surrey, UK: Grower.

Rupp, D. E., Snyder, L. A., Gibbons, A. M., & Thornton, G. C., III. (2006). What should developmental assessment centers be developing? *Psychologist-Manager Journal, 9,* 75–98.

Rupp, D. E., Thornton, G. C., III, & Gibbons, A. M. (2008). The construct validity of the assessment center method and usefulness of dimensions as focal constructs. *Industrial and Organizational Psychology: Perspectives on Science and Practice, 1,* 116–120.

Schleicher, D. J., Day, D. V., Mayes, B. T., & Riggio, R. E. (2002). A new frame for frame-of-reference training: Enhancing the construct validity of assessment centers. *Journal of Applied Psychology, 87,* 735–746.

Schmidt. F. L., & Hunter, J. E. (1998). The validity and utility of selection methods in personnel psychology: Practical and theoretical implications of 85 years of research findings. *Psychological Bulletin, 124,* 262–274.

Shore, T. H., Thornton, G. C., & Shore, L. M. (1990). Construct validity of two categories of assessment center dimension ratings. *Personnel Psychology, 43,* 101–116.

ter Muerlen, A. (2001). Logic and natural language. In L. Goble (Ed.), The *Blackwell guide to philosophical logic* (pp. 461–483). Malden, MA: Blackwell.

Thornton, G. C., III. (1992). *Assessment centers in human resource management.* Reading, MA: Addison-Wesley.

Thornton, G. C., III, & Byham, W. C. (1982). *Assessment centers and managerial performance.* New York: Academic Press.

Thornton, G. C., III, & Gibbons, A. M. (2009). Validity of assessment centers for personnel selection. *Human Resource Management Review, 19,* 169–187.

Thornton, G. C., III, & Krause, D. E. (2009). Selection versus development assessment centers: An international survey of design, execution, and evaluation. *The International Journal of Human Resource Management, 20,* 478–498.

Thornton, G. C., III, & Mueller-Hanson, R. A. (2004). *Developing organizational simulations: A guide for practitioners and students.* Mahwah, NJ: Erlbaum.

Thornton, G. C., III, & Rupp, D. R. (2006). *Assessment centers in human resource management: Strategies for prediction, diagnosis, and development.* Mahwah, NJ: Erlbaum.

van Emmerik, I. J. H., Bakker, A. B., & Euwema, M. C. (2008). What happens after the developmental assessment center?: Employees' reactions to unfavorable performance feedback. *Journal of Management Development, 27,* 513–527.

Woehr, D. J., & Arthur, W. Jr. (2003). The construct-related validity of assessment center ratings: A review and meta-analysis of the role of methodological factors. *Journal of Management, 29,* 231–258.

Woo, S. E., Sims, C. S., Rupp, D. E., & Gibbons, A. M. (2008). Development engagement within and following developmental assessment centers: Considering feedback favorability and self-assessor agreement. *Personnel Psychology, 61,* 727–759.

Part 3

Task-Based Assessment Centers

8

Task-Based Assessment Centers

Theoretical Perspectives

Duncan J. R. Jackson
University of Seoul

The previous three chapters have focused on the dimension-based approach to AC design and implementation. Dimension-based ACs (DBACs) have reigned, almost exclusively, as the most popular approach in both the practitioner and academic realms. Relatively little has been written, however, on an alternative task-based conceptualization of AC ratings. In this chapter, I explore and develop theory relating to the task-based approach to ACs. This type of AC has adopted several labels over the course of its relatively short history, including *task-based assessment*, *task-specific ACs*, *outcome-based ACs*, *role-based ACs*, and *task-based ACs* (Goodge, 1988; Hoffman et al., 2007; Lance, 2008a; Lowry, 1997). In the following three sections, the term *task-based AC* (TBAC) will be used for simplicity.

TBACs represent theoretical grounding that differs from traditional approaches and utilize AC-related scores in a unique manner. Despite these distinctions, a TBAC is still classified as a bona fide AC according to the latest guidelines (International Task Force on Assessment Center Guidelines, 2009). TBACs present a promising set of opportunities for academics and practitioners alike, as well as a range of practical approaches to the scoring of ACs.

As an overview, the major surface-level difference between TBACs and DBACs relates to the manner in which these respective approaches are scored. Both TBACs and DBACs utilize behavioral information as their scoring foundation. TBACs, however, aggregate behavioral ratings to exercises that represent samples of work role constructs. Conversely, DBACs aggregate to dimensions, which represent underlying work-related constructs. As such, TBACs are intended to measure role-based constructs specific to each exercise rather than dimensions scored across exercises. While the distinction here may initially seem superficial, it leads to substantive theoretical differences between the approaches.

Background on Task-Based Assessment Centers

In order to appreciate TBACs, it is important to understand their origins. While their distant historical underpinnings are the same as those for ACs generally (see the relevant historical section in this volume), their recent history signifies notable divergences from other approaches. Pre-World War II AC-related procedures in the late 1930s focused on a holistic approach to summarizing the human psyche (Highhouse, 2002). In keeping with these early procedures, TBACs do not seek to atomize complex behavioral responses into various subcomponent dimensions (see Iles, 1992; Vernon & Parry, 1949). Instead, they regard AC output behavior as a representation of knowledge, skills, abilities, traits, situational influences, and a myriad of other factors. This does not mean that TBACs denigrate psychological constructs. Rather, the approach views such variables as sub-components of a much larger global behavioral framework that is made up of innumerable, interacting parts.

In terms of assigning scores to participants, pre-World War II procedures were primarily qualitative and aimed to assess the "whole personality" (Ansbacher, 1941, p. 370). In contrast, behavioral outcomes are assessed in TBACs using standardized scoring procedures. In this regard, TBACs formalize their assessment around task lists that are specific to each AC exercise. These task lists are aggregated within exercises to reflect work related role constructs. As with ACs generally, TBACs are influenced by the work of Flanagan (1954), who endorsed standardized behavioral scoring procedures for simulation exercises.

From the late 1940s onwards, cross-exercise dimension scoring in ACs took the lead in empirical research. Despite the popularity of dimensions from this point, almost three decades ago, Gorham (1978) implied that it would be feasible or even preferential to develop ACs without using dimensions scored across exercises. He stated that while dimensions and their associated titles can be "convenient collecting ground for a number of behaviors, unfortunately in many instances the rating with these names is all that eventually gets put into the record or finds its way to the decision maker" (p. 5). In other words, the ultimate emphasis in DBACs is placed on dimension titles rather than exercises.

When presented with dimension scores, the temptation may be to conceptualize them as though they are underlying psychological constructs; as is well documented in the literature on attribution theory (Carr, 2003; Jackson, Stillman, & Atkins, 2005; Woodruffe, 1993) and has been debated in the AC literature where evidence for cross-exercise stability in AC scores is rarely found (Lance, 2008a). On the contrary, the typical finding is that correlations among same dimensions assessed *across* exercises tend to be much weaker than correlations among different dimensions assessed *within* exercises; culminating in what have been labeled "exercise effects" (Lance, 2008a, 2008b; Lance, Lambert, Gewin, Lievens, & Conway, 2004; Sackett & Dreher, 1982). This presents a problem for DBACs because exercise effects suggest that it would be more meaningful to summarize AC scores within exercises than by dimensions across exercises.

Sackett and Dreher's (1982) now famous study on exercise effects signaled a criticism of the conceptualization of dimensions as psychological constructs, akin to those presented in personality theory. However, the study also inadvertently provided some of the first empirical evidence in favor of TBACs. The common finding of variables that correlate strongly within exercises is problematic for the DBAC approach. However, such patterns are consistent with the theoretical perspectives on TBACs that follow. Researchers since Sackett and Dreher (1982) have often focused on attempts to make dimensions function as variables that manifest with relative stability across exercises (Lance, 2008a). However, a lesser-known research stream has involved investigating an approach to developing ACs that does not involve using cross-exercise dimensions. Iles (1992, p. 80) states that while the dimension-based approach is used in most AC procedures,

> recent British centres (in the form of "task-based centres" and "collaborative centres") have, however, begun to diverge from this model. They have begun to incorporate such innovations as the assessment of global performance on tasks, not on dimensions, the extensive use of observer check-lists, and the use of substantial amounts of self-assessment and joint assessment.

Initial recommendations for the development of TBACs were presented by Goodge (1988). In particular, Goodge suggested formalizing assessment around a single global rating for each exercise, emphasizing the job-relevance of AC exercises, and using supplementary behavioral checklists as an aid to scoring. Goodge's checklists were indicators of whether a behavior had occurred or not (similar to Flanagan, 1954; see also Hedge & Teachout, 1992) and were merely proposed as a supplementary guide to scoring.

The next set of guidelines to emerge displayed greater cohesiveness in terms of their task-based outlook. Lowry's (1997) course of action presented several developments for the TBAC and formalized assessment around a modified version of the behavioral checklists that Goodge (1988) had previously treated as supplementary. Like Goodge, Lowry emphasized within-exercise ratings and the job-relevance of exercises. However, rather than providing a single global score for each exercise, he suggested providing a checklist of multiple generalized responses that were deemed relevant to a particular exercise. Rather than indicating the presence or absence of the listed responses, Lowry suggested scoring the quality of each response on a scale. He also emphasized the use of job analysis (particularly, task analysis) in the development of such checklists. The current AC guidelines specify that behavioral classification within exercises and the use of behavioral checklists are acceptable scoring foundations for ACs (International Task Force on Assessment Center Guidelines, 2009).

In summary, contemporary TBACs are based on task analyses, include multiple simulation exercises (e.g., more than two) that are "job-related to the extent practicable" (Lowry, 1997, p. 57), utilize checklists of responses nested within exercises, and provide ratings for each of these responses on a scale representing varying performance standards (see Table 8.1). A key distinction here, when compared with DBACs, is that TBACs do not incorporate dimensions scored across exercises other than an assessment of overall or general performance. In this regard, Lowry suggests that the TBAC approach simplifies several practical matters with respect to scoring. Both Goodge and Lowry were primarily practitioners, so, in many ways, the TBAC can be considered a practitioner-initiated design. In more recent years, however, academia has shown interest in the approach and has revealed that TBACs represent a fascinating set of alternative theoretical perspectives on AC-related behavior.

Below, an array of theoretical viewpoints will be presented with a view to fostering an understanding of the foundations underlying TBACs. First, it will be shown that TBACs borrow heavily from a range of behavioral approaches, including the literature on performance

Table 8.1 Key Features of Task-Based Assessment Centers

	Feature	Task-Based Representation
1.	Job analysis	Emphasized as an important basis, particularly the use of task-analysis.
2.	Status of simulation exercises	Considered to be behavioral measures of contextualized work roles.
3.	Number of simulation exercises	Because they constitute the foundation of task-based assessment centers, more than two exercises are commonly endorsed.
4.	Job-relevance of simulation exercises	Should be as job-relevant as possible.
5.	Scoring basis	Behavioral items that are specific to (i.e., nested in) simulation exercises. Such items should be specific enough to refer to a particular exercise but general enough to allow for multiple, relevant behavioral manifestations. Items are scored on a scale reflecting the quality of a given participant response.
6.	Overall exercise ratings	Used to represent general performance. Arithmetic integration (e.g., the average rating) is encouraged.
7.	Feedback	Always behavioral and based on exercise or role performance.
8.	Theoretical basis (internal workings)	Systems theory is used to provide a framework for understanding how an array of variables feed into the AC process and interact to produce behavioral output. Each exercise reflects a contextualized management role or set of roles that simulates roles found in criterion performance.
9.	Theoretical basis (criterion-related)	Behavioral consistency explains relationships among simulated work roles and similar criterion roles.
10.	Perspective on output from assessment centers	Considered to be the result of complex interactions among psychological and situational variables that manifest as aspects of general and situationally-specific behavioral performance.

Note. The information presented in this table summarizes that in the extant literature on task-based assessment centers (Goodge, 1988; Jackson, et al., 2007; Jackson, Stillman, et al., 2005; Jackson et al., 2010; Lance, 2008a, 2008b; Lievens, 2008; Lowry, 1997).

feedback and applied behavior analysis. Second, systems theory (Kast & Rosenzweig, 1972; Katz & Kahn, 1978) and the literature on management roles (Hogan, Broach, & Salas, 1990; Mintzberg, 1971, 1973) will be used to describe the constructs that TBACs purport to measure. Third, behavioral consistency (Wernimont & Campbell, 1968) will be presented to add insights into the potential usefulness of TBACs for predicting work-related outcomes.

Task-Based Assessment Centers and Behavioral Approaches

TBACs apply concepts from performance feedback and applied behavior analysis (Jackson, Stillman, et al., 2005). With reference to performance feedback, it is routinely suggested that developmental information is best specified in behavioral terms (Kluger & DeNisi, 1996). As Murphy and Cleveland state, feedback "that is specific and behaviorally-oriented is more likely to be useful than feedback that is general and vague" (1995, p. 92). Likewise, Armstrong (2006, p. 99) recommends relating feedback to "specific items of behavior." Rudman (2003) also suggests focusing on "behaviour that can be changed" (p. 130). This idea is mirrored in other feedback applications, including clinical settings (Hartmann, Roper, & Bradford, 1979) and has previously been discussed in various forms in other areas of the AC literature (Joyce, Thayer, & Pond, 1994; Thornton, Kaman, Layer, & Larsh, 1995; Woodruffe, 1993). TBACs emphasize contextual influences on behavior because feedback, here, is organized in terms of how it pertains to each exercise.

TBACs formalize assessment around lists of behavioral responses that balance a degree of specificity with sufficient generality in order to allow for multiple manifestations of behavior to emerge (Jackson, Atkins, Fletcher, & Stillman, 2005; Jackson, Barney, Stillman, & Kirkley, 2007; Jackson, Stillman, et al., 2005). This is to account for the influence of situational characteristics whilst, at the same time, recognizing that there may be multiple versions of "acceptable" or "unacceptable" behavior. Take, for example, the checklist item "Speaks clearly and annunciates appropriately" in response to a customer service scenario (from Jackson, Stillman, et al., p. 219). This item is typical of those seen in TBACs and is somewhat specific in that it refers to a particular customer service interaction. However, it allows for a class of potential responses, each of which could vary in terms of its level of acceptability. Thus, upon being trained, the aim for assessors is to accurately identify the relevant class of behaviors and the appropriate level of acceptability. The behavioral anchor here is also similar to those seen in DBACs. The difference here is that it does not form part of a dimension that is scored across exercises and, in a TBAC, it is considered in the context of a particular exercise.

In terms of cognitive load, within-exercise behavioral judgments like this have been argued as presenting a much easier task for assessors to process when compared to drawing inferences about underlying dimensions based on manifest behavior (Jackson et al., 2007;

Lance, 2008a; Lowry, 1997). Although the use of behavioral checklists is not new to the AC literature, they are often suggested for use as an aid to dimension assessment (Donahue, Truxillo, Cornwell, & Gerrity, 1997; Lievens, 1998; Reilly, Henry, & Smither, 1990). Conversely, in the TBAC framework, scaled behavioral checklists are the focal indicators of interest. Analogous checklists have been widely and successfully utilized in applied behavior analysis for the modification of behavior in clinical and developmental settings (Cooper, Heron, & Heward, 2007).

One of the clear advantages of focusing on work roles specific to exercises for assessment and for providing feedback is a minimization of internal attributions. Luecke and Hall (2006, p. 57) state that the focus, when providing performance feedback, should be based "on behavior, not character, attitudes, or personality. This practice will prevent the other person from feeling personally attacked." This idea relates directly to *attribution theory* and the study of causes that are assigned to behavioral responses (Martinko, Douglas, & Harvey, 2006). In particular, providing feedback on the basis of role-based responses (rather than dimensions) is likely to assist in terms of avoiding *fundamental attribution errors.* The fundamental attribution error, identified by Ross (1977), refers to the tendency for people to infer internal, dispositional causes for behavior, even in the presence of obvious situational influences. Although AC dimensions were not necessarily intended as internal measures of traits (Howard, 2008), there is the risk that, in practice, they might be interpreted that way (Lance, Baranik, Lau, & Scharlau, 2009), particularly given their cross-exercise scoring configuration that looks similar to a multitrait-multimethod (MTMM) matrix (Campbell & Fiske, 1959). Focusing on contextualized role responses helps to minimize the likelihood of such attributions (Feldman, 1981).

In sum, TBACs use assessment procedures analogous to those employed in applied behavior analysis. These procedures hold the advantages of providing clarity, brevity, and lower cognitive demands on AC participants and raters. Job-relevant exercises are utilized in ACs, and, as such, pertinent situational influences are introduced to the assessment. Yet another advantage of the TBAC approach is that it potentially avoids internal attributions by focusing on behavioral responses. The apparent simplicity of this approach presents a tidily packaged set of interacting psychological and situational variables. However, there are still unanswered questions here relating to the constructs that TBAC exercises measure.

Systems and Role-Based Conceptualizations of Task-Based Scores

Systems theory (Kast & Rosenzweig, 1972) presents a useful framework for understanding the AC process from a broad perspective. At least some of the ideas presented in this section are consistent with another approach that has gained popularity in the AC literature, namely *trait activation theory* (TAT, e.g., Lievens, Chasteen, Day, & Christiansen, 2006). Although TAT holds promise, it is possibly somewhat restrictive in terms of its focus on the priming of traits given certain situations. Systems theory, on the other hand, not only acknowledges interactions among traits and situations, but also a range of other variables, their interactions, as well as the temporal ordering of events in ACs.

Figure 8.1 presents a systems framework applied to ACs (from Jackson, Stillman, & Englert, 2010). The first component of the framework depicts a host of *input* variables, incorporating participant factors (e.g., traits, knowledge, skills, abilities, cultural background), organization factors (e.g., organizational culture), and design factors (e.g., whether the AC has been designed according to current guidelines). The next component refers to the *environment* that is created when all of the input variables interact during the time that the AC takes place. At this point, input factors interact in complex ways to produce *output*, which constitutes the third component of the systems framework. The output from the interaction process involves, under a TBAC view, aspects of both general and situationally-specific (i.e., exercise- or role-specific) behavioral performance (Jackson et al., 2010). These components of

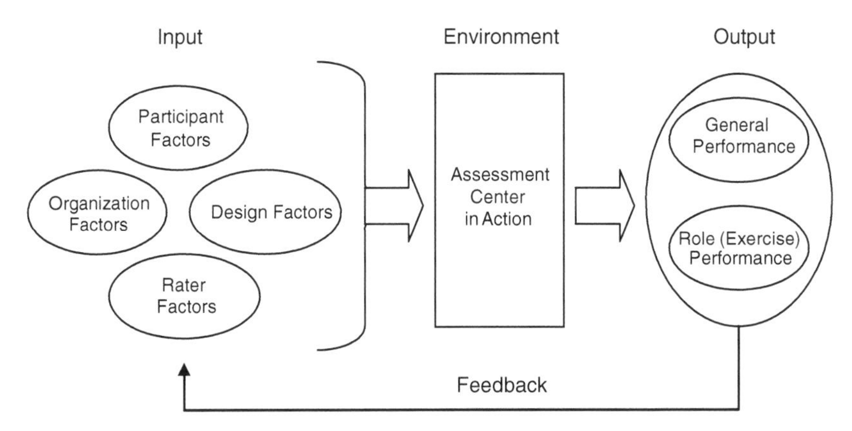

Figure 8.1 A systems approach to the assessment center process (adapted from Jackson, et al., 2010, used with permission).

performance reflect all of the factors and their interactions that feed into the AC process. Systems theory provides a broad framework for understanding how these components work together as a Gestalt (Brown, 1936; Kast & Rosenzweig, 1972). Individually, the factors that make up the AC process may be relatively inert. But, when activated in concert, they form a rich aggregate of interacting features.

The lower portion of the systems model in Figure 8.1 also incorporates the notion of feedback loops. These link outputs back to inputs and imply that the latter hold a perpetual influence over the former. In practical terms, such patterns could manifest in multiple ways, including information on how to design AC exercises more effectively based on the manner in which participants perform. For example, participants may find a particular exercise to be overly difficult and this information could be used to modify exercises for later use. Another example is where participants are provided with developmental behavioral feedback. This may have a direct effect on the overall performance of the organization. Yet another example is where the organization is provided with useful information on which to base employment selection decisions. The system, thus, is continuous and evolves as it continuously feeds information back to itself.

Systems theory provides a broad overview of a range of processes in ACs. However, it does not inform on the specific constructs that TBAC measure. It is vital to isolate the constructs involved in an assessment procedure (Arthur & Villado, 2008) and TBACs treat exercises as substantive measures, in and of themselves. But what do these exercises measure? From a theoretical perspective, what are the constructs that AC exercises tap? Which constructs could be associated with commonly used AC exercises?

The literature on managerial roles, particularly that based on Mintzberg's research (1971, 1973), can be used to help define the constructs that exercises measure. Mintzberg developed a taxonomy comprising *interpersonal* (management through people), *informational* (management through data), and *decisional* (management through action) meta-roles. Under each meta-role, he defined more specific sub-roles, comprising the interpersonal sub-roles (*figurehead, leader, liaison*; relating to interpersonal exchanges), informational sub-roles (*monitor, disseminator, spokesperson*; relating to the processing of information), and decisional sub-roles (*entrepreneur, disturbance handler, resource allocator, negotiator*; relating to decision-making in organizational environments). These role constructs focused on offering explanations for interactions between managers and work contexts.

Mintzberg's management roles have been applied to in-basket tests, which are commonly used in ACs (Shapira & Dunbar, 1980). Moreover, a role framework very similar to that presented by Mintzberg has been applied in military settings. Hogan et al. (1990) found evidence for three broad task categories, which they labeled the *thing-oriented taxon* (relabeled here as *instrumentality*, which incorporates action and manipulation associated with objects, machinery, or other items), the *data-oriented taxon* (solving problems associated with the presentation of information), and the *people-oriented taxon* (involving interpersonal tasks). Specific to the AC realm, Russell and Domm (1995) presented a role framework that also bears similarities to Mintzberg's roles. The Russell and Domm framework covers *judgment* (quality of decisions), *organization and planning* (effective regulation of work), *forcefulness* (impact of behavior), *initiative* (orientation toward action), *energy* (level of work activity), *decisiveness* (quality of choices), *behavioral flexibility* (appropriately modifying behavior), *impact* (creating a favorable impression), *leadership* (guidance toward task accomplishment), *oral communication* (clarity of expression), and *social sensitivity* (detection of environmental cues).

Under a TBAC view, each exercise can be thought of as a substantive measure of a particular role. Such roles can be defined broadly (like the meta-roles presented in Hogan et al., 1990; Mintzberg, 1971, 1973) or more narrowly (like the sub-roles in Mintzberg; or the roles in Russell & Domm, 1995). An appealing feature of these roles is that they specify exercise scores in construct terms, which is a more meaningful way to communicate such ideas to managers and also aligns TBAC scores with outcome measures of job performance specified around competency constructs (Borman, Bryant, & Dorio, 2010). Also, previous studies have shown evidence for the generality of role constructs in managerial contexts (Joyce et al., 1994; Mintzberg, 1971; Russell & Domm, 1995; Shapira & Dunbar, 1980), across cultures (Pearson & Chatterjee, 2003), and in non-managerial contexts (Hogan et al., 1990).

Behavioral Consistency and Task-Based Assessment Centers

Over 40 years ago, Wernimont and Campbell (1968) published a fascinating paper that still holds a great deal of relevance to contemporary organizational studies and psychology. The authors began their article by discussing developments in assessment during World Wars I and II, which focused on "general intelligence and aptitude tests" (p.

372). They then stated that, within this context, "an unfortunate marriage occurred" between the classic validity model and the use of tests as indicators of underlying predispositions or "signs," rather than as "samples" of actual behavior.

There are three important concepts presented in this passage. First, *signs* are presented as indicators of predispositions (e.g., traits, personality) thought to underlie or cause behavior. Second, *samples* are presented as indicators of actual behavioral performance distinguished from signs. Third, a critique is implied that in organization studies, our focus is on signs as predictors, when "it would be much more fruitful to focus on meaningful samples of behavior" (Wernimont & Campbell, 1968, p. 372). A reasonable take on the literature in industrial-organizational psychology and human resource selection suggests that signs, 40 years on, still present much more of a focus than samples. Little seems to have changed since Wernimont and Campbell stated that in most texts dealing with employee selection "signs seem to take precedence over samples" (p. 374). To reflect this, in respectable contemporary texts on the subject of assessment (e.g., Gatewood, Feild, & Barrick, 2008), signs, as indicators of personality, ability, or integrity, are often given more prominence, or are allocated more space, than samples. Wernimont and Campbell (p. 376) explicitly referred to ACs as samples rather than signs.

The behavioral focus of ACs as samples is a clear advantage associated with this technique (Ballantyne & Povah, 2004). Relative to other perspectives, the focus on ACs as samples is amplified in TBACs. While traditional dimensions run the risk of being misinterpreted as though they are traits (Howard, 2008; Lance et al., 2009), TBACs place a greater emphasis on the sample feature of ACs. Behavioral responses in any AC are, by definition, contextualized within work-related simulation exercises (International Task Force on Assessment Center Guidelines, 2009). Aggregating scores within such simulations both formalizes and emphasizes the idea that an AC comprises a set of samples of work-relevant behavior.

The TBAC view is that the theoretical basis for the criterion-related validity of ACs is predicated on emphasizing the notion that ACs are samples. ACs, here, are considered to be measures of roles that are tied to work related contexts. The inclusion of multiple simulations creates an important distinction from individual performance tests and allows for a greater sampling of behavior across a range of work-related situations. Moreover, the presence of multiple tests allows for the assessment of general performance across a number of situations.

This leads to Wernimont and Campbell's (1968) argument with regard to criterion-related validity. They propose that in order to predict a work-related outcome, a predictor test should be consistent with that outcome. Thus, our aim might be to predict job performance, which is often considered to be behavioral and a result of a number of psychological and situational influences (Murphy & Cleveland, 1995). In order to predict job performance, therefore, Wernimont and Campbell argue that a predictor test should be conceptually similar to the criterion. In this regard, the criterion-related validity of TBACs is explained by the concordance between *simulated* behavior in multiple work-relevant performance tests and *actual* work behavior (Jackson, 2007).

An example from an executive management position in the construction division of a conglomerate based in South Korea, will serve to demonstrate the relevance of behavioral consistency. South Korean construction companies frequently negotiate contracts with foreign countries and have clients in locations such as Russia, North America, and Arabia. As a hypothetical example, a job analysis for such an organization might reveal that negotiating with parties from diverse cultures, allocating appropriate resources to complete projects, influencing others, and communicating effectively with stakeholders (e.g., environmental groups) form challenging tasks for executive managers. Turning to Table 8.2, the *negotiator, resource allocator, leader,* and *liaison* roles are relevant to these tasks. Exercises could be developed, using guidance from the extant literature (e.g., Thornton & Mueller-Hanson, 2004), which simulate contextual elements of these roles. One exercise could be used for each role, such that (a) the negotiator role could involve a business game covering a negotiation with a client in Russia, (b) the resource allocator role could involve an analysis simulation where a limited number of resources must be optimally used to complete a project, (c) the leader role could involve a group discussion requiring influence, and (d) the liaison role could involve a role play with an individual from an environmental group who has concerns requiring action.

Under a behavioral consistency view, criterion-related validity would be based on the association between the simulated roles covered in the TBAC and similar roles in which executive managers will engage as part of their real world job performance. Both the simulated and real world roles will involve multiple, interacting psychological and situational variables. In a TBAC, relative to other AC approaches, the scores of the simulated roles are reflected in aggregates of exercise

Table 8.2 Assessment Center Exercises Matched to Role Frameworks

Exercises	Role Frameworks			
Howard (2006)	Russell & Domm (1995)	Mintzberg (1971) Sub-Roles	Mintzberg (1971) Meta-Roles	Hogan et al. (1990)
In-basket	Judgment	Monitor	Informational	Data
Planning	Organization and planning	Disseminator, Spokesperson		
Fact-finding	Forcefulness	Disturbance handler		
Business game	Initiative Energy	Entrepreneur, Negotiator	Decision-making	Instrumentality
Analysis	Decisiveness	Resource allocator		
Group discussion	Behavioral flexibility Impact Leadership	Figurehead, Leader		
Presentation	Oral communication	Liaison	Interpersonal	People
Role play	Social sensitivity			

Note. Suggestions are presented above for common exercises matched to role constructs based on definitions in the references provided. Different matches are possible depending on exercise content.

performances. Each exercise, in the example above, represents a job-relevant managerial role (or, potentially, multiple roles). Scoring for each exercise (role measure) would be based on a behavioral checklist derived from task analyses (Lowry, 1997).

Summary and Conclusion

The task-based approach to ACs represents an important alternative conceptualization of AC ratings. Although TBACs were formally suggested in the late 1980s, there has been little theoretical development of the approach in the literature. This chapter suggests that the TBAC approach holds advantages in terms of avoiding internal attributions and enhancing developmental feedback and employment decisions. A systems approach facilitates an understanding of the broad workings of ACs. Systems theory acknowledges the myriad factors that feed into and interact within an AC to produce behavioral output. It is suggested that AC exercises can be thought of as measures of managerial roles. In terms of their potential for criterion-related validity, behavioral consistency suggests that simulated work role behavior will be consistent with role manifestations in similar work situations.

TBACs present a number of new opportunities for researchers and practitioners and consider ACs and their theoretical basis in a manner that elevates the status of exercises to that of substantive role measures. As such, they have the potential to influence theory in other areas of assessment (e.g., performance management, interview-based assessment). The systems and role approaches, although relatively unexplored in the assessment realm, present broad perspectives and useful frameworks for summarizing a host of complex ideas. The key to uncovering further theoretical insights into TBACs lies in information garnered from empirical research. TBACs present important directions for future research efforts in industrial-organizational psychology.

References

Ansbacher, H. L. (1941). German military psychology. *Psychological Bulletin, 38,* 370–392.

Armstrong, M. (2006). *Performance management: Key strategies and practical guidelines* (3rd ed.). London: Kogan-Page.

Arthur, W., Jr., & Villado, A. J. (2008). The importance of distinguishing between constructs and methods when comparing predictors in personnel selection research and practice. *Journal of Applied Psychology, 93,* 435–442.

Ballantyne, I., & Povah, N. (2004). *Assessment and development centres* (2nd ed.). Aldershot, England: Gower.

Borman, W. C., Bryant, R. H., & Dorio, J. (2010). The measurement of task performance as criteria in selection research. In J. L. Farr & N. T. Tippins (Eds.), *Handbook of employee selection* (pp. 439–461). New York: Routledge.

Brown, J. F. (1936). *Psychology and the social order.* New York: McGraw-Hill.

Campbell, D. T., & Fiske, D. W. (1959). Convergent and discriminant validation by the multitrait-multimethod matrix. *Psychological Bulletin, 56*(2), 81–105.

Carr, S. C. (2003). *Social psychology: Context, communication and culture.* Queensland, Australia: Wiley.

Cooper, J. O., Heron, T. E., & Heward, W. L. (2007). *Applied behavior analysis* (2nd ed.). Upper Saddle River, NJ: Pearson/Merrill-Prentice Hall.

Donahue, L. M., Truxillo, D. M., Cornwell, J. M., & Gerrity, M. J. (1997). Assessment center construct validity and behavioral checklists: Some additional findings. *Journal of Social Behaviour and Personality,* (12), 85–108.

Feldman, J. M. (1981). Beyond attribution theory: cognitive processes in performance appraisal. *Journal of Applied Psychology, 66*, 127–148.

Flanagan, J. C. (1954). Some considerations in the development of situation tests. *Personnel Psychology, 7*, 461–464.

Gatewood, R. D., Feild, H. S., & Barrick, M. R. (2008). *Human resource selection* (6th ed.). Mason, OH: Thomson South-Western.

Goodge, P. (1988). Task-based assessment. *Journal of European Industrial Training, 12*, 22–27.

Gorham, W. A. (1978). Federal executive agency guidelines and their impact on the assessment center method. *Journal of Assessment Center Technology, 1*, 2–8.

Hartmann, D. P., Roper, B. L., & Bradford, D. C. (1979). Some relationships between behavioral and traditional assessment. *Journal of Behavioral Assessment, 1*, 3–21.

Hedge, J. W., & Teachout, M. S. (1992). An interview approach to work sample criterion measurement. *Journal of Applied Psychology, 77*, 453–461.

Highhouse, S. (2002). Assessing the candidate as a whole: A historical and critical analysis of individual psychological assessment for personnel decision making. *Personnel Psychology, 55*, 363–396.

Hoffman, B. J., Thoresen, C. J., Lance, C. E., Thoresen, J. D., Jackson, D. J. R., Foster, M. R., et al. (2007, April). *The Assessment Center Validity Paradox: Alternative Analytic and Design Methodologies*. Paper presented at the Society for Industrial Organizational Psychology, New York, NY.

Hogan, J., Broach, D., & Salas, E. (1990). Development of a task information taxonomy for human performance systems. *Military Psychology, 2*, 1–19.

Howard, A. (2006). Best practices in leader selection. In J. A. Conger & R. E. Riggio (Eds.), *The practice of leadership: Developing the next generation of leaders* (pp. 11–40). San Francisco, CA: Jossey-Bass.

Howard, A. (2008). Making assessment centers work the way they are supposed to. *Industrial and Organizational Psychology: Perspectives on Science and Practice, 1*, 98–104.

Iles, P. (1992). Centres of excellence? Assessment and development centres, managerial competence, and human resource strategies. *British Journal of Management, 3*, 79–90.

International Task Force on Assessment Center Guidelines. (2009). Guidelines and ethical considerations for assessment center operations. *International Journal of Selection and Assessment, 17*, 243–253.

Jackson, D. J. R. (2007, April). *Task-specific assessment centers: Evidence of predictive validity and fairness.* Paper presented at the Society for Industrial and Organizational Psychology, New York, NY.

Jackson, D. J. R., Atkins, S. G., Fletcher, R. B., & Stillman, J. A. (2005). Frame of reference training for assessment centers: Effects on interrater reliability when rating behaviors and ability traits. *Public Personnel Management, 34*, 17–30.

Jackson, D. J. R., Barney, A. R., Stillman, J. A., & Kirkley, W. (2007). When traits are behaviors: The relationship between behavioral responses and trait-based overall assessment center ratings. *Human Performance, 20*, 415–432.

Jackson, D. J. R., Stillman, J. A., & Atkins, S. G. (2005). Rating tasks versus dimensions in assessment centers: A psychometric comparison. *Human Performance, 18*, 213–241.

Jackson, D. J. R., Stillman, J. A., & Englert, P. (2010). Task-based assessment centers: Empirical support for a systems model. *International Journal of Selection and Assessment, 18*, 141–154.

Joyce, L. W., Thayer, P. W., & Pond, S. B. (1994). Managerial functions: An alternative to traditional assessment center dimensions? *Personnel Psychology, 47*, 109–121.

Kast, F., & Rosenzweig, J. E. (1972). General systems theory: Applications for organization and management. *Academy of Management Journal, 15*, 447–465.

Katz, D., & Kahn, R. L. (1978). *The social psychology of organizations* (2nd ed.). New York: Wiley.

Kluger, A. N., & DeNisi, A. (1996). The effects of feedback interventions on performance: A historical review, a meta-analysis, and preliminary feedback theory. *Psychological Bulletin, 119*, 254–284.

Lance, C. E. (2008a). Why assessment centers do not work the way they are supposed to. *Industrial and Organizational Psychology: Perspectives on Science and Practice, 1*, 84–97.

Lance, C. E. (2008b). Where have we been, how did we get there, and where shall we go? *Industrial and Organizational Psychology: Perspectives on Science and Practice, 1*, 140–146.

Lance, C. E., Baranik, L. E., Lau, A. R., & Scharlau, E. A. (2009). If it ain't trait it must be method: (Mis)application of the multitrait-multimethod methodology in organizational research. In C. E. Lance & R. J. Vandenberg (Eds.), *Statistical and methodological myths and urban legends: Doctrine, verity and fable in organizational and social sciences* (pp. 337–360). New York: Routledge.

Lance, C. E., Lambert, T. A., Gewin, A. G., Lievens, F., & Conway, J. M. (2004). Revised estimates of dimension and exercise variance components in assessment center postexercise dimension ratings. *Journal of Applied Psychology, 89*, 377–385.

Lievens, F. (1998). Factors which improve the construct validity of assessment centers: A review. *International Journal of Selection and Assessment, 6*, 141–152.

Lievens, F. (2008). What does exercise-based assessment really mean? *Industrial and Organizational Psychology: Perspectives on Science and Practice, 1*, 112–115.

Lievens, F., Chasteen, C. S., Day, E. A., & Christiansen, N. D. (2006). Large-scale investigation of trait activation theory for understanding assessment center convergent and discriminant validity. *Journal of Applied Psychology, 91*, 247–258.

Lowry, P. E. (1997). The assessment center process: New directions. *Journal of Social Behavior & Personality, 12*, 53–62.

Luecke, R., & Hall, B. J. (2006). *Performance management: Measure and improve the effectiveness of your employees*. Boston, MA: Harvard Business School Press.

Martinko, M. J., Douglas, S. C., & Harvey, P. (2006). Attribution theory in industrial and organizational psychology: A review. In G. P. Hodgkinson & J. K. Ford (Eds.), *International review of industrial and organizational psychology* (Vol. 21, pp. 127–187). Hoboken, NJ: Wiley.

Mintzberg, H. (1971). Managerial work: Analysis from observation. *Management Science, 18*, 97–110.

Mintzberg, H. (1973). *The nature of managerial work*. New York: Harper & Row.

Murphy, K., & Cleveland, J. N. (1995). *Understanding performance appraisal: Social, organizational and goal-based perspectives*. Thousand Oaks, CA: Sage.

Pearson, C. A. L., & Chatterjee, S. R. (2003). Managerial work roles in Asia: An empirical study of Mintzberg's role formulation in four Asian countries. *Journal of Management Development, 22*, 694–707.

Reilly, R. R., Henry, S., & Smither, J. W. (1990). An examination of the effects of using behavior checklists on the construct validity of assessment center dimensions. *Personnel Psychology, 43*, 71–84.

Ross, L. (1977). The intuitive psychologist and his shortcomings: Distortions in the attribution process. In L. Berkowitz (Ed.), *Advances in experimental social psychology* (Vol. 10, pp. 173–220). New York: Academic Press.

Rudman, R. (2003). *Performance planning and review: Making employee appraisals work* (2nd ed.). Crows Nest, New South Wales, Australua: Allen & Unwin.

Russell, C. J., & Domm, D. R. (1995). Two field tests of an explanation of assessment centre validity. *Journal of Occupational and Organizational Psychology, 68*, 25–47.

Sackett, P. R., & Dreher, G. F. (1982). Constructs and assessment center dimensions: Some troubling empirical findings. *Journal of Applied Psychology, 67*, 401–410.

Shapira, Z., & Dunbar, R. L. M. (1980). Testing Mintzberg's managerial roles classification using an in-basket simulation. *Journal of Applied Psychology, 65*, 87–95.

Thornton, G. C., III., Kaman, V., Layer, S., & Larsh, S. (1995, May). *Effectiveness of two forms of assessment center feedback: Attribute feedback and task feedback*. Paper presented at the 23rd International Congress on the Assessment Center Method, Kansas City, Kansas.

Thornton, G. C., III., & Mueller-Hanson, R. A. (2004). *Developing organizational simulations: A guide for practitioners and students*. Mahwah, NJ: Routledge.

Vernon, P. E., & Parry, J. B. (1949). *Personnel selection in the British Forces*. London: University of London Press.

Wernimont, P. F., & Campbell, J. P. (1968). Signs, samples, and criteria. *Journal of Applied Psychology, 52*, 372–376.

Woodruffe, C. (1993). *Assessment centres: Identifying and developing competence* (2nd ed.). London: Institute of Personnel Management.

9

How to Design and Implement a Task-Based Assessment Center

Carl J. Thoresen and Joseph D. Thoresen

Cornerstone Management Resource Systems

Hanging 15 feet above the fire trucks in Station #6 on East Avenue in Livermore, California is a simple light bulb. It was turned on in the summer of 1901 and has provided light for firefighters ever since (http://www.centennialbulb.org). Some ascribe its longevity to a carefully controlled power supply and the fact that it has almost never been turned off. It seems unlikely that these are the only reasons why it appears in the *Guinness Book of World Records* (Glenday, 2007) as "The Centennial Light." It also seems possible that the company that made this bulb appreciated that they were engaged in a relatively new but important endeavor and over-engineered their product.

As scientist-practitioners, we have been accused of over-developing (engineering) our task-based assessment centers (TBACs). When we created our first TBAC in 1998, there was some research to provide us ideas and direction but no existing models to guide our efforts. Many aspects of the *Guidelines and Ethical Considerations for Assessment Center Operations* did not apply. Because we abandoned the traditional dimension-based approach, our programs could only loosely be considered "assessment centers." We recognized and accepted responsibility for the fact that our programs would impact the lives and careers of participants and the effectiveness of client organizations. In addition, we appreciated that we were breaking new ground in a profession that relies heavily on tradition and past practices. To further complicate matters, our client companies operated in an industry that has always been very concerned about anything potentially litigious. Over-engineering seemed prudent.

We mention this only to illustrate that not all TBACs need to replicate or parallel the methodology that will be described in this chapter. Different situations require different responses, and the operational details of successful TBACs sometimes differ from what we will present. Some may require less rigor, fewer simulations, or perhaps different evaluation procedures. Some, undoubtedly, will need to be more lengthy and sophisticated. We have been asked to write this chapter because our time and experience with TBACs has allowed us to develop processes that test the limits and leverage the strengths of this methodology. In addition, our programs have been extremely well received by clients who apply and use them in real world situations.

The Need for Change

Traditional dimension-based assessment centers (DBACs) have been used by a variety of organizations worldwide for promotional decision making and employee development for over 40 years. Few, if any, significant changes regarding the core assumptions underlying these programs have occurred during this period. As a result, it is tempting to assume that a change in this traditional methodology is unnecessary. As scientist-practitioners, we disagree. Although we do not understand why, it seems to us that core DBAC methodology has remained unchanged for so long because a large group of practitioners and researchers has ignored a significant body of research challenging some fundamental underpinnings of this methodology. In our view, the body of research that runs counter to traditional DBAC methodology is of such a magnitude and importance that a critical reexamination and overhaul of the process is warranted. We feel that this overhaul should not be limited by loyalty to the past or the inertia of current practice. Instead, it should begin by recognizing that traditional methodology was—by necessity—designed without the benefit of the voluminous body of research that has followed it. As scientist-practitioners, we have attempted to capitalize on this research. To explain the rationale behind this work, it is first necessary to review some operational issues that have frequently been overlooked by both DBAC researchers and practitioners and address some practical implications of each.

Some Neglected Issues in the Application of the Assessment Center Method

The Construct Validity Issue

As noted in previous chapters, a consistent finding in the assessment center literature is the failure of DBAC exercises to accurately measure the attributes or dimensions they purport to measure—a finding known as the "construct validity problem" (Lance, 2008; Lance, Lambert, Gewin, Lievens, & Conway, 2004; Lievens, 1998, 2002; Lievens & Conway, 2001 Sackett & Dreher, 1982). Research-based efforts to improve the construct validity of assessment center dimensions have either proven futile—or at best—produced modest results (Arthur, Day, McNelly, & Edens, 2003; Gaugler & Thornton, 1989; Reilly, Henry, & Smither, 1990; Woehr, Arthur, & Bowler, 2002). Perhaps because ACs and their associated dimensions have levels of predictive validity comparable to or greater than other widely used selection methods (Arthur et al., 2003; Meriac, Hoffman, Woehr, & Fleisher, 2008), at least in the applied realm, the construct validity problem has been virtually ignored.

To date, many DBAC practitioners seem blissfully unaware of this research or the suggestion offered by some researchers to abandon the dimension-based approach altogether (Jackson, Stillman, & Atkins, 2005; Joyce, Thayer, & Pond, 1994; Lance, 2008). The common assumption seems to be that if a dimension or attribute can be conceived, it can be accurately measured via a DBAC. Thus, reliance on the traditional model continues unabated. Organizations continue to invest in these programs and the lives and careers of participants are influenced, perhaps arbitrarily, by the results.

Unproven Developmental Value of DBACs

Although originally designed for selection purposes, DBACs have increasingly been used for diagnosing employee developmental needs. In fact, many organizations utilize DBACs in an attempt to accomplish both objectives in what Thornton and Rupp (2006) label as "hybrid centers" (p. 75). From a research perspective, the use of DBACs for developmental purposes is problematic for at least four reasons. First, when developmental feedback is provided in a DBAC, it is invariably structured around dimension evaluations. If DBACs cannot consistently and reliably measure these constructs, developmental recommendations created from them are, at best, suspect. Second, dimensions that are often targeted for development are generally person-focused. In fact, major models of personality such as the "Big Five" have been utilized as a lens through which to evaluate the relevance of dimensions to particular DBAC exercises (e.g., Lievens, Chasteen, Day, & Christiansen, 2006). This is problematic, as these types of personal attributes show considerable temporal stability and resistance to change in adults (McCrae & Costa, 1994; Srivastava, John, Gosling, & Potter, 2003). Third, DBAC feedback is often limited to descriptions of observed behavior (what was done at the DBAC) and contains no prescriptive component (what one could do to improve skills). Without some prescriptive component, feedback cannot be expected to result in skill development (Rupp et al., 2006). Finally, because the prima facie purpose of DBAC exercises is to generate data relevant to dimensional constructs, DBAC exercises may have little in common with actual job tasks. Hence, feedback that describes how to more effectively handle these situations may have little potential to result in meaningful coaching.

These concerns are supported by the finding that no longitudinal field-based research on employed adults has ever demonstrated meaningful change in levels of dimensional scores as a result of DBAC feedback and subsequent coaching efforts (Thornton & Rupp, 2006). Given the widespread use of DBACs for the development of leadership and management competencies, this is both surprising and disappointing.

The Use of an External Selection Model for Internal Selection

Currently, the most frequent organizational application of traditional assessment centers is associated with internal selection and promotion timing (Eurich, Krause, Cigularov, & Thornton, 2006). We contend that this practice of applying an *external* selection model based on predictive validity for *internal* selection and promotion results in unintended negative consequences. The use of an external (predictive) model when hiring from outside an organization goes back to the early days of industrial psychology, and it is entirely appropriate when organizations have no investment in or commitment to external candidates. Organizations can reject the vast majority of applicants in order to make effective use of the imperfect (i.e., with an operational validity < 1.00) predictive measure. It does not matter that, even if validity is relatively high, a large number of "false negatives"—people who would have performed effectively if hired—are created (Taylor & Russell, 1939).

Early in the history of the assessment center method, programs were used primarily for foreman or supervisory selection (Thornton & Byham, 1982). Hourly employees were evaluated for promotion into management. This was, in essence, an application of an external selection model, as there were many willing candidates to choose from. In order to take advantage of moderate predictive validity, only a small percentage of candidates "passed," and many false negatives were created. These false negatives were viewed as unfortunate, but acceptable.

This model becomes problematic, however, when DBACs are used internally to promote *professional individual contributors* into leadership positions. In these situations, assessment center participants are typically highly valued employees. Organizations usually have significant financial investments in these people, who are top performers in their current roles. Promotion procedures that result in high failure rates and create large numbers of false negatives in this group waste valuable human resources. In addition, if candidates who "fail" the assessment believe that their career options have suddenly become limited, they can be expected to seek advancement opportunities outside the organization.

In our experience, organizations sometimes try to respond to negative reactions from high-value internal candidates and their managers (we have heard these programs called "assassination centers") by simply "passing" more DBAC candidates. In so doing, they promote more false positives into leadership roles and reduce the impact and utility of the process. The dilemma represents a classic tradeoff between Type I and Type II errors. From the perspectives of both the organization and the candidates who are assessed, there is no good answer. Of course, it is important to note that this problem is not unique to DBACs, which have repeatedly been shown to possess levels of validity greater than or comparable to other methods used in managerial selection (Arthur et al., 2003; Meriac et al., 2008). Obviously, no such method—or combination of methods—will ever achieve perfect operational validity. Our point is that, at least in our experience, organizational decision makers are totally unaware of this dynamic and too often *assume* these programs are highly accurate tools for making internal promotion decisions. They often do not understand or appreciate the limitations of using an external hiring model for internal promotion, and they do not realize the hidden costs of this practice.

Task Based Assessment Centers as an Alternative to Traditional Dimension-Based Assessment Centers

We believe the recent attention given to TBACs (Jackson, Barney, Stillman, & Kirkley, 2007; Jackson et al., 2005; Lance, 2008) represents a major positive development in AC literature and that TBACs have the potential to resolve many of the concerns outlined above. Lance and colleagues have suggested that DBACs possess predictive validity largely because the exercises represent content-valid work samples (Lance, Foster, Gentry, & Thoresen, 2004). Lance (2008) also indicated that DBAC performance is cross-situationally specific rather than dimension-driven, thus exercises—not dimensions—represent the true "building blocks" of DBACs.

From a general perspective, TBACs simply build upon this logic, supported by job sample methodology (Roth, Bobko, & McFarland, 2005), and replace DBAC exercises with *high-fidelity simulations* designed to sample key *functions* and responsibilities of the target job. Simulation performance is evaluated using a task or outcome-based approach that capitalizes on the "exercise effect" finding uncovered by research demonstrating problems with DBAC construct validity. In this alternative model, the "constructs" are neither dimensions nor exercises. The focal construct is *exercise performance itself.* Programs are structured to retain many of the positive characteristics of DBACs, while practices not supported by research are abandoned.

Structural and Methodological Similarities to Traditional DBACs

First, as with DBACs, multiple raters evaluate performance in multiple simulations. Using multiple simulations allows for the content of the target job to be sampled comprehensively. Use of multiple raters reduces the potential influence of positive or negative evaluator bias. Whenever possible, a 1:1 evaluator to candidate ratio is used to further reduce the possibility of bias, encourage a detailed evaluation of performance, and prevent evaluator cognitive overload.

Second, as in DBACs designed to improve construct validity, a highly structured and behaviorally based evaluation process is utilized. This rating process may be facilitated by the use of behaviorally anchored rating scales (BARS) or behavioral checklists in an effort to simplify the evaluation process and increase objectivity and accuracy (Reilly et al., 1990). Because they have the potential to provide for more detailed feedback, we usually prefer the use of checklists. Due to space limitations, an example of an evaluation guide used in a TBAC simulation is explained and provided in Appendix A, which may be viewed along with other sample materials at http://www.tbacs.org.[1]

Finally, evaluation teams in our TBACs rely on a consensus-based rating approach to determine the level of readiness—analogous to the "overall assessment rating" (OAR)—demonstrated by each participant. As in DBACs, individual simulation performance is described, and individual simulation ratings are reviewed and finalized (Thornton & Rupp, 2006). We recognize that numerous AC researchers have long cautioned against the use of the consensus-based procedure. Instead, many favor an arithmetic or statistical approach in which ratings typically are averaged over simulations or exercises (e.g., Goodge, 1988; Jackson et al., 2007; Sackett & Wilson, 1982; Wingrove, Jones, & Herriot, 1985). However we consider the consensus-based procedure more compatible with the goals and objectives of the programs we will be describing. This issue will be addressed in detail later in this section.

Departures from Traditional DBAC Methodology

Despite these similarities, we have identified six key points of divergence between dimension- and task-based assessments. Before providing detail on these differences, several basic issues and assumptions underlying our view of TBAC methodology deserve mention. First, I/O psychologists (ourselves included) are trained to view employment testing through the lens of predictive validity. As a result of our training, we understand and appreciate this perspective. However, we contend that *achievement* or *licensure* testing can also have an important role in promotion/selection decisions and suggest that TBACs are uniquely compatible with this methodology. Second, we recognize that achievement or licensure tests are not specifically intended to predict levels of future performance. In this context, they simply address whether or not candidates currently possess the necessary knowledge and skills to effectively perform the basic requirements of the target job. We see this goal as being compatible with the intent of internal selection. Third, in TBACs, performance in the simulations (exercises) replaces dimensions as the focal constructs being assessed. Finally, when TBAC simulation content does not reflect actual job content to a reasonable degree, both the content- and construct-related validities of TBACs are compromised.

Difference #1: The Role of Job/Task Analysis and Simulation Design

Depending upon the goals of the program, the type and importance of job analysis and its impact on the development of simulation content can represent a very significant departure from the practices normally associated with traditional DBACs. The role of job analysis in the development of DBACs is to identify the constructs (dimensions) associated with performance on the target-level job. In some cases, the job analyst may draw upon an organization's competency model as an a priori guide for these efforts (Thornton & Rupp, 2006). From the perspective of exercise content, the job analyst in effect works backward, deductively creating a scoring key to be used in the determination of test (exercise) content. By its very nature, this is a highly inferential process that requires expert understanding of dimensional and/or competency-related constructs and their presumed relationships with job performance. In our experience, the relationship between job content and exercise content in DBACs is typically somewhat casual and, when it exists at all, has as its primary purpose the development of exercises that are "face valid in the eye of users and participants" (Thornton & Rupp, 2006, p. 82).

In contrast, the purpose of job analysis in the development of a TBAC is to gather enough information about functions of the target job in order to create simulations that reflect the primary job tasks. From the perspective of the simulations, the job analyst works *forward* by developing test content *before* determining how it will be evaluated. The role of psychological inference is minimized in this process, as both simulation content and evaluation issues become the responsibility of subject matter experts or job content experts (JCEs)—usually first and/or second-level supervisors of the target position.

In summary, the job analysis techniques used in the development of a TBAC are very different from those used in the creation of a DBAC. The differences exist because the construct and content-related validities of TBACs are dependent upon how well simulation content reflects actual job content. As it turns out, the use of high-fidelity simulations also increases the utility of TBACs in a number of other important operational areas.

Difference #2: "Silo-ed," Outcome-Based Performance Measurement

Among the most notable departures of TBAC methodology from DBAC programs is the manner in which candidate behavior is analyzed and performance is measured. Traditional DBACs use one of two structural processes to make dimensional evaluations from observations of performance on exercises (Lance, Foster, et al., 2004; Thornton & Rupp, 2006). Individual assessors may provide dimensional evaluations immediately after the observation of exercise performance, or conversely, the assessor team may make these evaluations during the integration session after performance on all exercises has been observed. Regardless of which process is utilized, only dimensions are evaluated. No effort is made in any way to review exercise performance as such. The evaluation of dimensional performance is *horizontal*, as evaluation team members create overall dimension ratings from observed behavior *across* different exercises. In fact, previous research that uncovered the exercise effect problem did so through exploratory (Sackett & Dreher, 1982) or confirmatory (Lance, Foster, et al., 2004; Lance, Lambert, et al., 2004; Lievens & Conway, 2001) factor analytic techniques, and not direct measures of exercise performance.

In contrast, participant attributes or characteristics are not in any way addressed in a TBAC. While the DBAC evaluation process is person focused, TBACs address only *outcomes* or performance on the functional aspects of high-fidelity simulations. Although more structured and detailed, the method used in the evaluation of TBAC performance is similar to that used in the evaluation of actual job performance. In a sense, the goal of TBAC evaluation to create virtual performance reviews of people in jobs they do not yet hold.

The behavior used to make these evaluations is typically broken down and organized under subheadings or *performance components* which are evaluated independently. When developing an overall evaluation for simulation performance, these individual performance components are reviewed and "rolled up" into an overall evaluation. Because performance components are only relevant to the simulation in which they are measured, the evaluation process is vertical or "silo-ed" within each simulation.

Figure 9.1 illustrates this "silo-ed" structure. The actual TBAC was designed to evaluate the readiness of pharmaceutical sales representatives to assume first-level sales manager responsibilities. It consists of six simulations that reflect the key functions of the managerial job (Business Review, Struggling New Sales Representative, Disengaged Sales Representative, Insubordinate Sales Representative, Office Day/Inbox, and Sales Team Meeting).

As an example of the evaluation process, consider the Insubordinate Sales Representative simulation (see the "Sample TBAC Evaluation Guide" section Appendix A, downloadable from http://www.tbacs.org.) Overall simulation performance is derived from evaluations of *Information Gathering* (questioning the employee in order to better understand the situation), *Initiating Change* (effective use of interpersonal or leadership tactics to stimulate performance improvement), and *Solution Development* (developing and implementing strategies/tactics for increasing employee job performance). Note that part of the functional evaluation of performance in this simulation is the temporal aspect of the performance components. In order to effectively handle the simulation, the participant must first understand the nature of the problem and convince the employee of the need for change. Only then can a realistic plan for correcting the performance deficiency be developed.

Performance components are *not* to be confused with dimensions. They are performance-based subcomponents of the overall task, much as catching a ground ball and throwing it to the first baseman are performance-based components of a shortstop's task of throwing out a batter. There is no concern about "style points" (analogous to descriptive dimensions of performance captured in a DBAC evaluation). The focus is on whether or not the participant's response met the performance demands of the situation and achieved the necessary outcome. If a participant fails to meet the standard of overall simulation performance because of a failure to successfully handle a performance component, feedback on this performance issue can be useful in developing the skills necessary to perform the associated job function more effectively.

Performance components are specific to the content of each simulation. When simulations share similar challenges (e.g., the Disengaged Representative and the Insubordinate Representative), the names of the performance components may be similar. However, because of the operational differences in the simulations, their successful achievement may require very different actions or behaviors. Thus, it is not necessary—and in fact may be improper—to look horizontally across these simulations to make inferences about underlying dimensional constructs.

	1 Significantly Short of Requirements	2 Somewhat Short of Requirements	3 Meets Requirements	4 Somewhat Exceeds Requirements	5 Significantly Exceeds Requirements
BUSINESS REVIEW					
Descriptive Understanding		2			
Information Utilization		2			
Summary		2			
STRUGGLING NEW SALES REPRESENTATIVE					
Issue Identification			3		
Constructive Support		2			
Summary			3		
DISENGAGED SALES REPRESENTATIVE					
Information Gathering				4	
Initiating Change			3		
Solution Development			3		
Summary			3		
INSUBORDINATE SALES REPRESENTATIVE					
Information Gathering		2			
Initiating Change			3		
Solution Development	1				
Summary		2			
OFFICE DAY / INBOX					
Operational Issues			3		
Personnel Issues		2			
Summary		2			
SALES TEAM MEETING					
Message Delivery			3		
Establishing Leadership			3		
Solution Development			3		
Summary			3		

Readiness Estimate: Not Ready – Additional Development Required. Paul's performance in the simulation indicated that he is not yet ready for promotion to first -level sales manager. An estimated 6–12 months of focused development in several functional areas is required.

Figure 9.1 Sample TBAC performance summary with "vertical" (task-based) evaluation structure

Evaluation of the Office Day/Inbox simulation, which uses a task-based process to evaluate item-level performance, does not lend itself to this structure. Instead, the evaluation is organized functionally under the headings of *Operational Issues* (in this case items dealing primarily with administrative tasks, adherence to organizational or industry compliance policies, allocation of resources such as budgets, and customer relations) and *Personnel Issues* (items dealing primarily with human resource-related concerns, providing positive or corrective individual feedback, responding to conflicts between subordinates).

Difference #3: Description and Evaluation of Candidate Performance

All performance evaluations are made against the standard of whether or not observed performance meets what is expected and required of an effective new manager. In the current example, a 5-point Likert scale (Figure 9.1) is used to make these evaluations. In addition, job analysis results may stipulate very specific behavioral responses as basic requirements for achieving a rating of 3 (Meets Requirements).

After the members of the evaluation team share their individual evaluations and reach agreement on the level of performance achieved on each of the simulations, this information is reviewed to develop a consensus summary evaluation—an estimate of each participant's *readiness* for promotion. This is very different from the DBAC process of making estimates of management potential from a dimensional performance profile.

If a participant's performance meets or exceeds the "effective new manager" standard on all simulations, he/she is obviously ready for immediate promotion. This is the highest performance level a participant can achieve. When a participant does not meet this standard, the members of the evaluation team must identify the skills that must be developed prior to promotion and scale the overall readiness evaluation accordingly. This process and the process of identifying the activities most likely to positively impact observed skill deficiencies (developmental activities) can require considerable discussion among members of the evaluation teams. For these reasons, we prefer the use of a consensus-based procedure instead of an arithmetic or statistical approach that results in an overall performance score.

Difference #4: The Importance of Job Content Experts as Evaluators

A core requirement in our TBACs is that simulation evaluations be made by *job content experts,* typically high-performing managers, second-level managers, management trainers, and human resource professionals. This differs from the DBAC approach, in which assessment teams may consist of managers, psychologists, or some combination of the two (Thornton & Rupp, 2006). The practice of exclusive reliance on managers or other job content experts for evaluating TBAC performance runs counter to the recommendations of many noted AC researchers. Gaugler et al. (1987) presented meta-analytic data demonstrating that evaluation teams consisting of psychologists produced ratings with slightly higher predictive validity than those of managers, a finding that lead these authors to recommend that psychologists always be represented on AC evaluation teams. It is worth noting that neither the statistical nor the practical significance of this difference was clearly established in their study.

If psychological constructs (i.e., dimensions) are being (or even *can* be) evaluated using assessment center methodology, it stands to reason that psychologists should be involved in these assessments. If content-valid task or simulation performance is being evaluated and leadership/management development is a primary goal of the program, effective managers in the target job, higher-level managers who supervise people in the target job, and those in special functions who are very familiar with requirements for job success should make the evaluations. These people not only understand job requirements, they can also provide practical information and insights regarding developmental strategies likely to impact observed performance shortcomings. Using psychologists to evaluate TBAC performance would be equivalent to having them evaluate the actual job performance of managers without the understanding or appreciation of many critical issues associated with successful—or unsuccessful—performance. Note that we are *not* suggesting that I/O psychologists and professionals in allied disciplines have no role to play in the implementation of TBACs. We are only suggesting that their roles are different. We believe that I/O psychologists are critical to the design, implementation, and on-site facilitation of TBACs. However, they should *not* function as evaluation team members.

In our experience, the requirement that managers who serve as assessors in DBACs engage in extensive training (e.g., Archambeau,

1979; Fleenor, 1996; Harris, Becker, & Smith, 1993; Lievens, 2001; Russell, 1985; Schleicher, Day, Mayes, & Riggio, 2002) does not extend to evaluation team members in TBACs. In contrast, we have found that rater training of experienced managers and job content experts is greatly simplified. There is no need to train evaluators on construct (dimension) definitions and exercise content. Evaluator training on simulations of familiar content, in conjunction with a highly structured evaluation process, can be accomplished within a single day. Thus, rater training can be self-contained within a single TBAC administration. This is because managers are required to evaluate task and simulation performance that is very closely aligned with job performance they typically evaluate in their supervisory roles. In addition, TBAC evaluations are made under controlled conditions using a structured evaluation process is that is far superior to what typically occurs when actual job performance is evaluated. Finally, there is no requirement that behavioral observations be forced through dimensional "filters" before they can be evaluated.

Difference #5: The Limited Need for Assumptions and Inferences

One of the primary design goals of our TBAC methodology was to reduce the level of inference required in all facets of program design and implementation. The inherent content-related validity of a well-developed TBAC evaluation process is much less dependent upon inference than traditional DBACs. There is no need to rely on abstract constructs (i.e., dimensions) to predict future job performance because *performance outcomes* per se are captured by the tasks of interest. Thus, performances represent true samples of content-relevant future work behavior (Wernimont & Campbell, 1968).

The primary assumption in a TBAC is that the simulations represent the most critical job functions. The primary inference is that performance on the simulations will be closely replicated by performance on the job. Both issues can be controlled by careful job analysis and the development of high-fidelity simulations that are supported by detailed evaluation tools that focus on the appropriate performance outcomes. When all is said and done, the goal for developing a TBAC should be to create a process that results in *performance reviews of people in jobs they do not yet hold*. The level of inference that exists in a TBAC is dependent upon how well this goal is achieved.

Difference #6: Functionally-Oriented Versus Trait-Based Feedback

An important point of departure between DBAC and TBAC methodologies involves the form and nature of feedback that is provided to participants and the client organization's decision makers. This is a critical and very important difference. Feedback from DBAC performance is necessarily person-focused, or structured around the dimensions the program is intended to measure. Candidates are provided with recommendations as to how they might improve with respect to competencies or personal characteristics such as initiative, decisiveness, stress tolerance, leadership, organization, etc. In contrast, TBAC feedback is strictly *task based* and deals with specific job function *skills* that must be developed in order to improve readiness to assume job responsibilities. As mentioned previously, the use of performance component measurement points within each simulation allows this feedback to be highly task-specific and fine-tuned.

Focusing simulation performance and developmental feedback on job-related functions and tasks as opposed to personal characteristics is advantageous to participants and organizations for at least two reasons. As indicated earlier in this chapter, TBAC feedback is directed at skills that are tangible and malleable, rather than competencies, traits, or personal attributes that may be resistant to change. Second, task-focused feedback should lead to increased acceptance on the part of the candidate—particularly if the feedback is not positive. Meta-analytic research on Feedback Intervention Theory (FIT; Kluger & DeNisi, 1996) has shown that feedback efforts tend to have greater influence when directed at the task rather than the person. Task-focused feedback is regarded as less threatening to self-esteem and thus tends to be received more openly. Likewise, the transparency of the TBAC evaluation process should lead to more positive perceptions of procedural justice, which has been linked to greater feedback acceptance in a broad array of domains (Brockner & Wiesenfeld, 1996; Thornton & Rupp, 2006). In fact, the limited research that exists on this subject suggests that, in the AC context, individuals prefer task-based to person- or dimension-based feedback (Joyce et al., 1994).

An example of the feedback possibilities that exist in a TBAC is provided in Appendix A of http://www.tbacs.org. The latter section of Appendix A (Items 47A through 47H) illustrates a series of task-related developmental activities. After observing a candidate engage in the

Insubordinate Sales Representative simulation and evaluating performance, an evaluator can refer to this list to choose the developmental activities most likely to improve the handling of similar situations that would occur on the job. The content presented represents only a sample of possible activities that an evaluator may suggest for this particular simulation. Different activities (not shown here) are offered for each of the six simulations which make up this particular TBAC.

Three noteworthy characteristics of these developmental feedback options deserve mention. First, as indicated in the instructions, each of these activities was identified by a panel of job content experts (i.e., experienced sales managers and trainers rather than psychologists) as a means of increasing proficiency in each job function. Second, the activities listed are highly specific to each job function and are directed to the development of specific skills. Third, the evaluator is not limited to this list of developmental options but can call upon his/her experience, knowledge of the job, and awareness of organizational resources to augment these possibilities.

In addition to the developmental plans and strategies initiated by performance on the simulation, receipt of TBAC feedback *itself* can represent a significant developmental intervention. Feedback is structured and organized to not only recognize effective actions and behavior but also to identify what the participant *could have done differently* to improve his/her performance (Appendix B, http://www.tbacs.org). Feedback is no longer passively descriptive, and because simulation content closely parallels the content of actual job tasks or functions, feedback becomes a *coaching intervention.* (An excerpt from an actual feedback report is provided in Appendix B of http://www.tbacs.org.)

Design and Implementation of an Operational TBAC

Developing Simulation Content

Job Analysis. An I/O psychologist conducting a job analysis for a DBAC is responsible for identifying the dimensions associated with success on the target job. This person attempts to utilize his/her knowledge of dimensional constructs to identify important dimensions from descriptions of job tasks, behavior and responsibilities. He or she is clearly in an expert role. In contrast, the responsibility of the I/O psychologist conducting a TBAC job analysis is to learn enough about the job to design high-fidelity simulations that reflect the most critical job functions (tasks). Based on this information, he or she then designs instruments for evaluating simulation performance that reflects the standards of the organization. In this situation, the I/O psychologist is not in the role of a *functional* or *content* expert. Instead, the I/O psychologist functions as a *process expert.* He or she becomes the content expert when designing the simulation and evaluation material.

The purpose of our TBAC programs is to create a realistic scenario that requires participants to deal with the types of problems and situations that managers in the target job will have to handle successfully in order to be effective. Extreme situations should be avoided. Critical incidents are usually too extreme and occur too infrequently. Although sometimes useful when determining DBAC dimensions, they are not sufficiently representative for use in a TBAC. Situations that involve knowledge of policies or procedures that candidates have no reason to be aware of should also be avoided, as should issues that will be addressed in the basic training and orientation that new managers will receive once they are promoted.

Remember that simulation performance will be evaluated by reviewing the quality of participants' responses. Problems and situations included in simulations should have the potential to elicit a variety of responses that exist on a continuum of effectiveness. The only significant distortion in simulation content should be the speed at which the problems occur. Simulations allow time compression, thereby reducing the problem solving and decision making that occurs over an extended period of time into a matter of hours (it should be noted that DBACs require this same constraint). However, even this issue should not be overly exaggerated. People should be able to complete simulation content in the time provided, and TBACs should be considered *power* tests, not speeded tests.

With these objectives and parameters in mind, the job analysis should be initiated. In preparation for meeting with line management, it is important to:

1. Review available written information on job content, requirements and responsibilities. Attend to lists of competencies only to the extent that they convey information about job activities.
2. Discuss major areas of job content (responsibilities, challenges, performance requirements, etc.) with knowledgeable staff personnel who will be involved in the program and members of the human resources (HR) department. The HR perspective can be useful background information.

3. Develop a plan for the remainder of the job analysis. With the help of a point person responsible for the program, make decisions about such issues as:
   a. Whether or not job content experts (JCEs) will be interviewed as a group or as individuals.
   b. The number and identity of the people to be interviewed. At this stage, a broad spectrum of potential stakeholders and end users should be asked to participate. In our experience, when these persons express skepticism about the mission, process, or content of the program itself, participation in program development is often enough to allay their concerns.
   c. The creation of a formally recognized "Management Advisory Board" (MAB)—or some other appropriate title—if JCEs are to be interviewed as a group. This will convey the importance of the project to the organization, facilitate communications and usually result in high-visibility JCEs identifying with and supporting the program.
   d. The development of timelines for all important aspects of the program. Work backward from the time the initial program is to be administered and provide generous time for simulation design.

After developing a basic understanding of job content, arrange a meeting with a sample of high-level line management stakeholders who will ultimately use the results for promotion decisions. Some of these people may have been involved in the decision to create a TBAC and will have an appreciation of its purpose and content. If this is not the case, make a presentation that will provide them with this information. If stakeholders understand that an effective TBAC will make their jobs easier by enhancing the effectiveness of the organization's newly promoted managers, they can be expected to be cooperative. Issues appropriate for this discussion include:

1. Current performance issues and why the program is needed.
2. Anticipated changes in the content or importance of current job functions.
3. Perspectives on the most important tasks or job functions that managers in the target job must perform.

After this meeting you will probably have sufficient information to create an interview guide. This will be needed if you are conducting individual meetings or meeting with a MAB. At a minimum, this guide should include:

1. An introduction or presentation to explain the purpose of the session and what must be achieved.
2. Open-ended questions based on the insights developed at this point in the job analysis process, such as:
   a. What are the most challenging tasks the managers have to deal with?
   b. What activities consume the bulk of the manager's time?
   c. When managers perform poorly, what tasks seem to be associated with their most significant challenges?

Whether using a MAB or interviewing individuals, it is a good idea to inform people to be interviewed of the meeting's purpose and allow them to begin thinking about things to discuss in advance of your questioning. If using a MAB, it is a good idea to have a high-level manager initiate the first meeting by describing the importance of the project, reiterating the purpose of the meeting, and demonstrating his/her commitment to the process. If interviewing individuals, a letter or e-mail from such a person is suggested. Whether you are meeting with individuals or a MAB, it is a good idea to be briefed by your point person about what to expect from the individuals who will be interviewed. Your goals for this initial meeting (individual or group) are to:

1. Identify major job functions (what incumbents spend their time doing).
2. Develop an appreciation of the relative importance of the different job functions.
3. Understand the most significant challenges associated with performance of the different job functions.
4. Determine patterns of responses that differentiate highly effective managers from less effective managers at specified job functions.

If possible, it is appropriate for those being interviewed to describe situations when managers were either particularly effective or ineffective when engaged in a specified job function. Techniques for getting the most from these meetings include:

1. Asking open-ended questions and allowing sufficient time for responses and discussion.
2. Encouraging and reinforcing detailed input.
3. Questioning and following up aggressively.
4. Checking frequently for understanding.

5. Summarizing issues discussed by reviewing your notes and conveying insights developed. Seeking and encouraging feedback regarding the accuracy of your understanding of key information.

During the meeting, take detailed notes and associate managers' names with the comments and contributions they make. This will be useful if you have follow-up questions about specific issues. Before concluding the meeting, be sure to ask the managers if you can contact them again to follow up on things that may need additional explanation or clarification.

After you have reviewed your notes and developed an outline of your findings, actively seek detailed feedback in writing to ensure understanding of important issues. This can be done by:

1. Developing a questionnaire that describes the job functions and the issues associated with them in detail. An excerpt from one of these questionnaires is provided in Section I of Appendix C of http://www.tbacs.org. Following the functional approach of Fine and Cronshaw (1999), this questionnaire should capture the frequency and importance of engaging in the job-related behaviors listed, as well as the mode (e.g., meetings, phone calls, written communications, etc.) by which these issues are likely to be addressed. The behaviors that are deemed relevant for inclusion in the program can be grouped together to create a job function or individual simulation. If a written or electronic questionnaire is administered, it is also important to be sensitive to other demands on the time of respondents and avoid redundancy in questionnaire content.
2. Summarizing your understanding of the major job functions and associated challenges in a report that is sent for confirmation to the people interviewed.

The use of the questionnaire described above will result in an audit trail that will serve as a useful design document and help establish and document the content-related validity of both the simulation and the evaluation tools.

Developing Simulation Content. The separation of job analysis from the creation of simulation content is at least somewhat artificial. Although separated physically in time, ideas associated with possible simulation content will probably occur spontaneously during the job analysis process. As you become comfortable with your knowledge of job content, it is appropriate to test ideas for simulation content on the JCEs being interviewed.

As a general rule, simulation content should be developed as directly as possible from job analysis findings. As in conducting the job analysis, the role of the I/O psychologist is not to make interpretive judgments but to convey the job and its challenges as they were described. There should be no tricks or gimmicks in simulation content (e.g., efforts to artificially induce participant stress, use of deception, etc.). Such efforts will serve no purpose and reduce program credibility.

As a designer, your primary audience for credibility is the team of JCEs—not the participants. It is unlikely that participants will be aware of the range of problems and situations handled by their supervisors. The people participating in the program have, in all likelihood, been effective, conscientious employees throughout their careers. They will have little appreciation for the range of problems some of their peers may have caused for their managers.

Some important suggestions associated with enhancing the realism of simulation content include:

1. Avoid placing the simulation in the actual client or focal organization. Although this can enhance realism, there can be unintended consequences associated with this strategy. For example, small changes in the organization (a new product, a merger with another organization, a policy change, etc.) can create major distractions and result in otherwise unnecessary redesign. Instead, create a fictitious organization that closely parallels the structure and operating environment of the target organization. Candidates will still relate to simulation content, but the program will not require as much redesign and will better protect potentially sensitive information.
2. Integrate all simulation content into a coordinated story line, where all simulations are placed in the same organization and occur within a clearly delineated timeframe.
3. Design the TBAC so that evaluation of performance in the various simulations is not *interdependent*. In other words, performance on one simulation should not directly impact performance on another, and performance within each simulation should be evaluated independently. By necessity, some simulations will be naturally and inextricably associated with others. For example, if candidates are required to analyze sales or manufacturing data in order to prepare a business assessment that will be presented to their new boss, this information may also be used as background for handling inbox problems, preparing for one-on-one meetings with subordinates, preparing for a team meeting, etc. A fail-

ure to conduct an effective business analysis should, at least indirectly, have a negative impact on the performance of related simulations. Even so, we strongly recommend that simulations linked in this manner be *evaluated* separately as stand-alone events.

4. Do not make candidates work with the individual simulations in a vacuum. In addition to background provided by quantified information such as that described above, provide general background information that managers would likely have at their disposal. Information on products, subordinates, competitors, etc., can provide a realistic context for decision making and problem solving.
5. Make one-on-one leadership interactions as realistic as possible. The problems and the situations portrayed by the role-players (who should be the evaluating managers) should come directly from the job analysis. Reponses to likely comments and tactics initiated by the candidates should be consistent with job analysis findings and be carefully scripted and studied by role-players. Although some companies have used professional actors for role-players, we do not recommend this practice. These events are not the place for contrived drama, and it is much more important for role-players to be JCEs who can draw from their personal experiences and knowledge of the job to develop realistic, job-related responses to unanticipated candidate questions and tactics. We also recommend that the setting for the interaction be as natural as possible. For example, it is not necessary for an evaluator to be in the room taking notes. Instead, we recommend that the interaction be captured in an unobtrusive manner (e.g., audio, video, or digital recording). After playing the role, the evaluation team member can review the interaction and evaluate performance. This reduces the cognitive load on the evaluator, who does not have to simultaneously engage in the role play while evaluating performance. The ability to review the interaction should further enhance the accuracy of the assessment.
6. Develop inbox or office day simulation items as directly as possible from job analysis findings. In our experience, only problems likely to be encountered through e-mail or telephone should be addressed in this setting. Appendix C (Section I, Column 3, "Mode of Resolution"; see http://www.tbacs.org) indicates how this can be determined. To further enhance the reality of this simulation, we offer the following recommendations:
   a. Allow participants to respond directly and electronically to e-mails that are presented on their computers. If organizational resources permit, a simulated e-mail inbox environment is very useful for this purpose.
   b. Allow candidates to respond to some issues via voice mail. Actual voice mailboxes, condenser microphones with required software

installed on participants' computers, or even small handheld microcassette recorders are helpful in this regard.

c. Present some issues via voice mail. Again, actual voice mailboxes or small tape recorders can be used.
d. Interrupt work on the items with telephone calls. Based on job analysis results, develop scripts for the role players making the calls. These calls may come from various sources (e.g., customers, employees, supervisors or peer managers). As with all face-to-face interactions, these calls should be recorded so that role players can separate playing the role from making evaluations. Small tape recorders with embedded recording devices or the use of speaker phones make this process simple to administer.
e. Advise participants to read through all e-mails before taking action on any issue. Some of the issues will be related, and this information will provide additional context for decision making.

TBAC inboxes are substantially different from inboxes used in traditional assessment centers in several key aspects. Item content is more realistic. Again, because they are achievement measures and participants will be evaluated on the quality of their solutions, TBAC inboxes are *power tests*. Thus, participants should be given sufficient time to complete the items. In our experience, candidates should be given at least 5 hours (optionally broken into 2 different periods if candidate fatigue is a concern) to complete a 15-item inbox.

There are no hard and fast rules for the number or content of simulation elements that are used in a TBAC. Depending on the complexity of the target managerial job, the TBACs we have designed and administered have utilized between 4 and 6 independent simulations, which can typically be completed in 1½ to 2½ days.

Reviewing and Confirming Simulation Content. After simulation content has been developed, it must be reviewed by the team of JCEs used in the job analysis process. If you have contacted them individually with questions as you developed content, major changes may not be required. Conversely, if the job analysis was conducted with the assistance of a MAB, this group should be reconvened. To conserve their valuable time, the simulation should be given to each member in advance of the meeting. Be sure to remind them of the security requirements associated with handling and discussing this material (i.e., program content should not be distributed within the organization so that it could be viewed by potential candidates). These meetings can be handled face-to-face or through a series of conference calls. When they have been completed and the MAB is satisfied with simulation content, it is time to develop the evaluation methodology.

Developing Evaluation Standards. The determination of evaluation standards occurs after the JCEs have agreed upon what candidates must accomplish in each simulation. The standard is typically what JCEs, as managers of people in the target job, would expect of effective new managers. (Higher performance standards and expectations would naturally be applied to experienced, effective managers.) Through the years, we have noticed that some organizations require significantly different standards than others. Again, it is not the role of the I/O psychologist to challenge an organization's performance standards. It is, however, the psychologist's role to structure the evaluation process to ensure that effective new manager performance remains the consistent standard for all evaluations.

Performance standards or outcome requirements must be developed for each simulation. Much of this detail can be developed directly from the job analysis questionnaire (Section II of Appendix C). To ensure the accuracy and comprehensiveness of this content, it is critical to elicit very specific behavioral detail from members of the MAB during job analysis interviews or group meetings. The inbox can provide a unique challenge for the development of performance standards. When addressing the inbox with the MAB, treat each item as an independent case study and have them develop minimum performance objectives or desired outcomes for each item.

After all performance standards or outcomes have been established, the structure of the evaluation process can be developed. Usually the outcomes agreed upon by the MAB fall into rather well-defined performance objectives. As stated previously, inbox items may be grouped into *Operational* and *Personnel* issues, with some items likely containing elements of both. Performance on each inbox item can be evaluated and the evaluations organized under these headings. In the example we have provided (see Figure 9.1), performance in one-on-one leadership meetings is clustered under the performance objectives *of Information Gathering, Initiating Change*, and *Solution Development*. Performance under these subheadings is considered when determining an overall evaluation for each simulation. Depending upon the preference of the organization, these summary evaluations may be derived mathematically, or by consensus of the evaluation team members. As mentioned earlier in this chapter, when leadership/management development is a serious program objective, we recommend the team consensus approach.

Evaluation of each performance objective is supported by structured evaluation processes directly associated with the performance standards identified by the JCEs. In some cases, such as in the analysis of sales data, there are "correct" answers to questions. In some situations, members of the evaluation team must determine whether or not actions taken by candidates would have achieved certain clearly stated objectives (e.g., motivated a subordinate to increase job effort, satisfied an external customer, delivered a compelling message while leading a team meeting). In cases where judgment is required in the evaluation process, accuracy is enhanced by the degree of realism or fidelity of the scenario to the target job, the evaluator's knowledge of what is required for successful performance, and the fact that the evaluation is made by a team.

Final Thoughts

We believe that TBAC methodology offers a practical, research-based, common-sense alternative to the traditional assessment center approach. Many of the advantages we see to the TBAC approach result from the shift from an aptitude-based (i.e., dimensional) to a licensure-based (i.e., task) paradigm for managerial selection and development. In fact, as scientist-practitioners we are somewhat puzzled as to why the status quo adherence to the traditional dimension-based approach has persisted for so long. Since Sackett and Dreher's original study in 1982, nearly heroic statistical machinations have been offered in an effort to defend DBAC construct validity and the legitimacy of dimensions as building blocks of AC structure (Arthur et al., 2003; Lievens, 1998, 2002; Lievens et al., 2006; Lievens & Conway, 2001; Woehr & Arthur, 2003). At best, the general conclusion is that the construct validity problem may not be quite as severe as originally believed (Woehr & Arthur, 2003), but it has not yet been resolved. Furthermore, no compelling theoretical or practical justifications as to why dimensions *should* be retained have *ever* been presented.

In contrast, task- or functionally-based assessment is more aligned with the type of performance evaluation that occurs on the job. It results in the type of information that organizations typically use for decision making, and it provides developmental feedback that is pragmatic and actionable. In our experience, the direct relevance of simulation content and the transparency of the process generate positive reactions and greater acceptance of performance feedback among candidates. Finally, TBAC evaluations provide organizational decision makers with an assessment of candidate readiness to take up the mantle of leadership which does not rely so heavily on inference. We hope that traditional DBAC practitioners will consider the TBAC approach when cultivating future leaders and that our work and ideas will stimulate research that assists in the evolution and refinement of this methodology.

Note

1. All materials may also be downloaded as PDF files. We recommend that the reader print copies of these materials, as they will frequently be referenced throughout the remainder of this chapter.

References

Archambeau, D. J. (1979). Relationships among skill ratings assigned in an assessment center. *Journal of Assessment Center Technology, 2*, 7–19.

Arthur, W., Jr., Day, E. A., McNelly, T. L., & Edens, P. S. (2003). A meta-analysis of the criterion-related validity of assessment center dimensions. *Personnel Psychology, 56*, 125–154.

Brockner, J., & Wiesenfeld, B. M. (1996). An integrative framework for explaining reactions to decisions: Interactive effects of outcomes and procedures. *Psychological Bulletin, 120*, 189–208.

Eurich, T. L., Krause, D. E., Cigularov, K., & Thornton, G. C., III (2006, April). *Assessment centers: Current practices in the United States.* Paper presented at the meeting of the Society for Industrial and Organizational Psychology, Dallas, TX.

Fine, S. A., & Cronshaw, S. F. (1999). *Functional job analysis: A foundation for human resources management.* Mahwah, NJ: Erlbaum.

Fleenor, J. W. (1996). Constructs and developmental assessment centers: Further troubling empirical findings. *Journal of Business and Psychology, 10*, 319–335.

Gaugler, B. B., Rosenthal, D. B., Thornton, G. C., III, & Bentson, C. (1987). Meta-analysis of assessment center validity. *Journal of Applied Psychology, 72*, 493–511.

Gaugler, B. B., & Thornton, G. C. (1989). Number of assessment center dimensions as a determinate of assessor accuracy. *Journal of Applied Psychology, 74*, 611–618.

Goodge, P. (1988). Task-based assessment. *Journal of European Industrial Training, 12*, 22–27.

Glenday, C. (2007). *Guinness book of world records.* London: Guinness World Records.

Harris, M. M., Becker, A. S., & Smith, D. E. (1993). Does the assessment center scoring method affect the cross-situational consistency of ratings? *Journal of Applied Psychology, 78*, 675–678.

Jackson, D. J. R. (2007, April). *Task-specific assessment centers: Evidence of predictive validity and fairness.* Paper presented at the 22nd annual meeting of the Society for Industrial and Organizational Psychology, New York, NY.

Jackson, D. J. R., Barney, A. R., Stillman, J. A., & Kirkley, W. (2007). When traits are behaviors: The relationship between behavioral responses and trait-based overall assessment center ratings. *Human Performance, 20,* 415–432.

Jackson, D. J. R., Stillman, J. A., & Atkins, S. G. (2005). Rating tasks versus dimensions in assessment centers: A psychometric comparison. *Human Performance, 18,* 213–241.

Joyce, L. W., Thayer, P. W., & Pond, S. B., III (1994). Managerial functions: An alternative to traditional assessment center dimensions? *Personnel Psychology, 47,* 109–121.

Kluger, A. N., & DeNisi, A. (1996). The effects of feedback interventions of performance: A historical review, a meta-analysis, and a preliminary feedback intervention theory. *Psychological Bulletin, 119,* 254–284.

Lance, C. E. (2008). Why assessment centers do not work the way they are supposed to. *Industrial and Organizational Psychology: Perspectives on Science and Practice, 1,* 84–97.

Lance, C. E., Foster, M. R., Gentry, W. A., & Thoresen, J. D. (2004). Assessor cognitive processes in an operational assessment center. *Journal of Applied Psychology, 89,* 22–35.

Lance, C. E., Lambert, T. A., Gewin, A. G., Lievens, F., & Conway, J. M. (2004). Revised estimates of dimension and exercise variance components in assessment center postexercise dimension ratings. *Journal of Applied Psychology, 89,* 377–385.

Lievens, F. (1998). Factors which improve the construct validity of assessment centers: A review. *International Journal of Selection and Assessment, 6,* 141–152.

Lievens, F. (2001). Assessor training strategies and their effects on accuracy, interrater reliability, and discriminant validity. *Journal of Applied Psychology, 86,* 255–264.

Lievens, F. (2002). Trying to understand the different pieces of the construct validity puzzle of assessment centers: An examination of assessor and assessee effects. *Journal of Applied Psychology, 87,* 675–686.

Lievens, F., Chasteen, C. S., Day, E. A., & Christiansen, N. D. (2006). Large-scale investigation of the role of trait activation theory for understanding assessment center convergent and discriminant validity. *Journal of Applied Psychology, 91,* 247–258.

Lievens, F., & Conway, J. M. (2001). Dimension and exercise variance in assessment center scores: A large-scale evaluation of multitrait-multimethod studies. *Journal of Applied Psychology, 86,* 1202–1222.

McCrae, R. R., & Costa, P. T., Jr. (1994). The stability of personality: Observations and evaluations. *Current Directions in Psychological Science, 3,*173–175.

Meriac, J. P., Hoffman, B. J., Woehr, D. J., & Fleisher, M. (2008). Further evidence for the validity of assessment center dimensions: A meta-analysis of internal and external correlates. *Journal of Applied Psychology, 93,* 1042–1052.

Reilly, R. R., Henry, S., & Smither, J. W. (1990). An examination of the effects of using behavior checklists on the construct validity of assessment center dimensions. *Personnel Psychology, 43,* 71–84.

Roth, P. L., Bobko, P., & McFarland, L. A. (2005). A meta-analysis of work sample test validity: Updating and integrating some classic literature. *Personnel Psychology, 58,* 1009–1037.

Rupp, D. E., Gibbons, A. M., Baldwin, A. M., Spain, S. M., Woo, S. D., Brummel, B., et al. (2006). An initial validation of developmental assessment centers as accurate assessments and effective training interventions. *Psychologist-Manager Journal, 21,* 171–200.

Russell, C. J. (1985). Individual decision processes in an assessment center. *Journal of Applied Psychology, 70,* 737–746.

Sackett, P. R., & Dreher, G. F. (1982). Constructs and assessment center dimensions: Some troubling empirical findings. *Journal of Applied Psychology, 67,* 401–410.

Sackett, P. R., & Wilson, M. A. (1982). Factors affecting the consensus judgment process in management assessment centers. *Journal of Applied Psychology, 67,* 10–17.

Schleicher, D. J., Day, D. V., Mayes, B. T., & Riggio, R. E. (2002). A new frame for frame-of-reference training: Enhancing the construct validity of assessment centers. *Journal of Applied Psychology, 87,* 735–746.

Srivastava, S., John, O. P., Gosling, S. D., & Potter, J. (2003). Development of personality in early and middle adulthood: Set like plaster or persistent change. *Journal of Personality and Social Psychology, 84,* 1041–1053.

Taylor, H. C., & Russell, J. T. (1939). The relationship of validity coefficient to the practical effectiveness of tests in selection: Discussion and tables. *Journal of Applied Psychology, 23,* 565–578.

Thornton, G. C., III, & Byham, W. C. (1982). *Assessment centers and managerial performance.* New York: Academic Press.

Thornton, G. C., III, & Rupp, D. E. (2006). *Assessment centers in human resource management: Strategies for prediction, diagnosis, and development.* Mahwah, NJ: Erlbaum.

Wernimont, P. F., & Campbell, J. P. (1968). Signs, samples, and criteria. *Personnel Psychology, 52,* 372–376.

Wingrove, J., Jones, A., & Herriot, P. (1985). The predictive validity of pre- and post-discussion assessment centre ratings. *Journal of Occupational Psychology, 58,* 189–192.

Woehr, D. J., & Arthur, W. (2003). The construct-related validity of assessment center ratings: A review and meta-analysis of the role of methodological factors. *Journal of Management, 29,* 231–258.

Woehr, D. J., Arthur, W., Jr., & Bowler, M. (2002, April). *A meta-analytic examination of the impact of methodological factors on assessment center validity.* Paper presented at the meeting of the Society for Industrial and Organizational Psychology, Toronto, ON.

10

Research into Task-Based Assessment Centers

Charles E. Lance
The University of Georgia

The purpose of this chapter is to review the existing research on task-based assessment centers (TBACs). I will provide a(nother) brief sketch of the history of assessment centers (ACs) as backdrop to the recent resurgence in interest in TBACs as an alternative design strategy to more traditional dimension-based ACs (DBACs), summarize what is known about TBACs to date, and suggest some directions for future research on TBACs.

A(nother) Brief History of the AC

As Highhouse and Nolan (Chapter 2, this volume) point out, there are usually a number of different ways to construct and report a history, including the history of a personnel selection technique such as ACs. I will structure this brief history in terms of four eras that I will refer to as the Wartime Era, the Industrial Application Era, the Construct Validity Era, and the Current Era.

The Wartime Era can be characterized as the application of holistic assessments such as psychiatric interviews, psychological tests, physical activities, and situational exercises in the selection of officers in the German, British, American, Australian, and New Zealand military in World War II. I will not summarize the state of the practice during this era as comprehensive reviews have already been provided by Highhouse (2002; Highhouse & Nolan, Chapter 2, this volume), Howard (2010), Murray (1990), and Thornton and Byham (1982). The Industrial Application Era saw the evolution and transportation of these wartime selection efforts to (primarily) managerial selection in (again, primarily) American companies such as AT&T, SOHIO, GE, IBM, and Sears in the 1950s through the 1970s. These efforts have also been documented and reviewed in such seminal works as Bray (1989), Bray, Campbell, and Grant (1974), Finkle (1976), Howard (2010), Moses and Byham (1977), and Thornton and Byham (1982).

Then, in 1982 the Construct Validity Era began with Sackett and Dreher's publication of what they referred to as some "troubling empirical findings" (p. 401). As is described by Thornton and Rupp (Chapter 7, this volume), one scoring strategy in DBACs is to obtain dimensional ratings after the completion of each exercise, yielding what are now often referred to as post-exercise dimension ratings (PEDRs). Sackett and Dreher found that factor analyses of these PEDRs resulted in factors defined *not* by the dimensions that were assessed in the ACs they studied, but by the exercises that were used to assess the dimensions.[1] When viewed through a multitrait-multimethod (MTMM) matrix lens, where the dimensions represent the traits and the exercise represent the methods, these findings are indeed troubling because PEDRs apparently do not reflect the dimensions (traits) they were designed to assess but instead reflect the methods employed to assess them. And it was this basic pattern of findings, replicated dozens of times in the 1980s through the 2000s (see Lance, Lambert, Gewin, Lievens, & Conway, 2004), that sent AC researchers on a 25-year-long mission to solve the AC construct validity problem. Researchers investigated variations in such factors as the number of dimensions assessed, participant-to-assessor ratios, assessor qualification (e.g., managers vs. psychologists), type and extent of assessor training, and AC purpose (Lievens, 1998) in efforts to increase relationships between like dimensions assessed in different exercises (i.e., increase "convergent validity") and reduce correlations among different dimensions assessed in the same exercise (increase "discriminant validity"). Unfortunately, these (often very clever) "design fixes" had little or no effect on convergent and discriminant validity (in a traditional MTMM sense) and when they did, their effects were often in the opposite direction. For example, Woehr and Arthur's (2003) meta-analysis showed that PEDR discriminant validity was better for psychologist (vs. manager) assessors, and when assessor training was conducted (as would be expected), but discriminant validity was also better for *greater* numbers of dimensions, *high* participant-to-assessor ratios, and *shorter* (vs. longer) rater training programs (counter to expectations). Thus it appeared that AC construct validity (in this traditional MTMM sense) had little or no chance of being salvaged.

The beginning of the end of the Construct Validity Era might be traced to a series of studies by Lance and colleagues in the 2000s (Lance, Foster, Gentry, & Thoresen, 2004; Lance, Foster, Nemeth, Gentry, & Drollinger, 2007; Lance et al., 2000; Lance, Lambert, et al., 2004) that suggested that perhaps ACs need not be fixed in the first place. One critical point that these studies established was that the Exercise factors that are invariably found in factor analysis of PEDRs should *not* be interpreted as representing performance-irrelevant common method bias (as is implied by a MTMM lens on the AC design fix challenge) but as representing true cross-situational (i.e., cross-exercise) specificity in candidate performance. That is, performance overall, and with respect to the PEDRs assessed in each exercise would be *expected* to vary across exercises because the situational characteristics, performance demands, and associated knowledge, skill, and ability requirements themselves vary across the different exercises. These robust findings also led Lance and colleagues to suggest that ACs could profitably be re-engineered away from the assessment of (what were presumed by some to be cross-situationally consistent) dimensions and toward the assessment of what ACs are apparently assessing already—performance in distinct simulated tasks. That is, why not move toward a more task-based assessment if that is the way ACs apparently already work anyway?

If Lance and colleagues' studies can be viewed as marking the beginning of the end of the Construct Validity Era, the exchange of articles in the inaugural issue of *Industrial and Organizational Psychology: Perspectives on Science and Practice* (IOP) could perhaps be viewed as signaling the beginning of the Current Era. In my feature article, I reviewed the AC construct validity literature and concluded that (a) AC candidate performance is inherently cross-situationally (i.e., cross-exercise) specific, (b) assessors are generally quite accurate at observing and rating candidate performance, and (c) that ACs should be redesigned toward task- or role-based assessments and away from traditional dimension-based assessment (Lance, 2008a). My message was generally *not* well received. Critics' comments expressed their unwillingness to give up dimensions in ACs, their reluctance to give up on design fixes and suggested that the assessment of construct validity involves more than just the MTMM approach. In my rebuttal (Lance, 2008b), I replied to these critiques and argued that it was an unfortunate adoption of the MTMM "urban legend" (Lance, Baranik, Lau,

& Scharlau, 2009; Lance & Vandenberg, 2009; Vandenberg, 2006) that was responsible for "sending researchers on a 25-year long detour to fix an organizational intervention that was not broken in the first place" (Lance, Dawson, Birklebach, & Hoffman, 2010, p. 441). The main benefit from this exchange of ideas was to bring to the surface several current controversies concerning the design and implementation of, and research on ACs and one of these controversies was the legitimization of task-based approaches to assessment.

TBAC Research

Pre-Current Era Literature

But in fact, these ideas had already been expressed years earlier. For example, Griffeths and Allen (1987) and Goodge (1988) argued how, in "breaking with tradition" (Griffeths & Allen,1987, p. 18) task-based ACs could be designed under the guiding principles of (a) sampling critical tasks or job functions as exercises for assessment, (b) eliminating assessment according to skills (i.e., dimensions), (c) providing assessors with observational checklists for assessment, and (d) substituting mechanical combination of assessor judgments for clinical combination during consensus meetings. Griffeths and Allen and Goodge argued that task-based (versus more traditional skill-based) assessments would insure content validity, reduce subjectivity, and substantially reduce the costs of assessment.

Around the same time, and in the context of the Construct Validity Era research effort other researchers became keenly aware of the robustness of findings such as those presented by Sackett and Dreher (1982) and suggested that since AC performance seemed to be clustered around tasks rather than dimensions, that a task-based focus for assessment would be a very reasonable alternative (e.g., Iles, 1992; Robertson, Gratton, & Sharpley, 1987). Also, Lowry (1995, 1997) described in detail procedures for the development, implementation, and evaluation of TBACs in the public sector, including job analysis, selection of job simulations, development of task checklists, assessor training, and procedures for assessing interrater reliability (IRR) in and content validity of TBACs. Preliminary evidence from these studies indicated that (a) assessors preferred the concrete task checklists in TBACs over dimension-based assessment in DBACs, (b) IRRs were in the .80s up to .95 range, and (c) candidates preferred the more specific task-based feedback afforded by TBACs over more traditional DBAC-based feedback. However, these early works went largely unacknowledged for many years.

In one unique study that bridges the Construct Validity and Current Eras, Lovler, Rose, and Wesley (2002) developed an unusual (at the time) AC that contained three exercises (Employee Discussion, Problem Analysis, and an In-Basket) and eight dimensions (Analytical Thinking, Problem Solving, Coaching, Planning/Time Management, Flexibility, Interpersonal Skills/Relationship Building, Oral Communication, and Written Communication). What was unusual about their AC was that PEDRs were not measured using traditional dimension ratings, but lists of behavioral checklist items nested within dimensions. As such, a PEDR-level assessment was attained by aggregating checklist-level ratings within dimensions for each exercise separately. What was interesting about this study was that when PEDR-level aggregate scores were factor analyzed, factors clearly defined by exercises emerged (as in virtually every other Construct Validity Era study). However, when checklist-item-level ratings were factored *within* exercises, factors clearly defined by *dimensions* emerged. As suggested by the authors, these findings indicate that AC dimensions are construct valid at the dimension *X* exercise level, but not as cross-situationally (i.e., cross-exercise) stable constructs because performance itself is cross-situationally (i.e., cross-exercise) specific.

Several other pre-current era studies also investigated the reliability and validity of tasks that are often included as individual AC exercises, but independent of the construct validity question. For example, Bass (1954) provided an early review of research on the leaderless group discussion (LGD) conducted in several samples of college students, ROTC cadets, and sales, management, and administrative personnel. LGD IRRs were in the .80s and .90s, the average test-retest reliability across 8 studies reviewed was .69, and the median correlation between LGD ratings and independent peer rating and nomination criteria was .39 across 17 studies. Also, the average correlation between LGD ratings and various measures of cognitive ability was .28 across 12 studies.

A number of other pre-current era studies also investigated the reliability and validity of in-basket tasks (e.g., Brass & Oldham, 1976). Schippman, Prien, and Katz (1990) provided a narrative review of these studies, concluded that both IRR and validity of in-basket scores varied considerably across studies and, consequently, questioned the utility of in-basket tasks. More recently, Collins, Schmidt, Sanchez-Ku, Thomas, McDaniel, and Le (2003) conducted a large-scale meta-analysis (MA) of individual difference predictors of AC ratings. While their MA focused mainly on predictors of AC overall ratings, they did report mean uncorrected correlations of .32 and .36 between general cognitive ability and LGD and in-basket performance, respectively. Thus pre-current era research provides some support for the reliability and validity for two tasks (LGD and in-basket) that are often included in operational ACs and the idea that performance in both tasks is related to candidate cognitive ability. Related to this latter point, Goldstein, Yusko, Braverman, Smith, and Chung (1998) showed that performance in some exercises (e.g., two in-baskets and a team preparation exercise) were more strongly related to cognitive ability that were others (e.g., subordinate meeting, group discussion) and that exercise scores' relationships with supervisor ratings collected as part of a 360-degree performance measurement system changed very little once cognitive ability scores were partialed out. Thus, Goldstein et al.'s results suggest that although cognitive ability is a stronger determinant of some AC exercises than others, performance in AC exercises retains incremental validity in predicting job performance above and beyond cognitive ability.

Current Era Research

More recently, and more clearly as part of the Current Era of research on ACs, Jackson and colleagues have spearheaded much of the recent research on TBACs (e.g., Jackson, 2007, 2010; Jackson, Ahmad, & Grace, 2010; Jackson, Barney, Stillman, & Kirkley, 2007; Jackson, Englert, & Brown, 2009; Jackson, Englert, & Stillman, 2010; Jackson, Stillman, & Atkins, 2005; Jackson, Stillman, & Englert, 2010; Stillman & Jackson, 2005). Some of this research has aimed at assessing and documenting IRR of TBAC checklist ratings. Note that other forms of reliability estimates are inappropriate as candidate performance true scores are not expected to be consistent across exercises (in fact this is one the major findings from the Construct Validity Era; thus retest reliability estimates are obviated) or consistent across task elements within exercises (obviating internal consistency estimates). For example, Jackson et al. (2009) replicated Lowry's (1995) earlier findings in showing IRR for TBAC checklist ratings in the .83 to .95 range. Also, Stillman and Jackson (2005) used Signal Detection Theory to analyze TBAC data and showed that checklist ratings were reliable but somewhat lenient. Jackson et al. (2005) and Jackson (2010) used generalizability theory to parse variance in TBAC checklist ratings into various variance components and estimated ratings' dependability coefficients (analogous to reliabilities) to be in the .80s and .90s. Finally, in an extension of work relating to multisource performance ratings (e.g., Hoffman, Lance, Bynum, & Gentry, 2010), Hoffman, Melchers, and Kleinmann (2010) showed that first-order idiosyncratic assessor factors loaded strongly on second-order exercise factors, demonstrating (a) high IRR among assessors, and (b) once again, that exercise factors represent cross-situationally specific candidate performance and not mere halo in assessors' ratings. Thus, while research in this area is still young, there appears to be accumulating evidence that TBAC raters' checklist ratings are highly reliable.

As regards another major psychometric criterion—validity—there is less research on TBACs, especially as it relates to criterion-related validity. In one of two studies to date, Jackson (2007), using a managerial sample, showed that a task-based overall rating correlated .42 (uncorrected for attenuation or range restriction) with supervisor ratings of candidates' on-the-job performance obtained one year later using the host organization's existing performance appraisal instrument. Jackson also found that TBAC ratings were unrelated to ethnicity and gender and only weakly related to age (r = -.18). In a second study, Lance et al. (2007) compared dimension-based and task-based scoring systems in an AC used as part of a promotional system for police officers. They found that a general performance factor derived from both the dimension-based ratings and the task-based ratings correlated r = .29 with supervisor performance ratings obtained six months later for research purposes only and that exercise-specific factors correlated moderately (rs ranged .14–.28) with performance ratings and job knowledge test scores that were used, in part, to screen candidates into the AC. Thus although very limited, the evidence to date indicates that TBACs have criterion-related validities that are on the order of, or perhaps higher than those of DBACs (Gaugler, Rosenthal, Thornton, & Bentsen, 1987; Hardison & Sackett, 2004).

Other studies have sought direct comparisons of the internal structures of DBAC and TBAC scoring systems. In the first of these, and consistent with Lance et al.'s (2004) Construct Validity Era findings, Jackson et al. (2005) supported an Exercise-only factor structure for both DBAC and TBAC scoring systems. On the other hand, Lance et al.

(2007) found support for a 3-Exercise/1-Dimension (i.e., a general performance factor) confirmatory factor analysis (CFA) solution for both dimension- and task-based ratings. Jackson, Englert, et al. (2010) found support for a 4-Exercise only model for TBAC data but a 3-Exercise/1-Dimension model for DBAC data. Finally, Jackson, Ahmad, et al. (2010) argued that TBAC ratings are not necessarily entirely situationally specific, and supported a 4-Exercise/1-Dimension model for TBAC task checklist ratings. Collectively, these findings are consistent with Lance et al.'s (2004) findings—the internal structure of ACs is almost always characterized by factors representing cross-situationally specific exercise performance, but may include also a general factor that represents the extent to which candidates perform generally well or not so well across all exercises. Why does the general factor appear sometimes and sometimes not? We return to this question later.

One final area concerns rater training in TBACs. Jackson et al. (2005) found that frame of reference training (FORT) benefitted IRR in both a TBAC and a DBAC but that DBAC raters benefitted more. This suggests that the more concrete TBAC checklist ratings are naturally easier and require less training for raters to "get on the same page" as compared to more traditional dimension-based ratings (see also Goodge, 1988). In a second study, Jackson et al. (2009) demonstrated that IRR increased progressively across trials in a FORT program for three different groups of TBAC assessors. Thus from these few studies it appears that the beneficial effects of FORT (Woehr & Huffcutt, 1994) generalize to TBAC checklist ratings.

Tentative Conclusions and Directions for Future TBAC Research

I began this chapter by claiming that there is not yet much research on TBACs to summarize in this chapter. By understanding that research on TBACs really only began at the commencement of the Current Era, it is understandable why—the Current Era began somewhere around 2002 to 2008. Yet already one can draw some conclusions from research that has been reported that likely will stand the test of time and additional scrutiny:

1. TBAC assessors' checklist ratings have high IRR and are at least as reliable as more traditional DBAC ratings. As suggested by Goodge (1988) nearly 25 years ago, this likely stems from the fact that checklist items

refer to directly observable and easily evaluated behaviors and do not require additional inferences regarding dimensional category membership that more conventional DBAC judgments require (see also Jackson, Stillman, et al., 2010, for an elaboration of this argument).

2. Like DBAC-based PEDRs (Lance et al., 2004), TBAC checklist ratings' internal structure is largely cross-situationally (i.e., cross-exercise) specific, though sometimes a general performance factor that represents generally good or poor performance across all or most exercises also emerges. Because this structure emerges almost identically for DBAC and TBAC data, I suspect that this structure reflects the inherent latent structure of candidate performance, and not some aspect of the manner in which the rating data are collected (Lance, 2008a).
3. TBACs are perceived as fair, job-related, and as providing useful specific feedback, especially in comparison to more traditional DBACs. Because of the concreteness of checklist items, ratings should be perceived as being more behaviorally based, more objective, more closely tied to on-the-job performance requirements, and instrumental in diagnosing areas for performance improvement as compared to more traditional DBAC ratings. As one example, Thornton, Kaman, Layer, and Larsh (1995) found that task-based feedback was found to be at least as effective as more traditional attribute- (i.e., dimension-) based feedback in terms of recipient reactions and subsequent behavior change.
4. TBACs are at least as good a predictor of job performance as are DBACs. This should not be surprising as TBACs may in some sense be viewed as a hybrid of more traditional DBACs and traditional work samples, which have also been researched for years (Truxillo, Donahue, & Kuang, 2004; see Jackson, 2010, for an excellent discussion of distinctions between TBACs and work sample tests) and so in some sense it might be expected that the validities of TBACs would fall somewhere in between those of more traditional DBACs (around .37) and work sample tests (around .54; Schmidt & Hunter, 1998).

Despite these optimistic but tentative conclusions, TBACs will be slow to be accepted and integrated into selection and performance appraisal practice, and for at least three reasons. For one, change is itself thought to be uncomfortable and a source of stress (Holmes & Rahe, 1967). Second, most companies have their own competency model(s) which they often seek to measure, directly or indirectly, using an AC. Of course, this (almost) always leads to a dimension- (trait-) based AC because competencies are more easily conceived of and translated into dimension labels than they are actual tasks.

Relatedly, traditional DBACs "work," are perceived as fair, and have demonstrated validity and utility in performance appraisal (Meriac,

Hoffman, Woehr, & Fleisher, 2008) so why fix something that ain't broke? Because TBACs have not (yet?) been demonstrated as a preferable alternative to traditional DBACs. This is the another reason why additional research is needed.

But what kind of additional research? One answer is "more." I suspect that the internal structure of TBACs is now known and has been known for some time, but additional documentation will bolster the confidence of this conclusion. I suspect that the same can be said with respect to the high IRR of TBAC checklist ratings and the acceptability of TBACs to assessors, candidates and sponsoring organizations. However, documentation of TBACs' criterion-related validity is sorely needed. So, one area of needed research is on the basic psychometric characteristics of TBACs especially in relation to their DBAC counter parts (Brannick, 2008).

More research is also needed on the inherent cross-situational (i.e., cross-exercise) specificity in AC performance. One question raised earlier is why ACs' internal structure is sometimes characterized by absolute situational specificity and why sometimes a general performance factor also emerges. One possible explanation is as a result of methodological artifacts, that is use of exploratory factor analysis (EFA) versus CFA. CFA would be more prone to detection of a general factor because of (a) the ease with which one is parameterized, and (b) the power of the chi-squared test used to test for differences in fit between nested models. EFA would be biased against the detection of a general factor due to (a) the subjectivity of some factor retention rules (e.g., scree test, interpretability), and (b) rotation of distinct factors toward simple structure. A second possibility is that because dimension labels are more subjective that task checklist items, they may more likely tap into a general performance factor (Viswesvaran, Schmidt, & Ones, 2005), making it more likely that DBACs would more likely yield a general factor than TBACs. A third possibility is that regardless of scoring system, an AC would more likely yield a general factor to the extent that the exercises themselves are more similar.

But this raises an even more fundamental question—*why* is situational specificity in AC performance so robust when the majority of known performance predictors (e.g., general mental ability, conscientiousness, integrity; Schmidt & Hunter, 1998) trait-based? The most popular line of research attempting to answer this "why" question is in connection with trait activation theory (TAT; Lievens & Christiansen, Chapter 4, this volume; Tett & Burnett, 2003; Tett & Guterman,

2000). As summarized by Lievens (2009) "[t]he trait activation potential of a given situation is primarily determined by the relevance and strength of that situation. A situation is considered relevant to a trait if it provides cues for the expression of trait-relevant behaviour" (p. 111). Behavior should be more cross-situationally consistent to the extent that the situations are similar in strength and activate the same trait(s) and there is general support for TAT (Lievens, Chasteen, Day, & Christiansen, 2006). However, the effect sizes associated with TAT are incommensurate with those associated with cross-situational specificity in AC performance and so TAT is likely an incomplete explanation, at best. What is needed is a program of research directed at adapting existing work (e.g., Ten Berge & De Raad, 1999, 2001; Tett & Burnett, 2003; Van Heck, 1984, 1989) toward a general taxonomy of work situations and AC exercises in particular to model situational causes, along with their interaction effects with candidate characteristics, on AC performance.

Among other needed methodological advances include the need to move beyond MTMM-type models of AC performance. One possible extension that Jackson (2010) has already explored is the use of multivariate generalizability theory to partition variance components in ACs. A second possibility is the use of more general CFA models that account for the inherent hierarchical and nested structures of AC data (e.g., Hoffman et al., 2010). A third example is the possible application of analytic techniques such as linear mixed models (Putka, Le, McCloy, & Diaz, 2008) that are appropriate for what are referred to as "ill structured" data arrays as many operational ACs are.

The nomologial validity of TBACs needs to be continued to be explored. In one study, Jackson, Stillman, et al. (2010) demonstrated the predictability of task performance in a TBAC on the basis of cognitive ability and personality variables. More research along these lines and like that reported by Lance et al. (2007) in which differential relationships were shown between personality predictors and job knowledge and job performance outcomes and general (i.e., a general AC performance factor) and exercise-specific AC performance was demonstrated is needed to locate AC performance in a larger nomological network of work-related predictor and criterion constructs.

Penultimately, more links need built and more collaborative relationships established between efforts in related areas such as multisource performance appraisal, interview research, and educational assessment. There are many commonalities across these bodies of literatures (data design issues, rater modeling issues, etc.) where advances in one area could well inform progress in another.

Finally, Goodge (1988) claimed nearly 25 years ago that TBACs would likely be less expensive and more readily embraced by organizations, assessors, and candidates as compared to more traditional DBACs. Research on user acceptance and cost-benefit analysis is lacking and is sorely needed and is likely necessary before TBACs see widespread adoption and implementation.

Note

1. Interestingly, Turnage and Muchinsky (1982) published similar findings in the same year, but Sackett and Dreher are usually "credited" with initiating the spate of "construct validity fix" studies that ensued for over 25 years.

References

Bass, B. M. (1954). The leaderless group discussion. *Psychological Bulletin, 51*, 465–492.

Brannick, M. T. (2008). Back to basics of test construction and scoring. *Industrial and Organizational Psychology, 1*, 131–133.

Brass, D. J., & Oldham, G. B. (1976). Validating an in-basket test using an alternative set of leadership scoring dimensions. *Journal of Applied Psychology, 61*, 652–657.

Bray, D. W. (1989). History of the assessment center in the United States. In J. Wilson, G. Thomson, R. Millward, & T. Keenan (Eds.), *Assessment for Teacher Development* (pp. 15-24). Philadelphia, PA: The Falmer Press.

Bray, D. W., Campbell, R. J., & Grant, D. L. (1974). *Formative years in business: A long-term AT&T study of managerial lives*. New York: Wiley.

Collins, J. M., Schmidt, F. L., Sanchez-Ku, M., Thomas, L., McDaniel, M. A., & Le, H. (2003). Can basic individual differences shed light on the construct meaning of assessment center evaluations? *International Journal of Selection and Assessment, 11*, 17–29.

Finkle, R. B. (1976). Managerial assessment centers. In M. D. Dunnette (Ed.), *Handbook of industrial and organizational psychology* (pp. 861–888). Chicago: Rand McNally.

Gaugler, B., Rosenthal, D., Thornton, G., & Bentsen, C. (1987). Meta-analysis of assessment center validity. *Journal of Applied Psychology, 72*, 493–511.

Goldstein, H. W., Yusko, K. P., Braverman, E. P., Smith, D. B., & Chung, B. (1998). The role of cognitive ability in the subgroup differences and incremental validity of assessment center exercises. *Personnel Psychology, 51*, 357–374.

Goodge, P. (1988). Task-based assessment. *Journal of European Industrial Training, 12*(6), 22–27.

Griffeths, P. J., & Allen, B. (1987). Assessment centres: Breaking with tradition. *Journal of Management Development, 6*(6), 18–29.

Hardison, C. M., & Sackett, P. R. (2004, April). *Assessment center criterion-related validity: A meta-analytic update.* Paper presented at the Meeting of the Society for Industrial and Organizational, Psychology, Chicago, IL.

Highhouse, S. (2002). Assessing the candidate as a whole: A historical and critical analysis of individual psychological assessment for personnel decision making. *Personnel Psychology, 55*, 363–396.

Hoffman, B. J., Lance, C. E., Bynum, B. H., & Gentry, W. A. (2010). Rater source effects are alive and well after all. *Personnel Psychology, 63*, 119–151.

Hoffman, B. J., Melchers, K. G., & Kleinmann, M. (2010, April). *Disentangling assessment center exercise and rater effects.* Paper presented at the meeting of the Society for Industrial and Organizational Psychology, Atlanta, GA.

Holmes, T. H., & Rahe, R. H. (1967). The social readjustment rating scale. *Journal of Psychosomatic Research, 11*, 213–218.

Howard, A. (2010). The management progress study and its legacy for selection. In J. J. Farr & N. T. Tippins (Eds.), *Handbook of employee selection* (pp. 843–864). New York: Routledge.

Iles, P. (1992). Centres of excellence? Assessment and development centres, managerial competence, and human resource strategies. *British Journal of Management, 3*, 79–90.

Jackson, D. J. R. (2007, April). *Task Specific assessment centers: Evidence of predictive validity and fairness.* Paper presented at the meeting of the Society for Industrial and Organizational Psychology, New York, NY.

Jackson, D. J. R. (2010). *Patterns of dependability among raters in task-based assessments.* (Unpublished manuscript)

Jackson, D. J. R., Ahmad, M. H., & Grace, G. M. (2010, April). *Are task-based assessments best represented by absolute situational specificity?* Paper presented at the meeting of the Society for Industrial and Organizational Psychology, Atlanta, GA.

Jackson, D. J. R., Barney, A. R., Stillman, J. A., & Kirkley, W. (2007). When traits are behaviors: The relationship between behavioral responses and trait-based overfall assessment center ratings. *Human Performance, 20*, 415–432.

Jackson, D. J. R., Englert, P. & Brown, G. S. (2009, April). *Interrater reliability of behavioral checklists in task-based assessment centers.* Paper presented at the meeting of the Society for Industrial and Organizational Psychology, New Orleans, LA.

Jackson, D. J. R., Englert, P., & Stillman, J. A. (2010). *Seeking a resolution: A data-driven comparison between dimension- and task-based assessment centers.* (Unpublished manuscript)

Jackson, D. J. R., Stillman, J. A., & Atkins, S. G. (2005). Rating tasks versus dimensions in assessment centers: A psychometric comparison. *Human Performance, 18*, 213–241.

Jackson, D. J. R., Stillman, J. A., & Englert, P. (2010). Task-based assessment centers: Empirical support for a systems model. *International Journal of Selection and Assessment, 18*, 141–154.

Lance, C. E. (2008a). Why assessment centers do not work the way they are supposed to. *Industrial and Organizational Psychology: Perspectives on Science and Practice, 1*, 84–97.

Lance, C. E. (2008b). Where have we been, how did we get there, and where shall we go? *Industrial and Organizational Psychology: Perspectives on Science and Practice, 1*, 140–146.

Lance, C. E., Baranik, L. E., Lau, A. R., & Scharlau, E. A. (2009). If it ain't trait it must be method: (Mis)application of the multitrait-multimethod methodology in organizational research. In C. E. Lance & R. J. Vandenberg (Eds.), *Statistical and methodological myths and urban legends: Doctrine, verity, and fable in organizational and social research* (pp. 337–360). New York: Routledge.

Lance, C. E., Dawson, B., Birklebach, D., & Hoffman, B. J. (2010). Method effects, measurement error, and substantive conclusions. *Organizational Research Methods, 13*, 435–455.

Lance, C. E., Foster, M. R., Gentry, W. A., & Thoresen, J. D. (2004). Assessor cognitive processes in an operational assessment center. *Journal of Applied Psychology, 89*, 22–35.

Lance, C. E., Foster, M. R., Drollinger, S. M., Sorensen, K. L., Gentry, W. A., & Nemeth, Y. M. (2007). *A comparison of task-based versus dimension-based scoring procedures in an operational assessment center (AC).* Paper presented at the meeting of the Society for Industrial and Organizational Psychology, New York, NY.

Lance, C. E., Foster, M. R., Nemeth, Y. M., Gentry, W. A., & Drollinger, S. (2007). Extending the nomological network of assessment center construct validity: Prediction of cross-situationally consistent and specific aspects of assessment center performance. *Human Performance, 20*, 345–362.

Lance, C. E., Lambert, T. A., Gewin, A. G., Lievens, F., & Conway, J. M. (2004). Revised estimates of dimension and exercise variance components in assessment center post-exercise dimension ratings. *Journal of Applied Psychology, 89*, 377–385.

Lance, C. E., Newbolt, W. H., Gatewood, R. D., Foster, M. R., French, N., & Smith, D. E. (2000). Assessment center exercise factors represent cross-situational specificity, not method bias. *Human Performance, 13*, 323–353.

Lance, C. E., & Vandenberg, R. J. (Eds.), (2009). *Statistical and methodological myths and urban legends: Doctrine, verity, and fable in organizational and social research* New York: Routledge.

Lievens, F. (1998). Factors which improve the construct validity of assessment centers: A review. *International Journal of Selection and Assessment, 6*, 141–152

Lievens, F. (2009). Assessment centres: A tale about dimensions, exercises and dancing bears. *European Journal of Work and Organizational Psychology, 18*, 102–121.

Lievens, F., Chasteen, C. S., Day, E. A., & Christiansen, N. D. (2006). Large-scale investigation of the role of trait activation theory for understanding assessment center convergent and discriminant validity. *Journal of Applied Psychology, 91,* 247–258.

Lovler, B., Rose, M., & Wesley, S. (2002, April). Finding assessment center construct validity: Try behaviors instead of dimensions. Paper presented at the meeting of the Society for Industrial and Organizational Psychology, Toronto, Ontario.

Lowry, P. E. (1995). The assessment center process: Assessing leadership in the public sector. *Public Personnel Management, 21,* 171–184

Lowry, P. E. (1997). The assessment center process: New directions. *Journal of Social Behavior and Personality, 12,* 53–66.

Meriac, J. J. P., Hoffman, B. J., Woehr, D. J., & Fleisher, M. S. (2008). Further evidence for the validity of assessment center dimensions: A meta-analysis of the incremental criterion-related validity of dimension ratings. *Journal of Applied Psychology, 93,* 1042–1052.

Moses, J. L., & Byham, W. C. (Eds.). (1977). *Applying the assessment center method.* New York: Pergammon.

Murray, H. (1990). The transformation of selection procedures: The War Office Selection Boards. In E. Trist, & H. Murray (Eds.), *The social engagement of social science: A Tavistock anthology* (pp. 45–67). Philadelphia: The University of Pennsylvania Press

Putka, D. J., Le, H., McCloy, R. A., & Diaz, T. (2008). Ill-structured measurement designs in organizational research: Implications for estimating interrater reliability. *Journal of Applied Psychology, 93,* 959–981.

Robertson, I. T., Gratton, L., & Sharpley, D. (1987). The psychometric properties and design of managerial assessment centres: Dimensions into exercises won't go. *Journal of Occupational Psychology, 60,* 187–196.

Sackett, P. R., & Dreher, G. F. (1982). Constructs and assessment center dimensions: Some troubling empirical findings. *Journal of Applied Psychology, 67,* 401–410.

Schippman, J. S., Prien, E. P., & Katz, J. A. (1990). Reliability and validity of in-basket performance measures.. *Personnel Psychology, 43,* 837–859.

Schmidt, F. L., & Hunter, J. E. (1998). The validity and utility of selection methods in personnel psychology: Practical and theoretical implications of 85 years of research findings. *Psychological Bulletin, 124,* 262–274.

Stillman, J. A., & Jackson, D. J. R. (2005). A detection theory approach to the evaluation of assessors in assessment centers. *Journal of Occupational and Organizational Psychology, 78,* 581–594.

Ten Berge, M. A., & De Raad, B. (1999). Taxonomies of situations from a trait psychological perspective: A review. *European Journal of Personality, 13,* 337–360.

Ten Berge, M. A., & De Raad, B. (2001). The construction of a joint taxonomy of traits and situations. *European Journal of Personality, 15,* 253–276.

Tett, R. P., & Burnett, D. D. (2003). A personality trait-based interactionist model of job performance. *Journal of Applied Psychology, 88,* 500–517.

Tett, R. P., & Guterman, H. A. (2000). Situation trait relevance, trait expression, and cross-situation consistency: Testing a principle of trait activation. *Journal of Research in Personality, 34,* 397–423.

Thornton, G. C., & Byham, W. C. (1982). *Assessment centers and managerial performance.* San Diego, CA: Academic Press.

Thornton, G. C., III, Kaman, V., Layer, S., & Larsh, S. (1995, May). *Effectiveness of two forms of assessment center feedback: Attribute feedback and task feedback.*. Paper presented at the meeting of the International Congress on the Assessment Center Method, Kansas City, KS.

Truxillo, D. M., Donahue, L. M., & Kuang, D. (2004). Work samples, performance tests, and competency testing. In J. C. Thomas (Ed.), *Comprehensive handbook of psychological assessment, Vol. 4: Industrial and organizational assessment* (pp. 345–370). Hoboken, NJ: Wiley.

Turnage, J. J., & Muchinsky, P. M. (1982). Transsitutaional variability in human performance within assessment centers. *Organizational Behavior and Human Decision Processes, 30,* 174–200.

Vandenberg, R. J. (2006). Statistical and methodological myths and urban legends: Where, pray tell, did they get this idea? *Organizational Research Methods, 9,* 194–201.

Van Heck, G. L. (1984). The construction of a general taxonomy of situations. In H. Bonarius, G. L. Van Heck., & N. Smid (Eds.), *Personality psychology in Europe: Theoretical and empirical developments* (pp. 149–194). Lisse, Netherlands: Swets and Zeitlinger.

Van Heck, G. L. (1989). Situation concepts: Definition and classification. In P. J. Hettema (Ed.), *Personality and environment: Assessment of human daptation* (pp. 53–70). Chichester, UK: Wiley.

Viswesvaran, C., Schmidt, F. L., & Ones, D. S. (2005). Is there a general factor in ratings of job performance? A meta-analytic framework for disentangling substantive and error influences. *Journal of Applied Psychology, 90,* 108–131.

Woehr, D. J ., & Arthur, W. Jr. (2003). The construct-related validity of assessment center ratings: A review and meta-analysis of the role of methodological factors. *Journal of Management, 29,* 231–258.

Woehr, D. J., & Huffcutt, A. I. (1994). Rater training for performance appraisal: A quantitative review. *Journal of Occupational and Organizational Psychology, 67,* 189–205.

Part 4

Mixed-Model Assessment Centers

11

Dimensions AND Exercises

Theoretical Background of Mixed-Model Assessment Centers

Klaus G. Melchers, Andreja Wirz, and Martin Kleinmann
Universität Zürich, Switzerland

The *Guidelines and Ethical Considerations for Assessment Center Operations* (hereafter referred to as the *Guidelines*) put forth by the International Task Force on Assessment Center Guidelines (2009) give a prominent role to two aspects of the assessment center (AC) method: dimensions and job-related simulations (i.e., exercises). According to the *Guidelines*, dimensions should be a result of a job analysis used to determine behaviors that are important for job success. These dimensions should reflect meaningful and relevant categories. During the AC, these categories are then used to classify behaviors that are displayed by AC participants in the different exercises.

As illustrated in the previous chapters of this book, there is some disagreement in the AC literature whether dimensions or exercises are the more important of these two aspects. This issue, however, has some resemblance to the person-situation debate in personality theory, that is, to the debate regarding whether traits or situations are the primary determinant of behavior. Many researchers in the personality domain agree that both the person (as characterized by traits, abilities, and other individual difference variables) and the situation are important determinants of human behavior (see, for example, the articles published in a recent special issue of the *Journal of Research in Personality* edited by Donnellan, Lucas, & Fleeson, 2009). Similar to this interactionist view, mixed-model ACs give weight to both sources of variance in the behavior of AC participants.

The aims of the present chapter are, first, to give an overview about the role that dimensions and exercises play as sources of variance for candidates' behavior in an AC, second, to review theoretical work that might help to understand the interplay of dimensions and exercises, and third, to describe implications for designing and conducting ACs and for using information obtained from these ACs.

Dimensions and Exercises as Sources of Variance for Candidates' Behavior

In different domains in industrial and organizational psychology—or in psychological assessment in general—it has been found that variance in evaluations of candidates' performance can be traced to the different targeted performance dimensions as well as to the different situations (which are often modeled as "method" factors). Thus, in ACs, dimensions and exercises contribute to variance in post-exercise dimension ratings (PEDRs) that are made by assessors to evaluate candidates' performance in the different exercises (e.g., Anderson, Lievens, van Dam, & Born, 2006; Arthur, Woehr, & Maldegen, 2000; Kleinmann, Kuptsch, & Köller, 1996). Similarly, in structured interviews, dimensions and different interview components (e.g., past-oriented vs. future-oriented interview questions) contribute to variance in ratings of interviewees' performance (e.g., Klehe, König, Richter, Kleinmann, & Melchers, 2008; Van Iddekinge, Raymark, Eidson, & Attenweiler, 2004), and in multisource feedback, dimensions and different rater sources (i.e., supervisors vs. peers vs. subordinates) contribute to variance in ratings' of employees' performance (e.g., Hoffman, Lance, Bynum, & Gentry, 2010). Furthermore, the usual finding in all of these domains is that dimensions account for less variance than the respective "method" factors (for the AC domain, see, for example, the results from meta-analytic and other large-scale investigations by Bowler & Woehr, 2006; Lance, Lambert, Gewin, Lievens, & Conway, 2004; Melchers, Henggeler, & Kleinmann, 2007; or Woehr & Arthur, 2003).

An important question concerning these and related findings is whether method factors reflect unwanted variance (i.e., error) or true cross-situational variability. Error variance would be psychologically irrelevant in the assessment of candidates' performance, whereas true cross-situational variability would provide information that is psychologically informative and useful for selection and assessment.

A long-held concern is that method factors in ACs, multisource performance ratings, or other selection and assessment procedures are indicative of measurement error (see Lance, Dawson, Birkelbach, & Hoffman, 2010, for a review). As measurement error impairs measurement of the targeted dimensions, evidence for method factors (as in the case of AC exercise factors) is usually considered to be undesirable. Recent research, however, has confirmed that these method factors are substantively meaningful and represent a valid and meaningful source of information (Lance et al., 2010). In the AC domain, for example, significant correlations between exercise factors and job performance ratings, cognitive ability, and individual difference variables have been found (Lance, Foster, Gentry, & Thoresen, 2004; Lance, Foster, Nemeth, Gentry, & Drollinger, 2007; Lance et al., 2000). Furthermore, meta-analytic research has long confirmed that using a larger number of different exercises in ACs contributes to higher criterion-related validity (Gaugler, Rosenthal, Thornton, & Bentson, 1987).

Another important question, however, is why dimensions in ACs account for so much less variance than exercises and what role exercises play for the assessment of dimensions. In the past, exercises were mainly seen as means to simulate task, social, and organizational demands (cf. Lievens, Tett, & Schleicher, 2009). According to the *Guidelines* (International Task Force on Assessment Center Guidelines, 2009), exercises should be designed to provide the necessary information for evaluating the targeted dimensions. Furthermore, ACs should include a sufficient number of different exercises to provide enough opportunities to observe candidates' behavior related to each dimension. The latter point provides part of the answer to the initial question because it implies that a single exercise usually does not suffice to elicit behavior that is indicative of all the targeted dimensions. Instead, different exercises pose different demands for candidates so that different kinds of behavior are needed to handle each of these exercises successfully (Howard, 2008; Neidig & Neidig, 1984). Thus, to ensure that all targeted dimensions can be evaluated appropriately, different exercises are needed to elicit behaviors for each dimension and these exercises should be designed in such a manner that they elicit enough dimension-relevant behavior. As will become more evident in the following sections, exercises that pose very different demands for candidates activate different underlying traits and trigger different behavioral patterns. This, in turn, limits the chances to find behavioral convergence across exercises and thereby restricts the variance that can be accounted for by dimensions that are evaluated in several of these different exercises. At the same time, this increases the proportion of variance that is attributable to exercises.

Theoretical Background of Mixed-Model Assessment Centers

In the personality domain, conceptions that acknowledge that person variables as well as situation variables influence behavior have a long tradition. For example, Lewin (1946) assumed that behavior B is a function of two sources, the person and the environment, leading to the axiomatic expression B = *f*(P, E), where P stands for the person and E stands for the environment, or more specifically, for the specific situation an individual is confronted with. According to such an interactionist view, individuals can behave consistently across different situations but different people can also behave similarly in a specific situation. Furthermore, the specific situation influences the degree to which individual difference variables like traits influence an individual's behavior. Thus, "[t]raits and situations, in this light, are inseparable, forming two sides of a single coin" (Lievens et al., 2009, p. 108). Applied to the AC domain, this suggests that individual difference variables, as well as exercise characteristics, influence candidates' behavior and that the degree to which dimensions and exercises account for variance in PEDRs depends on the interplay of these two sources.

Trait Activation Theory

Trait activation theory (TAT, Tett & Burnett, 2003; Tett & Guterman, 2000) represents an application of interactionist principles to the work domain and explains how personality traits come to be expressed as work behavior and how such behavior is related to job performance. In recent years, several researchers (e.g., Haaland & Christiansen, 2002; Lievens, Chasteen, Day, & Christiansen, 2006; Lievens et al., 2009) have suggested considering TAT to understand the interplay of person and situation variables in ACs. An extensive review of TAT and discussion of its application to ACs can be found in a recent article by Lievens et al. (2009).

TAT has at least two important implications for ACs. First, individuals only show trait-related work behavior if a situation provides trait-relevant cues. This means that the standing of an AC participant on a given trait will only lead to trait-related behavior in an exercise if this exercise activates the specific trait by providing relevant cues, or said differently, if the trait-activation potential is high for the trait in question. In a similar vein, Reis (2008) speaks about situations as social affordances, meaning that they represent opportunities for acting and interacting. Sociability, for example, is more likely to lead to trait-related behaviors when a candidate has to interact with other people than when there is no need for behaviors related to Sociability, such as in situations in which no social interaction is required. Similarly, Conscientiousness is more likely to lead to trait-relevant behavior when a candidate has to handle complex and detailed materials in a systematic manner than in situations that provide no opportunities for trait-related behaviors because they do not require detail, precision, orderliness, and the like. As a consequence of this, convergence of behavior across situations can only be expected if different situations have high trait-activation potential for the trait in question.

Second, in addition to trait-relevance, expression of a trait as actual behavior also depends on the strength of the situation. Situation strength reflects the degree to which a situation leads most or even all individuals to respond in the same manner (Mischel, 1973, 1977). Thus, traits will only influence candidates' behavior if a situation is relatively weak so that different individuals can handle it differently. However, if a situation is too strong, this will override the effects of individual differences in behavioral propensities. The level of Conscientiousness, for example, will only be predictive of an individual's behavior in situations that require trait-related behaviors if the individual has the choice to show—or not to show—Conscientiousness-related behavior. Accordingly, inter-individual differences in Conscientiousness will not predict behavior in situations with clearly defined roles and close supervision that lead all individuals to act similarly (cf. Tett & Burnett, 2003). Thus, situations—or exercises in the case of ACs—are seen as moderators of trait expression (e.g., Haaland & Christiansen, 2002).

An important challenge for personality research is to determine the fundamental dimensions that characterize social situations (Reis, 2008). One approach offered by TAT in this regard is to classify situations in terms of the traits that they activate. In the first application of TAT to ACs, for example, Haaland and Christiansen (2002) determined the trait-activation potential of the exercises used in a promotional AC by collecting expert ratings of the degree to which each of these exercises activates each of the Big Five traits. Using this approach, they found that ratings of dimensions linked to a given Big Five trait showed stronger convergent correlations when they stemmed from exercises judged to be high in trait-activation potential for this trait than ratings from exercises that were low in trait-activation potential for this trait (also see Lievens et al., 2006).

Cognitive Affective Personality System Theory and the Importance of Peoples' Understanding of Situations

An approach that is similar to TAT and more general in scope is Mischel and Shoda's (1995) cognitive affective personality system (CAPS) theory. According to CAPS theory, personality is considered as a set of intra-individually stable *if* ... *then* ... situation-behavior relations, meaning, stable and distinct patterns of actions that an individual shows in response to different types of situations. Specifically, CAPS theory postulates, amongst other things, that features of the situation trigger a series of affective and cognitive mental representations. Depending on the activated representation, certain behavioral scripts are prompted. In comparison to TAT, the CAPS framework has even more power to explain individual and situational consistency and inconsistency of behavior across different situations because of its recognition of individual differences in the perception of a situation. Thus, CAPS theory offers an explanation for the variance of behavior in situations like those that candidates face in different AC exercises (cf. Jansen, Lievens, & Kleinmann, 2011; Kleinmann et al., 2011): If Candidate A's perception of the situation activates the cognitive representation of Assertiveness, since he or she assumes the AC exercise to measure this dimension, the behavioral script being primed is that of Assertiveness. If Candidate B, however, interprets the situation differently and activates his or her Cooperativeness script, for example, a behavioral pattern may follow that differs from Candidate A's behavior. Furthermore, consistency of an individual's behavior across situations can only be expected if he or she interprets different situations similarly, so that similar behavioral scripts are activated.

Thus, for CAPS theory, the distinction between nominal situations and psychological situations becomes important (Block & Block, 1981; Reis, 2008). Nominal situations refer to situations that are perceived in the same manner by different individuals, whereas psychological situations refer to situations as they are perceived and interpreted by a particular individual. This distinction is important because, as implied by Mischel and Shoda's (1995) CAPS framework, individuals will only behave similarly in relation to different situations when these situations are functionally equivalent in meaning (Mischel, 2009). However, even when two situations are nominally equivalent, an individual might understand them differently so that the two situations are psychologically different to him or her. This important aspect is a key feature of CAPS theory that is not included in TAT (Tett & Burnett, 2003).

For the AC domain, an implication of the distinction between nominal and psychological situations is that it is important to consider candidates' perceptions of the situational demands in the exercises as this will influence the traits that are activated in the different exercises and, ultimately, the kind of behavior that candidates show. Consistency of behavior across different exercises can only be expected if a candidate perceives similar situational demands in the different exercises. In this regard, research on candidates' ability to identify evaluation criteria (ATIC) in selection procedures like ACs or selection interviews is informative. This research revealed that candidates differ considerably in the degree to which they identify the evaluation criteria, that is, the targeted dimensions (Kleinmann, 1993; Kleinmann et al., 2011; Melchers et al., 2009). Thus, different candidates may have a very different understanding of what is required in these exercises, and empirical evidence supports that this understanding influences dimension measurement in ACs in line with the CAPS framework: First, it has been found that convergence of assessors' ratings was higher when two exercises targeted the same dimension and when candidates correctly discerned this dimension in both exercises (Kleinmann, 1993). This suggests that individuals' behavioral consistency is higher when the psychological situations are more similar. And second, Jansen et al. (2011) found that the correctness of the situation perception moderated the way in which individual difference variables were related to performance in AC exercises. In particular, Jansen et al. found that people who were high on Conscientiousness and Agreeableness and who correctly identified targeted AC dimensions that were conceptually related to these two traits received higher performance ratings on the corresponding dimensions. Thus, when there was a match between the nominal situation and candidates' perception of the psychological situation, relevant traits led to more trait-related behavior and ultimately to higher performance ratings in the AC. Conversely, candidates who were high on these traits but who were not able to correctly identify the situational demands (i.e., for whom there was no match between the nominal situation and the psychological situation) received lower ratings.

Traits and Dimensions and their Role for Candidates' Behavior in AC Exercises

Even though AC dimensions initially came out of a personality tradition (so that some early ACs actually aimed at assessing personality, e.g., Handyside & Duncan, 1954; see also Chapter 2 of this volume), it is important to acknowledge that they are usually not conceptualized or considered as traits. Instead, as, for example, pointed out by Howard (1997, p. 22), AC dimensions "have always been muddled collections of traits (e.g., energy), learned skills (planning), readily demonstrable behaviors (oral communication), basic abilities (mental ability), attitudes (social objectivity), motives (need for achievement), or knowledge (industry knowledge), and other attributes or behaviors." This has several important implications.

First, one has to consider which of the different traits that are potentially activated in a given exercise are related to the different targeted dimensions. If a trait is related to more than one dimension, this will lead to a situation where behavior indicative of all of these dimensions is triggered (Lievens et al., 2009). As a consequence, within-exercise ratings of these dimensions should correlate more strongly than ratings of dimensions that are related to different traits. One of the consequences of this is that factor analyses of the corresponding PEDRs will reveal stronger exercise-factors when dimensions are related to the same underlying traits than when they are not.

Second, AC dimensions also vary considerably in their breadth. A broad dimension like Leadership, for example, is related to more traits (e.g., Assertiveness, Decisiveness), learned skills (e.g., Delegation), attitudes (e.g., a valued participative decision style), and other attributes or behaviors than a much narrower dimension like Short-term planning. Thus, in comparison to narrow dimensions, dimensions that are broader in scope have a larger range of dimension-related behaviors, and this larger range of behaviors is more likely to be triggered by several different traits.

Third, research in the personality domain has repeatedly found that specific traits are better at predicting behavior in specific situations or predicting specific outcomes (e.g., see the research reviewed by Hough & Oswald, 2008). Thus, for specific exercises, there might be closer correspondence between traits and dimensions for narrow traits and narrow dimensions than for broader traits and broader dimensions. Accordingly, traits measured at the facet level of the Big Five personality factors, for example, might make better predictors for PEDRs on narrow AC dimensions than traits measured at the domain level. Finally, especially when specific exercises are used that allow the evaluation of specific narrow AC dimensions, convergence of the dimension ratings across exercises should be good if the different exercises are actually conceptualized as parallel measures. This is because exercises in such a situation would activate exactly the same narrow traits and thus require the same behaviors to be handled successfully (see Brannick, 2008, for a similar argument), at least as long as these exercises are also perceived to be psychologically equivalent. On the other hand, across exercises that are different in scope and therefore represent psychologically different situations, a potential drawback of specific narrow dimensions is that the targeted dimensions and the situations (i.e., exercises) are too specific to allow for behavioral consistency, and it might not even be possible to rate a given narrow AC dimension in another exercise if this exercise represents a situation that is too different. Thus, little behavioral consistency and little convergence of the dimension ratings across exercises can be expected.

The above mentioned implications pose a problem for those who want to take measures to improve the construct-related validity of PEDRs and who—in line with the *Guidelines* (International Task Force on Assessment Center Guidelines, 2009)—also want to include a set of relatively different exercises in an AC so as to ensure that the most relevant tasks and situations that job incumbents may face are all included in the AC. As noted above, research on the criterion-related validity of ACs suggests that including a larger number of different exercises that simulate different job-relevant tasks is beneficial for criterion-related validity (Gaugler et al., 1987). However, it is unlikely that candidates perceive these different exercises as psychologically similar. Consequently, different traits are activated across exercises, so that candidates show different kinds of behavior. Thus, when specific narrow dimensions are to be observed in such an AC, little convergence across exercises can be expected and dimensions will account for very little variance in assessors' PEDRs.

A potential solution in such a situation—or for ACs in general that do not include several parallel versions of an exercise—would be to group together conceptually related narrow dimensions so that these form kind of a broader meta-dimension (Hoffman, Melchers, Blair, Kleinmann, & Ladd, 2011; see also Chapter 12 of this volume). On a conceptual level, similar dimensions are likely to be related to the same underlying trait when this trait is also measured at a broader level (i.e., at the domain level of the Big Five instead of the facet level). Thus, from a TAT or CAPS perspective, it seems unlikely that similar dimensions allow ratings that are distinct from each other (especially when several similar dimensions are rated within the same exercise). For example, when Leadership and Persuasiveness are both targeted in an exercise, both of these dimensions are likely to be related to Extraversion and Emotional Stability and similar behaviors might be used as indicators of both. As a consequence, assessors' ratings of both dimensions are likely to have a high correlation. Usually, such a result would have been considered as indicating a lack of discriminant validity. However, quite in contrast to this view, finding high intercorrelations between ratings of two similar dimensions is something that is expected on the basis of TAT and CAPS theory and should be interpreted as evidence for convergence between dimensions that are similar in scope and that are fed by the same underlying traits.

Furthermore, on a psychometric level, using more than one dimension as an indicator of a broader underlying meta-dimension has the advantage that the number of indicators for this meta-dimension is larger than for the original narrow dimension. It might often even help to avoid the problem that dimension ratings reflect single-item measures that suffer from limited reliability. Instead, when several related dimensions are rated within an exercise, these dimension ratings can be used in combination in order to improve the reliability of dimension measurement at a broader level.

An important issue in this regard is how one can derive a set of potential meta-dimensions when designing an AC. Fortunately, over the years, different classifications for AC dimensions or for dimension structures in the general managerial performance literature have been put forth that might provide feasible meta-dimensions (cf. Hoffman et al., 2011). The major difference between these classifications is the number of categories that they assume. However, the scope of the suggested categories is necessarily broader when fewer categories are assumed (and assuming fewer categories has the effect that narrow dimensions might be grouped together that are not always fed by similar underlying traits).

Shore, Thornton, and Shore (1990), for example, suggested a categorization scheme in which AC dimensions were specified as indicators of only two broad factors—a "performance style" factor and an "interpersonal style" factor. These two factors roughly correspond to task performance and interpersonal performance. In contrast to this, based on a content analysis of the dimensionality of managerial performance, Borman and Brush (1993) proposed a structure that differentiates more between dimensions related to the interpersonal style factor. This structure consists of three meta-dimensions (as well as a fourth, "other" category) that could be used to classify narrow performance dimensions: Communication and interpersonal facilitation, Technical activities/mechanics of management, and Leadership and supervision. A related structure has been suggested in prior AC research, where Kolk, Born, and van der Flier (2004) suggested a very similar categorization scheme with three categories that they illustratively labeled as Feeling, Thinking, and Power. Finally, Arthur, Day, McNelly, and Edens (2003) put forth a seven factor taxonomy of AC dimensions to classify manifest AC dimensions into broader latent factors. Broad dimensions specified in Arthur et al.'s taxonomy include: Communication, Consideration and awareness of others, Organizing and planning, Problem-solving, Influencing others, Drive, and Tolerance for stress/uncertainty.

Implications for AC Design

The theoretical background described above has several implications that should be considered for designing and conducting ACs. First, different situations activate different sets of traits. For ACs, this means that not all exercises are equally important for all dimensions (Howard, 2008) and that not all dimensions are equally important for all exercises (Lievens et al., 2009). Thus, a fully-crossed exercise-dimension matrix, in which each dimension is to be rated in each exercise, does not seem appropriate for most ACs. Instead, it seems more appropriate to design ACs so that assessors only have to observe and rate dimensions in an exercise that are related to traits for which the trait activation potential in this exercise is high. Such an approach will ensure that trait-relevant behaviors will be triggered in an exercise so that assessors can make meaningful observations and have sufficient information to evaluate the respective AC dimensions appropriately.

Second, in addition to both (a) choosing exercises so as to ensure that they reflect important tasks of the target job and (b) specifying which dimensions can potentially be observed in a given exercise, it is also important to ensure that the different exercises sufficiently activate those traits that are related to the targeted dimensions. Thus, besides choosing exercises that are potentially relevant for a given set of traits, it is also important to provide sufficient cues for these traits and to include enough opportunities within an exercise so that candidates can show trait-relevant behavior. If these steps are not taken, there is a risk that relevant traits are not triggered appropriately and/or that there are too few occasions on which candidates can show trait-relevant behavior. This in turn increases the risk that there will be little variance in candidates' behavior and therefore also little variance in assessors' ratings (Haaland & Christiansen, 2002). Potential means to increase the trait activation potential of an exercise include adaptations of exercise content, the use of exercise instructions that contain trait-relevant cues or role-players that provide cues in their behavior (cf. Lievens et al., 2009).

Third, given that candidates vary considerably with regard to their understanding of the different AC exercises (Kleinmann, 1993), steps might be taken to ensure (a) that candidates agree more on the psychological situations that the different exercises represent and (b) that the psychological situations show a closer match with the nominal situations that the AC designers had in mind. One way to accomplish this would be to administer the AC transparently, meaning that candidates are informed explicitly about the targeted dimensions in the different exercises (e.g., Kleinmann et al., 1996; Kolk, Born, & van der Flier, 2003). This should help to ensure that candidates correctly perceive the situations that the different exercises reflect and, consequently, to ensure that relevant behavioral scripts for these situations can be activated. This should, ultimately, lead to more behavior related to the targeted AC dimensions. As a consequence, measurement of these dimensions should be facilitated in transparent ACs as compared to nontransparent ACs.

Fourth, in addition to ensuring that exercises activate the targeted dimensions, it is also important to pay attention to the situational strength of these exercises and to consider whether the exercises allow candidates to approach these situations differently. As pointed out by Lievens et al. (2009), when exercises are designed in such a way that they include only clearly defined tasks and require very specific predetermined steps that need to be taken, candidates have little opportunity to handle these situations differently on the basis of their individual propensities. Thus, candidates' behaviors should not be constrained too much by exercise instructions. Instead, instructions should leave enough room so that differences can emerge in how candidates approach and handle a given exercise.

A potential problem that AC designers might face when they consider the last two implications together is that transparency of the targeted dimensions helps to increase the trait-activation potential for traits that are conceptually related to the targeted dimensions but that transparency might also increase the situational strength of an exercise. As pointed out by Lievens et al. (2009), revealing the targeted dimensions to candidates reduces the vagueness and ambiguity of an exercise, which in turn reduces differences in how candidates perceive and handle this exercise. Thus, when dimensions are made very explicit to candidates (e.g., by telling candidates which dimensions are targeted in any given exercise and by also informing them about specific behaviors that are related to each dimension, cf. Kleinmann et al., 1996) this might cause candidates to show more dimension-related behaviors, but these behaviors can no longer be interpreted as being indicative of candidates' standing on traits that are conceptually related to the targeted dimensions. As a consequence, transparency might lessen the personality loading of AC exercises and thereby reduce the relationship between traits and behavioral ratings from AC exercises (Smith-Jentsch, 2007). Instead, transparently administered AC exercises would allow a purer measure of candidates' ability to show certain kinds of behavior, that is, of their maximum performance with regard to the targeted dimensions (Smith-Jentsch, 2007). Thus, when information on candidates' maximum standing on these dimensions is needed as might be the case when ACs are used for developmental or training purposes, then AC dimensions should be made transparent. However, when it is more important to know how candidates handle different exercises so as to forecast how they might approach similar situations later on the job, then it might be more advisable not to make dimensions too transparent. In line with this, transparency of the targeted dimensions might even lower the predictive validity of ACs (cf. Kleinmann et al., 2011).

Fifth, the use of exercises that are similar in content—so that they are perceived similarly and thus activate similar traits—is beneficial for convergence in behavior across exercises. Thus, using similar exercises in an AC is beneficial for the convergent validity of dimension ratings across exercises (e.g., Schneider & Schmitt, 1992). However, as noted above, AC exercises are usually not chosen to be parallel measures but to reflect the most relevant tasks and situations of the target job (Howard, 2008; Neidig & Neidig, 1984). Therefore, even though using only similar exercises might lead to better assessment of those dimensions that are relevant for these specific exercises, it might jeopardize the prediction of job performance when important job-related tasks are not reflected in the choice of exercises used in an AC.

A final implication related to the previous issue concerns the question of at which level dimensional information should be measured and used in ACs. If personality is reflected by a set of distinctive but stable *if* ... *then* ... situation-behavior relations as assumed by CAPS theory, then it is obvious that behavioral information across different situations is needed to draw valid conclusions about an individual's personality. For ACs, this means that in order to draw valid conclusions about a candidate's standing on a given dimension, it is necessary to observe dimension-relevant behavior across a set of different exercises. However, the relevant unit to interpret dimensional information in such a case would not be a single PEDR but information across different exercises, that is, the overall dimension rating (Howard, 2008). As noted above, it might even be advisable to categorize similar dimensions together and to take an average of these similar dimensions across all the different exercises (Hoffman et al., 2011). This information on candidates' cross-situational standing on a limited set of broad dimensions might then be used in combination with information on how well a candidate could handle specific exercises (as indicated, for example, by the average of all ratings from each exercise, cf. also Jackson, Barney, Stillman, & Kirkley, 2007). These two pieces of information can be used together both for selection as well as for developmental purposes. Knowledge about particular strengths and weaknesses concerning specific dimensions as well as specific tasks can be used to make placement decisions in the context of personnel selection and to provide feedback or to tailor training programs to the specific needs of candidates in the context of training and development.

Conclusion

The theoretical background reviewed in this chapter shows that ACs generate information on dimensions and exercises. Both sources of information—as well as their interaction (as, for example, in the case where behavior in a specific exercise does not fit with the overall pattern of information gained in an AC concerning a candidate's performance on a set of dimensions and across a set of exercises)—are valuable and can be employed for important purposes in the context of personnel selection as well as training and development. Mixed-model ACs acknowledge the importance of both of these sources and try to give appropriate weight to them.

Acknowledgments

Preparation of this chapter was partially supported by a grant from the Swiss National Science Foundation (Schweizerischer Nationalfonds; Grant 100014-117917). We would like to thank Filip Lievens for long and stimulating discussions related to the issues of this chapter.

References

Anderson, N., Lievens, F., van Dam, K., & Born, M. (2006). A construct-driven investigation of gender differences in a leadership-role assessment center. *Journal of Applied Psychology, 91*, 555–566.

Arthur, W., Jr., Day, E. A., McNelly, T. L., & Edens, P. S. (2003). A meta-analysis of the criterion-related validity of assessment center dimensions. *Personnel Psychology, 56*, 125–154.

Arthur, W., Jr., Woehr, D. J., & Maldegen, R. (2000). Convergent and discriminant validity of assessment center dimensions: A conceptual and empirical reexamination of the assessment center construct-related validity paradox. *Journal of Management, 26*, 813–835.

Block, J., & Block, J. H. (1981). Studying situational dimensions: A grand perspective and some limited empiricism. In D. Magnussen (Ed.), *Toward a psychology of situations: An interactionist perspective* (pp. 85–102). Hillsdale, NJ: Erlbaum.

Borman, W. C., & Brush, D. H. (1993). More progress toward a taxonomy of managerial performance requirements. *Human Performance, 6*, 1–21.

Bowler, M. C., & Woehr, D. J. (2006). A meta-analytic evaluation of the impact of dimension and exercise factors on assessment center ratings. *Journal of Applied Psychology, 91*, 1114–1124.

Brannick, M. T. (2008). Back to basics of test construction and scoring. *Industrial and Organizational Psychology: Perspectives on Science and Practice, 1*, 131–133.

Donnellan, M., Lucas, R. E., & Fleeson, W. (2009). Introduction to personality and assessment at age 40: Reflections on the legacy of the person-situation debate and the future of person-situation integration [Special issue]. *Journal of Research in Personality, 43*, 117–119.

Gaugler, B. B., Rosenthal, D. B., Thornton, G. C., III, & Bentson, C. (1987). Meta-analysis of assessment center validity. *Journal of Applied Psychology, 72*, 493–511.

Haaland, S., & Christiansen, N. D. (2002). Implications of trait-activation theory for evaluating the construct validity of assessment center ratings. *Personnel Psychology, 55*, 137–163.

Handyside, J. D., & Duncan, D. C. (1954). Four years later: A follow-up of an experiment in selecting supervisors. *Occupational Psychology, 28*, 9–23.

Hoffman, B., Lance, C. E., Bynum, B., & Gentry, W. A. (2010). Rater source effects are alive and well after all. *Personnel Psychology, 63*, 119–151.

Hoffman, B. J., Melchers, K. G., Blair, C. A., Kleinmann, M., & Ladd, R. T. (2011). Exercises AND dimensions are the currency of assessment centers. *Personnel Psychology, 64*, 351-395.

Hough, L. M., & Oswald, F. L. (2008). Personality testing and industrial-organizational psychology: Reflections, progress, and prospects. *Industrial and Organizational Psychology: Perspectives on Science and Practice, 1*, 272–290.

Howard, A. (1997). A reassessment of assessment centers: Challenges for the 21st century. *Journal of Social Behavior and Personality, 12*, 13–52.

Howard, A. (2008). Making assessment centers work the way they are supposed to. *Industrial and Organizational Psychology: Perspectives on Science and Practice, 1*, 98–104.

International Task Force on Assessment Center Guidelines. (2009). Guidelines and ethical considerations for assessment center operations. *International Journal of Selection and Assessment, 17*, 243–253.

Jackson, D. J. R., Barney, A. R., Stillman, J. A., & Kirkley, W. (2007). When traits are behaviors: The relationship between behavioral responses and trait-based overall assessment center ratings. *Human Performance, 20*, 415–432.

Jansen, A., Lievens, F., & Kleinmann, M. (2011). Do individual differences in perceiving situational demands moderate the relationship between personality and assessment center dimension ratings? *Human Performance, 24*, 231–250.

Klehe, U.-C., König, C. J., Richter, G. M., Kleinmann, M., & Melchers, K. G. (2008). Transparency in structured interviews: Consequences for construct and criterion-related validity. *Human Performance, 21*, 107–137.

Kleinmann, M. (1993). Are rating dimensions in assessment centers transparent for participants? Consequences for criterion and construct validity. *Journal of Applied Psychology, 78*, 988–993.

Kleinmann, M., Ingold, P. V., Lievens, F., König, C. J., Melchers, K. G., & Jansen, A. (2011). A different look at why selection procedures work: The role of candidates' ability to identify criteria. *Organizational Psychology Review, 1*, 128-146

Kleinmann, M., Kuptsch, C., & Köller, O. (1996). Transparency: A necessary requirement for the construct validity of assessment centres. *Applied Psychology: An International Review, 45*, 67–84.

Kolk, N. J., Born, M. P., & van der Flier, H. (2003). The transparent assessment centre: The effects of revealing dimensions to candidates. *Applied Psychology: An International Review, 52*, 648–668.

Kolk, N. J., Born, M. P., & van der Flier, H. (2004). A triadic approach to the construct validity of the assessment center: The effect of categorizing dimensions into a feeling, thinking, and power taxonomy. *European Journal of Psychological Assessment, 20*, 149–156.

Lance, C. E., Dawson, B., Birkelbach, D., & Hoffman, B. J. (2010). Method effects, measurement error, and substantive conclusions. *Organizational Research Methods, 13*, 435–455.

Lance, C. E., Foster, M. R., Gentry, W. A., & Thoresen, J. D. (2004). Assessor cognitive processes in an operational assessment center. *Journal of Applied Psychology, 89*, 22–35.

Lance, C. E., Foster, M. R., Nemeth, Y. M., Gentry, W. A., & Drollinger, S. (2007). Extending the nomological network of assessment center construct validity: Prediction of cross-situationally consistent and specific aspects of assessment center performance. *Human Performance, 20*, 345–362.

Lance, C. E., Lambert, T. A., Gewin, A. G., Lievens, F., & Conway, J. M. (2004). Revised estimates of dimension and exercise variance components in assessment center postexercise dimension ratings. *Journal of Applied Psychology, 89*, 377–385.

Lance, C. E., Newbolt, W. H., Gatewood, R. D., Foster, M. R., French, N. R., & Smith, D. E. (2000). Assessment center exercise factors represent cross-situational specificity, not method bias. *Human Performance, 13*, 323–353.

Lewin, K. (1946). Behavior and development as a function of the total situation. In L. Carmichael (Ed.), *Manual of child psychology* (pp. 791–844). New York: Wiley.

Lievens, F., Chasteen, C. S., Day, E. A., & Christiansen, N. D. (2006). Large-scale investigation of the role of trait activation theory for understanding assessment center convergent and discriminant validity. *Journal of Applied Psychology, 91*, 247–258.

Lievens, F., Tett, R. P., & Schleicher, D. J. (2009). Assessment centers at the crossroads: Toward a reconceptualization of assessment center exercises. In J. J. Martocchio & H. Liao (Eds.), *Research in personnel and human resources management* (Vol. 28, pp. 99–152). Oxford, UK: JAI.

Melchers, K. G., Henggeler, C., & Kleinmann, M. (2007). Do within-dimension ratings in assessment centers really lead to improved construct validity? A meta-analytic reassessment. *Zeitschrift für Personalpsychologie, 6*, 141–149.

Melchers, K. G., Klehe, U.-C., Richter, G. M., Kleinmann, M., König, C. J., & Lievens, F. (2009). "I know what you want to know": The impact of interviewees' ability to identify criteria on interview performance and construct-related validity. *Human Performance, 22*, 355–374.

Mischel, W. (1973). Toward a cognitive social learning reconceptualization of personality. *Psychological Review, 80*, 252–283.

Mischel, W. (1977). The interaction of person and situation. In D. Magnusson & N. S. Endler (Eds.), *Personality at the crossroads: Current issues in interactional psychology* (pp. 333–352). Hillsdale, NJ: Erlbaum.

Mischel, W. (2009). From Personality and Sssessment (1968) to Personality Dcience, 2009. *Journal of Research in Personality, 43*, 282–290.

Mischel, W., & Shoda, Y. (1995). A cognitive-affective system theory of personality: Reconceptualizing situations, dispositions, dynamics, and invariance in personality structure. *Psychological Review, 102*, 246–268.

Neidig, R. D., & Neidig, P. J. (1984). Multiple assessment center exercises and job relatedness. *Journal of Applied Psychology, 69*, 182–186.

Reis, H. T. (2008). Reinvigorating the concept of situation in social psychology. *Personality and Social Psychology Review, 12*, 311–329.

Schneider, J. R., & Schmitt, N. (1992). An exercise design approach to understanding assessment center dimension and exercise constructs. *Journal of Applied Psychology, 77*, 32–41.

Shore, T. H., Thornton, G. C., III, & Shore, L. M. (1990). Construct validity of two categories of assessment center dimension ratings. *Personnel Psychology, 43*, 101–116.

Smith-Jentsch, K. A. (2007). The impact of making targeted dimensions tranparent on relations with typical performance predictors. *Human Performance, 20*, 187–203.

Tett, R. P., & Burnett, D. D. (2003). A personality trait-based interactionist model of job performance. *Journal of Applied Psychology, 88*, 500–517.

Tett, R. P., & Guterman, H. A. (2000). Situation trait relevance, trait expression, and cross-situational consistency: Testing a principle of trait activation. *Journal of Research in Personality, 34*, 397–423.

Van Iddekinge, C. H., Raymark, P. H., Eidson, C. E., & Attenweiler, W. J. (2004). What do structured selection interviews really measure? The construct validity of behavior description interviews. *Human Performance, 17*, 71–93.

Woehr, D. J., & Arthur, W., Jr. (2003). The construct-related validity of assessment center ratings: A review and meta-analysis of the role of methodological factors. *Journal of Management, 29*, 231–258.

12

How to Apply a Mixed-Model Assessment Center

Jurgen Bank
BTS USA, Inc.

Sarah Brock, Anuradha Ramesh, and Joy Hazucha
PDI Ninth House

Introduction

As assessment practitioners, we are in the business of helping organizations achieve their goals by improving the quality of their leaders. In the world of Assessment Centers (ACs) this means supporting clients to make better individual and organizational decisions, including decisions for leader selection, succession, and development. This chapter begins with a key question: How can we create and implement an effective, applied AC that meets psychometric rigor and our stakeholder's business needs? We use the mixed-model AC to satisfy both requirements.

Consider the following situation:

> *A large, manufacturing company is looking to fill a regional VP role. In conjunction with HR, the hiring manager has identified the following critical skills: develop innovative solutions, motivate others to perform, drive execution through others, develop talent and demonstrate adaptability. In the client's view these skills are critical to success. The hiring manager has also pointed out significant business and job challenges that the regional VP would face: manage sales, services, local marketing and HR; lead the outsourcing of all the company's service offerings; accomplish results by empowering others; drive improved business results; coordinate work with peers across division lines; and renew key clients' commitment.*

In this situation, what kind of assessment should be used to identify the right person for the role? Should the focus be on the critical skills as measured in the dimensions or on assessing the individual's ability to meet these business challenges? This is the key question when choosing either a dimension approach or a task approach in a leadership assessment. In our practice the answer is obvious. We focus on both, measuring the critical skills *within* the context of specific business challenges. Despite the academic methodology debate between the relative merits of a dimension (Arthur, Day, & Woehr, 2008) or a task-based (Lance, 2008) approach to ACs, the market demands a rigorous assessment of skills or dimensions that predict a leader's performance when addressing specific business, industry, functional, or job challenges. The mixed-model approach supports criterion validity and face validity; both are relevant to our clients' acceptance of the assessment process and results.

To illustrate how practitioners apply the mixed-model AC, we will first examine the macro context and investigate how the business and work environment impact the design and use of the mixed-model AC. We will then move to a discussion of the micro aspects of the mixed-model AC, where we review how design and data management work and how the mixed-model AC handles tasks and dimensions. It is fair to say that the macro context has a tremendous impact on the micro view of the mixed-model AC, as it sets the parameters for tasks and dimensions. We will then circle back to the macro view to look at the business and work environment from the perspective of a specific assessment instance. We will discuss how the purpose of the assessment and the participant's macro environment influence the presentation of results. Finally, we will present future research directions.

The Macro View of the Mixed-Model AC

We use the term *macro* to refer to contextual issues, such as job specific requirements, corporate needs and organizational culture. This entails an understanding of critical job tasks, corporate strategy, specific leadership challenges, and related concurrent business challenges, corporate culture and how it shapes specific leadership style expectations and derailers, preferred aspirational aspects, and possible rewards on the career path.

The Concurrent State of the Business Matters

Business, industry, and leadership challenges can strongly impact AC design. External factors such as economic environment and industry trends have a direct influence on how business is conducted and drive leadership issues at any given time. This may be well illustrated in a straightforward example. The generally depressed economy and vast changes in how news became accessible on the internet in the last decade lead to a dramatic change of the newspaper business in the United States. Rich income sources (i.e., advertising) dried up as the advertisement revenue was progressively consumed by the internet. Concurrently the reader base shrank because consumers progressively satisfied their information needs online. This lead to an industry trend of decline and concentration. All of these aspects affected the way business was conducted, i.e., *doing more with less*, *downsizing supporting functions* and *stretching leaders by exposing them to dramatic and unwelcome surprises.* Specific leadership challenges for a particular executive in this context could have been, for example, *to prevent attrition of most talented employees, maintain morale, and to manage the acquisition of additional skills in the absence of support teams.* When designing an assessment center, it is critical that the nature of the simulations and the dimensions assessed reflect such macro context issues.

Motivators Need to be Understood

Understanding how a role will motivate an incumbent, including the rewards and the career path it provides, is also critical for the correct application of assessment data. For example, in some organizations mid-level leader field roles have significant autonomy. Success and rewards are largely driven by hitting the numbers. Leaders who are motivated by having autonomy and managing towards financial goals will experience a greater likelihood of satisfaction and success in the job than those who are motivated by executing clear supervisory directives. Contextual motivators impact the design of tasks and the choice of dimensions measured. A client wishing to assess mid-level field leaders, such as those described above, will receive more meaningful data if the boss simulation included tasks with little oversight or direction, a strong focus on performance metrics *and* measured dimensions related to initiative, financial savvy, and determination to achieve.

Derailers Flag Incompatibility with Organizational Culture

A final contextual variable might be best addressed with the term *derailers*, describing behaviors and preferences that may lead to failure

(Lombardo, Ruderman, & McCauley, 1988). We often identify derailers that are specific to a company's culture or a particular job. For example in businesses dominated by engineers a culture of precise project management is predominant. In such an environment a manager would likely be derailed unless he/she was able to define an approach to execution. When designing an AC for such a role, not only must the simulation invoke management of concepts or ideas but it also should include an opportunity to demonstrate his/her thoughts on execution. Thus, both the exercises and dimensions are informed by potential derailers specific to a given organizational environment. While many derailers may impact the scoring of certain competencies, we also recommend to point out explicitly the threats to a person's success in the client's work environment and business culture. Just as we showed how the motivational structure of the target environment is relevant to the AC design, so too can its culture impact the design of the assessment components. These results should be emphasized in the report.

We recommend to factor-in job context variables into the design and into the interpretation of the AC:

1. The macro-view grounds the mixed-model AC and provides the foundation for better design and more relevant interpretation of data.
2. Concurrent Business and Leadership challenges should impact the design.
3. Available motivators should be identified and reflected in the interpretation of data.
4. Derailers poignantly describe potential conflicts between personal style and organizational culture and must be identified and considered.

Designing a Mixed-Model AC

Critical Job Tasks Should be AC Simulation Tasks

Understanding the job tasks and evaluating their criticality for success in the job is the foundation of the AC design. As an illustration, a particular boss meeting simulation has a strong focus on identifying and initiating strategies. A simulation like this should be used when the target environment is undergoing significant change and strategic adjustments are necessary. While all jobs include a boss, we do not always include a boss meeting simulation in our ACs. For example, jobs that have a focus on execution of processes would warrant simulations such as an in-box and a direct report meeting. Thus, critical job tasks drive the decision to use one simulation over another. At the same time, these critical job tasks impact the dimensions considered in the AC design. The interdependence of tasks and dimensions on the macro level is further demonstrated in Table 12.1. Job tasks, simulation tasks and dimensions are inextricably linked in the content of ACs.

Table 12.1 Job Tasks, Simulation Task Categories, and Dimensions

Examples of Relevant Job tasks	Simulation Task Category	Dimensions
Manages others directly *Needs to drive execution through others*	Direct Report Meeting	*Use Insightful Judgment* *Financial Acumen* *Engage and Inspire* *Promote Collaboration* *Ensure Execution* *Drive for Results*
Manages vendors *Applies strategy to vendor management and support successful execution*	Vendor Meeting	*Use Insightful Judgment* *Strategic Thinking* *Financial Acumen* *Innovate* *Influence Others* *Promote Collaboration* *Build Relationships* *Drive for Results*
Manages external clients *Addresses and resolves customer concerns, and/or develop long-term client plans* *Ensures transfer of learnings within the organization*	Customer Meeting	*Use Insightful Judgment* *Financial Acumen* *Innovate* *Influence Others* *Promote Collaboration* *Build Relationships* *Ensure Execution* *Drive for Results*
Contributes to defining strategy *Aligns own areas with strategic planning* *Develops area specific initiatives to support strategies*	Boss Meeting	*Use Insightful Judgment* *Strategic Thinking* *Financial Acumen* *Innovate* *Influence Others* *Drive for Results*
Influences peers across the organization *Influences peers in order to drive own results*	Team Meeting	*Use Insightful Judgment* *Strategic Thinking* *Financial Acumen* *Innovate* *Influence Others* *Promote Collaboration* *Build Relationships* *Drive for Results*

Using Pre-Existing or Custom Simulations

When designing a mixed-model AC, a systematic classification of simulation categories might be helpful. We either select from a catalogue of pre-existing, well-developed and researched simulations, or we develop new simulations to capture the critical job tasks and challenges. Our goal is to optimize relevance, measurement rigor and efficiency—for each target role we search for a set of simulations that will best mimic the business challenges and job tasks and will allow for observations of the critical skills or dimensions. We like to work with the following list of possible AC simulation categories. *Inbox, meeting with a direct report, meeting with peers, leaderless group discussion, meeting with boss, meeting with customer, meeting with vendor, giving a presentation to all employees,* and *holding a press conference.*

We have established well-developed versions of these simulations for various levels in the organization (see more about hierarchical dimension models below) and for field and headquarter roles. Using pre-existing simulations has distinct advantages. First, using pre-existing simulations requires no additional time or capital investment which would otherwise be spent to draft, pilot and review materials and enable consultants for each specific AC project. Second, because of the pervasive use of the same content across a large number of AC projects, global calibration can be achieved with reasonable effort. Finally, the use of pre-existing simulations enables us to build vast databases and establish norms to monitor for trends, control item effectiveness and research long-term predictiveness in a systematic fashion. Custom developed simulations provide good value when they are part of large assessment projects that will run with hundreds of participants over many years so that they aggregate a critical mass of data.

Making Hard Choices to Optimize the Solution

Whether we use pre-existing or custom simulations, we generally experience that both task-focus and the dimension-focus result in the same design. As others have pointed out, the nature of the performance situation dictates the nature of the critical behaviors (Lievens & Christiansen, Chapter 4, this volume), and this interdependency leads both approaches to equal designs (also see Table 12.1).

We typically start by identifying the organizational level of the role, and then prioritize the challenges within the target role. The practical considerations of time and money must be balanced against comprehensiveness of coverage. As we develop a set of new simulations or make choices for a set of pre-existing simulations, we also explore the dimensions that are critical for success. We investigate whether or not the selected set of simulations provides sufficient data to evaluate the desired dimensions. In most cases it would not possible to replicate all the critical tasks or challenges associated with a job in one exercise. But high-fidelity, realistic simulations easily hit on a broad range of dimensions. Multiple exercises provide the additional opportunity to collate more data resulting in more robust dimension measurements. Intuitively one would assume that more exercises automatically lead to more reliable measures. This is in fact the case when the simulations are highly similar. Situations where the actual behaviors in two simulations are not well aligned, and the ratings are not expected to correlate, will result in lower observed reliability. See more about the construction of rating sheets to achieve across simulation convergence below.

We also consider delivery efficiency as a critical aspect in the applied setting of the practitioner, as both the participant's time as well as the consultant's time are a direct cost to the client. We may eliminate dimension ratings from a simulation even when the behaviors are observable, if we have the opportunities for more precise ratings in another simulation. To differentiate between included and excluded dimension ratings, we use the judgment of experienced observers, often in collaboration with the client. We also consider the variance in dimension ratings for each exercise. A dimension/exercise measure with a large rating variance is discriminating well between participants and is therefore preferred over one with smaller variance.

Our research and experience suggests that using two to four simulations is adequate to strike a balance between the cost and validity of the AC. The use of multiple observations allows us to understand pervasive strengths and development needs that emerge consistently across situations as well as those that might be specific to a given situation. As a rule of thumb we strive for at least two scores from different simulations for the same dimension but often include as many as four. In Table 12.2 we present all potential observations points associated with a cluster of dimensions and tasks. Table 12.3 displays a representative final design example of an integration grid.

Table 12.2 Integration Grid: What Is Observable

	In-Box	Direct Report Meeting	Boss Meeting	Peer Meeting	Team Meeting	Customer Meeting	Vendor Meeting
Judgment	x	x	x	x	x	x	x
Strategy	x		x	x	x	x	x
Financial Thinking	x	x	x	x	x		
Innovation			x	x	x	x	x
Global Thinking	x		x			x	
Influencing			x	x	x	x	x
Inspiring	x	x		x	x		
Collaborating	x	x		x	x		x
Talent Support	x	x	x				
Relationship Building		x		x	x	x	x
Execution Skills	x	x	x			x	
Drive	x	x	x	x	x	x	x
Customer Focus	x		x			x	
Courage		x	x	x	x		x
Trust Building	x	x		x	x	x	x
Adaptability			x	x	x	x	x

The final assessment design usually consists of a subset of the conceptually complete matrix. Based on the leadership framework, specification of context and efficient use of observation points, the appropriate tasks and dimensions are selected. In this decision process, we make hard trade-offs and both tasks and dimensions are scrutinized. A focus on pivotal tasks *and* the critical dimensions leads to the final design. Thus, in the design of this mixed-model AC, task and dimension aspects are equally considered.

We would like to summarize the following recommendations:

1. Simulation tasks should resemble job tasks.
2. Pre-existing simulations can be more economical, they often can be researched better, and they may be more effective.
3. The AC should focus on the most critical aspects in the target job (regarding dimensions and simulations).
4. It makes economic sense to optimize the number of dimensions rated in each given simulation.

Table 12.3 Integration Grid: Example

	In-Box	Boss Meeting	Team Meeting	Customer Meeting
Use Insightful Judgment	x		x	
Think Strategically		x	x	
Apply Financial Acumen	x	x		
Innovate		x		x
Display Global Perspective				
Influence Others		x	x	x
Engage and Inspire	x		x	
Promote Collaboration	x		x	
Build Talent	x	x		
Build Relationships			x	x
Ensure Execution	x	x		x
Drive for Results	x	x	x	x
Focus on Customers	x	x		x
Lead Courageously		x	x	
Inspire Trust	x		x	x
Adapt and Learn			x	x

The Micro View of the Mixed-Model AC

Brian Hoffman (Chapter 13, in this volume) raises conceptual questions regarding the meaning and interpretation of exercise effects. Connelly, Ones, Ramesh and Goff, (2008) have demonstrated, using data from our practice, that both exercises and dimensions provide valid variance in assessments, thus offering empirical support for a mixed-model. We will split our arguments into an exercise and a dimension focus. In our view, and as we already have expressed, these two views are more like two sides of the same coin. We systematically cross-reference the dimension and the task view.

Exercise Effect

Simulations Must Be Task Relevant. In our practice we do not engage a participant in an activity that is not obviously face valid. For example, it would not be palatable to our clients to engage in a call-center exercise if answering calls from customers was not part of the job. Or, even if we could provide an outstandingly powerful client meeting simulation that would measure pivotal competencies, such a simulation would not be acceptable if meetings with clients were not part of the participants' job.

However, the scenario need not be set in the industry of the target role. Often it is more valuable to design the business and leadership challenges in an altered setting as this takes participants out of their comfort zone and does not allow them to copy approaches from their current environment without additional reflection. Rather, a change of industry levels the playing field for participants from within the industry and from outside. For example, the AC scenario for a client looking to assess for the position of a restaurant chain's regional manager could resemble a regional manager role of a drugstore chain. As long as the AC tasks resemble job tasks and the participants are reasonably familiar with the subject matter the lack of actual, specific industry expertise does not mask skill measurement.

The fact that we employ exclusively job task relevant simulations may also contribute to equal importance of task and dimension data in our practice. When job tasks and simulation tasks are not aligned and the similarity between tasks in the simulation and in the role diminishes, validity will likely deteriorate even when dimensions still appear to be job relevant. In other words, relevant dimensions measured in irrelevant situations may lead to irrelevant results. For example, convincing others, measured in a sales meeting might not be relevant to the skill of convincing a group of peers.

Calibration Reduces Unwanted Variance. One methodological requirement for the AC is the reliability of the measure. We invest considerable effort in establishing and maintaining a consistent calibration of our raters, in order to minimize rating style differences. Ill-calibrated raters create error variance between simulations that needs to be avoided. Thorough calibration is of particular interest for a global practice that navigates the difference not only between individual raters, but also across their languages and cultural backgrounds. During the calibration sessions, a deliberate discussion establishes a common understanding of the minute dynamics of the simulation and how to best react to particular behavior of the participant. In the next step, calibration trainees observe a taped simulation and are asked to rate the participant. Finally, trainees compare their ratings with an expert rating, discussing and resolving any discrepancies. This process is repeated until a satisfactory calibration result is achieved. Consultants do not participate in our assessment practice until they have passed calibration.

We would also like to point out that besides the dimension-based ratings we also require the rating of the exercise as a whole, i.e., *Overall Performance, very strong.* Furthermore, we ask consultants to what degree they found that the participant met certain qualitative goals in the exercise, i.e., *Developed 3-5 strategies that will improve margin and support profitable growth*, or *Showed how the strategic priorities will affect customer value and competitive positioning.*

By training and calibration on the rating practice of competencies and simulations specific outcomes, consultants acquire a robust and shared understanding of desired behaviors in specific dimensions *and* desired behaviors outcomes on the task level. This practice fully supports a hybrid understanding of the AC as we include standards for competency scores and task outcomes.

Should We Expect that Exercise Scores Correlate with One Another. Looking at the AC design from a naïve perspective, one would expect that within the one person there is likely a difference between how well he/she performs in different tasks. We would agree with the task based view that different tasks can lead to independent measurements of performance. However, based on our experience we also accept the assumption that tasks that are related to similar behaviors are correlating with one another. (Below, when we discuss how we use behaviors, it will become clearer, that our process of allocating BARS to dimensions favors the correlatedness.) In conclusion we would say that we expect the degree of intercorrelatedness of exercise average scores to be dependent on the proportion of shared competencies they tap into.

We want to highlight the following suggestions when designing a mixed-model AC:

1. Simulations must be task relevant, but not necessarily in the same industry as the target job.
2. Calibration of raters is necessary to reduce unwanted variance across raters.

Dimension Effects

As we have pointed out before, we believe that job tasks and skills dimensions and exercises are inextricably linked. There are a number of applied issues that we would like to discuss involving the use of dimensions and their interplay with the nature of exercises.

Dimensions Should be Conceptually and Empirically Clean. Frequently, we are confronted with clients who expect us to use competency models that have already been adopted in their organizations. When reviewing such competency models, we find significant variability in quality and usefulness for the AC. In competency models that we find difficult to work with, some of the dimensions appear to be designed primarily with corporate goals in mind, not considering that measuring them requires association with distinct and observable behaviors. For example, the dimension, Getting things done through others taps into many independent components, such as ability to analyze the complexity of problems, ability to motivate others, ability to instruct others, ability to monitor others' work, ability to judge the ability of others, the ability to put together effective teams, and many other aspects. This competency would greatly overlap with a second dimension *Commitment to 100% quality* in many of the behaviors just listed. In other words, although there always will be some overlap between dimensions, it is important that the competencies refer to reasonably distinct behaviors. To avoid a host of measurement issues related to data interdependence, we prefer to tease convoluted competencies apart and replace them with more precise and independent dimensions.

Use of Similar BARS Across Simulations. Our rating sheets are made up of Behaviorally Anchored Rating Scales (BARS) that have been designed for each dimension. BARS rating data has also been scrutinized to optimize internal consistency and differentiation between dimensions.

On a pragmatic level, we would also like to point out that we prefer BARS of the same dimension to be as similar as possible across simulations (see Table 12.4). In order to support simulation-specificity, the BARS are paired with simulation-specific, concrete behavioral examples. For example, *made several suggestions on how the analysis of the quality issue could be approached.* These behavioral examples are different across the simulations. Thus, although the types of behavior associated with a given dimension are the same in different simulations, the specific behaviors, including specific reference to issues and people in the scenario, are worded to match the situation closely.

Table 12.4 Strength Anchors for Customer Orientation Dimension across Tasks

In-Box Simulation	Boss Simulation	Team Simulation
Sought relevant and specific feedback from customers to continuously improve processes, products, and services.	Exceeded customer expectations, providing significant value.	Made plans to solicit additional feedback from customers to continuously improve processes, products, and services.
Consistently ensured that customer issues were fully and effectively resolved.	Created systems and processes that made it as easy as possible for customers to do business with the company.	Consistently and proactively searched for solutions that would provide new and significant ways to improve the customer experience.
Fostered a customer-focused environment where people were fully committed to maximizing customer satisfaction, loyalty, and commitment.	Proactively identified and anticipated customer requirements, expectations, and needs.	Proactively identified and anticipated customer requirements, expectations, and needs.

It is most concerning when we find that dimensions measured within the same exercise are strongly correlated. As stated above, this may occur when an AC is designed with imprecise and overlapping dimensions. Other possible reasons for a lack of variance across dimensions within a given exercise could be that a simulation is too difficult, or not difficult enough, or that the BARS do not adequately reflect the task. If that applies, we would consider the simulation design a root cause for lack of variance and the re-engineering of the simulation would be required. The goal is to create rater data that shows acceptable independence between dimensions measured in the same exercise.

Should We Expect Scores Within the Same Dimension Across Simulations to Correlate? In a strict multiple trait, multiple-method, approach one would assume that dimension scores across the simulations should correlate. However, in the exercise section above, we mentioned the naïve assumption that different tasks should result in independent task scores. We believe that the key to the solution of this conundrum lies in the detail of how task, dimensions, and observation techniques are constructed and aligned. A general answer regarding tasks and dimension relevance seems not to make sense in the absence of a clear understanding how they are defined and what data ends up in the cells of the integration grid.

In our practice we prefer to use the *same* BARS across the tasks for the *same* dimension. This helps with convergent validity as well as with a greater variance in the across tasks average. The more similar the BARS, the higher the correlations between two measures, as long as the BARS are equally related to observable behavior evoked in the respective simulations. Two simulations that are so much alike that they use the same set of BARS in their rating sheets, we would assume, should correlate strongly and only the error of measurement would keep them from generating identical scores. (We have already made a similar point in the exercise section.)

Looking at real life data, however, we need to acknowledge, that in-basket data generally correlates less with social situations, and social situations of the same nature, correlate more with one another than those of a different nature.

Leadership Taxonomies and Layers of Organizational Structure. There are many different taxonomies of managerial performance that have been used to describe the skills and characteristics of effective managers and leaders (e.g., Borman & Brush, 1993; Dowell & Wexley, 1978; Tett, Guterman, Bleier, & Murphy, 2000; Yukl & Lepsinger, 1992; Mintzberg, 1980). These dimension based models of managerial performance consist of 7 (Dowell & Wexley, 1978) to 18 (Borman & Brush, 1993) or even more dimensions depending on the level of specificity applied by the researchers. Most models include categories such as strategic planning; motivating, guiding and developing subordinates; networking; and managing resources. In our practice we use a leadership framework that groups dimensions into four domains.

The first domain, *Thought Leadership*, includes the ability to gather, integrate, and analyze information; make sound decisions; exercise strategic judgment; think innovatively and multi-dimensionally; and reason both inductively and deductively in the business context. These abilities have been shown to be related to successful leadership (Hoffman, Woehr, Maldegan, & Lyons, 2011; Kirkpatrick & Locke, 1991; Lord, DeVader, & Alliger, 1986). The second domain, *People Leadership*, describes the ability to work well with others, engage a team, and collaborate. This dimension has been demonstrated to identify effective leaders, as they display consideration of individuals' needs, abilities, and aspirations; attentive listening; effective coaching; mentoring; and team building (Bass, 1999; Tichy & Devanna, 1986). The third domain, *Results Leadership*, includes the ability to coordinate resources to achieve goals, drive for results, and plan and execute actions. The final domain, *Personal Leadership*, focuses on an individual's ability to manage him- or herself and includes the competencies that focus on adaptability, learning, and self-development. In summary, these four broad categories represent key behavioral performance areas that have been shown in many research studies to be related to successful leadership (Kirkpatrick & Locke, 1991; Yukl & Lepsinger, 1992).

Beyond this conceptual separation of dimensions, we have developed a stratified taxonomy that contains critical behaviors associated with the level in the organization and the complexity of the leadership tasks. We differentiate between five leadership levels, from team supervisor to the CEO of a Global 500 corporation. Looking across a wide range of industries, we have found that key leadership challenges and tasks can be grouped across leadership roles on the same level. Many similar challenges can be observed in jobs on the same hierarchical level and of comparable scope. For example *direct report meetings* are generally important for leadership roles on supervisory, department and business unit level. *Boss meetings* typically have a strong strategic thinking component and are more relevant on higher levels in the organization. A number of simulations that we developed taps into the challenges and tasks typical at each level.

This practice is informed by a robust body of literature (Boyatzis, 1982; Dierdoff, Rubin, & Morgenson, 2009; Spencer & Spencer, 1993; Tett et al., 2000) The discrete set of dimensions with specific behavior definitions, each adapted to one of five levels of leadership, reflects a powerful and well-researched taxonomy of managerial effectiveness (Borman & Brush, 1993; Dowell & Wexley, 1978; Tett et al., 2000). At different levels in the organization different skills are needed. (Charan & Drotter, 2000; Mumford, Campion, & Morgenson, 2007) (see Table 12.5). On a general level one could say that the definition of a competency is consistent across the hierarchical levels, however, on the behavior level significant differences exist. Because different behaviors are needed to measure each dimension at different hierarchical levels, the hierarchical level also drives the nature of the simulations we use.

Table 12.5 Stratified Competency Labels of Four Exemplatory Dimensions

	Vision / Innovation	Drive for Results	Engage and Inspire	Adaptability
C-level	Provide Vision	Drive for Stakeholder Success	Inspire Passion	Demonstrate Resilience
Senior Executive	Display Vision	Drive for Organizational Success	Energize the Organization	Demonstrate Agility
Executive	Innovate	Drive For Results	Engage and Inspire	Adapt and Learn
Managing Managers	Think Creatively	Show Drive & Initiative	Motivate Others	Show Adaptability
Managing Others	Identify Improvements	Show Initiative	Encourage Commitment	Readily Adapt

1 Pertinent to the main theme of this book we focus on the variance coming from simulations only. However in our practice we also include an interview, algorithm driven competency scores based on a personality questionnaire and cognitive reasoning tests. This practice is supported by strong empirical findings that these methods increase the predictive variance of the integration grid.

2 We also allow our consultants to sway the final rating if they have instance-specific evidence that certain observation should be weighted higher than others.

3 Quite often we find a significant difference between the global description of the macro variables as we gather them from the organization and how they are represented by line managers and participants. During pre-assessment consulting and interview we explore the "local macro." During feedback we use the "local macro" to position our findings effectively and generate buy-in.

4 In the summary report to the organization typically the simulation task view is not represented because, for simplicity reasons, organizations prefer to discuss results in competency language.

When using pre-existing simulations we often also use generic competency models that ensure a good balance of domains and the time tested and well-researched rating sheets that were developed with that generic model. Our consultants can apply their calibration knowledge when working with the rating sheet content they are familiar with. Only in a second step do we generate client competency scores from the scores generated with the generic model. This approach provides a double benefit. It guarantees balanced, relevant, calibrated data, and allows for efficiencies in infrastructure and training. It also provides our clients with a data presentation layer that uses their competency language, looks familiar and is therefore easy to process for the target audience (i.e., line management).

In summary, we recommend the following:

1. Dimensions should contain distinct behaviors.
2. Dimension ratings should be correlating more across simulations. If dimension ratings do not correlate across simulations, both measurement and substantive reasons should be explored.
3. Dimension ratings should be correlating less within simulations.
4. A good simulation creates rating data with large variance.
5. Using pre-existing well-researched rating sheets is compatible with the mixed-model approach and may have psychometric and economic benefits.
6. A balanced mix of competencies across the four leadership domains. (Thought, Results, People, Personal) is desired ACs for leadership roles.

How to Discuss Individual-Specific Data

At the end of the process of a mixed-model AC, information is generated regarding how a participant performed in specific tasks (e.g., the direct report meeting or boss meeting) *and* on how he/she performed on the dimensions (e.g., decision-making; influencing others).[1] Both the integration grid rows (dimensions) and columns (tasks) presented in Table 12.3 provide unique information and both have a legitimate place in the discussion of results with the participant, the hiring manager and other stakeholders in the client organization.

As scientists we understand that there are a number of possible root causes for inconsistent dimension scores across tasks that are associated with error of measurement, caused by factors such as insufficient calibration, order of simulations, environmental events during the AC, participant's self-fulfilling prophecy in regard to a specific task, and true performance differences that are tied to different situations. Our pragmatic way to come to an overall dimension rating is to average dimension scores across the simulations[2].

When the Dimension Rating "Does Not Add Up"

When the ratings do not converge within a dimension (or row of the integration grid), the discussion generally shifts to explore what took place in the various simulations. Our feedback recipients often inquire in detail to confirm that inconsistencies between simulations are not due to poor calibration between the various consultants rating the simulations.

For example, if we had observed a participant who excelled at *influence* in the boss meeting but was lacking *influence* in the direct report or the peer meeting, we might conclude that the participant was strong on the influencing behaviors related to presenting sound rationale and logic to convince others, but may not have equally strong skills in identifying "what's in it for others" and engaging a direct report. In these feedback sessions we are interpreting dimension performance *in light of* the tasks.

Another approach to deal with cross exercise differences in a dimension is to formally *split* dimensional performance based on task-based differences when assigning final dimension ratings into various components. For example, a participant can receive two different scores for the same competency, one referring to settings with people and one for settings on paper. In our view, such splitting is best avoided by a more elegant competency design. To the degree that differences in competency design has been ruled out, this approach can give a richer view of assessee performance that can be gained by collapsing incongruent dimensional performance across exercises.

When the Dimension Scores in One Exercise Are Consistently High or Low

In particular instances one may also observe a lack of variability of dimension scores for the same exercise. A number of situations may explain why this happened. The rater may have been subject to the halo effect, or the participant was ill-prepared and was completely unsuccessful in the simulation, or the simulation was too hard or too simple for the participant. By using dimensions from all four domains elucidated earlier, we typically find variability in performance measures within one exercise.

The Overall Average Matters

Obviously, a critical piece of data from the AC is the overall assessment score. Now, in any type of matrix, the average of the row averages equals the average of the column averages. Whether we communicate row (dimension) *or* column (exercise), averages may be governed by what makes the feedback most effective, as we will discuss. Either way, it is the overall average (be it the exercise *or* dimension average) which is the most important single variable to evaluate leadership on the simulated level, especially when the AC will be used in decision-making contexts. Of course, we also believe that for the focus of a participant's development and for the analysis of organizational strengths and developmental needs a more nuanced approach to interpreting AC performance is required. It is our general practices to norm this integration grid average. We present this overall average as a percentile that indicates how well an individual participant performed compared to all other participants in this AC's norm base. Clients can interpret this *overall percentile* as a prediction of performance in the target job for two reasons: (a) we have established a correlation between assessment scores and job performance, and (b) we have established content congruence between key behaviors related to the accomplishment of key job challenges as observed in the simulations. A rich database—drawn from a dataset of over 120,000 completed mixed-model ACs—and the assurance of rater calibration allow for a confident application of norms and their interpretation.

Concluding Points

1. Averaging dimension scores across simulations is helpful.
2. Instances where dimension scores between simulations differ create opportunity for additional insight.
3. Instances where the dimension scores within one simulation do not vary are an indicator that something may have gone wrong.

4. The overall integration grid average is particularly meaningful and norming it adds to its usefulness.
5. The purpose shapes how results are presented.

We would like to show how we leverage our mixed-model approach to ACs by creating specific outputs depending on the purpose of the assessment, which can be a selection question, an information need for succession planning, or a plan to guide the participant's development. Depending on the purpose, we process the overall score and the macro variables[3] differently. Finally we would like to discuss the organizational uses of aggregated participant data.

A Measure of Fit for Selection

In selection assessments, one of our clients' key questions is whether a candidate represents a "good fit" for the job in question. When we predict fit, both the *overall percentile* and the performance in essential dimensions are important.[4] In order to go beyond the dimension and task data, we also consider the macro variables, career aspirations and motivation, experience, and style preferences. In each of these categories we rate how these macro variables match the requirements of the target environment. For prediction of best fit, we generate an index score that integrates the overall percentile with fit ratings of career aspirations and motivation, experience, and style preferences. Considering this holistic view of the participant maximizes the practical usefulness of the AC data (Hollenbeck, 2009; Bank, Crandell, Goff, Ramesh, & Sokol, 2009) for the purpose of fit prediction.

For Succession and Readiness

Readiness describes to what degree someone is ready to be promoted. We use the labels, *Develop in place*, *Broaden*, *Prepare,* and *Ready.* The readiness finding also points out what a person is missing if he or she is currently not *ready.* The readiness concept is of particular interest for succession planning where the focus is not on making a hiring decision, but on determining *when* to promote and *who* should receive often costly additional development activities. The question is not primarily related to fit with the job, but shifts to the individual's readiness for new challenges on a higher organizational level. As in the fit rating, we use the overall percentile, specific dimensions, and the macro variables. But in contrast to the fit rating we do not calculate an accumulative score. Instead we want to make sure that people receiving the *ready* ratings satisfied a good or better requirement in *each* aspect of readiness. For example, a participant who is lacking some critical experiences may be rated *prepare* and will not receive the rating *ready* until he/she has closed their experience gap. The readiness rating and its explanation indicate to the organization and the participants what needs to happen before they are considered to be prepared for the next career move. In this particular aspect of the AC, we are hard pressed to argue that the hybrid model is of particular usefulness beyond what was already stated about the origin of the *overall percentile* and the importance of extreme task or dimension specific findings.

Provide Insight for Development

The development goal of many ACs is to devise precise and quick development action. Dimension-based feedback is the most direct and may highlight specific areas of growth and potential focus; however, this dimensional feedback emphasizes both performance that is consistent across exercises and performance that differs depending on the exercise. Feedback also needs to create insight and motivation for behavior change. Our consultants are trained to use all approaches—the task based view, the dimensions based view and also macro variables such as experience, aspirations, style or derailers—whatever enables them to put together the best "story" to present to the participant so that he/she gains insight into the key findings. The simulation-specific feedback is tangible and therefore often easy to accept. And, as the human mind tends to look for simple patterns (Charter, 1999), we also invite participants to explore themes across the simulations. Often, participants will find a pattern in the information before the consultant can get to a discussion of the dimension view. Finding these patterns supports the development discussion as they allow the participant to *chunk* dimensional information for easy recall and application (i.e., Baddeley, 1994).

Providing dimension-based feedback *in light of* task-based results optimizes impact and motivation for behavior change. For example, feedback that a participant should improve his or her ability to *influence upwards using more data* when advocating for strategic change (as noted specifically in the boss meeting simulation) is more helpful than feedback that a participant should improve his/her influence or his/her boss meeting skills. Addressing identified development needs, explained with the help of situations or dimensions, will make a difference in the participant's motivation and focus to engage in develop action to prepare for real world tasks and business challenges.

At this point we would also like to discuss our practice of real-time coaching. In this approach to development ACs we interrupt the regular AC administration after each simulation and allow for the role-acting consultant and the participant to discuss their experience during the AC exercise. We have found that the immediacy of the feedback from the person who was minutes ago part of a business scenario, creates very powerful and memorable experiences for the participant. Insights that occurred during this unique opportunity to reflect on own leadership behavior with a coach is regularly documented as the most important take away from our development assessment participants. While this practice is focusing at one simulation at the time, we still consider it as part of the mixed model as we find that during the real-time coaching session behavior is discussed also in terms of competencies.

Analytics Allow for Organizational Benchmarking and Drive New Directions

A typical client is interested in AC analytics that use the aggregate assessment data to understand the strength and to identify organizational training and development needs of the participant group. Most clients prefer an initial presentation of aggregated AC data in the competency view. We often present graphics that depict strengths (i.e., highest rated dimensions) and development needs (i.e., lowest rated dimensions) for a particular group. However, as we consult around this data the discussion inevitably leads to mixed-model views when the client wants to understand *how, where*, and *why* we saw strengths or development needs on specific dimensions. In the discussion with the client, we are prepared to provide additional context information related to tasks that fully describes the detail of the simulation's design and how development might be possible. For example in a case where we found *develop talent* to be the lowest rated dimension, we might point out that providing *timely feedback* and *on-the spot coaching* during the *direct report meeting* were the lowest rated behaviors as opposed to the more typical themes during the boss meeting such as *uses consistent and fair processes to hire talent*; *understands what talent is needed*. This type of detailed, contextualized interpretation suggests that even in the talent consulting that uses AC results, the mixed-model approach is appropriate.

Summary

1. The fit measure considers the AC data in light of the context data and accumulates data to create a fit index that can directly compare participants in the selection process.
2. The readiness measure considers AC data in light of the context data and identifies gaps and categories of readiness.
3. The development report aims to motivate and focus the participant to work on the most critical development needs and leverage strengths.
4. Real-time coaching creates high-impact learning and personal insight opportunities.
5. AC analytics help the client organization to benchmark and identify competitive strengths and development needs.

Conclusion

The mixed-model has served us well in meeting many of our goals as science-guided practitioners. However, there are a few areas in which more research is required. As might have become apparent in this chapter, the dimension vs. task debate is not in the forefront of our concerns; we effectively utilize both aspects in our leadership focused practice.

More research should focus on understanding aspects of tasks that are specific to the hierarchical level and scope of leadership roles. The past two decades of work performance research has seen substantial attention to the development of performance taxonomies (Austin & Crespin, 2006), and in our practice we have implemented a stratified dimension model that is consistent with hierarchical taxonomies of managerial performance (Borman & Brush, 1993). Far less attention has been given to developing models of tasks which might be able to guide effective exercise selection.

Second, we would like to extend the academic focus on the approaches to feedback and how feedback can induce actual behavior change. We would like to better understand which leadership behaviors *can* be impacted and changed through development effort as compared to behaviors that will be difficult or impossible to change. For the mixed-model AC research, the question is about the appropriate format and emphasis of AC feedback. Specifically, can greater feedback acceptance and performance improvement be gained by presenting either exercise or dimension-based feedback or, what we assume, both.

Going forward, we welcome all research that provides better answers to the fit and readiness questions and induces targeted change and development with participants in our ACs. We believe that in our practice we have driven the mixed-model AC to a new level of maturity. We are striving to make organizations and their leaders—our leadership AC participants—more dynamic and competent so that they can master their challenges and make their organizations, and their consultants, successful.

Notes

1. Pertinent to the main theme of this book, we focus on the variance coming from simulations only. However, in our practice we also include an interview, algorithm driven competency scores based on a personality questionnaire, and cognitive reasoning tests. This practice is supported by strong empirical findings that these methods increase the predictive variance of the integration grid.
2. We also allow our consultants to sway the final rating if they have instance-specific evidence that certain observation should be weighted higher than others.
3. Quite often we find a significant difference between the global description of the macro variables as we gather them from the organization and how they are represented by line managers and participants. During pre-assessment consulting and interview, we explore the "local macro." During feedback we use the "local macro" to position our findings effectively and generate buy-in.
4. In the summary report to the organization typically the simulation task view is not represented because, for simplicity reasons, organizations prefer to discuss results in competency language.

References

Arthur, W., Jr., Day, E. A., & Woehr, D. J. (2008). Mend it, don't end it: An alternative view of assessment center construct-related validity. *Industrial and Organizational Psychology: Perspectives on Science and Practice, 1*, 109–115.

Austin, J. T., & Crespin, T. R. (2006). Problems of criteria in industrial and organizational psychology: Progress, problems, and prospects. *Performance measurement: Current perspectives and future challenges* (pp. 9–49). Mahwah, NJ: Erlbaum.

Baddeley, A. (1994). The magic number seven: Still magic after all these years? *Psychological Review, 2,* 353–356.

Bank, J., Crandell, S., Goff, M., Ramesh, A., & Sokol, M. (2009). Executive selection: Yes we can do better. *Industrial and Organizational Psychology, 2,* 151–154.

Bass, B. M. (1999). Two decades of research and development in transformational leadership. *European Journal of Work and Organizational Psychology, 8,* 9–2.

Borman, W. C., & Brush, D. H. (1993). More progress towards a taxonomy of managerial performance requirements. *Human Performance, 6,* 1–21.

Boyatzis, A. R. (1982). *The competent manager: A model for effective performance.* New York: Wiley.

Charan, R., & Drotter, S. (2000). *The leadership pipeline: How to build the leadership powered company.* San Francisco: Jossey-Bass.

Charter, N. (1999). The search for simplicity: A fundamental cognitive principle? *The Experimental Psychology Society, 52A,* 273–302.

Connelly, B. S., Ones, D. S., Ramesh, A., & Goff, M. (2008). A pragmatic view of assessment dimensions and exercises. *Industrial and organizational psychology: Perspectives on science and practice, 1,* 121–124.

Dierdorff, E. C., Rubin, R. S., & Morgenson, F. P. (2009). The milieu of managerial work: An integrative framework linking work context to role requirements. *Journal of Applied Psychology, 94,* 972–988.

Dowell, B. E., & Wexley, K. N. (1978). Development of a work behavior taxonomy for first line supervisors. *Journal of Applied Psychology, 63,* 563–572.

Hollenbeck, G. P. (2009). Executive Selection — What's right … and what's wrong. *Industrial and Organizational Psychology, 2,* 130–143.

Hoffman, B. J., Woehr, D. J., Maldegan-Youngjohn, D., & Lyons, B. D. (2011). Great man or great myth? A quantitative review of the relationship between individual differences and leader effectiveness. *Journal of Occupational and Organizational Psychology,84*(2), 347–381.

Kirkpatrick, S. A., & Locke, E. A. (1991). Leadership: Do traits matter? *Academy of Management Executive, 5,* 48–60.

Lance, C. E. (2008). Why assessment centers do not work the way they are supposed to. *Industrial Organizational Psychology: Perspectives on Science and Practice, 1,* 84–97.

Lombardo, M. M., Ruderman, M. N., & McCauley, C. D. (1988). Explanations of success and derailment in upper-level management positions. *Journal of Business and psychology, 2,* 199–216.

Lord, R. G., DeVader, C. L., & Alliger, G. M. (1986). A meta-analysis of the relation between personality traits and leadership perceptions: An application of validity generalization procedures. *Journal of Applied Psychology, 71,* 402–410.

McCauley, C. D., Ruderman, M. N., Ohlott, P. J., & Morrow, J. E. (1994). Assessing the developmental components of managerial jobs. *Journal of Applied Psychology, 79,* 544–560.

Mintzberg, H. (1980). *The nature of managerial work.* New York: Prentice Hall.

Mumford, M. D., Compion, M. A., & Morgenson, F. P. (2007). The leadership strataplex: Leadership skill requirements across organizational levels. *Leadership Quarterly, 18*, 154–166.

Spencer, L. M., & Spencer, S. (1993) *Competence at Work*. New York: Wiley.

Tett, R. P., Guterman, H. A., Bleier, A., & Murphy, P. J. (2000). Development and content validation of a "Hyperdimensional" taxonomy of managerial competence. *Human Performance, 13*, 205–251.

Tichy, N. M., & Devanna, M. A. (1986). *The transformational leader*. New York: Wiley

Yukl, G. A., & Lepsinger, R. (1992). An integrating taxonomy of managerial behavior: Implication for improving managerial effectiveness. In J. W. Jones, B. D. Steffy, & D. W. Bray (Eds.), *Applying psychology in business: The managers handbook* (pp. 563–572). MA: Lexington Press.

13

Exercises, Dimensions, and the Battle of Lilliput

Evidence for a Mixed-Model Interpretation of Assessment Center Performance

Brian J. Hoffman

University of Georgia

> It is computed that eleven thousand persons have at several times suffered death, rather than submit to break their eggs at the smaller end. (Jonathon Swift, *Gulliver's Travels*)

Introduction

Despite clear evidence for the presence, usefulness, and importance of dimensions and exercises in assessment centers (ACs), the majority of existing AC research presupposes that either dimensions *or* exercises are the appropriate focus for AC research and practice. As evidenced by the chapters in this book, there is compelling empirical evidence for both dimensions *and* exercises-based AC interpretations. Using this evidence as a springboard, the mixed-model perspective proposes that a complete interpretation of AC performance must include both dimension specific and exercise specific aspects of performance. To date, the evidentiary basis and inherent value underlying multifaceted interpretations of AC performance has rarely been explicitly articulated.

This chapter builds on existing AC literature in order to shed light on the meaning of the typical patterns of AC results, with a focus on interpreting both dimension and exercise variance as meaningful information in AC ratings. Based on this research, three perspectives of AC performance that consider both dimension and exercise-based assessment information are proposed, including: (a) an amended multitrait-multimethod (MTMM) model that includes broad dimensions, exercises, and general performance; (b) the dimensions within exercises model, emphasizing distinguishable performance dimensions in each exercise that don't necessarily converge across exercises; and (c) pattern approaches to AC performance, emphasizing the meaning of individual differences in patterns of AC performance. These three models will then be integrated with a focus on identifying the components of AC performance in order to facilitate a multifaceted and I believe, more complete interpretation of AC performance.

Mixed-Model Approaches

Although the three models take a very different approach to conceptualizing AC ratings, all three have in common the underlying assumption that dimension-specific and exercise-specific performance play a fundamental role in understanding assessee performance.

Mixed Model Perspective 1: MTMM-Based Conceptualizations

By now, the finding of strong correlations among different dimensions in the same exercise is well documented, as is the relatively weak correlation between the same dimension measured in different exercises (Lance, Lambert, Gewin, Lievens, & Conway, 2004; Sackett & Dreher, 1982). Substantial research has searched for evidence that ACs measure dimensions, and dimensions have almost universally been operationalized as trait variance in MTMM parlance. Although ACs are designed and interpreted based on dimensions, the vast majority of this research has not supported distinguishable performance dimensions in ACs. Based on these findings, some have concluded that that ACs do not measure dimensions and thus, dimensions should be removed from the design and interpretation of ACs and that ACs actually measure situational specificity in performance (Jackson, Chapter 8, this volume; Lance, Chapter 10, this volume). Based on limitations with existing MTMM research, I argue that these conclusions are premature (Bowler & Woehr, 2009; Lance, Woehr, & Meade, 2007) and review an alternative MTMM model that supports dimensions. On the other hand, others have argued that exercise based interpretations of AC ratings lack theoretical meaning (Arthur, Day, & Woehr, 2008).

However, below I review evidence showing that exercise specific variance contributes meaningful criterion variance to AC ratings and correlates meaningfully with nomological network variables. From the mixed model MTMM perspective, both dimension effects and exercise effects reflect performance relevant variance.

Problems with the Traditional MTMM Model. AC research has consistently been dogged by the inability to arrive at a suitable analytical and theoretical model that includes both dimensions and exercises. The argument that dimensions do not occupy a role in ACs stems from the heavy reliance on MTMM analyses and in particular, the application of confirmatory factor analysis (CFA) to model the traditional MTMM structure (Bowler & Woehr, 2009; Lance, Woehr, & Meade, 2007). Ironically and as reviewed by Lance (Chapter 10, this volume), the assumption that exercise variance reflects method bias is also a carryover from the application of MTMM approaches. Thus, before formerly elucidating the alternative MTMM model, a discussion of the statistical and conceptual limitations of past CFA-based MTMM research is needed.

Despite the frequent reliance of CFA analyses of MTMM matrices, the theoretical and analytical appropriateness of these models has been scrutinized. From an analytical perspective, Lance Foster, Nemeth, Gentry, and Drollinger (2007) used a Monte Carlo simulation to show that even when a dimensions plus exercise model was the actual (true) model, CFA-based MTMM results often supported other models, particularly in terms of model convergence and admissibility criteria. In other words, even when we know that the AC includes dimension and exercise effects by generating the data to make it so, CFA-based MTMM analyses often do not support this model! Indeed, this model often fails to converge unless the statistically biased correlated uniqueness model is used (cf. Lance et al., 2004; Lievens & Conway, 2001) or when post-hoc parameter constraints are applied (cf. Bowler & Woehr, 2006), both practices that undermine substantive conclusions. It is noteworthy that this method also suffers from similar issues when applied to methods other than ACs (cf. Lance, Dawson, Birklebach, & Hoffman, 2010).

There are reasons to expect that AC data will be particularly subject to improper solutions. For instance, CFA-based MTMM models are particularly prone to non-convergence when: (a) the sample size is low, (b) when each latent factor includes only a few indicators (Tomás, Hontangas, & Oliver, 2000), (c) when the model has a small number of traits and/or methods, and (d) when the ratio of indicators to factors is small (Marsh, 1989, 1993; Marsh & Bailey, 1991; Marsh, Hau, Balla, & Grayson, 1998). In other words, CFA-based MTMM of analyses are problematic in precisely the same circumstances under which AC data are typically analyzed. It seems absurd to dismiss the existence of personality and work attitudes on the basis on non-convergent models; yet this is precisely what has been argued in the context of AC dimensions.

Given persistent problems with this approach across domains, it seems more reasonable to conclude that CFA-based analyses specifying the traditional MTMM structure are problematic, not necessarily ACs. Some have advocated the use of linear mixed models (or Generalizability Theory [G-Theory] as it is commonly referred to in this literature) because this technique does not suffer from convergence and admissibility issues (Bowler & Woehr, 2009). However, past work has used univariate G-Theory, which operates under the dubious assumption that units of measurement are uncorrelated, much like the biased correlated uniqueness CFA model (Lance et al., 2004). Thus, CFA and G-Theory based analyses provide somewhat unique information (e.g., dimension effects in CFA are not analogous to the person x dimension interaction in G-Theory).

Conceptual Issues with MTMM-Based Analyses. In addition to empirical issues, there are conceptual issues that have precluded mixed model interpretations. First, based on the assumptions of MTMM research, AC research has equated exercises to method variance and thus a source of bias. As presented by Lance (Chapter 10, this volume), there is now compelling evidence that exercises reflect performance relevant variance. This research has been reviewed in detail previously in this volume and thus, will not be discussed here.

Second, insufficient care is given to appropriately defining the underlying dimensions and as a result, exercises often measure multiple conceptually similar dimensions which in turn, drives strong empirical overlap among dimensions measured in the same exercises. However, AC construct validity research commonly models all dimensions as unique factors, likely contributing to observed strong overlap among dimensions. In contrast, work performance research and theory frequently specifies the structure of performance by collapsing narrow manifest dimensions into broader latent factors based on the grounds of conceptual similarity. For example, conceptual taxonomies of managerial performance (Borman & Brush, 1993; Campbell, McHenry, & Wise, 1990), theoretical (Smith, Organ, & Near, 1983) and empirical (Hoffman, Blair, Meriac, & Woehr, 2007) models of organizational citizenship behavior, classic measures of leader behavior (Fleishman, 1957) and managerial skills (McCauley, Lombardo, & Usher, 1989), and investigations of the internal structure of multisource performance ratings (Hoffman, Lance, Bynum, & Gentry, 2010; Scullen, Mount, & Goff, 2000) routinely model the structure of performance by setting conceptually similar narrow manifest dimensions to load on broader dimension factors. Indeed, this same approach has been used with across exercise dimension ratings in ACs (Hoffman & Woehr, 2009; Shore, Thornton, & Shore, 1990). Yet, AC internal structure research has typically resisted specifying broad dimensions factors.

Thus, one reason for the consistent finding of indistinguishable dimensions in AC exercises is that many manifest dimensions in ACs are sufficiently similar to preclude discrimination. From this perspective, a strong correlation between conceptually similar dimensions (e.g., "analysis" and "judgment") should not be interpreted as a lack of discriminant validity; instead, it is most appropriately interpreted as evidence for the convergent validity of these dimensions, because theoretically, these variables should be very strongly related. However, past AC research typically models these dimensions as separate latent factors, which greatly influence the potential for inadmissible solutions. Given that existing research, which has argued for the exercise only interpretation has strictly modeled the espoused dimensions with neither care nor attention to the theoretical underpinnings of the underlying constructs (Arthur & Villado, 2008), the central conclusion that ACs do not assess dimensions is tenuous. AC research is advised to take a page from the broader managerial performance literature and collapse narrow manifest dimensions onto broad dimension factors based on theoretical and conceptual similarity. As outlined below, by amending MTMM models to include broad rather than narrow dimensions, stronger support can be found for dimensions.

In sum, prior AC internal structure research has heavily relied on the MTMM methodology and as a result has: (a) frequently found improper solutions when CFA is applied to examine the structure of AC ratings, (b) misinterpreted exercises as reflecting methods bias, and (c) extensively relied on the espoused dimensions, instead of testing theoretically meaningful broad dimension models. Accordingly, the findings of past AC internal structure research are tenuous, and alternative analytical approaches to investigating the structure and meaning of AC ratings are needed.

Alternative MTMM Model. Hoffman, Melchers, Blair, Kleinmann, and Ladd (2011) proposed an alternative MTMM model that included broad dimensions, exercises, and general performance. Importantly, this model applies lessons learned from past AC research in specifying broad dimension factors composed of narrow manifest dimensions. In addition, this model remedies issues associated with the traditional MTMM models by: increasing the number of manifest indicators for each dimension factor and decreasing the correlations among dimensions, which together, should enhance the potential for convergent and admissible solutions. Consistent with past AC research (Lance et al., 2000), the exercise and general performance factors are modeled as uncorrelated first order factors. See Figure 13.1 for a sample depiction of this model.

Hoffman et al. (2011) tested this model in four independent samples of AC ratings. In addition, multiple versions of this model were tested that varied the number and content of the broad dimension factors on the basis of past job performance models (e.g., Borman & Brush, 1993; Stogdill, 1963). Across the four samples, a total of nine models was tested that included broad dimensions, exercises, and general performance, and each of these models provided a closer approximation of AC ratings than was found with traditional models. Moreover, none of the broad dimension, exercise, and general performance models was

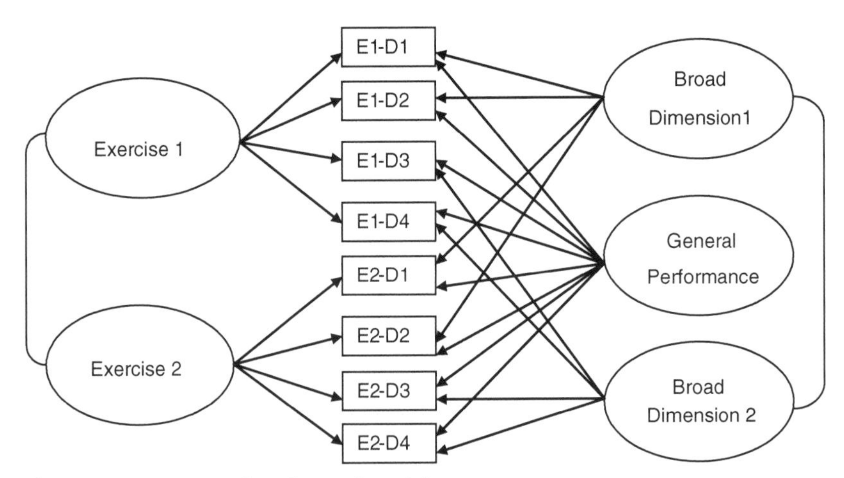

Figure 13.1 MTMM-based mixed model structure

hamstrung by the convergence and admissibility issues endemic to traditional CFA of MTMM matrices. Thus, this model appears to be a useful alternative to traditional MTMM models in terms of model fit, convergence, and admissibility. Despite the clear support for broad dimension factors in this study, it is important to note that broad dimensions explained much less variance in AC ratings than did exercises. Across the four samples, broad dimensions, general performance, and exercises accounted for an average of 15, 10, and 50% of the variance, respectively.

The articulation of a theoretically grounded model that consistently converges to admissible solutions is an important first step to supporting the perspective that dimensions and exercises are meaningful components of AC performance. However, based on the results of this model, it is clear that although dimensions clearly play a role in AC performance, the variance due to dimensions is somewhat small. Accordingly, it is reasonable to question their importance in accounting for the validity of ACs. In other words, to the extent that dimensions explain variance beyond exercises in criterion variables, evidence is provided for the importance of dimensions; if not, one must legitimately question the presence of and need for dimensions in ACs. I am aware of only three studies that have directly compared the influence of exercise and dimension variance on the criterion-related validity of ACs.

First, Connelley, Ones, Ramesh, and Goff (2008) briefly reported the results of a large sample study that compared the validity of exercises and dimensions. Their study showed that dimensions explained incremental variance beyond exercises in salary. Lievens, Dilchert, and Ones (2009) replicated these results by showing that dimensions explain variance beyond exercises in salary growth. Finally, Hoffman et al. (2011) again replicated these results in one sample using salary increase as a criterion and in an additional sample using supervisor ratings of performance as a criterion. In sum, the criterion-related validity of dimensions and exercises has been directly investigated in four independent samples, and in every case, the same conclusion emerges: both exercises and dimensions are "active ingredients" of the criterion-related validity of ACs.

Given consistent evidence that: (a) non-CFA based analytical approaches (e.g., G-theory) support dimensions and exercises in AC ratings, (b) both dimensions and exercises are valid indicators of salary and performance, and (c) dimensions explain variance beyond exercises in criterion variables and vice versa, it is clear that both cross-situationally consistent dimensions and situationally specific exercises are key components of AC performance. By extension, any argument to remove either exercises or dimensions from the interpretation of assessee performance does so at the peril of removing valid variance from a very expensive assessment tool.

Advantages and Disadvantages. The alternative MTMM model has several advantages and drawbacks that merit discussion. The primary advantage is that it appears to arrive at an admissible solution and a solution that provides a closer fit to the data than previously examined AC models. Given that improper solutions associated with MTMM-based CFA models have been the primary argument for the non-existence of dimensions, this advantage cannot be understated. In addition, a convergent model allows for the calculation of the magnitude of the components of AC ratings and the examination of the nomological network of multiple facets of AC ratings (cf. Hoffman et al., 2011; Lievens et al., 2009). Next, this model generalizes to other areas of performance in terms of both the use of broad dimensions and in terms of the components of performance specified (see Hoffman & Baldwin, 2012).

Despite these advantages, a few disadvantages merit discussion. Chief among them is that insufficient research has been conducted to evaluate the generalizability of this model. Although we did find supportive evidence in four samples, more research is needed to determine if the MTMM mixed model will demonstrate superiority in other ACs. Next, advocates of DBACs have argued that the use of within exercise dimension ratings is fundamentally inconsistent with the design of ACs. Although MTMM analyses of PEDRs should not be the only evidence by which construct validity is judged, valuable information can be provided by investigating the structure of within exercise dimension ratings using MTMM analyses of PEDRs (cf. Brummel, Rupp, & Spain, 2009). Thus, despite criticisms of within exercise dimension ratings, they are a vital component of the assessment process, and the analysis of within exercise dimension ratings is one of many useful methods to understanding the psychometric properties of AC ratings.

Mixed Model Perspective 2: Dimensions within Exercises

The dimensions within exercises mixed model proposes that (a) exercise performance is multifaceted and (b) one should not necessarily expect convergence across dimensions from different exercises. As depicted in Figure 13.2, this model specifies multiple broad dimensions in each exercise; however, common variance across exercises (e.g., dimension variance) is not explicitly modeled as a factor. This conceptualization of AC dimensions differs sharply from the ways in which past models have examined dimensions (Hoffman et al. 2011; Lance et al., 2000; Lance et al., 2004). Whereas previous AC internal structure research has exclusively modeled dimensions as being consistent across exercises, this model captures aspects of AC dimensions that are not cross-situationally consistent. In other words, dimensions are viewed as distinguishable within exercises but not necessarily consistent across exercises. For instance, instead of interpreting "influence" and role play performance separately, AC performance is in interpreted by nesting dimensions within exercises (e.g., influence in an leaderless group discussion [LGD]). This is in contrast to virtually all AC internal structure research that has implicitly assumed that (a) there are not distinguishable dimensions within exercises (as evidenced by unidimensional exercise factors) and (b) that the same dimension assessed in different exercises should strongly correlate (Lance et al., 2000).

Task-based assessment center (TBAC) research routinely parameterizes exercises using single homogenous exercise factors, underscoring the assumption by task-based advocates that situationally specific performance is "relatively undifferentiated … within exercises, counter to traditional AC theory" (Lance 2008a, p. 91). Nevertheless, there has been little conceptual work to explain the meaning of the systematic exercise effects. Why is it that nearly 100 years of research on human performance has supported the performance is multifaceted (Borman & Brush, 1993; Campbell, 1992; Hoffman, Blair, Meriac, & Woehr, 2007; Smith, Organ, & Near, 1983), yet performance in an AC exercises (a simulation of the work performance domain) is specified as a unidimensional construct? For TBAC approaches to be incorporated in any meaningful way, it is critical that the meaning of exercise effects be more clearly and rigorously articulated. After all, situational specificity has never been taken to mean that human behavior in a given situation will be homogenous and undifferentiated, at least not until the situational perspective was applied to ACs. For these reasons, the within exercise dimension model begins with the assumption that performance within exercises is not necessarily homogenous.

The assumption of past AC research that a dimension must be consistent across exercises is an unfortunate carry over from the extensive

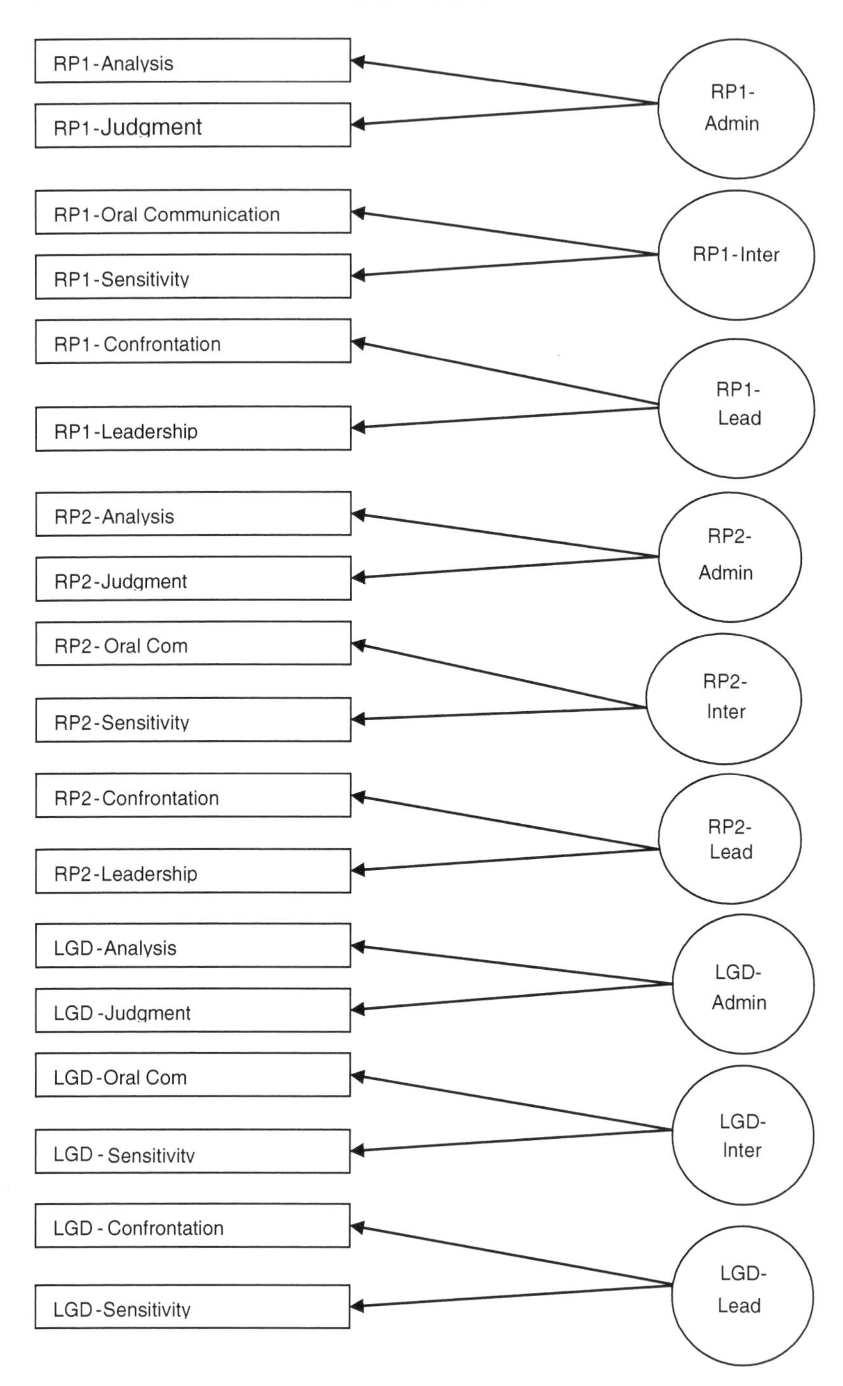

Figure 13.2 Dimensions within exercises. *Note:* All latent variables presumed to freely correlate. Correlations and uniqueness terms omitted for clarity.

reliance on MTMM based analyses and interpretations. For instance, Howard (2008) argued that AC ratings should have never been subjected to MTMM analyses, because AC exercises are explicitly designed to capture different aspects of similar underlying dimensions. According to Howard (2008), "If each exercise is equally capable of measuring each dimension, why measure [a given dimension] five different times? Given the costs associated with assessment centers, is this redundancy not an unnecessary waste of resources?" (p. 99). From this perspective, forcing the same dimension to load on a latent factor across exercises ignores that fact that different exercises capture unique aspects of dimensions. For instance, effective "influence" in a LGD entails persuading other group members to adopt a given proposal, building consensus among other group members, and diffusing disagreements among other group members, whereas effective influence in a role play would include motivating the role player, offering developmental guidance, or tactfully addressing sensitive topics. Although these behaviors all have influence as a central component, they are very different manifestations of influence (Yukl & Tracey, 1992). Therefore, a strong correlation among these different facets of influence should not be (and should never have been) expected. Accordingly, this within exercises dimension model does not parameterize convergence of dimensions across different exercises.

Hoffman and Meade (in press) directly tested this using confirmatory factor analysis. Specifically, we specified three broad dimensions tapped in each of three exercises. Results revealed that this model fit the data more closely than 3, 2, and 1 dimension models within each exercise and found that all three exercises (two role plays and an LGD) measured three correlated but distinct dimensions (interpersonal, problem-solving, and influence). Further, we also supported the measurement invariance (cf. Vandenberg & Lance, 2007) of different dimensions across exercises, supporting that the same dimension was measured on the same psychological rating scale across exercises. In addition, this model showed a similar fit to traditional AC models, and it did not suffer from convergence and admissibility issues. Thus, not only was performance differentiated within exercises but it was differentiated in similar ways across three unique exercises. In addition to these findings, Putka and Hoffman (2011) used a linear mixed model and found that the person × exercise × dimension interaction was the second largest source of reliably rated variance in AC ratings and was substantially larger than the person x dimension interaction. Unfortunately, limited research has explicitly considered this model.

However, the basic model is consistent with the core tenets of interactionist theories such as trait activation theory (TAT; Tett & Guterman, 2000) and the cognitive-affective personality system (CAPS) theory (Mischel & Shoda, 1995). To summarize from prior chapters in this book, TAT hypothesizes that behavior is a function of trait relevant cues of a given situation and that situations vary in their potential to cue different traits (see Lievens & Christiansen, Chapter 4 and Melchers et al., Chapter 11). Similarly, CAPs theory proposes that individuals perceive situations differently and that individual differences in subsequent behavior across situations correspond to differences in individual perceptions of a given situation. As applied to ACs, both theories imply that behavior will only be consistent across situations to the degree that the situation is similar or, according to CAPS, to the extent that a perceiver believes that the situation is similar. Note that both TAT and CAPS make two assumptions regarding the structure of ACs: (a) that behaviors should only be consistent in different exercises to the extent that the exercises are similar and (b) there are distinguishable dimensions of performance in a given exercise, rather than a single general factor for each exercise. Thus, these theories are more consistent with the dimensions within exercises model than traditional MTMM-based interpretations of ACs.

Although TAT is a relatively recent advancement in the AC literature, a growing literature base yields consistent, if not overly strong support for the basic hypotheses (see Lievens & Christiansen, Chapter 4). For instance, Haaland and Christiansen (2002) found that exercises that were characterized by high activating potential were more strongly correlated than those that are low in activating potential. In a systematic review of the literature, Lievens, Chasteen, Day, and Christiansen (2006) found that convergence increased when exercises activated the same trait. Yet, despite the consistent support for TAT, the effects of exercise similarity have been rather small. For instance, the mean correlation between dimensions assessed in exercises that activated similar traits was .36, relative to .25 for exercises that did not activate similar traits in the review by Lievens et al. (2006). Thus, although the demands of the exercise will clearly moderate the magnitude of cross exercise convergence, other moderators are likely operating.

Consistent with the central propositions of CAPS, assessee behavior is proposed to be driven by their perceptions of the demands of the situation. Assessees with the high levels of social awareness needed to accurately perceive the demands of the exercise will be more likely to attempt to display behaviors commensurate with these demands. Accordingly, assessees with a high degree of situational awareness should perform more effectively across situations, resulting in a higher degree of cross exercise consistency (Jansen, Lievens, & Kleinmann, 2009). On the other hand, if an assessee does not grasp targeted aspects of performance in a given exercise, they will be more likely to perform inconsistently, based on the their (mis)reading of the demands of each exercise. Although research is limited, preliminary research has supported the role of social awareness on cross-exercise convergence. Specifically, Jansen et al. (2009) found that assessees who were better able to "read" the demands of a given exercise performed more consistently across exercises. Accordingly, assessee situational awareness is proposed to be a key influence on the prominence of situationally specific and cross-situationally consistent aspects of AC dimensions.

Advantages and Disadvantages. The primary strength of this model is that it provides theoretical meaning to the ubiquitous exercise effect. Whereas the TBAC literature models AC exercises using homogenous exercise factors (single factors with no differentiable performance dimensions), the present model allows for distinguishable aspects of performance in a given exercise but consistent with Howard's arguments, does not assume that dimensions will be cross-situationally consistent.

A frequent criticism of TBACs is that they are not construct-oriented and that constructs are needed to advance the science. In other words, it has been argued that they lack psychological meaning. As noted by Arthur, Day, and Woehr (2008), what does it mean to give feedback to improve your in-basket skills? By providing construct-level representations of the behaviors displayed in AC exercises (e.g., nesting dimensional performance within exercises), the within exercise dimension approach can assign a more precise meaning to the focal construct. In addition, one factor underlying negligible relationships among individual differences and exercise factors (cf. Hoffman et al., 2011; Lance et al., 2000; Lance, Foster, et al., 2007) might be that combining all dimensions from a given exercise into a single factor results in a meaningless mash-up of information. For instance, combining problem solving skills and interpersonal skills measured in a role play will likely attenuate the relationship between problem solving skills and intelligence (see Hogan & Holland, 2003). In any case, a key theoretical advantage of the within exercise dimension model is the articulation of a more theoretically meaningful accounting of the ubiquitous exercise effect.

Next, this model seems to be the closest analytic model to date of the intent of the original managerial AC as well as the way that ACs are currently used in practice (Howard, 2008). For instance, when an assessee performs differently on a given dimension in different exercises, it is common to assign a "split" rating in the consensus meeting (e.g., a group vs. 1-on-1 dimensions such as initiative and influence are common). In addition, the standard procedure for developmental feedback reports is to embed dimensional performance with specific behaviors from specific exercises. For example, a feedback report might note that in the LGD, the assessee's interpersonal skills were strong, but in one-on-one meetings, interpersonal skills were weak. The traditional MTMM model does not allow for such divergences across exercises, even though AC practitioners well know that this is a common occurrence (see Bank et al., Chapter 12, this volume). Accordingly, from a practitioner's perspective, a major advantage of the within exercise dimension model is that it reflects what is actually done in ACs.

Despite these advantages, there are some clear disadvantages and avenues for future research associated with this model. First, only two studies have articulated the meaning of this model (Hoffman & Meade, 2008; Putka & Hoffman, 2011). Research that replicates this structure is clearly needed. Second, in the Hoffman and Meade study, despite evidence for a multidimensional within exercise structure based on the model fit, many of the dimensions in a given exercise were still very strongly correlated (latent factor correlations ranged from .55–.92). Thus, although we conclusively showed that dimensions were differentiable in a given exercise, a handful of the dimensions were sufficiently strongly correlated to generate concerns as to the practical value of treating them separately. It should be noted, however, that at least part of this overlap may be attributable to rater bias, rather than true dimension level overlap in a given exercise (cf. Hoffman, Melchers, & Kleinmann, 2010). It is important that future work continue to investigate the circumstances in which we should (and should not) expect convergence across exercises.

Mixed Model Perspective 3: The Within Assessee Approach

In the last decade, organizational researchers have called for using an integrated person-centered pattern approach to understand dynamic relationships when multiple processes are involved (Bergman,

Magnusson, & El-Khouri, 2003; Foti & Hauenstein, 2007; Katzell, 1994). In traditional variable or construct model approaches, each variable is examined as a discrete entity, and the focus is on the contribution that each variable has on explaining the criterion variable of interest. Importantly, construct centered approaches do not consider the interrelationship between constructs or how constructs interact to influence behaviors (Bergman et al., 2003). Bergman et al. (2003) argue that since "[an] individual develops as an active participant in an integrated person-environment system" (p. 7), person-centered pattern approaches are necessary to understand the dynamic interrelationships among behaviors. Thus, pattern approaches allow the complexity of the person and the complexity of the situation to be integrated and studied holistically (Foti & Hauenstein, 2007), rather than in a piece-meal way.

In the context of ACs, one would undertake a cluster analysis of within exercise dimension factors similar to those outlined in the within exercise dimension model. This would allow for the determination of the degree to which subsamples of assessees are characterized by different patterns of performance consistency across exercises. In essence, this approach shifts the question from "Are AC constructs valid?" to "For whom are ACs constructs valid?" Although these approaches are typically exploratory, it is illustrative and theoretically interesting to speculate on the groups that might emerge.

For instance, one would likely find a group corresponding to effective performance in all exercises and across all dimensions (superstars) and a group of ineffective performers in all dimensions in all exercises (low potential employees). It gets interesting when one considers the different groups that could correspond to different dimension and exercise combinations. A group consisting of higher performers on interpersonal dimensions but ineffective performance on problem-solving/administrative dimensions across all exercises (interpersonally skilled but lower levels of task related skills), or effective performers on all dimensions in written exercises but ineffective performers in all interpersonally oriented exercises (intelligence and conscientious but introverted assessees). There are numerous possibilities, and the number and composition of the groups is clearly an empirical question. The point here is that there will be certain AC performance profiles into which each assessee can be assigned. Once individuals are classified, the groups become the variable of interest. These groups can then be examined and predictors and outcomes of the groups can be investigated. It would be interesting to see if the emerging profiles were differentiated by certain aspects of personality and if they showed different patterns of relationships with criterion variables.

To my knowledge, AC research has not yet applied person-centered analyses to AC ratings. However, one study applied a quasi-person centered approach. Specifically, Gibbons and Rupp (2009) argued that (in) consistency in AC performance across dimensions is a meaningful variable in its own right. They estimated the variability across dimensions and found that assessee across dimension variability explained variance in outcomes beyond mean levels of performance on each dimension. Although focused on dimensions rather than consistency across exercises, this research nevertheless shows the value of person centered approaches. Indirect support for such a person centered interpretation is also evidenced in findings that ability to identify the dimensions measured in ACs (akin to social awareness) explains variance in convergence in performance across different exercises (Jansen et al., 2010) indicating that levels of cross exercise convergence likely differs by person. Similarly, as discussed below, AC practitioners interpret AC performance focusing on unique patterns of performance within and across dimensions and exercises, especially in developmental settings (see Bank et al., Chapter 12, this volume). Although this work represents a novel and exciting departure from traditional psychometric interpretations of ACs, far more work is needed to understand the form and function of patterns of assessee performance.

Advantages and Disadvantages. The primary strength of this approach is that it maps onto the ways ACs are interpreted by practitioners. In a consensus meeting, when delivering developmental feedback, and when making employment decisions, AC administrators regularly take a holistic approach to understanding AC performance (Howard, 2008). In other words, each candidate's pattern of performance within and across exercises is considered in developing the final dimension rating. To the degree that person-centered analyses match what is typically done in operational ACs, research investigating the nomological network and appropriate interpretation of various patterns could be very informative for practitioners. Next, by taking the analyses to the person level, this approach circumvents many of the problems with the analytical models usually used to investigate ACs. Instead of asking whether ACs are construct valid, this approach investigates what differences within and across exercises mean for a given assessee.

However, there are also some weaknesses associated with assessee centered mixed-model approaches. As with the mixed-model MTMM and the mixed-model dimensions within exercises perspective, there is a lack of empirical research for the assessee centered approach. Next, this approach is analytically complex and requires large sample sizes (or the use of a hold out sample). In addition, although this approach does provide important information about assessee performance, it does not provide the psychometric information that one can derive from factor analytic approaches.

Integrated Mixed Model

As should be evident to the reader, this chapter proposes that there are many meaningful ways to interpret AC performance. Just as this chapter proposes that the TBAC model and the DBAC perspectives are complementary, rather than competing models of AC performance, the three mixed-model perspectives outlined here are complementary, rather than competing perspectives of AC performance. In other words, the use of any of these models is contingent on the particular research question of interest. This multifaceted view of AC performance allows for a richer and more complete understanding of assessee performance than could be gained by focusing on either approach at the expense of the others.

Although the three mixed-model approaches articulated here have been implicitly examined in prior AC research and explicitly supported in a limited number of more recent studies, they have never been integrated conceptually or empirically. Figure 13.3 presents a conceptual combination of the three mixed models. Together, these models propose primary sources of performance relevant variance underlying ACs. Specifically, there are cross-situationally consistent aspects of dimensions (from the MTMM mixed model), situationally specific aspects of dimensions (from the dimensions within exercises model), a general performance factor (from the MTMM mixed model), and overall performance in a given exercise (from the MTMM mixed model). In addition, moderators are proposed to influence the prominence of these factors in specific ACs (e.g., exercise similarity, AC design) and for specific individuals (e.g., social awareness, behavioral flexibility, personality, and intelligence). This aspect of the model takes into account

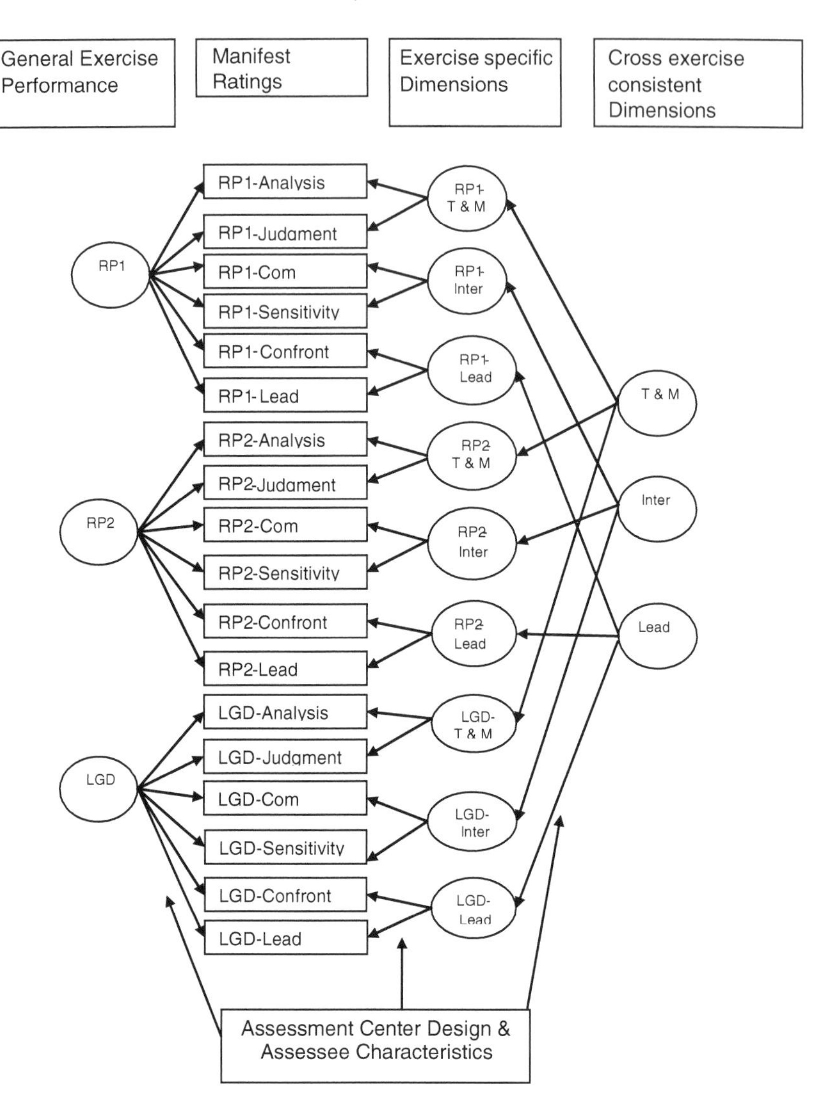

Figure 13.3 Integrated model of components of AC performance. *Note:* RP indicates Role Play. LGD indicates Leaderless Group Discussion. Inter indicates communication and interpersonal facilitation. Lead indicates leadership and supervision. T & M indicates technical activities and mechanics of management. The general performance factor, correlations, and uniqueness terms omitted for clarity.

the potential for unique patterns of performance for a given AC (the within assessee approach). This model is proposed as a means to frame multifaceted AC research and to identify under-examined areas of AC performance.

Dimensions. The application of MTMM analyses resulted in the widespread (mis)interpretation of dimensions as traits (Howard, 2008) that should be consistent across exercises. However, this model proposes that there are two aspects of dimensions that are meaningful in ACs: exercise specific aspects of dimensions and cross-exercise consistent aspects of dimensions. Past AC internal structure research has missed this central component of AC dimensions, the component of a dimension that is specific to a particular exercise. By pulling back from the interpretation of dimensions as traits, a clear picture of the nature of AC dimensions comes into focus, one that allows for both situationally specific and cross-situationally consistent aspects of performance dimensions.

The cross-situationally consistent aspect of dimensions is indicative of similar performance on a given dimension across multiple exercises. This component of variance is analogous to the "trait" factors in traditional MTMM-type analyses. On the other hand, situationally specific aspects of dimensions reflect patterns of behavior indicative of an underlying construct (e.g., a dimension), that are distinguishable from other patterns of behavior (e.g., distinguishable from other dimensions in a given exercise), and are specific to a given exercise (see Model 2 above). Using a linear mixed model approach, Putka and Hoffman (2011) found that the person × dimension × exercise interaction explained substantially more variance in AC ratings than the person x dimension interaction (dimension effects in MTMM parlance). Based on limited research to date, it appears that although assessee performance is distinguishable based on dimensions, these dimensions are largely independent across exercises. So, what will determine whether a given dimension manifests as specific to an exercise or consistent across exercises?

A variety of assessee characteristics and assessment center design characteristics are proposed to influence whether the dimensions assessed in a given exercise also converge across exercises. In terms of AC design characteristics, the most obvious is the nature of the exercises. Although AC exercises are designed to present unique aspects of the situation with which to measure certain dimensions, there should be some level of convergence among dimensions measured in more similar exercises. As noted above, investigations of TAT support this proposition. Yet, the effect sizes associated with TAT have been modest, leaving room for further exploration (Lievens et al., 2006). Given that AC exercises are designed to represent somewhat unique situations that will capture somewhat unique aspects of a given dimension (Howard, 2008), it is unlikely that TAT will ever yield strong effects in an operational AC. This is not a criticism of TAT; instead, TAT is very effective at explaining part of the reason for low levels cross-exercise convergence. However, TAT must be viewed in the broader context of variables that are expected to contribute to the convergence of assessee behavior across exercises.

It is also probable that assessee characteristics will determine the prominence of cross-situationally consistent dimensions and situationally specific dimensions (as proposed in Mixed Model 3 above). As mentioned above, situational awareness has been shown to play a key role in assessee cross exercise consistency. To the degree that an assessee can correctly identify the demands of a situation, she will be more likely to attempt to display behaviors that satisfy those demands. However this is only half of the equation. Although social awareness is an important first step, it alone does not guarantee that an assessee will have the ability to carry out the appropriate behaviors. Behavioral flexibility, or the ability to effectively adapt behaviors to meet the demands of a given situation, is frequently mentioned as the second necessary component for social intelligence (Zaccaro, 2007). In essence, just because one can ascertain the appropriate behaviors in a given situation, it does not mean that one has the behavioral repertoire to effectively meet the demands of the situation. Thus, situational awareness is necessary but not sufficient for consistent performance across situations. Future research investigating behavioral flexibility as a moderator of cross exercise performance consistency could prove informative.

Personality and intelligence would also likely play a role in the level of convergence and differentiation of an individual assessee's performance. One would expect smarter assessees to perform more effectively on problem-solving behaviors across all exercises but particularly so in written rather than verbal exercises (Hoffman et al., 2011). On the other hand, socially dominant assessees would likely perform well on competitive interpersonal tasks (e.g., a confrontation focused role play or a competitive leaderless group discussion), and more extraverted but empathetic assessees would perform more effectively on cooperative role plays (e.g., a cooperative LGD or a coaching role play).

Exercises. Although some portion of variance that has previously been attributed to exercises actually captures situationally-specific dimensional information, to some extent, assessees are likely to perform effectively overall in a given exercise due to factors such as cognitive ability, experience, conscientiousness, job knowledge, and motivation. For this reason, it is probable that an overall exercise effect will also remain, even after controlling for within exercise dimensional performance. For instance, smarter assessees should perform more effectively across all dimensions in written exercises (Collins et al., 2003). On the other hand, more extraverted or charismatic assessees are likely to perform more effectively across all aspects of interpersonal exercises. In addition, in contrast to MTMM based analyses equating exercise factors with method bias, evidence supporting the criterion-related validity of exercise factors (Hoffman et al., 2011; Lance et al., 2000) indicates that exercise effects reflect performance relevant variance.

There are also circumstances in which overall exercise performance might be expected to occupy a more prominent role in ACs. First, to the extent that the dimensions assessed in a given exercise are more homogenous or the exercise reflects a relatively narrow situation, assessees should perform more similarly in a given exercise. Similarly, if an assessee is able to ascertain all of the dimensions in a given exercise (via social awareness), he or she should perform more effectively on all dimensions in that exercise. Similarly, if a more intelligent assessee grasps key pieces of information in an exercise, they are likely to perform more effectively on all aspects of the exercise. This is consistent with the evidence of the observed relationship between intelligence, knowledge acquisition, and overall job performance stemming from the broader performance literature (Hunter, 1986). Additional research is needed investigating these and other interpretations of the meaning and theoretical underpinnings of the exercise effect and the underpinnings of exercise consistent and inconsistent performance at the assessee level.

General Performance. Typified by Guilford's (1954) general performance factor, Kenny and Berman's (1980) true correlation, Cooper's (1981) true halo, and *Viswesvaran*, Schmidt, and Ones's (2005) actual correlation, the idea of a *valid* general factor in performance ratings has persisted almost as long as ratings have been used to assess human performance. Although not traditionally part of the AC architecture, TBAC research replaced dimensions with a general factor in MTMM analyses (Lance et al., 2000; Lance et al., 2004; Lance et al., 2007), and more recent work has supported a structure including both dimensions and general performance (Arthur et al., 2003; Hoffman et al., 2011; Putka & Hoffman, 2011). This factor reflects consistency in assessee performance across all dimensions in all exercises. To the degree that general performance has consistently been found in the job performance literature (Hoffman, Lance, et al., 2010; Viswesvaran et al., 2005), the emergence of this factor in ACs provides evidence for the construct validity of AC ratings.

The AC general performance factor has been shown to be a correlate of intelligence (Hoffman et al., 2011; Lance et al., 2000), conscientiousness (Lance, Foster, et al. 2007), and social dominance (Hoffman et al., 2011). Consistent with these findings, the meta-analysis by Collins et al. found that intelligence and extraversion were the strongest individual difference predictors of the OAR. Research investigating other ratee antecedents (e.g., behavioral flexibility, experience, and social awareness) of overall performance is needed. Finally, design characteristics such as the similarity of the exercises (e.g., the use of all written or all interpersonal exercises) will likely influence the prominence of the general performance factor.

Conclusion

This chapter proposes that the past 60 years of AC research strongly points to a mixed-model of AC performance that includes multiple different aspects of assessee performance, including: exercise specific performance, exercise specific dimensional performance, cross exercise consistent dimensional performance, and overall general performance. Based on the accumulated, albeit indirect, evidence for the importance of a multifaceted interpretation, the adherence to a single approach is counterproductive and has stifled advances in the AC literature. Indeed, many AC practitioners either explicitly or implicitly operate their AC from a mixed-model perspective. Accordingly, recognizing existing evidence and in keeping up with practice, AC research is encouraged to investigate multiple aspects of AC performance. At a minimum, it is important to recognize that no one interpretation should be viewed as "more correct" than other interpretations. Instead of viewing facets of AC performance as competing explanations, they should be viewed as complimentary processes that will aid in the articulation of a far richer understanding of performance in ACs.

References

Arthur, W., Day, E. A., & Woehr, D. J. (2008). Mend it, don't end it: An alternate view of assessment center construct-related validity evidence. *Industrial and Organizational Psychology: Perspectives on Research and Practice, 1*, 105–111.

Arthur, W., & Villado, A. J. (2008). The importance of distinguishing between constructs and methods when comparing predictors in personnel selection research and practice. *Journal of Applied Psychology, 93*, 435–442.

Bergman, L. R., Magnusson, D., & El-Khouri, B. M. (2003). *Studying individual development in an interindividual context: A person-oriented approach.* Mahwah, NJ: Erlbaum.

Borman, W. C., & Brush, D. H. (1993). More progress toward a taxonomy of managerial performance requirements. *Human Performance, 6*, 1–21.

Bowler, M. C., & Woehr, D. J. (2006). A meta-analytic evaluation of the impact of dimension and exercise factors on assessment center ratings. *Journal of Applied Psychology, 91*, 1114–1124.

Bowler, M. C., & Woehr, D. J. (2009). Assessment center construct-related validity: Stepping beyond the MTMM matrix. *Journal of Vocational Behavior, 75*, 173–182.

Brummel, B., Rupp, D. E., & Spain, S. (2009). Constructing parallel simulation exercises for assessment centers and other forms of behavioral assessment. *Personnel Psychology, 62*, 135–170.

Campbell, J. P. (1992). Modeling the performance prediction problem in industrial and organizational psychology. In M. D. Dunnette & L. M. Hough (Eds.), *Handbook of industrial and organizational psychology* (pp. 687–732). Palo Alto, CA: Consulting Psychologists Press.

Campbell, J. P., McHenry, J. J., & Wise, L. L. (1990). Modeling job performance in a population of jobs. *Personnel Psychology, 43*, 313–333.

Collins, J. M., Schmidt, F. L., Sanchez-Ku, M., Thomas, L., McDaniel, M. A., & Le, H. (2003). Can basic individual differences shed light on the construct meaning of assessment center evaluations? *International Journal of Selection and Assessment, 11*, 17–29.

Connelly, B. S., Ones, D. S., Ramesh, A., & Goff, M. (2008). A pragmatic view of dimensions and exercises in assessment center ratings. *Industrial and Organizational Psychology: Perspectives on Science and Practice, 1*, 121–124.

Cooper, W. H. (1981). Ubiquitous halo. *Psychological Bulletin, 90*, 218–244.

Fleishman, E. A. (1957). The Leader Opinion Questionnaire. In R. M. Stogdill & A. E. Coons (Eds.), *Leader behavior: Its description and measurement* (pp. 120–133). Columbus, OH: Bureau of Business Research.

Foti, R. J., & Hauenstein, N. M. (2007). Pattern and variable approaches in leadership emergence and effectiveness. *Journal of Applied Psychology, 92*, 347–355.

Gibbons, A. M., & Rupp, D. E. (2009). Dimension consistency: A new (old) perspective on the assessment center construct validity debate. *Journal of Management, 35*, 1154–1180.

Guilford, J. P. (1954). *Psychometric methods* (2nd ed.). New York: McGraw-Hill.

Haaland, S., & Christiansen, N. D. (2002). Implications of trait-activation theory for evaluating the construct validity of assessment center ratings. *Personnel Psychology, 55,* 137–163.

Hoffman, B. J., & Bandwin, S. (2012). Modern managerial assessment: A comparison of assessment centers and multisource feedback. In G. Thornton & N. Povah, *Assessment Centers and Global Talent Management* (pp. 143–162). London: Gower.

Hoffman, B. J., Blair, C., Meriac, J., & Woehr, D. J. (2007). Expanding the criterion domain? A meta-analysis of the OCB literature. *Journal of Applied Psychology, 92,* 555–566.

Hoffman, B. J., Lance, C., Bynum, B., & Gentry, B. (2010). Rater source effects are alive and well after all. *Personnel Psychology, 63,* 119–151.

Hoffman, B. J., & Meade, A. (in press). Alternate approaches to understanding the psychometric properties of assessment centers: An analysis of the structure and equivalence of exercise ratings. *International Journal of Selection and Assessment.*

Hoffman, B. J., Melchers, K., Blair, C. A., Kleinmann, M., & Ladd, R. T. (2011). Exercises and dimensions are the currency of Assessment Centers. *Personnel Psychology, 64,* 351–395.

Hoffman, B. J., Melchers, K., & Kleinmann, M. (2010, April). *Disentangling assessment center exercise from raters effects.* Symposium presented at the 25th annual conference of the Society for Industrial and Organizational Psychology, Atlanta, GA.

Hoffman, B. J., & Woehr, D. J. (2009). Disentangling the meaning of multisource feedback: An examination of the nomological network surrounding source and dimension factors. *Personnel Psychology, 62,* 735–765.

Hogan, J., & Holland, B. (2003). Using theory to evaluate personality and job-performance relations: A socioanalytic perspective *Journal of Applied Psychology, 88,* 100–112.

Howard, A. (2008). Making assessment centers work the way they are supposed to. *Industrial and Organizational Psychology: Perspectives on Research and Practice, 1,* 98–104.

Hunter, J. E. (1986). Cognitive ability, cognitive aptitudes, job knowledge and job performance. *Journal of Vocational Behavior, 29,* 34–362.

Jansen, A., Lievens, F., & Kleinmann M. (2009, April). *The importance of situation perception in the personality—performance relationship.* Paper presented at the annual conference of the Society for Industrial and Organizational Psychology, New Orleans, LA.

Katzell, R. A. (1994). Contemporary meta-trends in industrial and organizational psychology. In H. C. Triandias, M. D. Dunnette, & L. M. Hough (Eds.), *Handbook of industrial and organizational psychology* (3rd ed., vol. 4, pp. 1–89). Palo Alto, CA: Consulting Psychologist Press.

Kenny, D. A., & Berman, J. S. (1980). Statistical approaches to the correction of correlational bias. *Psychological Bulletin, 88,* 288–295.

Lance, C. E. (2008a). Why assessment centers do not work the way they're supposed to. *Industrial and Organizational Psychology Perspectives on Research and Practice, 1*, 84–97.

Lance, C. E. (2008b). Where have we been, how did we get there, and where shall we go? *Industrial and Organizational Psychology: Perspectives on Research and Practice, 1*, 140–146.

Lance, C. E., Dawson, B., Birklebach, D., & Hoffman, B. (2010). Method effects, measurement error, and substantive conclusions. *Organizational Research Methods, 13*, 435–455.

Lance, C. E., Foster, M. R., Nemeth, Y. M., Gentry, W. A., & Drollinger, S. (2007). Extending the nomological network of assessment center construct validity: Prediction of cross-situationally consistent and specific aspects of assessment center performance. *Human Performance, 20*, 345–362.

Lance, C. E., Lambert, T. A., Gewin, A. G., Lievens, F., & Conway, J. M. (2004). Revised estimates of dimension and exercise variance components in assessment center postexercise dimension ratings. *Journal of Applied Psychology, 89*, 377–385.

Lance, C. E., Newbolt, W. H., Gatewood, R. D., Foster, M. R., French, N. R., & Smith, D. E. (2000). Assessment center exercise factors represent cross-situational specificity, not method bias. *Human Performance, 13*, 323–353.

Lance, C. E., Woehr, D. J., & Meade, A. W. (2007). Case study: AmMontecCarlo investigation of assessment center construct validity models. *Organizational Research Methods, 10*, 430–448.

Lievens, F., Chasteen, C. S., Day, E. A., & Christiansen, N. D. (2006). Large-scale investigation of the role of trait activation theory for understanding assessment center convergent and discriminant validity. *Journal of Applied Psychology, 91*, 247–258.

Lievens, F., & Conway, J. M. (2001). Dimension and exercise variance in assessment center scores: A large-scale evaluation of multitrait-multimethod studies. *Journal of Applied Psychology, 86*, 1202–1222.

Lievens, F., Dilchert, S., & Ones, D. S. (2009). The importance of exercise and dimension factors in assessment centers: Simultaneous examinations of construct-related and criterion-related validity. *Human Performance, 22*, 375–390.

Marsh, H. W. (1989). Confirmatory factor analyses of multitrait–multimethod data: Many problems and a few solutions *Applied Psychological Measurement, 13*, 335–361.

Marsh, H. W. (1993). Multitrait–multimethod analyses: Inferring each trait/method combination with multiple indicators. *Applied Measurement in Education, 6*, 49–81.

Marsh, H. W., & Bailey, M. (1991). Confirmatory factor analysis of multitrait multimethod data: A comparison of alternative methods. *Applied Psychological Measurement, 15*, 47–70.

Marsh, H. W., Hau, K., Balla, J. R., & Grayson, D. (1998). Is more ever too much? The numbe of indicators per factor in factor analysis. *Multivariate Behavioral Research, 33*, 181—220.

McCauley, C., Lombardo, M., & Usher, C. (1989). Diagnosing management development needs: An instrument based on how managers develop. *Journal of Management, 15*, 380–403.

Meriac, J. P., Hoffman, B. J., Woehr, D. J., & Fleischer, D. J. (2008). Furthe evidence for the validity of assessment center dimensions: A meta-analysis of the incremental criterion related validity of assessment center dimension ratings. *Journal of Applied Psychology, 93*, 1042–1052.

Mischel, W., & Shoda, Y. (1995). A cognitive-affective system theory of personality: Reconceptualizing situations, dispositions, dynamics, and invariance in personality structure. *Psychological Review, 102*, 246–268.

Putka, D., & Hoffman, B. J. (2011). *A closer look at reliable and unreliable sources of variance in assessment center ratings finally).* Unpublished manuscript.

Sackett, P. R., & Dreher, G. F. (1982). Constructs and assessment center dimensions: Some troubling empirical findings. *Journal of Applied Psychology, 67*, 401–410.

Scullen, S. E., Mount, M. K., & Goff, M. (2000). Understanding the latent structure of job performance ratings. *Journal of Applied Psychology, 85*, 956–970

Shore, T. H., Thornton, G. C., & Shore, L. M. (1990). Construct validity of two categories of assessment center dimension ratings. *Personnel Psychology, 43*, 101–116.

Smith, C. A., Organ, D. W., & Near, J. P. (1983). Organizational citizenship behavior: Its nature and antecedents. *Journal of Applied Psychology, 68*, 653–663.

Stogdill, R. M. (1963). *Manual for the Leader Behavior Description Questionnaire, Form XII.* Columbus, OH: Bureau of Business Research, Ohio State University.

Tett, R. P., & Guterman, H. A. (2000). Situation trait relevance, trait expression, and cross-situational consistency: Testing a principle of trait activation. *Journal of Research in Personality, 34*, 397–423.

Tomás, J. M., Hontangas, P. M., & Oliver, A. (2000). Linear confirmatory factor models to evaluate multitrait-multimethod matrices: The effects of number of indicators and correlation among methods. *Multivariate Behavioral Research, 35*, 469–499.

Vandenberg, R. J., & Lance, C. E. (2000). A review and synthesis of the measurement invariance literature: Suggestions, practices, and recommendations for organizational research. *Organizational Research Methods, 3*, 4–69.

Viswesvaran, C., Schmidt, F. L., & Ones, D. S. (2005). Is there a general factor in ratings of job performance? A meta-analytic framework for disentangling substantive and erro influences *Journal of Applied Psychology, 90*, 108–131.

Woehr, D. J., Putka, D., & Bowler, M. C. (2011). An examination of G-theory methods for modeling multitrait-multimethod data: Clarifying links to construct validity and confirmatory factor analysis. *Organizational Research Methods, 15*, 134-161..

Yukl, G., & Tracey, J. B. 1992. Consequences of influence tactics used with subordinates, peers, and the boss. *Journal of Applied Psychology*,77, 525–535.

Zaccaro, S. J. (2007). Trait-based perspectives of leadership. *American Psychologist, 62*, 6-16.

Part 5

A Summary of Three Perspectives on Assessment Centers

14

Dimensions, Tasks, and Mixed Models

An Analysis of Three Diverse Perspectives on Assessment Centers

Walter C. Borman

Personnel Decisions Research Institutes, Inc.

My task for this chapter is to summarize issues around three approaches to conceptualizing, developing, and operating contemporary assessment centers (ACs)—the dimension-based approach, the task-based strategy, and the mixed-model. Dimension-based centers use behavioral constructs as the dimensions of interest, behavioral-psychological variables determined by job analysis or related methods to be important for the target job(s). Task-based centers elevate exercises to the main focus and strive to evaluate assessees on a representative set of work-sample-like exercises designed to assess performance in highly job relevant tasks and roles, thus bypassing the requirement to abstract back to more psychological constructs. Finally, the mixed-model AC approach takes an interactionist position, that behavior in ACs is a function of both individual differences in behavioral tendencies and situational influences on behavior, that is, individual differences interact with exercise influences and demands, resulting in task *and* dimension relevant behavior.

Some scholars/researchers view these perspectives as competing and needing a resolution, a "winner." With this perspective, and a boxing analogy, it seems to me readers, as referees, need to give respect to the reigning champion, the dimension-based approach. This approach has been remarkably effective as a selection and development technique for more than 50 years, with excellent criterion related validity against job performance criteria, a track record of assessors' successfully observing, integrating, and evaluating behavior, with behavioral dimensions providing the foundation for the entire enterprise. Thus, this review begins with a brief statement of the dimension-based "position," including evidence for its usefulness and relevance. I do not review the mechanics of the dimension-based method, or of the task-based or mixed-model approaches, as they have been ably described in other chapters within this compendium.

Dimension-Based ACs

First, dimension-based ACs (DBACs) typically possess considerable content validity. Dimensions are identified and defined based on job analysis or some kind of related competency modeling method, making them highly relevant to the target job(s), exercises are selected or developed to be representative of the job(s) and to elicit behavior on the target dimensions, and assessors are trained to perform their evaluation task with alignment to the dimension content and the context of the target organization. Further, the principle of multiple assessors evaluating each assessee contributes to the fairness of the assessment process.

Second, the criterion-related validity of DBACs has been generally impressive. The early Gaugler, Rosenthal, Thornton, and Bentson (1987) meta-analysis validity estimate of the OAR against overall job performance was .37, corrected for restriction-in-ratings and the unreliability of the criterion. A more recent meta-analysis updating Gaughler et al. relating OARs to overall performance ratings provides a somewhat lower point estimate of .28 (Hermelin, Lievens, & Robertson, 2007). Two other recent meta-analyses examined relationships between the individual AC dimension ratings and overall performance ratings criteria (Arthur, Day, McNelly, & Edens, 2003; Meriac, Hoffman, Woehr, & Fleischer, 2008). Arthur et al. found dimensions such as Communication, Influencing Others, and Planning and Organizing having corrected mean correlations of from .25 to .39. The Meriac et al. estimates for the same AC dimensions were somewhat lower, varying from .16 to .35.

Third, DBACs have demonstrated incremental validity over other predictors against job performance. Meriac et al. (2008) found ΔR^2 of .097 ($p < .001$), when adding AC dimensions to general cognitive ability and Big 5 personality predictors.

Fourth, for selection, the target jobs have typically been supervisory or management-related, but others have included sales, military recruiters, factory workers, police work, leadership in the military, the pharmacy profession, vocational rehabilitation counselors, and the job of stockbroker. Types of criteria have included job performance ratings, objective performance, career progression, ratings of potential, salary progression, and sales.

Finally, dimensions have been a useful unit of measurement for providing feedback to assessees. Dimensions are understandable currency for assessees to grasp, although in the next section it is pointed out that convergent and discriminant validity evidence for DBACs provide problems for the veracity of this kind of feedback.

Difficulties with Interpreting Dimension-Based AC Data

This is becoming an often repeated tale, so I will cover the issue briefly. A consistent research finding beginning with Sackett and Dreher (1982) and Turnage and Muchinsky (1982) is that when dimension ratings are generated after each exercise, factor analyses of these data result in exercise rather than dimension factors. Thus, the correlations within exercise, across dimensions are greater than the within-dimension, across exercise correlations. This is "troublesome" as stated by Sackett and Dreher because it suggests either assessors are providing inaccurate or imprecise ratings, or that assessees' performance is inconsistent across exercises on individual dimensions, rendering feedback to assessees on dimensions (presumably consistent across exercises) as problematic. At one level, this finding strikes at the heart of the AC-for-development enterprise. How can assessees be provided with feedback on their effectiveness at the dimension level, when their scores on the dimension are sometimes inconsistent across exercises? Fortunately, AC practitioners over the years have adopted ways to give dimensional feedback that accounts for this inconsistency, when it occurs, and Hoffman (Chapter 13, this volume) offers a.theoretical model of how to explain these patterns of dimensional scores. But before discussing these points, we move to an AC approach that more directly and fundamentally addresses the convergent and discriminant validity problems with dimension-based centers, the task-based AC (TBAC).

Task-Based ACs

The TBAC strategy is at one level an elegant way to address head-on the construct validity problems with dimension-based ACs by paying attention to data and adjusting our AC design to align with those data. If dimension variance accounted for is generally low and exercise variance accounted for higher, why not focus the AC on tasks or exercises and abandon or at lease reduce focus on dimensions? In one stroke, this idea fits the data much better than with the dimension-based emphasis. From a scientific perspective, this sounds pretty good!

Interestingly, this strategy also has some more practice-related advantages. The TBAC approach places even more emphasis than DBACs on job analysis and sampling tasks to represent important performance and role requirements, something I/O psychologists are very experienced in and good at. Also, checklist behavioral items, highly recommended for assessors to use to generate ratings in TBACs (Jackson, Englert, & Brown, 2009) may provide more objective, readily observable, and more reliable AC ratings, and these exercise or role-based ratings may be easier to feed back to assessees compared to dimension ratings (e.g., for an exercise requiring counseling a poor performing supervisor, feedback might be, you addressed the most critical issues with the supervisor, but you set somewhat unrealistic goals to improve his performance), and may also be more acceptable and understandable to the assessee. Finally, with respect to validity, TBACs, with their similarity to work samples, should hopefully take advantage of that method's strong track record of high validity against job performance.

So, the TBAC approach (Jackson, 2007; Jackson, Barney, Stillman, & Kirkley, 2007; Lance, 2008) first uses job analysis and discussions with SMEs to select the most important tasks or roles to represent in the ACs. Then, I/O psychologists and SMEs design exercises that represent with high fidelity the important functional and role requirements of the target job(s), and a behavioral checklist or related assessment format is developed to evaluate performance in each exercise (see Thoresen & Thoresen, Chapter 9, this volume, for specific examples of how these steps may be accomplished). As pointed out by Jackson (Chapter 8, this volume), these exercise assessments are scored *by exercise* and are not combined across exercises as is done in dimension-based ACs. The TBAC assessment procedures are similar to those used in applied behavioral analysis for effecting change in a clinical or counseling setting.

In sum, TBACs represent an attractive alternative to DBACs in that: (a) TBAC procedures align better with empirical construct validity evidence accumulated over the past 25 years on DBACs; (b) TBAC rating procedures likely place less cognitive load on assessors and should provide more objective and reliable assessments; and (c) feedback to assessees on their exercise performances avoid the inferences and internal attributions that must be made by assessors in DBACs.

Evidence Related to AC Dimension and Exercise Effects and Methodological Issues with these Analyses

There have been many studies using confirmatory factor analysis (CFA) methods to estimate dimension and exercise variance accounted for in ACs. The "scorecard" is probably best provided by results from three meta-analyses that used CFA or related analyses to summarize these parameters. Unfortunately, the estimates are somewhat different, due to the studies sampled and the specific meta-analytic methods employed. Lievens and Conway (2001) found that dimension and exercise factors accounted for equal amounts of variance (34%). Lance, Foster, Gentry, and Thoresen's (2004) results were more favorable to exercises, with 52% due to exercises and only 14% apportioned to dimensions. Bowler and Woehr's (2006) results were more in the middle with 33% and 22%, respectively, due to these two sources. Thus, it is difficult to draw definitive conclusions here, except to say, although on balance, exercise factors seem to control more variance, dimensions account for a respectable up to comparable amount of this variance compared to exercises.

Another context for evaluating these kinds of variance accounted for effects is by comparing the factor structures of DBAC and TBAC scoring of the same ACs. As reported in Lance (Chapter 10, this volume), Jackson, Stillman, and Atkins (2005) found an exercise-only structure for both scoring systems, and in another study found a 4-exercise only model for TBAC data but a 3 exercise, 1 dimension structure for DBAC scoring. For the most part, this supports Lance et al.'s (2004) results of exercise factors plus a general factor, the latter indicating a perform-well/poorly in all of the exercises. This jibes with a practitioner view that some assessees, because of their relevant experience, general mental ability, and/or superior broad interpersonal skills, simply do generally better on all or most exercises.

Despite the variance accounted for findings just noted, researchers conducting these kinds of MTMM-CFA analyses on AC data know that often these analyses suffer serious problems with non-convergence, especially when sample sizes are low, when the model has a small number of traits or methods, and when the ratio of indicators to factors in the CFA is small (see Hoffman, Chapter 13, this volume, for a discussion of this and similar measurement issues, as well as approaches to address these problems). An additional study, damaging to CFA in the context of ACs, Lance, Foster, Nemeth, Gentry, and Drollinger (2007) showed that when data were generated in a Monte Carlo simulation to reflect both dimension and exercise effects, CFA results often supported other models besides the dimension + exercise structure.

Hoffman (Chapter 13, this volume) goes on to suggest that in DBACs, especially, more narrowly focused exercises tend to have multiple dimensions that are highly correlated, leading to reduced likelihood of dimension factors. Even exercises that are broader in focus may have relatively large numbers of dimensions fairly highly correlated within-exercise. However, if these dimensions can be reduced in number to broader factors that should be less highly intercorrelated, we may be more likely to tease out at least within-exercise dimensions factors, with the possibility of across-exercise dimension factors emerging. This kind of thinking is in part leading to the idea of mixed-model ACs, treating both exercises and dimensions as the "currency of the AC."

Mixed Model ACs

A third approach to AC design and subsequent interpretation is the mixed-model AC, where both exercises and dimensions are emphasized to provide interpretation of AC data at both the exercise and dimension levels. Hoffman (Chapter 13) provides rationale for such a strategy and three models that help explain why these may be reasonable interpretations of AC data. To me, the most important thrusts of the mixed model approach are: (a) an embracing of the powerful effect of exercises on AC ratings, especially when they represent very different job situations (which they should) and (b) a resurgent interest in dimensions if they can be formed as more general (non-specific) constructs that should be correlated less highly within exercises, allowing for better discriminant validity *within* exercises and the possibility that more convergent validity within dimension, across exercises may occur. Even if the latter is not realized, discriminant validity of dimensions within exercises can reflect the inherent multidimensional structure of performance in general and AC performance specifically, and will allow for reliable and valid dimension x exercise feedback to assessees if not overall dimension-across exercise feedback. The mixed models Hoffman described (Chapter 13) will be explained in the next couple of paragraphs.

Hoffman, Melchers, Blair, Kleinmann, and Ladd (2011) demonstrated some support for the usefulness of the broader-dimensions idea in that: (a) all nine CFA models they generated with broader, more general dimensions represented and then tested resulted in convergent and admissible solutions; (b) dimension effects accounted for 15% of the variance, although exercises accounted for 50% (and overall performance, 10%); and (c) dimension factors explained variance in salary and salary growth criteria beyond effects of exercise factors. The latter finding confirms results from Connelly, Ones, Ramesh, and Goff (2008) and Lievens, Dilchert, and Ones (2009) using the same two criteria.

Hoffman's second mixed model (Chapter 13) is especially appealing to my practitioner side, the dimension within exercise model that posits different dimensions are discriminable within exercises but even the same dimensions across exercise may not converge if the different exercises call for different kinds of behavior to perform effectively (e.g., leadership dimensions in competitive vs. cooperative exercises). As mentioned previously, most practitioners are comfortable with this model, realizing that dimensions are coherent constructs but manifest themselves differently in very different exercises, *and* that exercises *should* present a wide variety of situations to avoid inefficient redundancies in the AC. On this topic, Howard (2008) went so far as to opine that AC data should never have been subjected to MTMM analyses in the first place because different exercises *should* be designed to capture different facets of the same underlying dimensions.

The third mixed model is interesting from a historical perspective. Owens and colleagues at the University of Georgia (Owens, 1976) conducted person-centered research for several years in which they tested incoming freshmen at Georgia on ability, personality, and especially, biodata scales, performed cluster analyses to group together students with similar profiles on these predictors, and compared group means on different dependent variables such as college GPA, drug use, attainment of leadership roles, tendency to over- or under-achieve, and differences in tested creativity. Now, many years later at Georgia, Hoffman is suggesting a similar "whole person" strategy to form groups homogeneous in their patterns of consistency in, for example, differences in dimension performance across exercises (e.g., consistent versus variable), and then study whether different groups vary on dependent variables such as criterion job performance. Of course, this approach is in a very preliminary stage, and offers only one study that begins to evaluate its usefulness (Gibbons & Rupp, 2009).

Conclusions About the Three Approaches to AC Development, Operation, and Analyses

I generally like to be decisive (where reasonable) in I/O psychology issues; there is so much waffling in our field, "more research is needed," "there are pros and cons to each position," etc. But in this case I don't see any clear cut "winner" between the dimension- and task-based approaches. Back to the boxing referee analogy, I am reluctant to overthrow the dimension-oriented strategy champion when the match is so close.

Fortunately, it seems to me we can declare the mixed-model the winner in the sense that it contains, potentially, the best ideas from each of the first two strategies related to ACs. All of the practice and research-related wisdom may be taken from the DBAC side. Dimension identification and definition as well as assessors' ratings have evolved to be quite sophisticated, reflecting dimensions that are behaviorally well defined, comprehensively cover the target jobs' performance requirements, are relatively non-overlapping and distinct, and assessors are well trained in making ratings on these dimensions. This picture should get even better, with advances in trait activation theory (Tett & Guterman, 2000), helping further to create dimension x exercise assignments that encourage reliable and valid dimension-level ratings in each exercise.

The TBAC side brings best practice I/O processes in job analysis to bear on exercise identification and development, and more generally, provides a deep appreciation for the importance of situations for influencing behavior. This approach also offers the behavioral checklist evaluation technique to provide more objective and reliable ratings of AC performance (to be fair, DBACs have sometimes employed this technique, as well). Finally, the approach brings another orientation to assessee feedback that has proven successful—feedback on how well an assessee handles different situations important for effectiveness on the target job(s).

Thus, I see pursuing the mixed-model option as a best bet for optimizing the effectiveness of ACs, from development of dimensions and exercises to analysis of assessor rating data to providing feedback to assessees on their AC performance. Science is served by paying attention to data showing the importance of exercise factors but also the reasonably significant dimension factors, as well as the exercise x dimension effect that can be substantively interpreted and cogently fed back to assessees for development. More research is obviously necessary (and discussed in the next section), but the mixed-model offers a reasonably coherent scientific story and a practical way forward to contribute to the heretofore highly successful AC enterprise.

Suggestions for Future Research

In my view, the most important direction for future research is to learn more about the two relatively new models, the TBAC and mixed model AC. Compared to the DBAC model, very little research has been conducted to evaluate the overall usefulness of each of these two models for either selection or development purposes. For example, how do the criterion-related validities of these two types of ACs against job performance compare to validities obtained for DBACs? Because many of the elements of these ACs are very similar to those of DBACs, I suspect that the validities will be comparable, and early empirical evidence (Jackson, 2007; Lance et al., 2007) suggests this is the case.

A second direction for further study builds on a recommendation made by Woehr et al. (Chapter 3, this volume). They suggested bridging the gap between criterion-related validity studies and construct-related studies. One way to do this is to conduct what I have termed external construct validity research (Borman, Hanson, & Hedge, 1997). What this involves is identifying relatively broad AC dimensions similar to those generated by Arthur et al. (2003), for example, Influencing Others and Planning/Organizing, summarizing assessee ratings on each of these dimensions across exercises, and then testing for convergent and discriminant validity against job performance criteria matched to the content of the AC dimensions (e.g., supervisory performance ratings made on the dimensions with names and definitions similar to those for the AC dimensions). The hypotheses are simply significant and relatively high correlations between AC dimension ratings and job performance ratings on the matched criterion constructs, higher than the correlations between assessed AC ratings on these dimensions and performance criterion ratings on unmatched dimensions. Dissertation research at the University of South Florida (Ackerman, 1996) found some support for these hypotheses with management technical skills and interpersonal skills dimensions.

A final future research suggestion is to explore further the use of G-theory in analyses of AC convergent and discriminant validity. Woehr and colleagues (Woehr et al., Chapter 3, this volume; Woehr, Putka, & Bowler, 2012) have clarified links between variance components in univariate G-theory and both convergent and discriminant validity in the Campbell and Fiske (1959) framework. This is a highly useful development for AC research. Perhaps even more helpful is recent work done by Woehr, his colleagues, and others to consider using multivariate G-theory in analyzing AC data. The main advantage of using the multivariate case is it allows for non-zero correlations between dimensions, normally a realistic expectation for AC rating data. Finally, earlier restrictions with the use of G-theory such as software requirements and analytical limitations have been largely removed, and G-theory seems poised to play a more active role in AC research.

A summary comment, I teach a graduate level I/O course on assessment centers, and for several years we have discussed in that course basically two issues: (a) assessment center validities against different kinds of criteria, especially job performance vs. potential; and (b) construct validity problems with AC ratings. These topics are interesting but, frankly, quite limited. The content covered in this book considerably broadens the areas of consideration and, in my opinion, rejuvenates the study of assessment centers. There are theoretical, empirical, and even philosophical issues that have been introduced by the editors and authors, and the stage is set for productive discussions and debates around new topics and issues in AC research and practice. New models of ACs have emerged, analysis strategies have improved, with several limitations now removed, and practice has been enhanced by these theoretical and empirical contributions. I believe my AC course will be more interesting in the future!

References

Ackerman, L. D. (1996). *Investigation of the external construct validity of the assessment center method.* Ph.D. dissertation, University of South Florida, United States, Florida. Available from Dissertations & Theses @ University of South Florida - FCLA. (Publication No. AAT 9622219).

Arthur, W., Jr., Day, E. A., McNelly, T. L., & Edens, P. S. (2003). A meta-analysis of the criterion-related validity of assessment center dimensions. *Personnel Psychology, 56,* 125–154.

Borman, W. C., Hanson, M. A., & Hedge, J. W. (1997). Personnel selection. In J. T. Spence, J. M. Darley, & D. J. Foss (Eds.), *Annual review of psychology* (Vol. 48, pp. 299–337). Palo Alto, CA: Annual Review.

Bowler, M. C., & Woehr, D. J. (2006). A meta-analytic evaluation of the impact of dimension and exercise factors on assessment center ratings. *Journal of Applied Psychology, 91,* 1114–1124.

Campbell, D. T., & Fiske, D. W. (1959). Convergent and discriminant validation by the multitrait-multimethod matrix. *Psychological Bulletin, 56,* 81–105.

Connelly, B. S., Ones, D. S., Ramesh, A., & Goff, M. (2008). A pragmatic view of dimensions and exercises in assessment center ratings. *Industrial and Organizational Psychology: Perspectives on Science and Practice, 1,* 121–124.

Gaugler, B. B., Rosenthal, D. B., Thornton, G. C., & Bentson, C. (1987). Meta-analysis of assessment center validity. *Journal of Applied Psychology, 72,* 493–511.

Gibbons, A. M., & Rupp, D. E. (2009). Dimension consistency: A new (old) perspective on the assessment center construct validity debate. *Journal of Management, 35,* 1154–1180.

Hermelin, E., Lievens, F., & Robertson, I. T. (2007). The validity of assessment centres for the prediction of supervisory performance ratings: A meta-analysis. *International Journal of Selection and Assessment, 15,* 405–411.

Hoffman, B. J., Melchers, K., Blair, C. A., Kleinmann, M., & Ladd, R. T. (2011). Exercises and dimensions are the currency of assessment centers. *Personnel Psychology, 64,* 351–395.

Howard, A. (2008). Making assessment centers work the way they are supposed to. *Industrial and Organizational Psychology: Perspectives on Research and Practice, 1,* 98–104.

Jackson, D. J. R. (2007, April). *Task-specific assessment centers: Evidence of predictive validity and fairness.* Paper presented at the Society for Industrials and Organizational Psychology, New York, NY.

Jackson, D. J. R., Barney, A. R., Stillman, J. A., & Kirkley, W. (2007). When traits are behaviors: The relationship between behavioral responses and trait-based overall assessment center ratings. *Human Performance, 20,* 415–432.

Jackson, D. J. R., Englert, P., & Brown, G. S. (2009, April). *Interrater reliability of behavioral checklists in task-based assessment centers.* Paper presented at the meeting of the Society for Industrial and Organizational Psychology, New Orleans, LA.

Jackson, D. J. R., Stillman, J. A., & Atkins, S. G. (2005). Rating tasks versus dimensions in assessment centers: A psychometric comparison. *Human Performance, 18*, 213–241.

Lance, C. E. (2008). Why assessment centers do not work the way they're supposed to. *Industrial and Organizational Psychology Perspectives on Research and Practice, 1*, 84–97.

Lance, C. E., Foster, M. R., Gentry, W. A., & Thoresen, J. D. (2004). Assessor cognitive processes in an operational assessment center. *Journal of Applied Psychology, 89*, 22–35.

Lance, C. E., Foster, M. R., Nemeth, Y. M., Gentry, W. A., & Drollinger, S. (2007). Extending the nomological network of assessment center construct validity: Prediction of cross-situationally consistent and specific aspects of assessment center performance. *Human Performance, 20*, 345–362.

Lievens, F., & Conway, J. M. (2001). Dimension and exercise variance in assessment center scores: A large-scale evaluation of multitrait-multimethod studies. *Journal of Applied Psychology, 86*, 1202–1222.

Lievens, F., Dilchert, S., & Ones, D. S. (2009), The importance of exercise and dimension factors in assessment centers: Simultaneous examinations of construct-related and criterion-related validity. *Human Performance, 22*, 375–390.

Meriac, J. P., Hoffman, B. J., Woehr, D. J., & Fleischer, D. J. (2008). Further evidence for the validity of assessment center dimensions: A meta-analysis of the incremental criterion-related validity of assessment center dimension ratings. *Journal of Applied Psychology, 93*, 1042–1052.

Owens, W. A. (1976). Background data. In M. D. Dunnette (Ed.), *Handbook of industrial and organizational psychology* (pp. 609–644). Chicago: Rand-McNally.

Sackett, P. R., & Dreher, G. F. (1982). Constructs and assessment center dimensions: Some troubling empirical findings. *Journal of Applied Psychology, 67*, 401–410.

Tett, R. P., & Guterman, H. A. (2000). Situation trait relevance, trait expression, and cross-situational consistency: Testing a principle of trait activation. *Journal of Research in Personality, 34*, 397–423.

Turnage, J., & Muchinsky, P. (1982). Transsituational variabiity in human performance within assessment ceters. *Organizational Behavior and Human Performance, 30*, 174–200.

Woehr, D. J., Putka, D., & Bowler, M. C. (2012). An examination of G-theory methods for modeling multitrait-multimethod data: Clarifying links to construct validity and confirmatory factor analysis. *Organizational Research Methods, 15*, 134–161.

Index

Page locators in *italics* indicate figures and tables.